Human Resource Management in Europe

The European Union is expanding. Wide cultural, political and economic differences within the Union have a significant impact on the management of human resources, so crucial to the success of any enterprise. Businesses within the EU have regularly to re-evaluate the context in which they work, and for investors from other continents, notably the USA and Asia, the potential for expensive mistakes is only too real.

In this comprehensive new book, the varied and particular challenges for human resource management in the EU are fully explored. Written in conjunction with the European Association for Personnel Management (EAPM), the book offers country-by-country analysis from native authors, assessing the contexts faced by businesses working in thirteen different states: from founding EU members, such as France and Germany, to relatively new entrants, such as Latvia and Poland. The book also includes a chapter on Turkey, an emerging economy currently outside the Union. The key issues are addressed from both theoretical and practical perspectives, while each chapter is also complemented by best-practice case studies.

Human Resource Management in Europe is a key text for all students and managers interested in HRM and the different European contexts in which it operates.

Professor Dr Christian Scholz holds the chair of Business Administration, especially Organisation, HRM and Business Management at the University of Saarland, and is founding Director of the MBA programme at the same institution. He has written extensively on international and strategic human resource management issues.

Dr Hans Böhm was Executive Director of the German Association for Personnel Management 1992–2007, and is now a Leadership and People Management Consultant. He served as the Secretary-General of the European Association for Personnel Management (EAPM) from 2003 to 2007. He has published several books and articles on management development and the professionalisation of HR management.

Human Resource Management in Europe

Comparative analysis and contextual understanding

Edited by Christian Scholz and Hans Böhm

Taylor & Francis Group

LONDON AND NEW YORK

First published 2008
by Routledge
2 Park Square, Milton Park,
Abingdon, Oxon OX14 4RN

Simultaneously published in the USA and Canada
by Routledge
270 Madison Avenue, New York, NY 10016

*Routledge is an imprint of the Taylor & Francis Group, an informa
business*

© 2008 Christian Scholz and Hans Böhm editorial matter and
selection; the contributors for their contributions

Typeset in Times New Roman by Keyword Group Ltd
Printed and bound in Great Britain by CPI Anthony Rowe,
Chippenham, Wiltshire

British Library Cataloguing in Publication Data
A catalogue record for this book is available from the British Library

Library of Congress Cataloging in Publication Data
A catalog record for this book has been requested

ISBN13: 978-0-415-44761-4 (pbk)
ISBN13: 978-0-415-44760-7 (hbk)
ISBN13: 978-0-203-93794-5 (ebk)

ISBN10: 0-415-44761-5 (pbk)
ISBN10: 0-415-44760-7 (hbk)
ISBN10: 0-203-93794-5 (ebk)

Contents

Preface

It is a fact that the countries forming the European Union are so diverse that even European businesspeople suffer a lack of information on the cultural, political and economic differences, and this is still much more valid for potential US and Asian business partners and investors. Gathering good information on the most relevant facts and differences in the European countries is a precondition for avoiding fatal and expensive mistakes. Therefore it is a crucial challenge for those who have such information to deliver it to the interested public, to decision-makers in business, to scientists and students, and to integrate it into a comparative context. Within the growing and more and more integrating Europe it is highly desirable to support the development of better mutual understanding by good comprehensive information on the part of all the different countries, and to further the future development of a common European identity. For politically and economically interested people in other continents, it is useful to get more detailed information on the different socio-economic, political and cultural conditions prevalent in the various European countries.

With this book the editors and authors want to contribute to better and more detailed information relative to human resource management in its different stages on the way to becoming a real strategic business partner function in the different European countries. To deliver such detailed information on all European countries is an impossible task for one volume. So the editors decided to provide that information on those thirteen member countries of the European Association for Personnel Management (EAPM) who were ready and willing to participate.

This has resulted in a comprehensive overview of the situation of HRM in these thirteen European countries, which, individually, are of course quite different. The contributions in this book provide a comprehensive and instructive analysis of HRM in Europe. For each of the thirteen countries we offer an integrated overview of HRM in practice, science and, most importantly, in relation to HRM as a profession. This book is of enormous value for all those people who are interested in such solid scientific and practice-oriented information. This was only possible by an unprecedented close cooperation between high-profile scientists and practitioners from all cooperating countries.

This book will be of great interest, value and importance to the following potential readers and practitioners within HRM:

– scientists and students from all over the world who want to learn about or do research on HRM in the respective countries. For academic teaching, the best-practice case studies in particular will be of great value;
– practitioners in HRM who have to cooperate at any level with one or more of the case countries;
– HRM professionals who intend working or already work in one of these countries;
– entrepreneurs and managers as well as their HR specialists and consultants from all over the world who want to invest in the case countries or who intend to merge with a company from one or more of these countries; and
– HR consultants who want to learn more about these countries in order to develop their consultancy services.

The editors would like to express sincere thanks to all the co-authors and colleagues who have contributed to make this book an invaluable source for all (future) HR professionals; they also wish to thank Professor Volker Stein from the University of Siegen, Dr Roman Bechtel, Tanja Bollendorf, Daniela Büch, Dr Uwe Eisenbeis, Edith Niklas, Steffen Lay, Felix Eichhorn and Oliver Schilke from the University of Saarland, as well as Dorothee Ellerbrake from the DGFP, who have integrated the different texts, translated, gathered information, designed the figures contained in the book and liaised throughout with the authors and the publisher.

Without their great support we would not have been able to finish this book in a reasonable time.

Additionally, we wish to offer our grateful thanks to the German Association of Personnel Management (DGFP e.V.) for its generous sponsorship, as well as the EAPM for its active and effective support of this challenging project.

Every effort has been made to contact copyright holders and we apologise for any inadvertent omissions. If any acknowledgement is missing it would be appreciated if contact could be made care of the publishers so that this can be rectified in any future edition.

Prof. Dr Christian Scholz and Dr Hans Böhm

Figures

Tables

1 Introduction

Christian Scholz/Hans Böhm/Tanja Bollendorf

IN SEARCH OF A 'HUMAN RESOURCE MANAGEMENT'

Searching for a European approach to human resource management (HRM) is no easy undertaking. A look at the piles of books about European HRM published in recent years shows that the topic can be treated in many ways: we can look at how specific HRM issues interact from a European perspective (Supiot/Meadows 2001; Sofer 2004) at country-specific practices and context variables (Brewster *et al.* 1992; Brewster/Mayrhofer/Morley 2004); at country-specific approaches to specific HRM topics (Brewster/Mayrhofer/Morley 2000); and at international companies with their specific problems, such as international recruitment or management of expatriates (Harzing/Ruysseveldt 2004; Dowling/Welch 2005; Linehan/Scullion 2005).

Sparrow/Hiltrop (1997: 201) make a cautious attempt to distinguish European HRM from US HRM when they write: 'If European management exists, it is in terms of greater cautiousness, sophistication of methods, and pursuance of elitist reward and career systems'. They emphasise five characteristic features where they perceive qualitative or quantitative differences compared with HRM in the USA:

1. European HR departments are more restricted in their autonomy.
2. European HRM has traditionally been less exposed to market processes.
3. European approaches to HRM focus more on groups than on individuals.
4. European social partners, such as trade unions or employee representatives, are more influential than their US counterparts.
5. In the European arena, labour market politics is more regulated, i.e. there is a greater influence of governments on the management of businesses.

Although the characterisation of HRM in Europe addresses different influencing factors, such as socio-cultural traditions, the legislative framework and institutional context, these factors only provide a framework in which European HRM can be positioned relative to non-European HRM. The whole landscape of HRM in Europe becomes less consistent if the standard of comparison is to be changed or if HRM in Europe is to be analysed in more detail. Differences exist between approaches of countries and there is no single European pattern of HRM (Sparrow/Hiltrop 1997: 201).

In order to better handle the differences within Europe for comparative analysis, researchers tended to build clusters of countries with similar approaches to HRM, or they identified clusters of homogeneous countries in empirical analysis (Ronen/Shenkar 1985; Brodbeck *et al.* 2000). For example, Nikandrou/Apospori/Papalexandris (2005) find relatively independent and congruent north–west and south–east clusters with regard to HRM practices in Europe, whereas Communal/Brewster (2004) make a hierarchical distinction which considers overlappings between countries. The first level of their typology separates HRM in the UK from the rest of Europe, which is due to the cultural proximity between the UK and the USA. On a second level, three main clusters can be distinguished within the rest of Europe, namely HRM in the south, the north and the east of Europe. Each of these clusters can be further differentiated. As to the northern countries, Scandinavian countries have, for example, some characteristics in common that distinguish them from other northern countries, of which Germanic countries (Switzerland, Austria and Germany) as well as small countries (Belgium, the Netherlands, Luxembourg) form sub-clusters.

All in all, approaches to HRM are quite heterogeneous within Europe. A consistent view of what European HRM means does not exist in literature. Therefore it would be more correct to speak of 'HRM in Europe' or 'HRM with European characteristics' than of 'European HRM'.

The contribution of this book

This book is supposed to present the whole diversity of HRM in Europe. Thirteen teams of authors give a comprehensive overview of the conception of HRM in their respective countries. They do not reason about an abstract definition of the term, but instead present a picture of HRM roles, practices and discussions of each country's HRM.

This book therefore provides a reliable and authentic source of national viewpoints and approaches to challenges which are often global in nature. The great advantage is that there are no national biases in tracing out the field of HRM in Europe. Ethnocentric presentations have been prohibited by the editors, and our advice is that ethnocentric reading should be prohibited by everyone who deals with this book. This book therefore does not provide a definition of 'European HRM', but it certainly makes a contribution to clarifying the concept.

HRM IN EUROPE: ITS IMPACTS AND CONTEXTS

THE SIGNIFICANCE OF HRM ACTIVITIES IN GLOBAL COMPETITION

It has been argued, and proven sufficiently and convincingly, that HRM is one of the most sensitive and important fields of action for the future success of economic companies (Pickett 2000; Sparrow/Schuler/Jackson 2000; Evans/Pucik/Barsoux 2002; Hayton 2005). It has become an undeniable fact that the best HRM and leadership creates the most competent and strongest people and teams as a convincing basis for optimal achievement in global competition in terms of innovation, quality, speed and customer orientation. In a world in which mere customer knowledge in all disciplines and new scientific findings become more and more accessible to everybody, the most important success factors in global competition are the people: their competences, their motivation to learn and to perform, leadership and cooperation, corporate values and culture.

After years of disappointing approaches to implementing the 'Lisbon Strategy', decided by the European Union Council in March 2000, which aims at developing Europe into the world's most competitive and dynamic knowledge-based economy, it has become most urgent to concentrate on people management and development, people competences and leadership in the real world of economy and work.

In this context, HR activities become more and more important for companies to strengthen their economic position, since they can be directly linked to organisational value creation. The performance of a company's workforce depends on these very activities, and it is even possible to prove its value for the company on the balance sheets. Recent approaches to human capital management established the link between HRM in companies and the monetary value of the company's human capital (Scholz/Stein/Bechtel 2004), and so created a currency for assessing the quality of HRM activities and investment in people. Evans/Pucik/Barsoux (2002) present a study from the USA according to which the marginal value of investing in the human capital of a company is about three times greater than the value of investment in machinery. Tzafir (2006) demonstrated in an empirical analysis of several business sectors that besides training, employee participation also enhances organisational performance.

In detail, HRM comprises the following activities:

- the attraction of qualified and talented job applicants (personnel marketing);
- the placement of the right people in vacant positions (personnel selection);
- the knowledge update, education and training of employees (personnel development);

- the creation of incentive systems (motivation and encouragement of employees); and
- the determination of the employee's monetary value for the company (human capital management).

The significance of people becomes most evident in the discussion about strategic HRM. In this process of strategic realignment of the HR function with the company's business goals, the HR function becomes a business partner for the line management, which means that HR managers work hand in hand with line managers to institute and manage the process of accomplishing the company's goals – whether these goals are financial targets, balanced scorecards, visions, or others (Ulrich 1997). Key HRM policies and practices in gaining competitive advantage are, according to Sparrow/Schuler/Jackson (2000: 45–6):

- culture;
- organisation structure;
- performance management;
- resourcing; and
- communication and corporate social responsibility.

Theory about strategic HRM has been treated sufficiently in other contexts (Ulrich 1997; Evans/Pucik/Barsoux 2002). The editors of this book decided to provide practical examples, comprising all of the above listed fields of policies, always embedded in a specific national context. All in all, this book contains fourteen case studies of company-specific HRM systems or practices for a high-performance workforce – one per country except for the Netherlands, for which we present two examples.

THE INFLUENCE OF HR DEPARTMENTS ON CORPORATE PERFORMANCE

HR managers in companies have competences and roles which differ with regard to their working context and therefore also shape the HR profile of a company. Sparrow/Hiltrop (1997) distinguish five factors influencing the roles and competences of HR managers: the professional allegance (functional background); the HR experience (career route and line exposure); the strategic integration through representation, participation and formal process in the company; the decentralisation and devolvement of HR to the line management; and the level of outsourcing of specialist services.

Indeed, among the trends that can actually be observed in HRM in many countries are the implementation of (internally used) shared services and the (external) outsourcing of HR functions. Shared services can take the form of service, providing not only to a company's own departments, but also to external client organisations, and it can also aim at restructuring the service provision through recentralisation and the creation of an internal market system (Shen 2005).

HR outsourcing means the contracting out of specialist services and tasks which have traditionally been fulfilled by personnel departments. Outsourcing of

HR functions to personnel service providers can occur for cost reduction purposes, but the search for experts, focus on core competences, access to technology platforms and further reasons can also cause outsourcing activities. Shen (2005) quotes studies according to which between 62 per cent and 85 per cent of participating companies indicated outsourcing at least one HR function.

Although practised from time to time for economical reasons, the outsourcing of personnel departments is problematic. A company risks losing its competitive advantage when buying personnel services which are sold identically to several other companies and are not designed for the company's specific context. Some authors therefore refer to the risks of outsourcing HR services, such as the loss of in-house knowledge and capacity or the loss of long-term competitiveness (Cooke/Shen/McBride 2005).

The importance of the contribution of company-owned HR departments should not be neglected. When analysing the impact of HR departments, different perspectives can be applied. The multiperspectivity view from the field of strategic management distinguishes between the mechanic, the strategic, the organic, the cultural, the intelligent and the virtual dimension (Scholz 2000a).

The mechanic dimension

This is the structural backbone of a company and refers to the organisational and procedural structure of a company: process responsibilities need to be fixed, workflows have to be created and control mechanisms implemented. HRM aims at placing people with adequate capabilities and experience so that these workflows function optimally, but it aims also at preparing people for changed organisational procedures, and for adapting their capabilities under HR development programmes.

The strategic dimension

This refers to the alignment of the HR department's work with the company's goals. It is the basis of multiperspectivity, because the company's structures and processes can be judged against the background of the strategy. HR departments have great influence and few restrictions, i.e. they are free to resort to a broad range of instruments and practices to fulfil all tasks related to HRM, from personnel recruitment to contract designs and personnel dismissals.

The organic dimension

This analyses a company's internal dynamics as an organism with individual specifics. HRM has to analyse patterns of growth or development, of single employees as well as of the organisation as a whole. It focuses on the observation of employees' individual development and adaptation from their entry into the company to departure, it observes the development of the organisation and its interaction with the environment, and it has to respond to the needs associated with every developmental phase.

6

The cultural dimension

This affects the value system of a company and its environment. HR managers need to position their own corporate strategy within this more general cultural framework, to create a motivating and identity-supporting climate. In the cultural dimension, the focus lies on analysing (visible) artefacts, (more or less conscious) values and (unconscious) underlying assumptions of HR practices. These affect, for example, recruitment and dismissal practices, official commitments to employees' development and social relationships within organisations.

The intelligent dimension

This develops HR as the intellectual potential of a company, by creating a knowledge base which can be shared by all employees. It means, for example, the use of information systems for the management of knowledge or employee development, as in knowledge management systems which prevent knowledge from being lost when employees leave the company, or as in learning software for meeting development goals.

The virtual dimension

This focuses on new organisational structures caused by diminishing organisational orders. Flexible forms of employment like telework or project contracts require new forms of contracts, supervision and communication. Not only flexible forms of works but also multiple locations or subsidiaries of a company make management more complex. In huge groups division of labour might even be international. This expands HR managers' tasks, since it requires international recruitment, foreign assignment of managers and other employees, as well as the support of those expatriates.

The multiperspectivity view demonstrates that HRM affects all domains of organisational performance, and it illustrates the variety of tasks related to the HRM function.

THE ROLE OF HR INSTITUTIONS AND 'SOCIAL PARTNERSHIP'

The HR institutions of a country are strongly associated with the notion of 'social partnership', since HR institution means generally trade unions or works' councils, defending the workers' interests vis-à-vis their employers. The term 'social partnership' has a special note in the European context (Ferrer/Hyman 1998): it stands for a far more developed codetermination of such institutions than in other areas of the world, and affects several fields. The institutions concerned not only deal with nominal wages or salaries, but also have a legitimate role in representing employee interests in agendas, such as the level of tax and other deductions or social benefits and entitlements which their contributions provide – even if this legitimacy has been increasingly questioned in several countries (Ferrer/Hyman 1998: xviii).

In fact, the importance of HR institutions and especially trade unions seems to diminish, due to different trends in society (Ferrer/Hyman 1998: xvii): first of all, the manual working class, in which trade unions have their strongest holds, is declining throughout Europe. Second, a differentiation of interests between the winners and losers in economic restructuring has to be stated, as well as coexistence of 'company egoism' and 'wildcat cooperation'. This last point addresses a perceived common interest between management and workforce in securing competitiveness in a harsher product market environment.

Some authors describe this changing employer–employee relationship as the 'new deal of employment' (Cappelli 1999; Janssens/Sels/van den Brande 2003; Aselstine/Alletson 2006). Scholz (2003) refers to this phenomenon as 'darwiportunism', a term that is composed of Darwinism and opportunism, and describes the rules of the new working context. The first part of the term (Darwinism) refers to the company's attempt to adapt its recruitment and person-nel retention practices to fast-changing market conditions and not to engage in long-term relationships. The second part (opportunism) refers to employees' reduced loyalty towards their employer. This reduced loyalty is replaced by a commitment for single projects and one's own career. Employees are interested in optimizing their CVs (or résumés) and in steadily enhancing or maintaining their attractiveness for the job market, since their company cannot give them long-term guarantees.

Flexibility is the key characteristic of this new employer–employee relation-ship as described in the darwiportunism concept. Because of increased competition in a global economy, changing demands and technological advances, companies are striving towards more flexibility by creating new forms of employ-ment, such as part-time work, temporary work, shift work, subcontracting, shared work or teleworking. Flexibility is also seen as a means to reduce unemployment, although some authors warn about the effects on macroeconomics and social structures (Serlavós/Aparicio-Valverde 2000).

The developments sketched above actually affect all European countries, although there are differences in the level of intensity, and labour politics has created the new concept of the 'flexicurity challenge'. Flexicurity means the attempt to reconcile the demand for flexibility in the labour market by firms with the workers' demand for job security (Dewettinck *et al.* 2006). In societies where the effects of globalisation cannot be stopped or reversed without compromising economic competitiveness, and where the role of trade unions and other labour institutions becomes less important, politics is in demand: governments have to find new solutions and to rethink their labour market poli-cies. For the time being, no model solution to the flexicurity challenge seems to exist. European countries move between attempting to implement maximum flexibility in their labour market structures while maintaining maximum social security.

THE HR POLICY FRAMES

HRM personnel have to respect the regulatory frameworks which are put in place by governments, trade unions and other regulatory bodies. A further context variable influencing HR operations is the company's overall strategy to which HRM is aligned. Earlier attempts to describe the frameworks within which HRM personnel operate simply provided a description of HR practices (Murray/Dimick 1978; Murray/Jain/Adams 1976). These typically included administrative practices, such as recruiting and selection, training and development, compensation, benefits and services, and labour relations, although the criteria for grouping policies depended on the purpose of the groupings (Murray/Dimick 1978).

There is evidence that a company's HRM strategy, and especially the allocation of financial resources to several HRM fields and instruments, depends on a combination of different contextual factors, namely economic conditions, pressure from powerful outsiders and the advocacy of positive interest groups. These influence the perception of problems related to HRM, as well as the identification of general policy areas in which initiatives should be taken (Murray/Dimick 1978).

Weber/Kabst/Gramley (2000) tried to answer the question whether organisation-specific variables or country-specific circumstances have a greater impact on HR policies in European organisations by analysing seven HR policies. They found that training and development were determined by company-specific antecedents. The influence of country-specific antecedents was quite small concerning pay and benefits, employee communication, people management philosophy and high-fliers, a little higher in recruitment and selection, and highest in equal opportunities/diversity.

Just as personnel work becomes a strategic issue, the HR manager's tasks become more faceted. The attempts of many governments to foster deregulation in labour market policies, and at the same time the decreasing importance of institutions, such as trade unions and works' councils in many countries cede more responsibilities to the single HR managers and the companies in general.

Strategy of internationalisation

HR managers therefore have a variety of options with regard to the design of contracts, the use of external personnel services and decentralisation of responsibilities in their home markets. If a company acts in more than one country, further decisions about labour policies have to be made with regard to the degree of integration of local policies, i.e. policies at different locations. Companies having subsidiaries in different countries or outsourcing certain production units to other locations have to decide about the fundamental alignment of their HRM, which is discussed in the literature in terms of ethnocentric, polycentric, regiocentric and geocentric strategy (Scholz/Messemer/Schröter 1991; Caligiuri/Stroh 1995):

- Ethnocentric strategies have a clear focus of the company's home market or country of origin. The parent company's HRM practices are implemented in all subsidiaries, regardless of local contexts or cultural differences.
- Polycentric strategies permit the implementation of different HRM practices in every location where the company is based. Foreign subsidiaries have the greatest level of authority and can develop country-specific HR strategies.
- Regiocentric strategies in the context of HRM imply a certain degree of decentralisation and mean an adaptation of HRM practices to groups of countries with a similar cultural background. These strategies balance centralisation and decentralisation.
- Geocentric strategies aim at a worldwide integration of all a company's activities. National specifics are neglected in favour of functional HR practices which represent the lowest common denominator.

Depending on the overall strategy, the integration of a company's employee recruitment, selection, development and other practices in the local context can be more or less adapted to country specifics. International HRM strategies differ from local HRM strategies in many respects (Evans/Pucik/Barsoux 2002; Fenwick 2004; Harzing 2004; Lazarova/Caligiuri 2004; Sparrow/Brewster/Harris 2004; Tarique/Caligiuri 2004). Whereas, for example, a geocentric strategy may foster employee mobility with extensive expatriate programmes, and involve international recruitment and search for international profiles of candidates, a polycentric strategy might concentrate its recruitment on national markets, which involves a different set of HR management practices.

Further, reflections about a company's internationalisation strategy must address the integration of the different units, especially in the ethnocentric, regiocentric and geocentric strategies, where subsidiaries act more or less independently from the parent company. Integration functions mainly regarding communication, and hence communication technology, has considerable influence on a company's communication flows, mutual matching, integration of sub-units and implementation of strategies or policies.

This phenomenon is referred to as a virtual dimension in the strategic organisation of HRM literature (Heneman/Greenberger 2002; Scholz/Stein/Eisenbeis 2001), and it depends on three virtualisation dimensions: development of core competences; integration of personnel functions; and information technology (Scholz 2000b). Information technology allows the connection between single units and shapes the role of the HR manager. Information technology is considered to be a critical driver of HR's transition from an administrative function to a strategic function (Bell/Lee/Yeung 2006) and can lead to competitive advantages in international HRM (Hannon/Jelf/Brandes 1996).

It has been argued by Edwards/Kuruvilla (2005: 1) that the national context has not sufficiently been considered in research about international HRM, and that their inadequate conceptualisation has restricted research progress, using culture as an unsatisfactory 'catch-all' for national differences. They emphasise the national business system as being a useful frame for analysis of national influences on HRM, and they propose to consider country-specific institutions, varying levels of economic and political predictability and stability, and differing types of infrastructure.

Sparrow/Hiltrop (1997: 203) also count the institutional factors and business structure of a country among the factors that shape a company's HR policies. Institutional factors comprise the level of organisational autonomy, trade unions and representative arrangements, the level of provision of social security and welfare, the recency and scope of labour codification, the employer/employee bias in legislation, and corporate responsibilities and penalties for redundancy. The business structure is determined by the degree of state ownership, organisational performance criteria, the size of organisations, the organisation life expectancy and the length of employee tenure, as well as the level of single family stakeholders and the fragmentation of industrial sectors.

Political frame

The European Union also sets political frameworks for the development of HRM activities within Europe and has to be seen as an important collective actor and major change driver affecting individuals, organisations and nation-states (Larsen/ Mayrhofer 2006: 263). EU legislation in fact has had and still has a far-reaching influence on the member states and their populations in creating equal opportunities and a homogeneous market. It also assists its member states in coping with the impact of structural changes on employment due to globalisation (van Liemt 1998).

Recent EU developments which most affect HR practitioners and business leaders according to Sforza (2005) are pensions, people mobility and corporate governance. The adoption of an EU-wide legal regime for pension funds will, among others, give companies the opportunity to set up their pension fund everywhere in Europe, and it sets an end to the discrimination regarding the deductibility of contributions paid to foreign-based pension funds for tax purposes by some countries. Increased people mobility will give companies the opportunity to recruit globally and to allocate work more efficiently. As to corporate governance, the EU promotes the transparency of directors' remuneration and defines minimum standards for the creation, composition and role of the nomination, remuneration and audit committees.

More systematically, EU policy with a more or less indirect impact on HRM can be associated with four major policy domains: employment; education; competition; and the economy (Weidenfels/Wessels 2002). While some EU activities consist more in collecting information and giving recommendations (like the identification and publication of best-practice employment procedures), some have a much greater impact on member states (consider, for example, the restructuring of the whole European system of higher education which is currently taking place).

EU employment policy aims at promoting a high level of employment, coordinating the employment policies of EU member states, and on developing a coordinated employment strategy. To achieve these goals, the EU publishes a yearly schedule of employment policy guidelines of the Council, monitors the employment programmes of member states, identifies best-practice procedures, benchmarks, financially supports employment policy programmes and makes recommendations to member states.

Education policy is meant to contribute to a qualitatively high general and professional education, and to promote access to education and further education at a high level. For this purpose, the EU creates action programmes and guidelines for the mutual acknowledgement of diplomas. The implementation of the so-called Bologna process in all member states demonstrates the influence of EU legislation in the field of education: by 2010, all European education systems will be restructured to offer Europe-wide acknowledged Bachelor and Master degrees.

It is through competition and economic policy that the Single European Market can be achieved. It allows for an open market economy with free competition, and aims at improving the general economic conditions for growth, wealth and employment. Monetary union has been one of many instruments employed to achieve these goals.

The meaning and the long-range effects of the enlargement of the EU from 15 to 25 member states in 2004 cannot be overestimated. And Europe continues to grow: Bulgaria and Romania joined the EU in January 2007 and Croatia and the Ukraine have at least their foot in the door. The negotiations with Turkey have begun, and – whatever results they will bring – a systematic development of Turkey towards a full integration into a future Europe seems to be irreversible and rational. There is a new geo-political system emerging with an enormous potential in terms of politics, industry and trade, science and the integration of cultural diversities. About 500 million people with a gross economic product of 10,000 billion euro offer a most interesting market and investment opportunity for the global economy.

It is evident that the EU can only even out legal differences between its member states to the extent that those member states are ready to cede national political competences. The coexistence of different national approaches to Europe-wide joint political challenges such as, for example, reducing unemployment or an ageing workforce, and the management of diversity, are therefore also characteristic of Europe. From a EU perspective, European HRM means less European-wide structures and a binding legislation for all member states, but rather benchmarking successful national approaches and discussion of best-practice examples.

The contribution of this book

Both the action scope for HRM as well as the theoretical perspectives of HRM presented in this chapter are highly relevant for practitioners and researchers alike, and they are addressed throughout the book. As to the flexicurity challenge, the whole range of European approaches is described, from social partnership in Austria to the conception of flexibility according to US patterns (a country known for its 'hire-and-fire' approach), UK patterns and those of other countries.

HR managers must become aware now of the importance of people and not when they find they are faced with difficulties in recruiting the right candidates when vacancies arise. This is shown in the UK contribution, since it is actually concerned with a lack of talented or qualified people. Other countries (like Italy) show evidence that HRM can promote a high-performance culture if it is strategically aligned with the company's goals.

The case studies on best practice presented in this book give different images of organisations. Similar to Morgan (1986), they can be related to all perspectives of the multiperspectivity view of the strategic organisation approach (Scholz 2000a). The case studies give an impressive overview of the diversity of HRM approaches in companies throughout Europe, and these include:

- The mechanic perspective is, e.g., covered by the Polish case study, where the introduction of a housekeeping and thrift management programme at Polish Security Printing Works is described.
- The strategic dimension is, e.g., referred to in the contribution of Italy, presenting the redefinition of HRM as a business partner for the line.
- The organic dimension is, e.g., addressed in the Spanish contribution, where the Spanish authors present an extensive restructuring process within a bank.
- An example of the cultural dimension is given in the contribution from the Latvian authors, who analyse a company's culture, applying organisational culture theories.
- The intelligent dimension, referring to a model of organisational information sharing, is, e.g., addressed in the Czech contribution.
- And finally, evidence for the virtual dimension can, e.g., be found in the contribution of the UK, presenting an example of how a company facing explosive growth succeeds in aligning its global, regional and local HRM.

DIFFERENT APPROACHES TO HRM IN EUROPE: (STILL) STRIKING, BUT BLURRING?

GLOBAL VERSUS COUNTRY-SPECIFIC APPROACHES

As seen in the earlier discussion, there is only a vague idea of what European HRM might be. Not only have researchers and practitioners in the field of HRM failed to agree upon a universal European self-conception of HRM, but also the EU fosters a pluralistic policy of harmonizing and levelling out differences. Nevertheless, there is a Europe-wide trend in HRM to become a strategic business partner and to contribute to companies' value creation. This section deals with the instruments to achieve these goals, and examines whether they are universally applicable or whether they only function in specific national contexts.

The question of whether country-specific approaches to HRM are more effective and more apt to enhance competitiveness, or whether global competition justifies global HRM practices directly, addresses the debate whether successful HRM strategies are global or country specific. In this debate, the culture-specific management position (also referred to as contextual, see e.g. Sparrow/Brewster/Harris 2004) and the culture-free management position are opposed (Braun/Warner 2002). Advocates of both positions have developed good arguments and a lot of literature has been produced (see, for a discussion of the term globalisation, Sparrow/Brewster/Harris 2004).

Besides, there are concepts that 'bridge' these two positions: contingency theorists assume interactions between HR practices and contingency factors, such as sector of activity, company size, ownership or organisational structure (Nikandrou/Campos e Cunha/Papalexandris 2006). Performance in this view depends on a matching of HR practices and other organisational characteristics, and internal consistency. Certain bundles of HR practices are suitable for certain types of companies, regardless of their country of origin.

Rosenzweig/Nohria (1994) concluded that different HRM practices vary with regard to their cross-cultural transferrability. They write that the more technical tasks of an HR manager, such as recruitment or training, are less culture bound. Performance appraisal and financial compensation belong to those HRM practices which are induced by socio-cultural factors and therefore are distinctive from one country to another.

In fact, the convergence or divergence debate seems to be dissolved by the distinction between a macro-level of HRM and a micro-level of HRM. At a macro-level, HR managers deal with organisational structure and technological issues, while on a micro-level, they are concerned with behaviour of people within organisations. Child (1981) found that research showing a convergence of cultures repeatedly is mainly based on macro-level factors, and studies supporting the cultural divergence thesis concentrate on micro-level variables.

For the culture-free versus culture-specific debate in HRM this means that convergence and divergence are parallel processes in organisations that do not exclude each other. Organisations in different countries may become similar in terms of organisational structures and systems, but people in these organisations continue to behave differently within them (Sparrow/Hiltrop 1994).

THE 'IDEA OF MAN' OR CULTURAL VARIABLES IN MANAGING HUMAN RESOURCES

To have a closer look at the socio-cultural factors that cause different approaches in less 'technical' aspects of HRM, one has to consider the extensive works of cultural anthropologists or psychologists, such as Hall (1969), Hall/Hall (1976; 1990), Hofstede (1980; 1991; 1993; 2002) and Trompenaars (1993), which all students of international HRM get to know in their first academic year.

Their work provides evidence for cultural differences in value systems which influence our thinking and behaviour, that is: our collective programming of the mind, a term stemming from Hofstede (1980). His cultural dimensions are among the most commonly agreed upon in international HR science. Hofstede distinguishes five dimensions:

1. Power distance: this describes the extent to which the less powerful members of organisations or societies in general accept and expect that power is distributed unequally. This level of inequality is endorsed by the followers as much as by the leaders. The power distance dimension characterises the relationship between people, e.g., between employees and their superiors.
2. Individualism versus collectivism: this is the degree to which individuals are integrated into groups. In individualist societies, the ties between individuals are loose and everyone is expected to care for him- or herself and his or her immediate family. In collectivist societies, people are strongly integrated into larger groups as extended families including uncles, aunts and grandparents. The in-group protects its members in exchange for unquestioning loyalty.
3. Masculinity versus its opposite, femininity: this refers to the distribution of roles between the genders. Feminine cultures esteem values such as modesty and care for others, whereas masculine cultures promote values such as competition and assertiveness.
4. Uncertainty avoidance: this refers to a society's tolerance for uncertainty and ambiguity. It indicates to what extent members of a culture feel either uncomfortable or comfortable in unstructured, i.e. novel, unknown or surprising situations. Uncertainty-avoiding cultures try to minimise the possibility of such situations by strict laws and rules, safety and security measures. People in uncertainty-accepting cultures tolerate a variety of opinions and come along with few rules.
5. Long-term orientation versus short-term orientation: this deals with virtue regardless of truth. Values associated with long-term orientation are thrift and

15

perseverance; values associated with short-term orientation are respect for tradition, fulfilling social obligations, and protecting one's 'face'.

These fundamental values help to explain why members of different cultures think and behave differently, in private life as well as in working contexts. What is more, for research: values can be made measurable and therefore present a comparative framework for different management practices throughout the world. The studies by Hofstede show that cultural differences exist not only between European and Asian or US cultures, but also between European cultures (Hofstede 2002).

The impacts of cultural factors on HRM in companies are manifold: culture influences the definition of an effective manager, it influences feedback mechanisms, patterns of communication, negotiation and participation, internal career dynamics and mobility, reward systems, the manager–subordinate relationship as well as mindsets on decisions about structures (Sparrow/Hiltrop 1997).

To illustrate the impact of cultural value systems on research in HR we can pick up the flexibilisation of labour forms once more. Raghuram/London/ Larsen (2001) found evidence for intercountry variations with regard to flexible employment practices, which are explained by cultural differences: part-time work in their study was related to power distance and individualism, contract work was related to uncertainty avoidance and individualism. Shift work was related to uncertainty avoidance, power distance and individualism, while telework was related to femininity. They also stated a tendency for high uncertainty-avoidance cultures to utilise less telework, part-time work and temporary work.

THE FUTURE: STREAMLINING HRM BY EUROPEAN CONCEPTS?

Are concepts of HRM currently emerging that can be called European? The term 'concept' is chosen on purpose, providing enough space to subsume different aspects found in literature, including a supporting philosophy and a set of HRM instruments and practices helping HR managers to accomplish their role.

A study across seven European countries (Denmark, France, Germany, the Netherlands, Spain, Sweden and the UK) revealed HR management philosophies and practices which seemed to converge: this convergence affected the importance accorded to human resources in the countries that were included in the study, the devolution for responsibility for HR issues from national-level institutions to the firm and within this to line management, as well as the linking of corporate and HR strategies so that they are mutually reinforcing (Clark/Pugh 2000: 96).

Sparrow/Schuler/Jackson (1994; 2000: 64–5) found evidence for even a world-wide convergence in some HRM practices and policies implemented to enhance competitive advantage. These either affect cultural change, structure, performance management, resourcing or communication and corporate responsibility. The trends

16

they identified are higher employee empowerment and the promotion of a diverse and egalitarian culture, decentralisation of responsibility, a trend towards higher customer orientation which can provoke a greater sharing of risks and rewards (e.g. by performance-related remuneration schemes), flexibility with regard to job assignments and decisions, and a greater involvement of employees by ameliorated communication structures and sharing of the company's goals with all employees.

Nevertheless, literature in HRM failed to analyse systematically these practices in their national context to show how they are linked to organisational strategy, how they are implemented, with which expectations from the company's leaders as well as from the employees with whom they are concerned, and what their societal impacts are. Or, to cut to the chase: whether the conception of these practices is the same throughout Europe? Maybe only then can we answer the question as to whether a European concept exists.

CREATING FRAMEWORKS FOR THE ANALYSIS OF 'EUROPEAN' HRM OR HRM IN EUROPE

Several authors have provided theoretical frameworks or models for analysing the management of human resources (Schuler/Dowling/De Cieri 1993; Brewster 1995; Ulrich 1997; Sparrow/Brewster/Harris 2004). Theoretical frameworks provide a conceptual structure for the organisation and analysis of scientific topics. They present perspectives by defining the kinds of variables that are considered in analysis. Hendry/Pettigrew (1990) consider, for example, five kinds of variables:

- an organisation's outer, i.e. socio-economic, technological, political-legal and competitive, context;
- an organisation's inner context, comprising culture, structure, politics/leadership, task technology and business outputs;
- the HRM context, i.e. role and definition of HRM within a company, its organisation and outputs;
- HRM content, which refers to HR flows, work systems, reward systems, employee relations; and
- the business strategy content, i.e. business objectives, as well as strategy and tactics.

Other authors developed schemes for the description of management practices in an international context, which also serve to bridge the differences between corporate and country cultures, and respect endogenous factors, like structure and strategy of multinational companies, as well as exogenous factors, like country characteristics or inter-organisational networks within a country (De Cieri/Dowling 1999).

Theoretical frameworks provide a conceptual structure for the organisation and analysis of scientific topics. They present perspectives by defining the kinds of variables that are considered in analysis.

When using a framework for research purposes, e.g. for European comparative studies in HRM, in general the researcher chooses a deductive approach, using a framework and then analysing variables within that framework. The inverse approach would be inductive, i.e. creating a framework by accessing a broad range of easy available data or, in the case of European HRM, country reports. This can be very difficult if the information provided by different countries is not standardised.

The book *Human Resource Management in Europe: Comparative Analysis and Contextual Understanding* provides information in standardised categories. All contributions were supposed to cover the same range of topics, but how the different teams of authors coped with these topics, how detailed their treatment was, and what kind of information they provided, was the responsibility of the individual teams. Nonetheless, when reading the contributions, the reader will perceive some striking parallels in the selection of contents provided in the national contributions.

Nearly all of the contributions compiled in this book refer to a certain level of social partnership in the HRM system of their country as the traditional starting point, and state a movement towards increased business orientation or business partnership at the present time. The second topic that crosses all contributions is the shift of meaning of the personnel function, namely from an administrative to a strategic function.

For this reason, a framework emanating directly from the examples described in this book is one containing two dimensions: social partnership versus business partnership and personnel administration versus strategic HRM. The relative position of each participating country, as far as can be concluded from the texts, is presented in Figure 1.1.

Of course, other frameworks could be constructed, but the one presented here is the most salient one. It is also interesting because the move towards greater business orientation and strategic thinking has implications for further domains that are related to HRM, as stated by some authors of this book. The establishment of a business partnership with the line management needs highly qualified, strategic-thinking HR managers. This point addresses education and further education of HR managers. In addition to this, some of the authors also mention the need to develop country-specific approaches to challenges of HRM. Like education, the development of country-specific solutions is a field that can be promoted by universities, which turn out to be the main drivers of change in HRM. Exchange between HR experts as well as mutual learning from best practices are also considered important for the development of the HR profession. This learning process takes place within HR networks and national HR associations. This book takes account of these points and tries to consider all relevant streams of HRM in the participating countries.

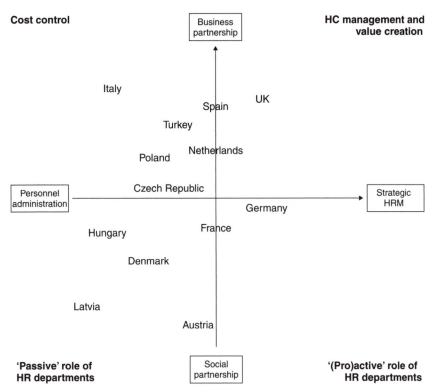

Figure 1.1 Development towards strategic HRM and business partnership

---

The contribution of this book

The appropriateness of global versus country-specific approaches to HRM is currently very topical in some European countries. Especially newer member states of the EU from East Europe are undergoing deep changes in society and working life, relating to the transition from centrally planned economies to free market economies. Obviously, new rules apply to this changed situation, and companies and individuals had to adapt at a rate that was too rapid for theoreticians to assist them and provide them with adequate solutions. The 'import' of general and HR management practices from western countries has therefore often been the most salient solution. There are also smaller countries in western Europe which lack both the necessary research and therefore knowledge of the conditions and factors influencing the success of HRM in their country.

This book presents some opinions in favour of the development of country-specific approaches to HRM. Some of our authors representing either the

19

academic or the practice field argue convincingly why their countries should not only import HRM concepts from the USA or other European countries, but also invest in research to develop their own solutions (see e.g. the contributions of Latvia, the Netherlands or Poland in this book).

The influence of cultural variables in the ways to manage people is shown in several contributions in this book. France and the Czech Republic use, for example, the dimensions of Hofstede as an explanatory frame.

The book features strategic HRM throughout and gives evidence that a streamlining in European HRM occurs at least with regard to the understanding of the HR function: it becomes a strategic partner for top management and a business partner for line management.

CHOOSING A COMPREHENSIVE APPROACH TO HRM IN EUROPE: THE STRUCTURE OF THE BOOK

THE COUNTRIES PRESENTED IN THIS BOOK

Since 1 January 2007, the EU comprises twenty-seven states. Besides the fact that these countries are all situated in the same continent, there are a lot of differences between their cultural, political and economic systems. Therefore, it is important for businesspeople to gather reliable information on the most relevant facts on and differences between the European countries. A lack of such information often results in catastrophic and expensive mistakes.

To meet this challenge, this book provides detailed information and knowledge on thirteen member countries of the European Association for Personnel Management (EAPM) who were willing to participate in this project.

This book delivers the HRM-related information relative to the following countries:

- France, Italy and Spain representing the 'Romanic' part of Europe;
- Poland and the Czech Republic the 'Slavic' part of Europe and as fast-developing new EU members, who had and have to manage a tremendously challenging process of transformation of the whole society, its economy and of course the HR function and profession (this applies equally to both Hungary and Latvia);
- Hungary, representing a former member of the 'Eastern bloc', was the first to open its boarders to western cooperation and influences;
- Latvia representing a new EU member from the Baltic States, which had previously been a part of the former Soviet Union;
- Denmark as a representative of Scandinavia;
- the Netherlands, the UK, Austria and Germany representing the 'Germanic' part of Europe and representing economies with quite different structures and industrial relations philosophies;
- Turkey, with its very special situation as a potential future member of the EU; it has been a fully integrated member of the EAPM for many years, and is working hard for harmonised cultural and political development towards European integration.

The information given about each country follows a certain structure, which is supposed to give room to the highest possible authenticity and at the same time grant comparability between the countries. The structure of the book is described in the following sections.

THE SOCIO-CULTURAL VARIABLES INFLUENCING HRM: BACKGROUND SECTIONS

The background sections follow immediately after the nutshell tables and they contain information about the socio-economic context of HRM in each country. These chapters embed HRM in a broader societal and/or economical context, as for example, the transition to a market economy in eastern European countries or demographical developments in the countries' population with an impact on actual or future personnel work.

They also provide a deeper understanding of cultural and historical factors in national HRM practices. Some authors describe the conception of HRM in their country or give a historical overview of the traditional employer–employee relationship and the development of the HR function over time. The role of labour unions or works' councils is also addressed in some contributions.

The authors of the individual contributions were free to choose the topics that they considered relevant for the understanding of HRM context in their country. The background sections are therefore highly authentic in reflecting the approach to HRM in each country, and the reader should always consider this as a reliable approach for gaining insight into a country's HRM.

CREATING NETWORKS THROUGH HRM ASSOCIATIONS: EAPM AFFILIATE SECTIONS

The countries presented in this book all have national associations for personnel management which are affiliated to the EAPM. Founded by national associations and professional institutions of personnel management in France, Germany, Switzerland and the UK in 1962, the EAPM forms an umbrella body of national organisations which represent personnel professionals. It is an experience-exchange organisation without profit-related objectives, and independent of all employers, trade union, state or political bodies.

The aims of the EAPM are to promote and develop knowledge of personnel issues, personnel activities and their importance to industry, commerce and both public and private sector administration. It grants exchange between its members by organising conferences, congresses and study visits, by publishing information and pursuing all other objectives which directly or indirectly correspond to the aims of the Association. Besides this, it establishes and maintains contacts with other national and international organisations, active in HRM or similar fields. EAPM today has twenty-seven member associations, thirteen of which are presented in this book. The national organisations present their work, which is targeted on their own country, in the EAPM-affiliate chapters.

RESEARCH TRADITIONS AND EDUCATION
OF THE FUTURE HRM THINK-TANK:
ACADEMIA SECTIONS

A separate section is dedicated to research and education in HRM in each country. The academia sections of this book present academic schools of thought in HRM, main topics of research, as well as curricula in the education for future HR managers and the main relevant universities and institutions for HRM education.

Universities play a key role in meeting a country's requirements in 'producing' human capital and in the education of future HR managers. The quality and thematic focuses of university HRM programmes determine the way a company's workforce is managed in the future and motivated for high-performance work.

Of course, HRM education programmes are not rigid but evolve over time and in accordance with economic needs, changing job specifications for HRM, or political requirements. Because of the Bologna process initiated by the EU, university programmes in HRM throughout Europe are actually undergoing far-reaching reforms. Some of them have already introduced BA and MA degrees including the indispensable European Credit Transfer System for students' transborder mobility, while others are still struggling with their transition, and discussing how to align their HRM programmes with BA/MA requirements.

The academia sections presented in this book focus either on research traditions, education or on both. Some of them describe the broad landscape of university programmes and research in their country, others focus on one or more examples which they consider as best practice or which they use to show crucial developments in the academia field. Again, the decision how to approach the academia field was the responsibility of the authors. It presents once more the European principle of allowing diversity within a thematic frame.

PRESENTING BEST PRACTICE: CASE STUDY SECTIONS

One section in each contribution is dedicated to the presentation of a case study in HRM. The case study on best practice example presents the work of an HRM department in a locally based company, which means HR development and training programmes or organisational culture analyses.

HR practitioners were ready to share their experiences in this book, and to give detailed insights into their company's HR strategy. Some of the contributions contain two case studies, provided by consultants and other practitioners with in-depth knowledge of the respective companies.

The companies described belong to very diverse economic fields: electricity production (Austria); insurance (Czech Republic); retail (Denmark); telecommunications (France, Latvia, the UK); medical and safety technology (Germany);

brewing (Hungary); banking (Italy, Spain); electronics (the Netherlands); oil and energy (the Netherlands); printing (Poland); and freight services (Turkey).

HRM solutions of the described companies provide impressive insights into specific implementations of Europe-wide HRM discussions into practice, at the same time considering national specifics. They also show the high HRM standards in the new EU member states as well as in the EU candidate Turkey, which at least in terms of HRM is revealed as an equal partner within the EAPM.

SUMMING-UP: SEVEN QUESTIONS TO THE AUTHORS OF THE CONTRIBUTIONS

Every team of authors answered seven questions from the editors. These questions address important topics, such as country specifics, most important achievements in HRM, 'do's' and 'don'ts' in each country, and so on, and they provide a short comparative overview of national specifics, similarities and differences.

HOW TO MAKE USE OF THIS BOOK

DIFFERENT APPROACHES TO HRM

The book *Human Resource Management in Europe: Comparative Analysis and Contextual Understanding* covers a wide range of HRM-related topics. Students and teachers of academic HRM courses can make use of this information in many valuable ways, depending on their fields of interest. In the following, we would like to present some possible ways of approaching HRM with this book.

The 'issue-related approach' to HRM consists of answering specific thematic questions: What are the main challenges of HRM in different European countries? Who are the most important theoreticians in the field of HRM in a certain European country? Which are the joint characteristics of HRM in southern European countries and what distinguishes them from northern European countries? What is an example of HRM in Turkey? How do HRM practices within telecommunication companies differ in different countries? Readers might have very specific questions with regard to HRM and this book can help to answer them. Nearly every topic relevant in actual and historical debates about HRM is treated by one or more of the teams of authors and these are embedded in a national discussion of HRM. When looking for specific issues, the table of contents as well as the index of this book should be consulted.

The 'country-related approach' means the individual study of different countries. Every country is accorded enough space in this book to give an overview of the HRM landscape and to treat in detail country-specific challenges. Therefore, single chapters can be consulted to get comprehensive information about HRM in a certain country. The country-specific approach will suit readers/users interested in academic courses on international HRM. This book gives a systematic, and at the same time authentic, overview of national HRM systems, practices, challenges and institutions for academic teaching.

The 'comparison-related approach' is self-evident because of the structure of the book. The structure of the book allows for comparisons to be drawn between countries. Information about HRM backgrounds, academia, HRM associations and best practices can systematically be explored and compared by cross-referring within the book. Direct possibilities for comparison are provided by the nutshells giving basic information on each country, as well as by the seven questions already referred to.

The 'institution-related approach' refers to professional associations for personnel managers. Each contribution in this book contains a section on the relevant national association for personnel management which is affiliated to the EAPM. The development of these associations, as well as their fields of activities and major concerns, can be directly compared. Many of the background sections to each country contain information about further national institutions like the role of trade unions or works' committees.

The 'theory-related approach' is obvious because of the academia sections. They contain comprehensive information about the whole academic field of HRM in each country, i.e. education programmes for HR managers, schools of thinking, fields of research and the associated theorists. These sections provide insight into the state of the art of HRM, since they reflect national debates across the whole field.

The 'positioning-related approach' suggests a more experimental approach to the reading of the book, since readers can create their own frameworks for the analysis of HRM in Europe, i.e. determine variables of interest, formulate questions and then read the relevant contributions for answers.

APPLICATION OF THE BOOK TO ACADEMIC COURSES: 'FOR STUDENTS ONLY'

Students and lecturers of HR courses can make use of this book in many ways, as shown by the different approaches presented above. This introductory chapter aims at providing a brief outline of the field of European HRM, which helps to classify and assess the information presented in the single contributions; the comparison of HRM systems in different countries is not possible without frameworks for analysis. Such frameworks help not least to assess the potential of national HRM systems to enable economic competitiveness within the country in which the system operates.

This book not only attempts to be thought-provoking and to encourage interpretations of national HRM strategies, for example, against the background of knowledge about Hofstede's cultural dimensions: it also contains extensive information on country specifics in HRM. The first learning target from reading this introductory chapter should therefore be the knowledge of factors influencing country-specific HR approaches as well as the discussion of problems related to the definition of the term 'European HRM'.

References

Aselstine, Kevin/Alletson, Keri (2006): A new deal for the twenty-first century workplace, in: Ivey Business Journal, 70(4): 1–9.

Bell, Bradford S./Lee, Sae-Won/Yeung, Sarah K. (2006): The impact of e-HR on professional competence in HRM: Implications for the development of HR professionals, in: Human Resource Management, 45(3): 295–308.

Braun, Werner/Warner, Malcolm (2002): The culture-free versus culture-specific management debate, in: Malcolm Warner/Pat Joynt (eds): Managing Across Cultures: Issues and Perspectives, 2nd edn, London, pp. 13–25.

Brewster, Chris (1995): Towards a 'European' model of human resource management, in: Journal of International Business Studies, 1/1995, www.fsa.ulaval.ca/personnel/vernag/REF/Textes/Brewster.htm (accessed 19 October 2006).

Brewster, Chris/Hegewisch, Ariane/Lockhart, Terry/Holden, Len (1992): The European Human Resource Management Guide, London.

Brewster, Chris/Mayrhofer, Wolfgang/Morley, Michael (eds) (2000): New Challenges for European Human Resource Management, New York.

—— (2004): Human Resource Management in Europe: Evidence or Convergence?, London.

Brodbeck, Felix C. et al. (2000): Cultural variation of leadership prototypes across twenty two European countries, in: Journal of Occupational and Organisational Psychology, 73(1): 1–29.

Caligiuri, Paula M./Stroh, Linda K. (1995): Multinational corporation management strategies and international human resources practices: Bringing IHRM to the bottom line, in: International Journal of Human Resource Management, 6(3): 494–507.

Cappelli, Peter (1999): New Deal at Work: Managing the Market-driven Workforce, Boston.

Child, John (1981): Culture, contingency and capitalism in the cross-national study of organisations, in: Barry M. Staw/Larry L. Cummings (eds): Research in Organisational Behaviour, 3, Greenwich.

Clark, Timothy/Pugh, Derek (2000): Similarities and differences in European conceptions of human resource management: Toward a polycentric study, in: International Studies of Management and Organisation, 29(4): 84–100.

Communal, Christine/Brewster, Chris (2004): HRM in Europe, in: Anne-Wil Harzing/Joris van Ruysseveldt (eds): International Human Resource Management, 2nd edn, London, pp. 167–94.

Cooke, Fang Lee/Shen, Jie/McBride, Anne (2005): Outsourcing HR as a competitive strategy? A literature review and an assessment of implications, in: Human Resource Management, 44(4):413–32.

De Cieri, Helen/Dowling, Peter J. (1999): Strategic human resource management in multinational enterprises: Theoretical and empirical developments, in: Patrick M. Wright/Lee D. Dyer/John W. Boudreau/George T. Milkovich (eds): Research in Personnel and Human Resources Management: Strategic Human Resources Management in the Twenty-first Century, Supplement 4, Stamford, pp. 305–27.

Dewettinck, Koen/Buyens, Dirk/Auger, Céline/Dany, Françoise/Wilthagen, Ton (2006): Deregulation: HRM and the Flexibility–Security Nexus, in: Henrik H. Larsen/Wolfgang Mayrhofer (eds): Managing Human Resources in Europe, London, pp. 45–62.

Dowling, Peter/Welch, Denice E. (2005): International Human Resource Management: Managing People in a Multinational Context, 4th edn, London.

Edwards, Tony/Kuruvilla, Sarosh (2005): International HRM: National business systems, organisational politics and the international division of labour in MNCs, in: International Journal of Human Resource Mangement, 16(1): 1–21.

Evans, Paul/Pucik, Vladimir/Barsoux, Jean-Louis (2002): The Global Challenge: Frameworks for International Human Resource, New York.

Fenwick, Marilyn (2004): International compensation and performance management, in: Anne-Wil Harzing/Joris van Ruysseveldt (eds): International Human Resource Management, 2nd edn, London, pp. 307–32.

Ferrer, Anthony/Hyman, Richard (1998): Introduction: Towards European industrial relations? in: Anthony Ferrer/Richard Hyman (eds): Changing Industrial Relations in Europe, 2nd edn, Oxford.

Hall, Edward T. (1969): The Hidden Dimension: Man's Use of Space in Public and Private, London etc.

—— (1976): Beyond Culture, Garden City.

Hall, Edward T./Hall, Mildred R. (1990): Understanding Cultural Differences: Germans, French and Americans, Yarmouth.

Hannon, John/Jelf, Gregory/Brandes, Deborah (1996): Human resource information systems: operational issues and strategic considerations in a global environment, in: International Journal of Human Resource Management, 7(1): 245–65.

Harzing, Anne-Will (2004): Composing an international staff, in: Anne-Will Harzing/Joris van Ruysseveldt (eds): International Human Resource Management, 2nd edn, London, pp. 251–282.

Harzing, Anne-Will/van Ruysseveldt, Joris (eds) (2004): International Human Resource Management, 2nd edn, London.

Hayton, James C. (2005): Promoting corporate entrepreneurship through human resource management practices: A review of empirical research, in: Human Resource Management Review, 15(1): 21–41.

Hendry, Chris/Pettigrew, Andrew (1990): Human resource management: An agenda for the 1990s, in: International Journal of Human Resource Management, 1(1):17–43.

Heneman, Robert L./Greenberger, David B. (eds) (2002): Human Resource Management in Virtual Organisations, Greenwich.

Hofstede, Geert (1980): Culture's Consequences: International Differences in Work-Related Values, Beverly Hills.

—— (1991): Culture and Organisations: Software of the Mind, London.

—— (1993): Culture's Consequences: International Differences in Work-related Values, Newbury Park.

—— (2002): Managing across cultures: issues and perspectives, in: Malcolm Warner/Pat Joynt (eds): Managing Across Cultures, 2nd edn, London.

Janssens, Maddy/Sels, Luc/van den Brande, Inge (2003): Multiple types of psychological contracts: a six-cluster solution, in: Human Relations, 56(11): 1349–78.

Larsen, Henrik H./Mayrhofer, Wolfgang (2006): European HRM: on the road again, in: Henrik H. Larsen/Wolfgang Mayrhofer (eds): Managing Human Resources in Europe, London, pp. 259–70.

Lazarova, Mila/Caligiuri, Paula (2004): Repatriation and knowledge management, in: Anne-Wil Harzing/Joris van Ruysseveldt (eds): International Human Resource Management, 2nd edn, London, pp. 307–32.

Linehan, Margaret/Scullion, Hugh (eds) (2005): International Human Resource Management: *A Critical Text*, Basingstoke.

Morgan, Gareth (1986): Images of Organisation, Beverly Hills.

Murray, V.V./Dimick, D.E. (1978): Contextual influences on personnel policies and programs: an explanatory model, in: Academy of Management Review, 3(4): 750–61.

Murray, V. V./Jain, Harish C./Adams, Ray J. (1976): A framework for the comparative analysis of personnel administration, in: Academy of Management Review, 1(3): 47–58.

Nikandrou, Iren/Apospori, Eleni/Papalexandris, Nancy (2005): Changes in HRM in Europe: a longitudinal comparative study among 18 European countries, in: Journal of European Industrial Training, 29(7): 541–60.

Nikandrou, Iren/Campos e Cunha, Rita/Papalexandris, Nancy (2006): HRM and organisational performance: universal and contextual evidence, in: Henrik Holt Larsen/Wolfgang Mayrhofer (eds): Managing Human Resources in Europe, London, pp. 177–98.

Pickett, Les (2000): People make the difference, in: Industrial and Commercial Training, 32(6): 225–9.

Raghuram, Sumina/London, Manuel/Larsen, Henrik Holt (2001): Flexible employment practices in Europe: country versus culture, in: International Journal of Human Resource Management, 12(5): 738–53.

Ronen, Simcha/Shenkar, Oded (1985): Clustering countries on attitudinal dimensions: a review and synthesis, in: Academy of Management Review, 10(3): 435–54.

Rosenzweig, Philip M./Nohria, Nitin (1994): Influences on human resource development practices in multinational corporations, in: Journal of International Business Studies, 25(2): 229–51.

Scholz, Christian (2000a): Strategische Organisation. Multiperspektivität und Virtualität, 2nd edn, Landsberg/Lech.

—— (2000b): Personalmanagement, 5th edn, Munich.

—— (2003): Spieler ohne Stammplatzgarantie. Darwiportunismus in der neuen Arbeitswelt, Weinheim.

Scholz, Christian/Messemer, Teresa/Schröter, Marco (1991): Personalpolitik als Instrument zur bewussten Kulturdifferenzierung und Kulturkoexistenz, in: Rainer Marr (ed.): Euro-strategisches Personalmanagement, 1, Munich, pp. 43–74.

Scholz, Christian/Stein, Volker/Eisenbeis, Uwe (2001): Die TIME-Branche: Konzepte – Entwicklungen – Standorte, Munich, Mering.

Scholz, Christian/Stein, Volker/Bechtel, Roman (2004): Human Capital Management: Wege aus der Unverbindlichkeit, Munich, Unterschleißheim.

Schuler, Randall S./Dowling, Peter J./De Cieri, Helen (1993): An integrative framework of strategic international human resource management, in: International Journal of Human Resource Management, 4(4): 717–64.

29

Serlavós, Ricard/Aparicio-Valverde, Mireia (2000): Flexible working practices: the challenges in Europe, in: Chris Brewster/Wolfgang Mayrhofer/Michael Morley (eds): New Challenges for European Human Resource Management, London, pp. 37–55.

Sforza, Leonardo (2005): EU developments and their impact on HR issues, in: Pensions, 40(4): 336–42.

Shen, Jie (2005): Human resource outsourcing: 1990–2004, in: Journal of Organisational Transformation and Social Change, 2(3): 275–96.

Sofer, Catherine (ed.) (2004): Human Capital over the Lifecycle: A European Perspective, Cheltenham etc.

Sparrow, Paul/Hiltrop, Jean-Marie (1994): European Human Resource Management in Transition, New York, London.

—— (1997): Redefining the field of European human resource management: A battle between national mindsets and forces of business transition?, in: Human Resource Management, 36(2): 201–19.

Sparrow, Paul/Brewster, Chris/Harris, Hilary (2004): Globalizing Human Resource Management, London.

Sparrow, Paul/Schuler, Randall S./Jackson, Susan E. (1994): Convergence or divergence: Human resource practices and policies for competitive advantage worldwide, in: International Journal of Human Resource Management, 5(2): 267–99.

—— (2000): Convergence or divergence: human resource practices and policies for competitive advantage worldwide, in: Mark Mendenhall/Gary Oddou (eds): Readings and Cases in International Human Resource Management, Scarborough, pp. 42–203.

Supiot, Alain/Meadows, Pamela (2001): Beyond Employment: Changes in Work and the Future of Labour Law in Europe, Oxford.

Tarique, Ibraiz/Caligiuri, Paula (2004): Training and development of international staff, in: Anne-Wil Harzing/Joris van Ruysseveldt (eds): International Human Resource Management, 2nd edn, London, pp. 283–307.

Trompenaars, Fons (1993): Riding the Waves of Culture: Understanding Cultural Diversity in Business, London.

Tzafir, Shay S. (2006): A universalistic perspective for explaining the relationship between HRM practices and firm performance at different points in time, in: Journal of Managerial Psychology, 21(2): 109–30.

Ulrich, David O. (1997): Human Resource Champions: The Next Agenda for Adding Value and Delivering Results, Boston.

van Liemt, Gijsbert (1998): Labour in the global economy: challenges, adjustment and policy responses in the EU, in: Olga Memedovic/Arie Kuyvenhoven/Willem T.M. Molle (eds): Globalisation of Labour Markets, Dordrecht, Boston, London, pp. 237–48.

Weber, Wolfgang/Kabst, Rüdiger/Gramley, Christopher (2000): Human resource policies in European organisations: an analysis of country and company-specific antecedents, in: Chris Brewster/Wolfgang Mayrhofer/Michael Morley (eds): New Challenges for European Human Resource Management, London, pp. 247–66.

Weidenfels, Werner/Wessels, Wolfgang (eds) (2002): Europa von A bis Z, Bonn.

2 HRM in Austria: behavioural school of thought

Dudo von Eckardstein/Julia Brandl/Hellwig Maier/Rudolf Thurner

Legend:
- Country portrait
- Participating countries

Austria: in a nutshell

In this chapter you will learn:

– that Austrian industrial relations cover three levels of responsibility (state, collective partners and organisational) which lead to a specific consensus culture;

– that HR academia in Austria is characterised by a strong fragmentation. Thus there is no summary of general topics to characterise the most important research fields; and

– that Verbund challenged the transition to a free market economy due to its HRM activities based on strategically targeted restructuring measures.

Capital:	Vienna
Area (sq km):	83,870 (land 82,444; water 1,426)
EU membership:	since 1995
Population:	8,192,880
Languages:	German (official nationwide); Slovene (official in Carinthia); Croatian (official in Burgenland); Hungarian (official in Burgenland)
Ethnic groups (in percentages):	Austrians 91.1; former Yugoslavs 4 (includes Croatians, Slovenes, Serbs and Bosniaks); Turks 1.6; German 0.9; other or unspecified 2.4 (2001)
Gross domestic product:	279.5 billion USD (2006)
Workforce (in percentages):	3.88 million: agriculture and forestry 3; industry 27; services 70 (2005)
Export commodities:	machinery and equipment, motor vehicles and components, paper and paperboard, metal goods, chemicals, iron and steel, textiles, foodstuffs

BACKGROUND: ECONOMY AND
SOCIAL PARTNERSHIP

🔳 .at

AUSTRIA: A GATEKEEPER FOR THE EAST

The Republic of Austria, situated geographically, historically and culturally in the heart of Central Europe, is a highly developed industrialised nation with an important service sector (e.g. banking and finance). The main feature of Austria's industrial and commercial sectors is a high proportion of small- and medium-sized enterprises. Austrian industry covers every branch of manufacture, from basic goods to the labour-intensive production of finished goods. Austrian industries are strongly export-oriented, with Germany the biggest traditional trading partner.

Since the opening of Eastern Europe in 1989 Austrian exports to this region have grown significantly faster than exports overall. Today, about one-third of all Austrian foreign investments are made in the Eastern European countries that recently became EU members – and the figure is rising. In some of these countries, up to one-tenth of direct foreign investment stems from Austria. Many Austrian companies have started developing markets in Eastern Europe by founding subsidiaries, transferring employees to these countries and so on. On the other hand, people from Eastern Europe have come to work in Austria.

These developments in the business orientation of Austrian companies have a number of implications for the way human resource management (HRM) is conducted. They are likely to present major challenges for the current attitude to HRM, which is in many ways similar to the German understanding of HRM (for details, see also Chapter 6 on Germany in this book). These similarities can be traced back partly to the common language, which facilitates the transfer of HRM concepts and practices between Germany and Austria. In addition, workforce mobility between Germany and Austria has encouraged companies to develop HRM practices that cater to employees from both countries.

> **In a few words, what would you say is the one fundamental strategic competitive advantage your country offers compared to others?**
>
> Austria is situated in the middle of Europe with a very good infrastructure and a high level of education. Moreover, Austria is not prone to industrial action, has a clearly structured legal system, offers a wide range of business promotion schemes and has a stable government.

ECONOMY: AN ASSEMBLY FOR SMALL- AND
MEDIUM-SIZED COMPANIES

As the structure of business in Austria is dominated by small and family-run businesses, responsibility for people management rests mainly with company owners.

In this context the use of formal HRM instruments (e.g. assessment centre for staff selection) is rather rare. Administrative HRM functions (e.g. payroll management) are either performed by a secretary/assistant or delegated to external service providers. Institutionalisation of a specialised personnel function and application of formal HRM instruments are found primarily in large companies. Even there, however, there is a dominant tradition of role-sharing between personnel specialists and line managers. Recruiting, planning and people development are tasks mostly performed by line managers, whereas HRM specialists focus on payroll management, having little influence on strategic decision-making.

Against the backdrop of increasing internationalisation, Austrian companies are finding they need a more integrated approach to HRM. The recent establishment of subsidiaries in Eastern Europe and acquisitions of Eastern European companies have brought up the question as to how HRM practices can be managed in an international context. As there is an increasing demand for expertise in HRM, this provides new opportunities for Austrian HRM specialists. However, in order to manage these developments, HRM specialists need to be familiar with languages, cultural backgrounds and working conditions (e.g. labour laws, industrial relations) in Eastern Europe. As many Austrian HRM specialists lack international gearing, this presents major challenges for the (academic) education and career paths of HRM specialists.

What is your advice for a foreign firm entering your country's market? What should managers especially care about and, what is more, be aware of?

We advise foreign firms to conduct a market analysis. They should also contact the Austrian Federal Economic Chamber for further information and assistance. Generally speaking, it is better not to move too close to megalopolis if it is not necessary.

ECONOMIC RELATIONS: THREE LEVELS OF RESPONSIBILITY

The Austrian system of industrial relations spans three levels (state, collective partners and organisational) with each level having its specific responsibilities and integration between the different levels. Collective bargaining in Austria is traditionally known for its 'consensus-oriented culture', with trade union and employers' representatives engaging in an intense dialogue. As a consequence, the number and duration of strikes is among the lowest in Europe. At the same time Austrian labour relations can be described as highly structured, with legal regulations providing a high level of protection for employees (e.g. regulations on dismissal pay). Employment conditions (e.g. remuneration, working time) can be generally seen as 'employee-friendly' as they provide a comparatively high standard of social and other benefits (e.g. overtime pay) for employees. As in other European countries, trade union membership in Austria has decreased in recent decades. Major reasons for this development are changes in industry and workforce structure (traditional trade union members are blue-collar workers, who are increasingly being replaced by white-collar workers) and employment conditions (e.g. standard employment contract erosion). In the long run, this will weaken the situation in Austria, raising the question whether its consensus-oriented culture will survive in the future.

Up to the present, the activities of Austrian companies in Eastern Europe have not had much impact on Austrian labour legislation and collective bargaining. However, with Austrian companies facing growing competition, there will be pressure on labour costs as well. The removal of mobility barriers for employees from Eastern European EU members from 2007 on is likely to increase the potential for highly qualified – and comparatively cheap – labour in Austria. Austrian companies need to harness this potential in order to strengthen their competitive position in the heart of Europe, so they need HRM strategies that will attract and integrate these employees.

> **What are you and other Austrian people extraordinarily proud of with respect to HRM?**
>
> Social peace, very low incidence of strikes.

AUSTRIA'S CONSENSUS CULTURE

Partly as a result of Austria's consensus culture, HRM activity is influenced by the view that companies have a duty to help ensure the welfare of the state and society. This attitude, which is commonly found in Austrian companies, has been recently formalised in the concept of 'corporate social responsibility' (CSR). The basic idea behind CSR is that a company's economic success and responsibility are interdependent – and that economic gain and responsible conduct do not constitute a contradiction. Among other things, CSR emphasises the need to involve others and strengthen commitment. Austria's leading employers' associations, the Federation of Austrian Industry (*Industriellenvereinigung*) and the Austrian Chamber of Commerce (WKO), have recently defined the kind of HRM activities that CSR entails.

> Involving others implies that employees are treated as partners, promoting social integration, taking the concerns of stakeholders into account and helping to improve the situation in other countries. A committed implementation effort emphasises the need for transparency through information policy, cooperation in a spirit of partnership and further development of promising measures.

35

In the context of the orientation of Austrian companies towards Eastern Europe two dissimilar developments are conceivable for current HRM practices. The first is that integrative HRM practices become less widespread. This, however, would mean giving up a major competitive advantage over companies from Eastern Europe, so Austrian companies would have difficulties attracting highly qualified workers in these markets. Therefore, the second option is that Austrian companies also transfer CSR to the foreign countries in question. This is also more probable because Austrian companies see 'improving the situation in other countries' as an element of CSR. Whatever strategy Austrian companies choose, they need to define strategies for dealing with differences between their current HRM practices and HRM practices in the new markets.

In the light of the circumstances noted above, the key challenges for HRM in Austria can be summarised as follows: (a) need for the development of highly qualified HRM specialists with specific expertise in HRM in the countries of Eastern Europe (e.g. language, labour law, culture); (b) need to attract and integrate highly qualified employees from Eastern Europe in order to stabilise and improve competitive positioning; and (c) development of strategies for dealing with differences in HRM between the Austrian context and Eastern Europe's emerging markets.

What is typical of your country in relation to the country itself (its culture, people, etc.) and its economy?

Even if, internationally, Austria is not considered to be a special case, there is still widespread agreement that cooperation and the coordination of interests between the federations is one of this country's distinctive features. The common definition for this type of cooperation is 'social partnership'.

EAPM AFFILIATE: ÖSTERREICHISCHES PRODUKTIVITÄTS- UND WIRTSCHAFTLICHKEITS-ZENTRUM (ÖPWZ)

:.at

FROM FOREIGN INFLUENCES TO INDEPENDENCE

The Austrian association for personnel management is called 'Österreichisches Produktivitäts- und Wirtschaftlichkeits-Zentrum (ÖPWZ)' in German, which translates into English as the 'Austrian Centre for Productivity and Efficiency'. ÖPWZ was one of the first institutions in Austria dedicated to the idea of social and economic partnership. The Centre was established by parliamentary resolution in 1950 in the wake of talks between representatives of the US Economic Cooperation Administration (ECA) mission in Austria and the Austrian Federal Government in 1949/50 – at a time when the Austrian economy was struggling to recover from the effects of the Second World War. The aim was to harness both intellectual and moral resources as well as Austria's natural assets in an endeavour to boost economic productivity. The venture was financed by an agreement between the ECA mission in Austria and the Federal Chancellor's Office, which is the central office for ERP (European Recovery Programme) affairs.

From 1960 onwards, ÖPWZ concentrated its activities on two business fields: (a) professional seminars for managers and specialists to develop and update competences and skills; and (b) a number of experience exchange groups were established, enabling managers in similar jobs to make contacts and benefit from the experience of their professional colleagues.

The first of these groups dedicated to personnel management was established on the basis of the German DGFP model (Deutsche Gesellschaft für Personalführung/German association for HRM and leadership) in 1966. During the 1970s, ÖPWZ continued designing and organising high-quality training programmes for managers and specialists across a broad range of topics and in a variety of formats such as seminars, conferences and congresses. The working and study groups continued likewise. Except during a short period of economic depression (the 'oil crisis') in the middle of the 1970s, demand for the ÖPWZ programmes increased. Predominant topics were personal and social–psychological development, organisational behaviour and management models. In-house courses proliferated and grew in significance, and even public organisations (on a federal as well as on a regional level) started to introduce special training programmes for their employees.

By the early 1980s, ÖPWZ had moved away from public funding and developed into an independent market-oriented institute dedicated to information transfer and training. Since then it has had a permanent staff of approximately forty persons. ÖPWZ stages more than 900 seminars, conventions, academies, training sessions (both in-house and external) and holds experience exchange meetings each year in many fields, e.g. leadership and personnel management.

In 2003 over 7,500 people took part in ÖPWZ seminars. These one- to two-day seminars serve to keep participants abreast of developments in their field. Academy programmes, on the other hand, are more time-consuming. They last one to three weeks and provide initial training in various fields. These include ÖPWZ Personnel Academy, ÖPWZ Purchasing Academy, ÖPWZ Sales Academy, ÖPWZ Payroll Academy, ÖPWZ-BWG Banking Academy, Training Course for Stockbrokers and Investment Advisors, VOIG-BWG Course in Capital and Portfolio Management.

💡.at

Historical transitions in eastern European countries and their repercussions on the Austrian economy have certainly had implications for ÖPWZ activities. On the one hand there was an objective to support the countries in their transition to a market economy; on the other hand, the imperative of the moment was to support Austrian companies in their attempt to open up the emerging markets.

'FORUM PERSONAL': BRANDING SERVICES

The economic independence of ÖPWZ derives from the organisation's two sources of income: (a) seminars and training; and (b) membership services. Both are maintained by fees from participants and members. Members in the field of HRM include some 400 private companies in the various economic sectors as well as organisations in the public sector.

The core service provided exclusively for members is what used to be called the Experience Exchange Group (*ARGE Personal*). Since 2003, all services and activities in the field of personnel management for members only are offered under the brand name 'Forum Personal' ('Personnel Forum') (see Figure 2.1).

The aim of the 'Personnel Forum' is to support HRM and HR development on a practical as well as on a theoretical level. This goal is achieved through the following activities.

Experience exchange groups

The member companies are divided into fourteen groups, each of which comes together four times a year, each member taking it in turns to host the meeting. The agenda of the meetings changes according to the needs defined by the group, but generally they start with a short presentation of the host company and relevant projects which have been undertaken in the company. Learning from best practices is one of the crucial points by which members profit. This is followed by an expert paper, which is discussed afterwards. Experts are either academics with an outstanding record or very experienced practitioners. Experience exchange is a very important item on each agenda. All the group members receive a copy of

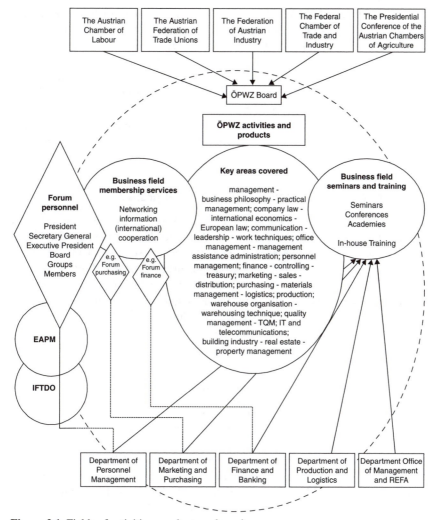

Figure 2.1 Fields of activities: products and services

the minutes taken. Another important aspect of these groups is that they create an environment of confidence, making benchmarking possible (e.g. concerning employee sickness absences or turnover rates). In short, it is all about learning through sharing professional knowledge.

Conferences/symposia for members only

In another major area of member services, ÖPWZ organises a range of conferences for members only. The most important one in terms of participant numbers is the Annual Meeting of Personnel Departments Heads. Up to one hundred people take part in this convention, consulting on issues such as labour law updates, addressing cutting-edge topics and, last but not least, taking the opportunity to discuss and socialise with colleagues. Another conference is the Austria–Germany–Switzerland Conference – a result of the intensive cooperation established between the German and Swiss associations and ÖPWZ in the 1960s. This meeting is organised in a joint effort by these countries, which are economically linked and share a similar business environment in certain key regards. The Alpen–Adria Conference is attended by HR managers from Austria, Italy and Slovenia; the focus of the Austria–Hungary Conference is on bilateral interests.

Seminars and conferences for broad target groups

In addition to these members-only events, ÖPWZ organises seminars and conferences for a broader target group. Personnel Forum member companies enjoy reduced participation fees if they use ÖPWZ seminars and courses to train their employees. For the target group HR managers, ÖPWZ offers approximately eighty different seminars a year (from one to three days' duration). In addition, the ÖPWZ programme includes a series of themed conferences with a broader HR focus. Here, the target group also includes executives with other functions, e.g. concerned with business ethics or reform of the Austrian pension system.

Academy for personnel management

ÖPWZ started in the 1970s with a five-week training programme specially developed for young HR professionals. The curriculum proved very successful and many executives participated in it. Two years ago the programme was relaunched in a shorter, three-week version and the curriculum remodelled. The decision to do so was based on the fact that companies are under increasing pressure to cut their training costs. The structure of the curriculum reflects the fact that an increasing number of people managers in Austria tend to be recruited from other parts of the company.

Surveys and studies

ÖPWZ conducts a wide range of surveys on a regular basis and provides benchmark data showing sectoral, regional, company-size related and so on, variations in various fields. To mention but a few, these include: (a) different ways of dealing with new regulations concerning the attachment of wages; (b) statutory regulations and practice concerning expatriates; (c) problems with high employee turnover rates; (d) employee sickness absence; (e) comparisons of different models of occupational pensions; and (f) starting salaries for university and college graduates. Some of these surveys are conducted in cooperation with universities, e.g. with the University of Applied Sciences Wiener Neustadt.

Consultancy: HRCC (Human Resource Competence Centre)

Recently a special group was established consisting of retired HR managers willing to share their knowledge and experience. They offer consultancy services (e.g. how to set up and analyse a system of key performance indicators) to companies, especially to SMEs, at a very reasonable cost. As the topic of demographic changes and age management is very prevalent nowadays, we consider this initiative – as well as similar projects in other European countries – to be very important.

Knowledge and information-sharing service – internet

Part of ÖPWZ's service package is to provide access to an internet information platform. State-of-the-art technology is harnessed to make available all kinds of resources relating to HR topics. There are also forums and a weblog. However, the ÖPWZ members have not yet tapped into the full potential of this feature. The platform also informs members about forthcoming events, results of surveys, and so on.

DEVELOPING THE HRM PROFESSION

The organisation has played a vital role in the development of professional personnel management. As has already been mentioned, the profession as we know it today has been defined and redefined in the course of the last fifty years. The establishment of networks is an outstanding and singular achievement and has had a major impact on the process of giving the profession a measure of self-assurance. Through this continuous exchange, HR managers – as they are called now – have helped each other in defining their role and getting to know their targets better. As we can learn from the archive, the issues HR managers tackle have not changed much over the years but tasks have expanded and their role has changed from an operational to a more strategic one.

'Who we are and how we want to be seen' is a matter of crucial importance for the success of both individual professionals and the profession as a whole. However, as HR managers deal with people, and people are a core asset for a company, this question has much wider implications. Different HR roles coexist. One important one is HR managers' part in collective bargaining. Other primary tasks are to implement legislation, to manage compensation and to be the social conscience of the business. But generally speaking, there is evidence of a fairly subtle shift in priorities regarding these various roles. As the goal of achieving business outcome and improving performance becomes more important, the relationship with the board of management is also changing. With less need to focus on operational issues, HR managers' sights and efforts are geared to developing a strategic partnership role with the board. Another 'new' role is as a consultant, providing advice for line managers.

41

The networks established by ÖPWZ have contributed – and are still contributing – significantly to this challenging and ongoing definition process. From the very outset, ÖPWZ monitored and promoted progressive change as a stable point of contact. What distinguishes ÖPWZ's services from those of other organisations in this field is the emphasis on a practical hands-on approach. Given its unique situation of having established excellent networks with both business and political decision-makers, ÖPWZ is in a position to respond to client requirements immediately and acquire first-hand information – something of major importance for a special, indeed distinctive Austrian feature: the system of social partnership, which has been a guiding principle in recent decades, making for close cooperation and coordination of interests between the federations and chambers on matters of income policy and certain aspects of economic and social policy, e.g. industrial safety regulations, labour market policy and principles of equal treatment.

From this background, the main item on the agenda of the 2003 meeting of heads of personnel departments focused on the demographic time bomb we are facing and the consequences for HRM at a strategic level. The conference therefore addressed the challenge of how to modify work organisation in order to make it possible for employees aged over 40 to stay longer with the company, remain healthy and be motivated to pass on their knowledge and experience to younger colleagues and co-workers. For example, this strategy was the subject of one of the conference's keynote papers given by the HR director of Voestalpine AG, one of the leading industry groups in Austria. There is growing evidence from a number of surveys that it is of immense importance to develop integrated, age-aware HR policies and provide flexible working patterns available to the workforce at all stages of life as well as tailor-made health and safety programmes capable of addressing age issues.

> **What would you like to teach foreign HR managers? What is important for them to know in your opinion?**
>
> It is very important for HR managers to know the Austrian system of 'social partnership', labour law and especially the collective agreements and payroll system.

VISION: BE THE NUMBER ONE CONTACT FOR HR

ÖPWZ's vision is to be the first and most important contact point for Austrian HR managers and its aim is to deliver a wide range of practical services to support its members in the HR profession, keep their competences and skills up to date and increase the efficiency of HR systems and processes. ÖPWZ offers a comprehensive knowledge base, enhanced by international links and two-way exchanges, a platform for exchanging experiences and engaging in dialogue as well as opportunities to make valuable personal contacts. ÖPWZ wants to contribute to

.at

the profession's reputation and standing in the business world. Its activities provide significant support at a practical level and pave the way for the anticipation of future trends, necessary developments or intellectually challenging debates.

There is little doubt that the future will see the development of more and more networked organisations because they are an effective answer to the continuous radical change sweeping the world of business. The reason for this development lies in the nature of this specific organisation form which can – temporarily – provide the strengths of a large organisation without the bureaucratic drawbacks. In the globalised economy, information and knowledge are of paramount importance and thus make cooperation indispensable. As the Personnel Forum has a great deal of experience of successful network management, ÖPWZ wishes to continue down this road and promote cooperative networking among members to help to ensure their economic well-being. ÖPWZ considers the network approach vital for the continued improvement of the HR profession.

ÖPWZ wishes to be regarded as an organisation helping HR managers to stand their ground and make more headway, because it considers people management as a crucial business function which contributes much to and is therefore indispensable for business success.

What would you say one ought not to do? What are the 'don'ts' in your country?

It may not be advisable to enter the Austrian market without a knowledge of the economic and legal situations and systems.

HR ACADEMIA: HRM AS AN ACADEMIC DISCIPLINE

ACADEMIC RESEARCH AND EDUCATION SINCE THE 1980s

Today, HRM is a well-established field of academic research in Austria. At least eight academic institutions at university level deal with HR topics (Table 2.1). One particularly Austrian characteristic is that only a few departments are exclusively dedicated to the discipline of HRM. HRM is mostly found embedded in organisation studies or management science.

Table 2.1 Academic HR institutions in Austria

University and faculty/institute	*Department name (year of establishment): academic responsibility*
University of Graz, Institute for Economics and Social Sciences	Organisation and Human Resource Management (since 1968): Herbert Kraus
University of Linz, Institute for Business Management	Organisation (since 1976): Gerhard Reber
University of Klagenfurt, Institute for Business Sciences	Organisational, Human Resources and Management Development (OHM, since 1980): Heijo Rieckmann
University of Innsbruck, Institute for Organisation and Learning	Personnel and Work (since 1980): Stephan Laske
Vienna University of Economics and Business Administration, Institute for Management and Education Science	Human Resource Management (since 1982): Wolfgang Weber (until 1985); Dudo von Eckardstein (until 2006)
Vienna University of Economics and Business Administration, Institute for Management and Education Science	Renamed in 1997 Interdisciplinary Department for Management and Organisational Behaviour (since 1997): Michael Hofmann (until 1987); Wolfgang Mayrhofer
Vienna University of Economics and Business Administration, Institute for Management and Education Science	Change Management and Management Development (since 1991): Helmut Kasper
University of Linz, Institute for Business Management	Human Resource Management (since 1992): Wolf R. Böhnisch
University of Vienna, Department for Business Management	Human Resource Management (since 1993): Christian Scholz acting as permanent visiting professor
Danube University Krems, Department for Business Management	General Management and Executive Education (since 1994)
PEF University, Vienna	(since 2002): Karl Zehetner

Historical development

The development of the academic discipline can be traced back to the 1970s when university departments dedicated to research in organisation, management and other related fields showed increasing interest in human aspects of their research and started to conduct a number of research projects in these fields. In some departments these activities were later institutionalised by adding the term 'human resource management' to the official department name (e.g. at the University of Graz). Others such as Gerhard Reber from the University of Linz later reverted to their regular research fields. Academic departments within the management discipline see HRM as a topic of growing relevance today. They increasingly integrate HR issues into their programmes without changing their department name. However, because HRM ultimately remains a peripheral field at these institutions (related to their core disciplines), the extent to which HR topics are investigated varies widely. Also, the focus on HRM is predetermined by their core discipline.

The first departments explicitly dedicated to HRM were established in Austria at the beginning of the 1980s – at the University of Innsbruck and at Vienna's University of Economics and Business Administration. The institutionalisation of the latter department, which was managed by Wolfgang Weber until 1985, was strongly encouraged and also co-financed for several years by the Austrian Federal Economic Chamber and the Federation of Austrian Industry. In 1992 a third HR department was set up at the University of Linz, so that in Austria today there are three academic departments whose core discipline is HRM. In contrast to the departments where HRM is seen as a peripheral discipline, these institutions cover a wide range of HR topics. The reforms to the academic system in Austria in the 1990s have resulted in the foundation of new types of academic institutions, including universities of applied sciences (*Fachhochschulen*) and privately run universities. A number of these institutions also contribute to the HR field, as they offer HR-related study programmes at postgraduate level (e.g. Danube University Krems, PEF University Vienna). However, these institutions focus exclusively on teaching. They employ hardly any staff of their own; instead, they conduct their programmes with practitioners and with academics from other universities.

Institutional structure

Generally HRM is located within the field of business administration. As the classification in Table 2.2 shows (see p. 49), HR departments in Austria either belong to faculties of economics and business administration or they are integrated into institutes with a focus on management or organisational studies. The number of academic staff regularly employed by the departments varies between four and seven, including the department head. This number obviously increases when those working on research projects and external lecturers are also taken into account. The way the departments are integrated into the universities and the size of the departments have remained largely unchanged for many years now. The 2002 Austrian university reform, which is currently being implemented, aims at a further concentration of resources, greater flexibility on the part of academics and the reorganisation of academic units themselves. So it is very likely that the present structure and staff numbers in the HR departments will undergo major changes in the near future. This is supported by the fact that two of the three department heads from the core HR departments will retire within the next few years.

ACADEMIC RESEARCH

The research orientation of HRM in Austria can be best summarised by the dominance of the behavioural approach as the overall research paradigm, by the heterogeneity of sub-theories and research topics and by a strong orientation towards the German academic community with regard to international activities. When talking about general orientations of academic research, academic scholars often distinguish between economic and behavioural approaches. The dominant research paradigm in Austria today is the behavioural school of thought. Economic theories are applied occasionally, but they receive no systematic attention. At first glance, this situation seems surprising because in Germany (which has a strong influence on the Austrian HR community in many ways), a micro-economic orientation in HRM has established itself in recent years and now dominates academic HR discourse. A possible explanation why Austria still focuses on the behavioural school could be the lack of turnover in personnel, since at the time when the Austrian academic HR institutions were established and staff recruited, the behavioural school was the recognised paradigm.

Within the behavioural paradigm there are many different theoretical traditions. Three theoretical approaches can be identified as relevant in Austria, although their diffusion in the academic institutions varies considerably:

1. The most important tradition is the functionalist approach. It has a strong pragmatic orientation as its aim is to provide theoretically founded instruments for HR practitioners in order to help to solve current problems in HR practice (e.g. HR development, staff reduction). As most Austrian HR researchers conduct studies within this context, the functionalist approach can be seen as the most important or even the dominant theoretical approach to Austrian HR research.
2. Systems theory also plays an important role in HRM. This school of thought emphasises the importance of structural aspects in HRM and tries to understand HRM from a more general viewpoint which also includes organisational aspects. Hence it acts as a counterbalance to traditional individualist or more people-oriented approaches to HR research. This school of thought is mainly represented by the Vienna University of Economics and Business Administration and the University of Klagenfurt. Austrian scientists have contributed to this school by developing original theoretical models for

analysing HRM from a systems perspective (Rieckmann 1982; Kasper/ Mayrhofer/Meyer 1998; Mayrhofer 2004).

3. The approach known as the critical management school is represented by the University of Innsbruck (Auer *et al.* 1993). In contrast to the previously discussed schools of thought the critical management school analyses HRM from perspectives that seem to be underrepresented by the functionalist research orientations. This category includes HR perspectives of minorities, gender studies, ethical questions of HRM and so on. The critical HRM school in Austria contributes to the HR field mainly by analysing negative effects of HR practices on employees and on society in general.

> Research topics within the HR discipline in Austria are characterised by strong fragmentation. Topics vary across academic departments, as different departments conduct research on the same topic. They also vary within academic departments, as different research interests within one department also occur.

This situation allows neither a ranking of the most important research fields nor a summary of 'general' topics. Listed below are some research fields in which two or more departments are involved. However, this list of research topics does not give information about the intensity in which a research field is explored, nor does it provide a complete list of research fields of Austrian HR researchers.

– On a macro or social level, questions concerning the management of work in changing social structures have become an important research topic in Austrian HR research. In this area several empirical projects have been conducted recently and HR researchers are planning to get involved here more in the future. One project in this context is the 'work–life balance' study that was conducted at the Vienna University of Economics and Business Administration and in which the compatibility of family and work was investigated. Other topics in this area are: elderly employees (von Eckardstein 2003a; 2003b); diversity management (Laske/Weiskopf 1996); healthcare at work (von Eckardstein *et al.* 1995; Böhnisch/Freisler-Taub/Schütz 1998).

– Closely related to this topic are issues of industrial relations and employment policy. This field analyses how changing social structures affect HR practices and employment policies. Here topics such as compensation, employment forms (e.g. atypical employment) and staff reduction are discussed. In the field of compensation the Department of HRM at the Vienna University of Economics and Business Administration (von Eckardstein 2001; 2003c) has established a leading role within the German-speaking scientific community. The growing importance of this field for research can be explained by the strongly regulated and mostly consensus-oriented Austrian industrial relations system and also by the relatively high labour costs in Austria compared to eastern European neighbours, such as Slovakia and Hungary.

Whereas the topics listed previously have their focus on a collective level, the next collection of issues draws on the relationship between organisation and individual from an HR developmental perspective. In this perspective the development of individual and organisational competences, management development (Rieckmann 1999; 2005); learning and careers (Mayrhofer *et al.* 2005a; 2005b) are investigated. In their internationally acknowledged Vienna Career Panel Project (Vi-CAPP), Mayrhofer and his team investigate career paths of management students and practitioners in a panel study. Growing attention is being given to international aspects of management development.

The research conducted in the topics mentioned above covers various industries. However, there is particular experience in the field of non-profit organisations (von Eckardstein/Brandl 2004;von Eckardstein/Ridder 2003); universities (Laske *et al.* 2000; von Eckardstein/Oechsler/Scholz 2001); and multinational companies (Kasper/Haltmeyer 2002). Because of the predominately small and medium-scale structure of businesses in Austrian industry, researchers also have expertise in specific HR issues in these types of enterprises.

The Austrian scientific community is not isolated but should be seen as an integral part of the German-speaking community. Austrian HR researchers are members of the *Verband der Hochschullehrer für Betriebswirtschaft e.V.* (VHB), the Association of University Professors of Management, a German network of academic researchers within business administration sciences. As a consequence, international research activities of Austrian researchers are mostly focused on the German-speaking scientific community. Activities which have also received high recognition in the English-speaking international field are, for example, the cooperation within the Cranfield project on European Human Resource Management (CRANET), a longitudinal survey instrument for HR practices coordinated for Austria by Wolfgang Mayrhofer. In addition, various Austrian HR researchers participate in the European Group for Organisational Studies (EGOS), an international network which also covers HR topics. Furthermore, there are numerous bilateral university-level projects with Anglo-Saxon countries (e.g. Australia, the USA) as well with Asian countries (e.g. the People's Republic of China).

ACADEMIC TEACHING

HRM teaching traditionally plays an important role in the Austrian academic system. This is due partly to the strong practical tradition in Austrian academic institutions and partly to the largely unfavourable student–supervisor ratio at Austrian universities.

The Austrian academic education system distinguishes between undergraduate, graduate and postgraduate students. HR courses are offered at all student levels; specialisation topics in HRM, however, are possible only for graduate students.

For undergraduate students, most universities offer introductory courses to HRM as a regular and essential field within the business administration study programmes (where HRM is a common body of knowledge).

Graduate students of business administration interested in further specialising in HRM can choose between several programmes in Austria (Table 2.2). However, the relative weight of HR core topics strongly differs between the programmes, as the study topics listed in Table 2.2 indicate. Among the programmes established at present, only three can be labelled HRM core programmes, meaning that they propose a clear HR focus and provide a wide range of HR topics. The other programmes provide specialisations in HR-related fields and offer HR topics as a way of enriching their curriculum.

Table 2.2 HR programmes for graduate students in Austria

University and programme title	*HR topics;[1] note graduates per year; lessons*
Vienna University of Economics and Business Administration: Human Resource Management; International Human Resource Management	Concepts of HRM, HR development, leadership, social competencies, strategic HRM, HR accounting, compensation; 120; 16
University of Innsbruck: Personnel	Personnel policy and leadership, theories of HRM, concepts and practices in personnel policy, research in personnel policy; 120; 10 (15)[1]
University of Linz: Human Resource Management	Fields of HRM, organisational behaviour, presentation skills, labour time, compensation, change management, strategic HRM; 50; 8 (16)[3]
Vienna University of Economics and Business Administration: Organisational Behaviour, International Organisational Behaviour	Change and stability, team development, complexity and decision-making, intercultural training, organisation and individual, management and culture, communication in a multicultural context; 120; 16
Vienna University of Economics and Business Administration: Change Management and Management Development	Change management and management development, leadership and teamwork management, organisational psychology, HR development; 120; 16
University of Graz: Master of Management and International Business (Organisation, Marketing, Human Resources, Innovation and Knowledge)[2]	HR concepts; 200; 4
University of Klagenfurt: Organisational, Human Resource and Management Development[2]	Leadership, HR development, organisational development and change, social competencies, teamwork; 50; 1

[1] Table contains only the HRM or HRM-related topics in the curriculum.
[2] In this Master's programme HRM is an integral part and not a specialisation field.
[3] The lessons in parentheses stand for secondary HRM specialisation tracks.

49

The number of students receiving a Master's degree in business administration with a specialisation in HRM or HR-related disciplines ranges between 50 and 500 per year depending on the specific programme. Postgraduate students following a Ph.D. programme in Austria can take courses in HRM as part of their doctoral programme, where HR-specific research issues (methods, theories) and aspects of the doctoral thesis are discussed with the department staff. MBA students can take HR courses either as a part of executive and general management programmes (for instance, as provided by the Danube University Krems) or they can even do an HRM-specific MBA programme, as provided by the PEF University in Vienna (postgraduate Master's programme Human Resource Management and Organisational Development).

The topics listed in Table 2.2 indicate that the teaching programmes for graduate students are largely similar at all academic institutions. Nearly all curricula offer courses in social competences, leadership and HR development (also extended to the team and organisation level). In contrast relatively little attention is given to topics such as compensation, labour time and HR accounting. These latter topics are exclusively addressed by core HR programmes. This confirms that these programmes provide a broader insight into issues relevant to HRM than curricula which offer HRM as part of a general programme.

A further characteristic of Austrian academic teaching practice is the importance of the relationship between theory and practice. To support this goal, MBA programmes require their students to do internships in order to gain practical experience, and universities encourage their (under)graduate students to do internships as well and invite practitioners to their courses for theory and practice dialogues.

Recent education programme developments show that cultural aspects of human behaviour (e.g. intercultural training) and international HR topics – formerly conducted on an irregular basis – have now become integral parts of many HRM teaching programmes. This suggests that academics recognise that HRM is receiving ever more importance in an international context.

BEST-PRACTICE CASE: VERBUND – AN ELECTRICITY COMPANY ON ITS WAY TO THE FUTURE

Q.at

HIGH-VOLTAGE HRM

Verbund was founded in 1947 on the basis of the second Nationalisation Act with a mission to assess the growth of current consumption, build and operate power stations with the help of special companies, develop and operate the supra-regional high-voltage grid, and carry on trade with foreign countries in the power sector. The company was partially privatised in 1988. Since then, it has been 51 per cent owned by the Republic of Austria, the other 49 per cent of shares being held by institutional investors and in free float. Over the years the company has become Austria's leading electricity company in the free market. It generates around 50 per cent of Austria's demand and transports 80 per cent of the high-voltage power within the country. Verbund generates over 80 per cent of its electricity from clean, renewable hydropower and is therefore one of the most environmentally friendly electricity producers in the EU. It sells its 'green' electricity to third-party suppliers and business customers in Austria and all parts of Europe. Because of Verbund's successful trade in electricity, over 50 per cent of its sales are generated abroad. The group owns and operates the Austrian high-voltage grid with lines running to neighbouring markets. As an independent grid operator, Verbund makes its lines available to all market players on equal terms.

Personnel strategy

The deregulation of the European electricity market set new standards for corporations such as Verbund. The Verbund group realised early on that it had to adjust to these new challenges of a free market economy. The group primarily focused on two, quite different, objectives:

- restructuring and massively reducing costs across the group; and
- strengthening and building on the group's market position in Europe.

These strategic measures also formed the basis of HRM. It was therefore the task of HR to forge a link between the reduction in personnel expenses and the increase in productivity per employee. Streamlining the group's organisation, setting up companies which are geared to the market and accountable for results, reducing the number of organisational units and hierarchical levels, and lowering the number of employees and payroll expenses in a socially compatible way was the focal point of Verbund's HR strategy. Another focal point concerned the qualification of employees, the creation of incentives to boost performance, the establishment of a working environment that was conducive to learning and motivating, as well as preparations for meeting the new challenges of a free market economy. These two approaches are inseparably linked to each other and thus a requirement

51

for optimising excellent human capital and ensuring that employees take an active part in the changes at Verbund triggered by liberalisation. Three fields have to be presented in detail.

HR division

For Verbund, the HR division is a factor crucial to the group's success. HR strategies are directly derived from corporate strategy and can be adapted quickly to new situations. Verbund's personnel policy is already in compliance with the Green Book of the EU Commission (http://europa.eu.int) and has been implemented in HR guidelines, personnel management, the organisation of HRM, HR planning, personnel development, training/further training and personnel controlling. The HR guidelines provide guidance on internal and external cooperation for the managing board, all executives and employees. The shift in corporate culture that came with liberalisation is particularly reflected in these guidelines.

Modern leadership approach

Personnel management is based on a modern leadership approach. Employee interviews are conducted systematically, and management style is based on 'management by objectives'. Executives are carefully selected according to the above criteria and this system has already begun to bear fruit. External experts have also confirmed the high quality of management: a management appraisal, carried out in cooperation with an international and reputable consultant, praised the high quality of the group's executives – and this appreciation was based on an assessment that was above average even by European standards. An anonymous survey among employees also painted a positive picture of the conduct of Verbund executives.

Effective personnel planning

Employees are selected on the basis of objective and logical criteria, thus ensuring that no one is hired who does not meet the requirements that come with the new challenges at Verbund. Needs-based, systematic and comprehensive personnel development as well as training and further training are the prerequisites for employees to advance within the organisation, but they also provide an opportunity for career development. Short- and medium-term personnel planning is carried out in coordination with the various companies and takes account of the targets that need to be met. Corporate planning, as decided upon, is integrated in the group plan, which then has to be endorsed by the Verbund Supervisory Board. Side by side with quantitative payroll planning, there is also qualitative planning, which is geared to the qualification structure. Personnel planning is part of overall planning and is reflected in labour-cost planning.

HR is now structured and established under strategic Human Resource Management/Holding, which assumes central control of personnel policy on the one hand, and supervises the operative, decentralised personnel departments (payroll administration and accounting) on the other hand. Personnel controlling is the tool used for sustainable HRM control. For example, education controlling monitors and continuously improves the entire set of HR measures, thus achieving sustainable effects (iterative process). The following sections will deal in greater detail with the individual aspects of HRM and the conditions under which it operates against the backdrop of moves to establish corporate social responsibility as a quality feature.

Effects of competition

In order to enhance its competitiveness in an extremely competitive environment, Verbund has been forced to continue its staff reduction programme. In full observance of its social responsibility towards employees, staff reductions have been realised in a socially compatible manner and, as in previous years, there have been no layoffs for operational reasons. The internal 'job market' has played a very significant role throughout the restructuring process. Transfers across Austria mean that employees have had to be extremely mobile and flexible. In the development of performance figures, Verbund focuses particularly on increasing employee productivity. This ratio is computed by dividing sales – excluding external electricity trade – by the average number of employees for the respective period. Since 2000, productivity in relation to sales – excluding external electricity trade – has increased by 21.2 per cent, from 383,700 EUR to 464,900 EUR. The average age of staff at the end of 2003 was 43.1 (women: 40.6, men: 43.5). The average length of service came to nineteen years (women: 17.3, men: 19.3). In 2003, the fluctuation rate for the entire group – on the basis of the BDA formula (voluntary resignations/average number of employees) – was 1.5 per cent.

Personnel development

To advance personally and to ensure the success of the organisation, each employee needs to be open to professional development. The needs-based range of training and personnel development programmes is available to all employees without exception. To promote the concept of equal opportunities and to ensure open and fair – i.e. clear and logical – access to different forms of professional development, annual employee interviews are held providing a framework for employees – in cooperation with executives – to prepare personal development plans.

New employees

Tailored programmes for new employees/trainees, promising employees and managers are found at the heart of the group's training activities. Each new employee is actively and personally supported from day one by the personnel development department; in addition, he/she will be assigned a mentor from his/her department. This training programme, which comprises four seminar/workshop modules, is completed by the employee during the first one and a half years. The group-wide trainee programme is currently based on a pool of eighteen employees.

The target groups are graduates of technical secondary schools, colleges and universities. Since 1996, Verbund has systematically operated a talent pool/executive training programme. Every two years, a group of around twenty-five to thirty employees is nominated. To ensure a maximum degree of objectivity, candidates undergo a two-day assessment under the supervision of external experts. In the personnel development sessions that follow, the results are evaluated and measures are planned together with the executives. Here, great care is taken to adapt the programme to changing conditions.

Executives

Executives, as a group, play a very significant role in the personnel development process. They are responsible for motivating employees and also have a decisive 'model' role. Verbund attaches great importance to systematic executive development with a focus on purpose-designed, target group-oriented programmes. Verbund is anxious to ensure that it will have access to an adequate number of specialists in the future and for this reason, specially designed programmes are conducted on a regular basis for promising employees. After very strict selection and Development Assessment Centre processing, these promising employees complete a two-year basic programme. When newly appointed executives take up their positions, they receive coaching and attend special events in preparation for their company-specific management tasks. All other executives participate in such special events as required.

Enhanced communication and executive networking represent another focal point which aims at the creation of a platform for the exchange of best-practice know-how. A special 'executive club' with its own purpose-designed internet platform has been set up in cooperation with the group's chief executives. An extended concept for management replacements was developed on the basis of an existing management potential study carried out in 2002. Using the results of the survey conducted among employees in the course of employee interviews in 2002, the documents were adapted and a series of practice-oriented training sessions for employee interviews was carried out. In one business area, a follow-up executive development process has been initiated. Its aim is the practical implementation of a management model, which will later be subjected to long-term evaluation in conjunction with employees. The management replacement concept has been implemented in 2004. In addition, key qualifications will be planned for all senior executives. In response to the growing trend towards internationalisation, the executives will also be offered a foreign-language course.

Apprentices

The training of apprentices to become specialists in their respective fields is an essential component of operational training and further education at Verbund. The year 2002 saw the establishment of a modern educational facility which provided training in the latest technologies for an increased number of apprentices. This is

Verbund's answer to addressing the shortage of skilled workers while making a crucial contribution to the reduction of youth unemployment. The main areas of training are electrohydraulics, electropneumatics, measuring and control technology and IT. Courses in communications technology commenced for the first time in autumn 2003. Apprentices are selected on the basis of an internally developed, objective process. This has produced excellent results, reflected by numerous prizes from competitions and examinations in which Verbund apprentices have participated. This success can, among other things, be attributed to the 'Learn to Learn' project run by a team of teachers and psychologists who prepare apprentices for upcoming examinations. At Verbund, apprentices are trained not only in technological disciplines, but also in social competence. In autumn 2003, twenty-seven new apprentices participated in a special course on team training.

Equal opportunities

At Verbund, employees and applicants are treated equally regardless of race, faith or religion, colour, nationality, ethnic origin, political conviction, gender, sexual orientation, disability or marital status. Verbund aims to increase the quota of women within the group from the current level of 15.3 per cent to over 20 per cent in the next few years and for this reason will give precedence to women with equal qualifications when recruiting new staff. This also applies to appointments at management level. As of 31 December 2003, the percentage of women in executive positions was 4.6 per cent, among young executives, 11.1 per cent. In the context of equal opportunities, the integration of disabled persons in the working process should not be forgotten. Verbund has 122 disabled employees. The percentage of disabled employees thus remains unchanged compared to the previous year at 4.7 per cent.

Compensation policy

Verbund operates an up-to-date and competitive wage and salaries system to guarantee that our employees are paid fairly and according to market rates. The collective agreement of the electricity companies is used as a basis here. The only relevant criterion is the performance of Verbund's employees. Verbund's wages and salaries level is, in part, still based on in-company payment systems established in the past, which are now difficult to correct. This is why the company started to look into new salary models at a very early stage. In 1998, the company created a performance-based salary model which paves the way for the equalisation of different groups of employees and which, at the same time, is equipped with fixed and variable salary components in line with current market trends. This model was implemented under the proviso that the existing situation of any employee would not be adversely affected. The performance-based salary model is based on the Procurement Executives Council collective agreement for employees, with effect for new hirings as of 1 January 1998. The works council was included in the project group, project management and the entire decision-taking process during the initial implementation project.

Working-time models

It is an established fact that flexible working hours translate into greater employee loyalty and satisfaction, which is why Verbund has increasingly turned to this system. In this context, the company is dedicated to recognising new trends, such as new forms of employment and alternative working-time models. Basically, the plant agreement on flexitime applies to all employees, provided they are not exempt due to a special rule or provision. By concluding such a plant agreement, Verbund took an important step towards enhancing flexibility. Employees covered by the 'new salary model' work hours based on an 'honour system'. Employees can shape their working week as they like; they just need to comply with the statutory provisions on working hours and coordinate their time with their superiors. Verbund has also launched a pilot project for telecommuting. Building upon the findings, it has entered into the same kind of individual agreements with telecommuters as it has concluded with others. As of 31 December 2003, the percentage of part-time workers was 3.4 per cent.

Fringe benefits

Voluntary fringe benefits contribute substantially to employee loyalty. Verbund complies with this principle by offering employees additional benefits such as health insurance, accident insurance and a pension plan. The additional health insurance held by the group and all employees covers any hospitalisation costs (special category: multiple-bed room) that are necessary and justified medically. The private accident insurance provides cover for active employees who suffer permanent disability or death due to an accident. Verbund offers its employees a company pension scheme to supplement the state pension. It is a contribution-based scheme providing an old-age pension, a widow/widower and orphans' pension or a disability pension. Under this scheme, employees can make contributions up to the amount of the employer contribution to increase their supplementary pension. Performance-based pension commitments still exist under contracts of employment entered into before 1994. In compliance with the law on employee severance payments, Verbund also pays 1.53 per cent of the respective monthly salaries of employees whose employment contracts commenced after 1 January 2003 into a corporate employee benefits fund which handles the investment of these funds. Severance obligations arising from employment contracts which were entered into before this date will be honoured.

Working atmosphere and etiquette

To ensure that dealings with staff are always effected in a respectful manner, the Verbund group adheres to the following principles of management, cooperation and communication:

• Corporate actions are determined by clear goals that are jointly defined by management and employees.

- Employees work in teams and the group promotes performance, innovation, keenness and creativity.
- Efficiency and willingness to show initiative is increased by allowing employees to work independently and by granting them the highest possible level of freedom with regard to decision-making.
- Cooperation, trust, openness, fairness and mutual respect are hallmarks of work and leadership styles.
- The skills and abilities of employees are promoted through future-oriented personnel development.
- Cooperation extends through all areas of the company. This allows Verbund to strengthen its corporate identity and enhance competitiveness as an international group.
- The organisation is project and process oriented.
- Communication is open and transparent and dialogue is encouraged.
- The group's actions are customer and service oriented.
- The overall aim is to be among the best in the market in all business areas.

Internal communication is a critical element of information flow; information is mainly disseminated through the intranet and the company newsletter *Kontakt*. Apart from day-to-day communications, executives and employees communicate directly within the framework of annual employee interviews.

Employees have ample opportunity to voice their opinions on any number of issues. In the coming years, the company plans to introduce more in-depth employee interviews and initiate a 'commitment index'.

In October 2003, Verbund held its sixth executive summit, with all the members of the Managing Board present. This gave eighty-six managers from all areas of the group an opportunity to discuss the strategic orientation and objectives of Verbund with the managing board.

Health

Having healthy employees is an essential prerequisite for performance and is thus the key to the company's success. Our medical care focuses on prevention and thus also meets statutory requirements. This includes a medical check-up at the time of recruitment, vaccinations, inspections and workplace-related examinations.

SUMMARY

In recent years, Verbund, the biggest electricity producer in Austria, has had to adapt to the liberalisation of the European electricity market. This new competition situation also affected HRM: through strategically targeted restructuring measures, the head count was reduced by 48.1 per cent (or 2,848 heads) between 1994 and 2003, from 5,164 to 2,680 – all the cuts effected in a socially responsible manner. Over the same period, total personnel costs were reduced by 41.5 per cent to 263.7 million EUR. This development was supported by HR development measures and tailored training methods. The introduction of a performance-related payment system helped keep up morale and motivation. This is most impressively expressed by an increase in productivity by 21.2 per cent since the year 2000.

Which people play key roles in your country? Which names should one know?

Heinz Fischer, Alfred Gusenbauer, Elfriede Jelinek, Wolfgang Eder, Jörg Haider, Gerhard Randa, Claus Raidl, Boris Nemczic, Elisabeth Gürtler, Hermann Maier, Hans Hollein, Manfred Deix, Wolfgang Ruttensdorfer, Christof Schönborn, Klaus Albrecht Schröder, Niki Lauda, Willi Resetarits, Franz Küberl, Michael Haneke, André Heller, Ludwig Scharinger, Swarovski, Dietrich Mateschitz, Walter Eselböck.

References

.at

Auer, Manfred/Gorbach, Stefan/Laske, Stephan/Welte, Heike (1993): Mikropolitische Perspektiven der Personalentwicklung, in: Stephan Laske/Stefan Gorbach (eds): Spannungsfeld Personalentwicklung. Konzeptionen – Analysen – Perspektiven, Wien, pp. 153–69.

Böhnisch, Wolf/Freisler-Traub, Andrea/Schütz, Robert (1998): Personalorganisation im Krankenhaus – Die Strategieorientierung des Human Resource Managements als kritischer Erfolgsfaktor, in: Christian Scholz (ed.): Innovative Personalorganisation, Neuwied, pp. 368–80.

Kasper, Helmut/Haltmeyer, Beate (2002): Knowledge sharing in multinational organisations, in: Journal of Cross-Cultural Competence and Management, 3: 279–313.

Kasper, Helmut/Mayrhofer, Wolfgang/Meyer, Michael (1998): Manager-Handeln nach der systemtheoretisch-konstruktivistischen Wende: Die Betriebswirtschaft, 58(5): 603–21.

Laske, Stephan/Weiskopf, Richard (1996): Personalauswahl – was wird denn da gespielt?: ein Plädoyer für einen Perspektivenwechsel, in: Zeitschrift für Personalforschung, 4: 295–330.

Laske, Stephan/Scheytt, Tobias/Meister-Scheytt, Claudia/Scharmer, Claus O. (eds) (2000): Universität im 21. Jahrhundert. Zur Interdependenz von Begriff und Organisation der Wissenschaft Universität und Gesellschaft, Schriftenreihe zur Universitätsentwicklung, 1, München, Mering.

Mayrhofer, Wolfgang (2004): Social systems theory and human resource management – more a blessing than a curse? Paper presented at the International Symposium on Human Resources and Economic Success, Paderborn, Germany, 27–28 February 2004.

Mayrhofer, Wolfgang/Meyer, Michael/Iellatchitch, Alexander/Schiffinger, Michael (2004): Careers and human resource management – a European perspective, in: Human Resource Management Review, 14: 473–98.

Mayrhofer, Wolfgang/Steyrer, Johannes/Meyer, Michael/Strunk, Guido/Schiffinger, Michael/Iellatchitch, Alexander (2005): Graduates' career aspirations and individual characteristics, in: Human Resource Management Journal, 15(1): 38–56.

Rieckmann, Heijo (1982): Auf der grünen Wiese. Organisationsentwicklung einer Werksneugründung. Sozio-technisches Design und Offene-System-Planung, Bern, Stuttgart.

—— (1999): Organisationsentwicklung und das Management komplexer Probleme und Systeme, in: Zeitschrift für Organisationsentwicklung, 3: 88–91.

—— (2005): Managen und Führen am Rande des 3. Jahrtausend. Praktisches – Theoretisches – Bedenkliches, 3rd edn, Frankfurt, Wien.

von Eckardstein, Dudo (ed.) (2001): Handbuch Variable Vergütung für Führungskräfte, München.

—— (2003a): Demographische Verschiebungen und ihre Bedeutung für das Personalmanagement, in: Zeitschrift Führung + Organisation, 3: 128–35.

—— (2003b): Nicht ohne die Alten, in: Frankfurter Allgemeine Zeitung, 8 October, p. 20.

—— (2003c): Leistungsvergütung für Professoren: Möglichkeiten und Probleme der Umsetzung auf Fachbereichsebene, in: Zeitschrift für Betriebswirtschaft, supplement booklet 3: 97–116.

von Eckardstein, Dudo/Brandl, Julia (2004): Human resource management in nonprofit organisations, in: Annette Zimmer/Eckhard Priller (eds): Future of Civil Society. Making Central European Nonprofit Organisations Work, Wiesbaden, pp. 297–314.

von Eckardstein, Dudo/Lueger, Günter/Niedl, Klaus/Schuster, Brigitte (1995): Psychische Befindensbeeinträchtigungen und Gesundheit im Betrieb. Herausforderung für Personalmanager und Gesundheitsexperten, München, Mering.

von Eckardstein, Dudo/Oechsler, Walter A./Scholz, Christian (2001): Personalmanagement und Dienstrechtsreform an deutschen Hochschulen – Eine kritische Analyse, in: Zeitschrift für Personalforschung, 1: 5–17.

von Eckardstein, Dudo/Ridder, Hans-Gerd (eds) (2003): Personalmanagement als Gestaltungsaufgabe im Nonprofit und Public Management, München, Mering.

The authors

Dr Dudo von Eckardstein (dudo.eckardstein@wu-wien.ac.at), full chair Professor of Human Resource Management at Vienna University of Economics and Business Administration. Main research: career management, compensation system, participation, quality management, psychological health disturbance, human resources management at universities and social non-profit organisations. Main publications: *Psychische Befindensbeeinträchtigungen und Gesundheit im Betrieb. Herausforderung für Personalmanager und Gesundheitsexperten* (with Günter Lueger, Klaus Niedl and Brigitte Schuster), Munich, 1995, *Formen und Effekte von Karriereplateaus. Eine theoretische und empirische Analyse* (with Wolfgang Elsik and Andreas Nachbagauer), Munich, 1997; *Muster betrieblicher Kooperation zwischen Management und Betriebsrat. Die Entwicklung von Lohnmodellen im System österreichischer Arbeitsbeziehungen*, Munich, 1998.

Dr Julia Brandl (julia.brandl@wu-wien.ac.at), Lecturer at Aarkus School of Business, at University of Innsbruck and at Vienna University of Economics and Business Administration. Main research: personnel departments, international personnel management, personnel management in non-profit organisations. Main publications: *Die Legitimität von Personalabteilungen. Eine Rekonstruktion aus Sicht der Unternehmensleitung* (Munich, 2005); *Human Resource Management in Nonprofit Organisations* (with Dudo von Eckardstein) (in: Zimmer, Anette/Priller, Eckhard (eds) *Future of Civil Society. Making Central European Nonprofit Organisations Work*, Wiesbaden, 2004, pp. 297–314); *Die Steuerungsfähigkeit Wiedererlangen – die Balanced Scorecard für das Management von Non-Profit-Organisationen* (with Markus Gmür) (in: Scherer, Andreas/Alt, Jens (eds) *Balanced Scorecard in Öffentlicher Verwaltung und Non-Profit-Organisationen*, Stuttgart, 2002, pp. 27–42).

Dr Hellwig Maier (hellwig.maier@opwz.com), ÖPWZ, Member of the Board, responsible for seminars, conferences and surveys in the range of HRM and payroll, among others Secretary General of 'Forum Personal', head of job training, EAPM further training delegate.

Dr Rudolf Thurner (rudolf.thurner@verbund.at), Österreichische Elektrizitätswirtschafts-AG, Head of the Human Resources Department, Managing President of 'Forum Personal' at the Austrian Centre for Productivity and Efficiency (ÖPWZ), and since 2007 President of the European Association for Personnel Management (EAPM).

Acknowledgements

Dudo von Eckardstein and Julia Brandl wish to thank their colleague Prof. Wolfgang Elšik for his comments on this chapter. They would also like to thank the members of HR-related academic departments in Austria for kindly providing them with information for this chapter.

3 HRM in the Czech Republic: striving towards a worldwide standard

Rostya Gordon-Smith/Michaela Tureckiová/Iveta Richter/Zdenek Simek/
Richard Dobeš

The Czech Republic: in a nutshell

In this chapter you will learn:

- that HRM activities in the Czech Republic have a common objective: to archieve the HR development that will ensure competitiveness for the country;

- that because of political change, the Czech Republic has no original HRM theory of its own. One of the major challenges for HR academia is the effective identification of and collaboration with talented people; and

- that since 2004 Česká Pojišťovna has become the most technologically modern insurance company, which entailed a steep learning curve for the company.

Capital:	Prague
Area (sq km):	78,866 (land 77,276; water 1,590)
EU membership:	since 2004
Population:	10,235,455
Languages:	Czech
Ethnic groups (in percentages):	Czech 94; Slovak 2; other 4 (Polish, German, Romany)
Gross domestic product:	221.4 billion USD (2006)
Workforce (in percentages):	5.31 million (2006): agriculture 4.1; industry 37.6; services 58.3 (2003)
Export commodities:	machinery and transport equipment, chemicals, raw materials and fuel

BACKGROUND: DEVELOPMENT OF STRATEGIC HRM AND RELATED CONCEPTS

FROM PERSONNEL DEPARTMENTS TO STRATEGIC HR DEVELOPMENT

In the Czech Republic, the discipline of HRM is built on the tradition of the social and personnel policy in industrial organisations developed during the period of the so-called first republic (1918–38). Challenges to the interrupted development of HRM became manifest, especially in the first half of the 1990s, when it was necessary to 'reinvent' HRM to a western Europe level and to restore its credibility in the eyes of employees and organisations. For forty years, the main emphasis had been on the administration of personnel and control of the political reliability of employees at all organisational levels.

The Czech Republic still has a lack of local, experience-based, senior and strategic HR expertise. In the last decade, multinational companies have introduced the notion that the application of HR strategies and processes is in direct correlation with business success. Today, the impact of that knowledge transfer can be seen in a fast-growing population of HR professionals, who today are at mid-management level, but represent a solid base for future Czech excellence in HRM.

HRM is still not a widely accepted term, especially in the public sector, healthcare and industry. The term 'human resources' is not readily accepted in the Czech business community because it translates too crudely into Czech as 'resources', being acceptable for only inanimate matter and provides no linguistic or historical linkage to the profession. In addition, there is a great deal of misconception about the role that HRM plays and its value-adding dimension. In most smaller scale Czech companies, HRM is still perceived as a luxury. It is often misconstrued as personnel management, which is – due to its historically coloured context – perceived by most people as a negative concept. Appreciation of HRM has yet to be built into Czech organisations.

The economic and social transformation of the Czech Republic (Czechoslovakia until 1992) and its gradual integration into European and global economic and political structures has been accompanied by problems related to the availability of a qualified and competent workforce in the country. Recruitment, management and development of HR have thus been constant – albeit often rather declaratively recognised – priorities at the level of organisations, regions and the national government.

Starting in 1989, when the so-called Velvet Revolution put an end to the centrally planned economy and the accompanying classification of people into castes based on political affiliations and loyalty to the regime, the management processes and instruments common in a market economy have also been gradually applied in the areas of HRM.

What is typical of your country in relation to the country itself (its culture, people, etc.) and its economy?

Despite some challenges, the economy is growing and offers interesting opportunities for foreign investment. People are generally friendly and hard-working; the younger generation has better entrepreneurial skills, is more willing to meet challenges and has better language skills. To sum up, the Czech Republic has a highly educated population with good manual skills and flexibility, fairly traditional norms of social behaviour, strong identification with historical events and growing economic wealth – which is associated with a widening social gap.

MAJOR THEORETICAL AND PRACTICAL APPROACHES TO HR DEVELOPMENT

Starting points

The transformation of personnel work in organisations and its anchoring in the conceptual principles of HRM took place spontaneously, especially in the first half of the 1990s. In that period, there was a shortage of experts able to distinguish, in terms of substance, the concepts of (tactical) personnel management from those of strategic HRM, to define the methods for making effective practical use of instruments available within these concepts and to do so comprehensibly, taking into account the specifics of Czech national and organisational culture. According to repeated researches applying the methodology of Geert Hofstede, the Czech Republic is a country with a medium power distance index made up of fairly high scores for uncertainty avoidance and individualism, a high masculinity index (with a tendency towards a relatively sharp decline) and a low Confucian dynamism index (Nový *et al.* 1996; Kolman 2001).

Both terms – personnel management and strategic HRM – were used indiscriminately and with a somewhat 'ideological' touch which further obscured the differences between them. (Incidentally, even today, there is still no consensus among Czech experts as to the relationship between the two terms and because of a widespread tradition of humanistic psychology, there is even a certain amount of lingering reluctance to use the term 'human resources'.) In practice, too, the two concepts coexisted and the management of organisations only gradually took on board the differences between the two.

Efforts to spread the concept of HRM as the then most recent instrument for people management and to familiarise the Czech professional public with trends in people management in organisations were reflected in the publication of translated works, mostly from US authors. The first domestic publication was written by Josef Koubek (1995), a professor at the University of Economics in Prague, and was designed for HR managers and students of the specialisation at newly emerging or 'renovated' university departments. The need to train or retrain practitioners of personnel work in organisations was also at its strongest in that period because the qualifications as well as the age and gender structure of personnel officers did not correspond to practical needs; it was necessary to upgrade and broaden their qualifications. For many, retraining had to be provided.

The period in question (and in many respects not only that period) was characterised by both a move to redefine the discipline's contents and a search for its links with other social and technical disciplines (for theory) and other management functions (in practice).

What are you and other Czech people extraordinarily proud of with respect to HRM?

Influenced to a great extent by the foreign/international companies that entered our market, HRM has reached a sound level. We have a number of Czech HR managers playing regional roles in parts of Europe and beyond.

The Czech Republic has a fast-growing community of HR professionals, who are now at mid-management level but represent a solid base for future excellence in HRM in the Czech Republic. HR expertise has grown exponentially in the last ten years and HR managers are now accepted in business partnerships. HR management in the Czech Republic in general is performance focused.

SEARCHING FOR HR COMPETENCES

Since the mid-1990s, several important pieces of research have been produced in the Czech Republic which confirmed expectations regarding:

- the diverse professional profile and background of HR practitioners (which itself highlighted their need for HR development, including harmonisation of their knowledge and experience base to make them equal partners for their colleagues in organisations – a precondition for 'business partnering'); and
- changes in the ratio between personnel functions administered by HR specialists and line managers.

The scope and relatively extensive powers invested in HR departments in the Czech Republic – possibly out of some 'post-revolution' euphoria and maybe also in the genuine belief that it was finally necessary to pay due attention to HR – have started to be gradually restricted again in companies in the Czech Republic. On the other hand, the competences of line managers and sometimes of employees themselves in most HR processes have been increasing (although this trend is not specifically Czech, it has met with rather negative responses in our country – probably because of the rapid pace and high demands of change).

67

This does not mean that the importance of HR departments or HR professionals has diminished. As pointed out by some Czech authors (among others, Stýblo 1998; Tureckiová 2004), their roles and functions are changing as the practical experience base grows.

MAJOR TRENDS IN HUMAN CAPITAL MANAGEMENT AND DEVELOPMENT

Strategic human capital development tools, whether they are competency- or knowledge-based management applications, or tools based on the learning-organisation concept, are among other areas to which major attention is being paid by the Czech academic community together with practitioners at top industrial organisations.

The linking of these theoretical inputs with company practice has recently resulted in a transition to methods and forms of company training which support mutual learning (to this end, some organisations in the Czech Republic have started to use the Investors in People methodology, while others are developing their own, customised models) and emphasise the development of key and talented workers.

The above human capital development trends in the Czech Republic naturally also have an international dimension. As a result of foreign investors coming into companies in the Czech Republic and the Czech Republic joining the EU in May 2004, it has also been necessary to deal with issues of inter-national and intercultural management. Experts in the Czech Republic focus primarily on the development of intercultural competences and cooperate with large companies in the Czech Republic by providing intercultural training and education. Prominent among these companies are players in the car industry, telecommunications and financial services (see also Nový *et al.* 1996).

At the other end of the spectrum of challenges faced by the 'Czech model' of HR development (HRD) is the task of finding HR professionals for small- and medium-sized enterprises and non-profit organisations.

Owing to the fast growth/promotion rates of the line management community, the overall business maturity of young managers is permanently at the stage of catching up with the last promotion, but is offset by an ability to learn and accept new challenges as well as by eagerness, ambition and hard work. A high level of people management skills is required but often not fully demonstrated, and, in reality, somewhat overestimated. Often, more importance and reliance is placed on systems than on processes, where the key role is played by managers, not tech-nology. As a result, HRM is required to perform administrative and traditional operational tasks to make up for the lack of people management knowledge at all levels. Consequently, strategic HR still has to show that its input is a significant catalyst of business success.

The activities described and outlined in this text have a common objective: to consolidate HR development which will ensure competitiveness for the Czech Republic and allow it to harness and develop fully the possibilities and, in the future, to actively create opportunities arising from both its membership of the EU and its involvement in a functioning and global knowledge-based society.

What would you like to teach foreign HR managers? What is important for them to know, in your opinion?

In most smaller scale Czech companies, HRM is still perceived as a luxury. HRM is often interpreted as personnel management, in its historically coloured context. The value of HRM has yet to be appreciated in Czech organisations.

The role of HR as people advocate versus business contributor is yet to be clarified and/or enhanced. Role modelling, setting a personal example, coaching and timely feedback are the most effective tools for transferring HR knowledge to the younger generation of Czech HR and line management professionals.

Some words of advice for foreign managers working in the Czech Republic:

• open communication: be pro-active;
• acquire a basic knowledge of the Czech language;
• acquire a basic knowledge of Czech culture and history; and
• show trust, delegate and cautiously control.

EAPM AFFILIATE: ČESKÁ SPOLEČNOST PRO ROZVOJ LIDSKÝCH ZDROJŮ (CSRLZ)

BRIEF HISTORY OF THE EAPM MEMBER ORGANISATION

CSRLZ, the Czech society for HR development, is a professional non-profit organisation, the only HR society in the Czech Republic which is a member of the European Association for Personnel Management (EAPM) and affiliated with the World Federation of Personnel Management Associations (WFPM).

CSRLZ was founded on 18 November 1993 by the Club of Czech Personnel Managers, the Czech Management Association and H. Neumann Consulting as a result of the growing need to support and network HR professionals requiring information about new trends in HR and the opportunity to access support and advice from fellow professionals.

THE ORGANISATION'S LEGAL STRUCTURE

CSRLZ is run by a voluntary board of directors comprising HR professionals from various industries and consulting organisations.

The board is headed by a president, who is assisted by vice-presidents responsible for various segments of HR, such as training and development; industrial relations; exchange meetings; conferences; *HR Forum Magazine*; international relations and education. The executive part is run by an executive director with a small staff at his or her specific disposal.

CSRLZ membership is open to any organisation, public or private, which operates in the Czech Republic, is involved with HR management and is willing to contribute towards its development.

CSRLZ members include organisations in heavy industries as well as in sales, consulting, financial, public sector and academic institutions. CSRLZ has a base membership of over 200 organisations with approximately 700 leaders and representatives from some of the largest organisations in the Czech Republic. CSRLZ is also a member of the Federation of Industry and Transportation, and through this has a say in the preparation of legislation in the HR field and an influence on collective bargaining between the unions and employers.

FIELDS OF ACTIVITIES: PRODUCTS AND SERVICES

CSRLZ organises national conferences with an international focus and presents the yearly HREA (HR Excellence Award) to the three best HR projects in the Czech Republic. It maintains links with partner organisations in the EAPM and WFPMA.

The society also publishes *HR Forum,* a national HR magazine, which is published in Czech with some articles in English. It is also active in the field of education, supporting the M.Sc. in SHRM (Strategic HR management), the first Master's degree for HR professionals in the Czech Republic.

Other CSRLZ activities include professional seminars, round-table discusions and local exchange meetings. Cooperation with non-HR managers is becoming increasingly important. The society provides support for the creation of active webpages as well as for HR libraries and job fairs. It is a partner for regional societies which need assistance in the fields of outplacement or HR recruitment.

THE ORGANISATION'S ROLE AND SIGNIFICANCE FOR HR MANAGEMENT

CSRLZ strives to develop active and respectful cooperation with line management. It lobbies for the recognition of HR management's value in organisations and promotes the HR profession in the market. Consequently, activities and events organised by CSRLZ aim at developing companies' awareness of the importance of strategic HR management, developing highly qualified HR professionals, establishing an excellent educational system, providing courses in HRM leading to credible international certification and degrees, as well as developing business partnerships and top management positions for HR professionals within organisations.

THE ORGANISATION'S VISION: TO BECOME PART OF THE INTERNATIONAL NETWORK

CSRLZ's vision is to develop HR up to worldwide standards through organised activities and international exchanges from Czech and international HR professionals. CSRLZ is ready to provide information, consulting, networking opportunities and support to the HR professionals in the Czech Republic. CSRLZ's information service is not only for members but also for the general public, and coordination and networking takes place with regional and other associations for HR professionals in the country.

CSRLZ's main goals are to become part of the international HR network and assure the transfer of knowledge gained through international experience, to facilitate the professional growth and performance of HR managers and specialists and to help to align HR management needs with the needs of business leaders.

Cooperation with other professional and government institutions is planned, as is the promotion of HR management's importance and impact as an integral part of organisations.

CONTRIBUTIONS TO NATIONAL HR DISCLOSURE

In the last fourteen years of CSRLZ's existence, the society has been involved continuously in all aspects of promoting the importance and effectiveness of strategic HR management within organisations. By organising support activities, the society has regularly gathered together and helped HR professionals in many aspects of their work and the challenges that they face. It has promoted active networking opportunities and cooperated with a number of other organisations (chambers of commerce, clubs, schools, non-government organisations (NGOs), government organisations) in order to promote and develop the standing of HR professionals in the Czech Republic. Through many activities and the *HR Forum* magazine, CSRLZ reaches out constantly to line managers and leaders to encourage support and appreciation of the HR role within organisations. CSRLZ has begun to plan a development strategy for young people in the future who might want to choose HR as a profession.

What would you say one ought not to do? What are the 'don'ts' in your country?

- Don't implement any 'good practice' from your own country without checking whether it will work locally. Don't underestimate knowledge, standard of living and culture.
- Don't expect high mobility and people going an extra mile to convince you of their abilities.
- Work hard to gain the trust of your peers and co-workers. Czechs are generally suspicious of any grand proclamations and tend to believe in more pragmatic statements supported and immediately followed by action.
- Don't underestimate the 'Czech way of doing things', as this is often an argument used by the Czech workforce if asked to undergo a mind-shift or participate in too much change.
- Czechs are traditionalists, they do not like change and generally do not cope well with it. When introducing change, do not expect overwhelming enthusiasm and immediate buy-in.
- Feedback is often seen as criticism. Czechs are not used to being praised too often. Recognition can be perceived very positively and has a great motivational upside if applied in a timely and sensitive manner.
- Be careful to know the difference between 'being friendly' and 'being friends', especially in the workplace.

HR ACADEMIA: A TALENT-DRIVEN SOCIETY

THEORETICAL APPROACHES TO HRM AND DEVELOPMENT

The free development of HRM theory was only made possible in the Czech Republic by a change of political regime towards the end of 1989 and the country's subsequent transition to a market economy and civic society based on personal abilities and responsibility. HRM theoreticians initially endeavoured to inform the broader professional public as fast as possible about the development of the discipline and its most recent trends. At first, numerous works were published and translated, then followed later by original Czech publications, which were still influenced by foreign works. For this reason, we cannot talk about an original Czech theory of HRM during that period of time. Nevertheless, most Czech publications are characterised by a sound approach to the study of the subject, including the presentation of links between HR management and other processes in an organisation, and by a good knowledge of the domestic situation, which shows especially in more recent publications in the sense that they modify theoretical inputs and adapt them to the best local practice (Koubek 1995, 1997, 2001; Stýblo 1998).

Starting in the latter half of the 1990s, two approaches to the concept of HRM began to take shape in the specialised literature. The first could be termed 'economic', focusing as it did on performance management and the application of the knowledge management concept (Koubek 2004; Truneček 2003), while the second, 'socio-psychological' approach focuses on 'soft' HR development using instruments based on the theory of adult education (andragogy), emphasising a strategic approach to further professional training and the HR training and development system (Petříková *et al.* 2002; Tureckiová 2004).

> **What is your advice to a foreign company entering your country's market? What should managers especially care about and, what is more, be aware of?**
>
> Any foreign manager needs cross-cultural training. Look for people who have worked for an international company, who are likely to meet your expectations and are familiar with the local market, history and culture. Also consider the following points:
>
> - we are not a third world country;
> - beware of the practice of 'passive resistance';
> - beware of 'do it our way' temptations; and
> - the Czechs spend significant time identifying and analysing problems, rather than finding solutions. Accepting personal responsibility and adopting a solution-oriented stance represent strong development opportunities for the new management generation.

ROLES AND COMPETENCES OF HR PROFESSIONALS

Nowadays, HRM (sometimes still referred to as personnel management) is taught as a separate subject at most universities preparing managers. It is possible to study HRM as a major subject at Palacký University in Olomouc, the University of Economics in Prague or Charles University in Prague, where it forms part of the Andragogy (Theory of Adult Education) and Personnel Management major. This unique combination of adult education theory and HRM actually reflects another characteristic feature of the theory and practice of HR management in the Czech Republic, namely the emphasis on HR development and gradual transition from the HRM concept to the application of the concept of developing a human capital pool of knowledge and skills (competences in more general terms). These knowledge workers are to become the future backbone and driving force for the development of the Czech economy because, unlike many other countries, the Czech Republic lacks major natural resources (oil, coal, gas, etc.) and therefore relies on human resources capital for its wealth.

In connection with the establishment and development of the HR profession – and, in a broader context, in line with the worldwide discussion on a global HR competence model – it was also necessary to create an accurate profile of the professional competences of those involved in the HR profession. Research in this area focused on mapping of the situation, primarily with regard to the educational structure of HR professionals (Česká společnost pro rozvoj lidských zdrojů 2000; Tureckiová/Pešková 2003a, 2003b; Tureckiová 2004). Academics from the same department authored publications defining the characteristics and development trends of the HRM major and the employment opportunities for its graduates (Beneš *et al.* 2001).

Summarising the above surveys confirms that the professional profile of HR specialists and managers in the Czech Republic is – as in other countries – highly diverse, which itself underlines the need to create a body, such as a professional chamber or association, which would verify, certify (guarantee) and further develop the professional competences of those involved in the HR profession. The above research, as well as reflections on best practice in the Czech Republic and numerous benchmarking studies, have also confirmed a gradual trend of transition from a tactical management level to a strategic one, evidenced by an outsourcing of traditional HR roles (data administrator and 'human factor' administrator) or by their transference to other employees within an organisation (primarily to line managers and partly also to the employees themselves).

HR specialists and managers have not been the only HR practitioners in organisations and this will continue to hold true in the future. The entire discipline is becoming increasingly generalised, and is placing new demands on its existing practitioners (including further necessary adjustments of the content of their professional training) as well as on other employees within an organisation, in particular the line managers, and on specialists in the field of labour law and adult education, who are turning into external HR service suppliers and, together with company HR professionals and line managers, rank among practitioners specialised in the HR area. Opportunities have been opening up for further professional training in the HR area as well as for a general management education (HRM for non-HR managers, trainers, coaches, advisers and consultants). This area is currently receiving a great deal of attention from both the academic community (adjustments of curricula) and commercial operators engaged in management training (graduate schools of business, trade colleges, private universities with a management bias and other educational institutions focusing on the development of managers).

HUMAN CAPITAL DEVELOPMENT

Main trends and concepts

Strategic tools for human capital development are among other areas being investigated by Czech academics, together with practitioners at leading organisations. This may involve competence-based management applications or applications based on the learning organisation concept, presented nowadays by a shift to methods and forms of employee training and development that promote mutual learning and the development of key and talented people in organisations.

Above all, as one of the strategic tools for application of the learning organisation concept, the methodology of knowledge management has a major impact on practice in organisations (particularly in international companies). Theoretical development of the knowledge management concept is represented in the Czech Republic by leading theoreticians such as Professor Jan Truneček of the University of Economics in Prague (Truneček 2003, 2004) and Professor J. Á. Jirásek (CMC Graduate School of Business), whose field also encompasses strategic management, including human resource development strategy (Petříková *et al.* 2002; Jirásek 2004).

HR development strategy: goals and challenges

Starting in 2000, several projects were launched with the objective of drafting a programming document for a 'Strategy of Human Resource Development for the Czech Republic' (Národní Vzdělávací Fond 2006). These projects were commissioned by the Ministry of Labour and Social Affairs of the Czech Republic and they were conducted under the guidance of the National Education Fund with the participation of a number of experts from universities. The resulting document, adopted by the Government of the Czech Republic in Resolution No. 210 of 3 March 2003, lists its first part five interconnected strategic objectives for HR development in the Czech Republic. These objectives not only accurately reflect the needs of Czech society and the Czech economy but also correspond fully with the above activities of HR management theoreticians in the Czech Republic.

The five strategic objectives are:

1. To establish lifelong learning as a common practice.
2. To prepare human resources for the challenges of a knowledge-based society and global economy.
3. To increase the international competitiveness of the Czech economy and its attractiveness for investors.
4. To increase the employability of the workforce and thus have a positive effect on employment.
5. To improve the use of limited resources and the mobilization of means for human resource development (strategy of HRD for the Czech Republic).

In a broader international context, the Czech Republic, as a small country with a steadily shrinking population, needs to ensure even more than larger developed countries that the talent of its citizens is well managed. The 'brain drain' is still in evidence, especially in certain professions and regions, and is being reinforced further by the process of globalisation and labour market liberalisation, including the free movement of labour within the EU. It is understandable that these tendencies cannot be eliminated and the challenge for experts in the field of human capital development for the future will be to rapidly identify talented individuals, develop them, manage them (talent management) and contribute to the development of social and economic conditions that will make the Czech Republic attractive for a local as well as an international workforce.

💡.CZ The identification and use of methods for effective collaboration with talented people and the development of key employees are among the major challenges for the development of the theory and practice of human capital development in the Czech Republic.

In a few words, what would you say is the one fundamental strategic competitive advantage your country offers compared to others?

- location in the heart of Europe;
- educated people; and
- stable economic and political climate.

BEST-PRACTICE CASE: ČESKÁ POJIŠŤOVNA a.s. – A LEARNING ORGANISATION

THE INITIAL SITUATION AT ČESKÁ POJIŠŤOVNA a.s.

Q.cz

Česká Pojišťovna a.s. is a modern Czech insurance company in Prague which has been offering its services since 1827. Its 5,000 employees and more than 6,000 sales agents cater for the long-term needs of its clients. The fruit of their labour is not only the strongest presence in the market but also client satisfaction with reliable services.

At the end of 2004, by introducing new technologies, altering the structure of the organisation, modifying processes, embracing an open-space culture and introducing continuous operations, Česká Pojišťovna was transformed into the most technologically modern insurance company in Central Europe. The company created three large computerised service centres for modern communication with the client. Česká Pojišťovna has the second biggest scanning centre in Europe and a client service operation that permits a quick standardised service for managing insurance and settling clients' claims without the need for personal face-to-face contact.

A modern company has been created with the most advanced technology, with growing requirements for professional knowledge, technology handling skills and management and communication skills. All such changes are naturally reflected in the requirements that need to be met in terms of employee preparation, development and education. Parallel to the traditional education in the category of daily trainings, a new direction in education was developed with a new approach which eventually completely involved all of the employees.

The new situation heightened the need for information-sharing and development across the company as a whole and, with the development of new technologies, an even greater need to emphasise internal education and evaluation of internal know-how.

Traditionally, education largely encompassed:

– daily training for communication centre operators;
– training for liquidators – client service damage estimators;
– development of specialists – specialised professionals, experts, lawyers; and
– development of managers at all levels of management in Manager 2000 and Euromanager 2005 programmes. The programmes were for all managers and compulsory. Each ran for two years and was geared to teaching basic managerial skills for line management, higher soft skills for middle management and top-level knowledge of processes, changes, projects and leadership for senior management.

NEW INFORMATION-SHARING AND KNOW-HOW RETENTION MODEL

The new model is based on the company's own mutual development practices and the following principles: sharing internal expertise, expanding the net of internal certified education, creating a net of voluntary expert education, creating a database of internal expertise (memoranda and records of lectures by top company experts). The overall vision is depicted in Figure 3.1. The new model required the involvement of all who excel at their work and are motivated to transfer their know-how to others. This programme has allowed the company to develop its own internal lecturers and helped to create an internal 'student' base.

In 2005, many successful forms of education were created or developed, which includes: afternoon expert seminars (already attended by 800 students); certified courses for managers called 'Euromanager' (already successfully completed by 420 employees in senior positions); a professional insurance pool (35 participants); an expert pool (85 participants); a talent management pool (for 45 selected participants); development of commercial coaches (preparation of 30 trainers, who will train 6,000 insurance agents); and a school of internal lecturers (approximately 50 regular internal lecturers).

ALL EMPLOYEES AS TARGET GROUP

The target group in the company encompasses all employees. Some participate as students, others as lecturers and coaches. This brings with it unprecedented

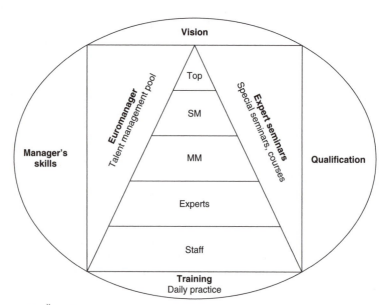

Figure 3.1 Česká Pojišt'ovna's information-sharing vision

interest in the voluntary afternoon's internal seminars, where young employees and specialists, in particular, have the opportunity to acquire direct know-how from experienced managers of the company and internal experts assuming the role of pedagogues for junior executive managers and specialists. These seminars are the most popular with employees; when they are announced, places are snapped up almost immediately, the majority being sold out within half an hour.

The company has managed to create a culture of mutual education and sharing of know-how. The following were the special focus groups:

- all line managers;
- university graduates and potential future experts;
- operators and leaders of the communication centre teams;
- mobile technicians and liquidators;
- project and product specialists and experts;
- net managers; and
- employees of the support function.

SOLUTIONS AND ADDED VALUE FOR EMPLOYEES AND THE COMPANY

The project was originally developed on the basis of the need to connect all forms of education and to enhance radically the professionalism of Česká Pojišt'ovna employees.

The original idea was to strengthen internal sources of training and development. However, from thorough preparation and after early positive feedback from the 'graduates' of individual modules, there developed a need to connect up the entire knowledge base of the company to form a long-term knowledge heritage. The first lecture memoranda were born.

The main contributions were: drawing attention to the development of individuals as well as teams, preserving know-how as a valuable source of information for further work in the area of company education, improving internal communication, making activities more effective in the new environment and creating a model for an internal university.

In the next phase, the new internal information database will be developed (identity of information carriers, knowledge derived from projects, conferences, seminars, and so on).

The aim is not to create a passive information source but to gain a map of active know-how.

CONCLUDING REMARKS

In 2005, after the successful transformation of Česká Pojišt'ovna with the creation of three major client centres, the Learning Organisation programme was launched.

In 2006, the focus was on the support and development of commercial and service personnel.

At the present, the project feels like an advance to a new level, meaning that if it is fully implemented, it will become a standard approach for solving the development and education of employees as well as working and harnessing the knowledge potential of the company.

The education programme in the past was geared to promoting the development of selected groups of employees. The new approach aims at sharing the knowledge base of the entire company. The objective is to provide broad support for the development of the company as a whole by harnessing the knowledge already acquired to maximum advantage. The success of the project can already be evaluated; evidence is furnished by both its financial impact and the active interest of employees themselves.

Which people play key roles in your country? Which names should one know?

- politicians and leaders: Tomáš Garrigue Masaryk, Václav Havel, Charles IV;
- Nobel Prize Laureates: Jaroslav Heyrovský (inventor of the polarographic method), Jaroslav Seifert (writer, poet);
- inventor/scientist: Otto Wichterle (developed material and technology for soft contact lenses);
- artists: Karel Čapek (writer, member of International PEN club, introduced the international word 'robot');
- composers: Leoš Janáček, Antonín Dvořák, Bedrich Smetana, Bohuslav Martinů;
- opera singer: Magdalena Kožená;
- sports personalities: Jaromír Jágr, Dominik Hašek, Martina Navrátilová, Kateřina Neumannová;
- educators: Jan Amos Komensky (Comenius).

References

Beneš, Milan *et al.* (2001): Marketing a práce s absolventy vysokých škol, Prague.

Česká společnost pro rozvoj lidských zdrojů (ed.) (2006): Průzkum odborného profilu profesionalů v říyzení lidských zdrojů, in: HR forum, 6/2000: 7.

Jirásek, Jaroslav Antonín (2004): Souboj mozků v řízení, Prague.

Kolman, Luděk (2001): Komunikace mezi kulturami, Prague.

Koubek, Josef (1995; 1997; 2001): Řízení lidských zdrojů – Základy moderní personalistiky, Prague.

—— (2004): Řízení pracovního výkonu, Prague.

Nový, Ivan *et al.* (1996): Interkulturální management, Prague.

Národní Vzdělávací Fond (2006): Strategie rozvoje lidských zdrojů pro Českou republiku. Online. Available HTTP: www.nvf.cz/rozvoj_lz/strategie.htm (accessed 6 February 2006).

Petříková, Růžena *et al.* (2002): Lidé – zdroj kvality, znalostí a podnikových výkonů (znalostní dimenze jakosti), Ostrava.

Stýblo, Jiří (1998): Moderní personalistika – Trendy, inspirace, výzvy, Prague.

Truneček, Jan (2003): Znalostní podnik ve společnosti znalostí, Prague.

—— (2004): Záverecná zpráva o plnění výzkumného úkolu GAČR 402/02/15, Prague.

Tureckiová, Michaela/Pešková, Lenka (2003a): Modelování HR rolí a kompetencí (I), in: HR forum, 4/2003: 30–1.

—— (2003b): Modelování HR rolí a kompetencí (II), in: HR forum, 5/2003: 36–7.

Tureckiová, Michaela (2004): Řízení a rozvoj lidí ve firmách, Prague.

.CZ

The authors

Rostya Gordon-Smith (gordonsmith@peopleimpact.com), Managing Partner, PeopleImpact. She has accumulated eighteen years of global experience in HRM, acquired in the Czech Republic, Canada, Great Britain, Hong Kong, Japan, Brazil, Estonia, Russia and other countries, and has practical experience in corporate culture development, processes implementation, management and leadership development and in all other aspects of HRM in international as well as local Czech organisations. She is founder of the PeopleImpact.s.r.o., an HR consulting company, and is a member of the Board of the Czech Society of HR Development (ČSRLZ). In 2000 she was named one of the fifty Top HR Leaders by *HR World*'s Global Leadership Agenda Survey, World Federation of Personnel Management Associations (WFPMA) and Cendant International Assignment Partners. In 2005 she was placed ninth in a group of twenty-five of the most successful women in the Czech Republic.

Michaela Tureckiová (michaela.tureckiova@ff.cuni.cz), Associate Professor at the Department of Adult Education and Personnel Management at Charles University in Prague. Academic adviser and guarantor of HRM programmes at the CMC Graduate School of Business, member of the Czech Association of Human Resource Development (ČSRLZ), Association of Management Trainers and Consultants (ATKM) and Association of Adult Education Institutions (AIVD) – certified trainer for the Czech and Slovak Republics. Main research: Human Resource Development, Theory of Management, and Organisational Behaviour. Main publications: *Marketing and Work with University Graduates* (2001, co-author); *Theory of Management* (2002); *People Management and Development in Firms* (2004); several articles on HR development and the roles and competences of HR professionals (published in *HR Forum* magazine in 2000 to 2004).

Iveta Richter (iveta.richter@cz.ey.com), HR Director, Ernst & Young. She studied economics in Prague and English in Washington, D.C. where she worked for the US Department of Commerce and USAID at the same time. Since 1993, she has been active in HR – first as Executive Search Consultant for FMCG and Media businesses, later as Regional HR Director for Warner Lambert, supporting the Czech Republic, Russia, Poland and Hungary. In 1999, she worked as HR Director of the Warner Lambert production plant. After the merger of Warner Lambert with pharmaceutical global leader Pfizer, she worked for Pfizer New York headquarters as European HR Director for Internal Communications, supporting fifteen countries in Europe and Canada. In 2001, she successfully supervised the HR aspects of Pfizer's merger with Pharmacia in the Czech Republic. She currently lives and works in Prague.

Zdenek Simek (zsimek@cpoj.cz), Česká Pojišt'ovna (a leading insurer in the Czech Republic), Head of HR. President of the Association of Banks and Insurance Companies. He has had different managerial experience in insurance business for twenty years, including nine years as an HR manager, finished exams in biology at Prague Agriculture University and HRM at Sheffield Hallam University (UK), gained HRM certificates and awards in Japan, Belgium, Germany. He is a member of the Czech Association of Human Resource Development (ČSRLZ). In 2003 he was named one of the ten top HR speakers, his HR team won an HR excellence award in the Czech Republic in 2002 and 2005. In 2007 he finished his MBA at Sheffield Hallam University.

.CZ

Richard Dobeš (richard_dobes@krauthammer.com), Krauthammer International, Managing Partner, central and eastern Europe. He is consultant, coach and trainer, co-author of two books on HRM, and lecturer on the MBA programme run by Sheffield University (UK) and the Czech Technical University in Prague. He makes contributions to the programmes of the Prague School of Economics, Prague, and the Anglo-American College. He is a member of the Prague School of Economics Scientific Board, a member of the Board of the Czech Society for HR development and a member of the Advisory Board of the Czech Management Society.

4 HRM in Denmark: on the top of Europe

Kim Staack Nielsen/Mette Nørlem/Anja Agerlin Leschly/Christina Grünbaum/
Henrik Holt Larsen

Denmark: in a nutshell

In this chapter you will learn:

- that the Danish economy is booming. For that reason it has become a challenge for Danish HRM to find, hire and retain qualified people;

- that Danish academia defines HRM as an interdisciplinary academic and practitioner-oriented field. This approach is taught at Danish universities at undergraduate, graduate and executive levels; and

- that Fakta involves humour as one of the leading values in its organisation. Combined with other HRM key success factors, the supermarket chain has become one of the most famous brands in Denmark.

Capital:	Copenhagen
Area (sq km):	43,094 (land 42,394; water 700)
EU membership:	since 1973
Population:	5,450,661
Languages:	Danish, Faroese, Greenlandic, German (English is the predominant second language)
Ethnic groups:	Scandinavian, Inuit, Faroese, German, Turkish, Iranian, Somali
Gross domestic product:	198.5 billion USD (2006)
Workforce (in percentages):	2.91 million (2006): agriculture 3; industry 21; services 76 (2004)
Export commodities:	machinery and instruments, meat and meat products, dairy products, fish, pharmaceuticals, furniture, windmills

BACKGROUND: PROFESSIONAL HRM AS A CHALLENGE

DANISH MONARCHY AND DEMOCRACY

Denmark is a monarchy, but at the same time it is a modern democracy.

Queen Margrethe II became the Queen of Denmark in 1972. The Danish Royal House can be traced back to Gorm the Old and his son Harald I Bluetooth. Gorm the Old became King of Denmark around the year 916. The two great lines of the Danish Royal House are the House of Oldenborg and the House of Glücksborg.

The Danish democracy was founded during the eighteenth century. All Danes are born free and equal; their personal liberties are guaranteed and protected. The political system of Danish democracy has a multiparty structure with 179 seats in the Parliament (Folketing). In February 2005 the Liberal Party and the Conservative Party were re-elected. The Liberals are the largest party represented in the Danish Parliament. The Liberal Party occupies twelve out of the nineteen ministries in the government. Since 2001 Mr Anders Fogh Rasmussen has been Prime Minister of the Danish government. The Faroe Islands and Greenland are part of Denmark, and have been so since the 1700s. They each have two representatives in the Danish Parliament. Both the Faroe Islands (since 1984) and Greenland (since 1979) have their own 'home rules' (regional legislation).

Denmark is a country with a highly developed welfare system. It is based on the idea that all citizens have equal rights to social security and education; this is probably one reason why Denmark has one of the highest taxations in the world.

DANISH ECONOMY AND WORKFORCE

Denmark is a highly developed service economy with continuing economic growth, with one of the highest employment rates in the world and the relatively low unemployment rate of 4.4 per cent. Exports (71.4 billion) exceed imports (62.7 billion) significantly. About one-third (920,000) of the whole Danish workforce (2,765,000) is employed in the public sector. Of the Danish workforce, 25 per cent has a diploma, Bachelor or Master's degree, which attests to the high qualification profile of the population.

Table 4.1 shows an estimation of ten important personal competences within the Danish population: the upper five items may be seen as special strengths whereas the lower five items must be interpreted as relative weaknesses of the Danes.

Table 4.1 The national competence accounting

Competence within	High	Middle	Low
Democratisation	53	40	7
Learning	51	38	11
Environment	39	49	12
Creative/innovative	37	45	18
Intercultural	39	44	17
Social	16	60	24
Study (read/write)	10	51	39
Communication	12	44	44
Health	1	53	46
Self-motivating	7	41	52

Danish employees are free to join a trade union; but the whole Danish workforce shows a remarkably high degree of union membership (80 per cent). The Danish Confederation of Trade Unions (LO) follows a global strategy for the Danish workforce under the title 'Denmark in a Globalised World'. The idea is to develop Denmark to become a central player in the global socio-economic development. The employers' organisation is the Confederation of Danish Employers (DA). DA leads and coordinates the collective bargaining negotiations with the unions and represents its members within the whole political system.

What is typical of your country in relation to the country itself (its culture, people, etc.) and its economy?

With only 5.4 million inhabitants, Denmark is among Europe's smallest countries. Even though it has one of the strongest economies in Europe, Denmark is well known for its well-developed welfare system and its high social security. In 2007, Denmark paid back the rest of its financial debt to foreign countries.

As with other European countries, Denmark is facing a demographically diminishing workforce – with a smaller number of young people and an increasing number of elderly people. Denmark therefore faces a future shortage of personnel. Due to this new demographical challenge, there will be an increasing need for public finance. To face this challenge, Denmark has already started to control public finance by launching political initiatives to force people to stay within the labour market for a longer period of time and to encourage younger people to finish their education and studies in a shorter time.

Denmark was formerly a traditional agricultural country, and it still has a well-developed export business in food products and beverages all over the world with well-known companies such as Arla, Tulip, Danish Crown, Carlsberg and Tuborg. However, Denmark also has other large and well-developed export areas with medical equipment/products, IT and communication technology/equipment, and not least in the area of the design of television and stereo products, furniture and household items.

Well-known Danish companies are Novo Nordisk, Ecco, Danisco, Lego, Bang&Olufsen, Danfoss, Grundfos, Louis Poulsen, Den Kongelige Porcelænsfabrik, and especially SAS, which is an airline joint venture between three countries: Sweden, Norway and Denmark.

DANISH HRM

A growing need for professional HRM

In 2002 the job market in Denmark was very bad, especially in certain business areas such as IT and telecommunications. The number of job vacancies showed a significant decrease. This was mainly a consequence of the insecure global economy triggered by the terrorist attacks on 11 September in the USA.

But now the situation has changed completely in Denmark: in 2006 the country was deemed to be a 'tiger economy', like many Asian countries some years ago. The economy is booming, and it has become a challenge to find, hire and retain qualified people. Many highly qualified Danish students find it attractive to study in larger countries either in Europe, the USA or Asia. Many of these highly qualified candidates stay in the country where they studied, especially because of the wider range of job opportunities. In order to attract these high-potential candidates not only do remuneration packages have to be taken into consideration, but also the company culture with its values, career opportunities, development plans and all the different fringe benefits that have an impact on the company's attractiveness.

Danish companies had to learn to adapt quickly to the fast-changing economic and labour market conditions. It was in such a context that the former President of the USA, Bill Clinton, named the Danish society a 'FlexSecurity System' (the remark from Bill Clinton was made during his two-day visit to Denmark in spring 2006). In 2005 the professional organisation for HR managers in Denmark Personalechefer I Denmark (PID) carried out a survey during its annual HR exhibition (Træfpunkt Human Resources). Some of the questions asked in that survey focused on which HR issues were considered most important for the future. The four most important issues were: (a) training and development (21.24 per cent); (b) HR visible on the bottom line (16.48 per cent); (c) talent management (16.12 per cent); and (d) lack of staff (11.35 per cent).

Looking at this distribution it is obvious that Danish companies are putting a major focus on retaining their good employees – especially at a time in which continuing low unemployment rates and a further booming economy are expected.

There is also a particular challenge for internationally active Danish companies to attract the right qualified and motivated candidates from foreign countries. In most cases they are expected to bring in their specific knowledge and experiences in foreign, regional or country situations which could be beneficial for the Danish employer. Therefore these kinds of recruiting companies also need to consider incentives and benefits to encourage employees to leave their home country and to live and work in Denmark, or elsewhere in the world for a Danish employer. This implies in many cases that the recruitment processes become quite complex, since the companies are hiring not only single employees, but whole families with all that that entails concerning housing, childcare, schools, language courses, social security and so on.

Core challenges for the Danish HRM

One of the most discussed issues in Denmark is the low birth rate, which will cause even more serious problems for companies, when they want to attract and recruit qualified working capacity in the years to come. On top of the low birth rate, future employees (born between 1977 and 1992) have different demands and expectations of their employment from the older generations. Therefore there will also be a change in the way the labour market is structured. The traditionally firm structure of the labour market will become more flexible, which is also mirrored in the wishes of the future employees.

Developing this line of thought, some scholars believe that future employees will not be employed on a permanent basis but only hired for the tasks and the duration of a certain project (free agents). Many employees will work more and more independently and often rather as freelance consultants than as regular permanent employees as we know them from the past. This creates a need for a new way of thinking of reward management in order to get highly qualified people to work for a certain company. Of course, this is not an option for all groups of employees, but for some of the knowledge-intensive groups the future will be similar to this.

Seven crucial fields of action for HR managers in the majority of Danish companies can be identified, and we outline these in turn.

Recruitment

When young future employees are asked what is the most important thing in their future job, the answer is clear: more than 50 per cent of students answer that the possibility of professional and personal development is a decisive factor when choosing where to work. Next comes the possibility of having influence in the job or assignment. The opportunity of flexible working hours also plays an important role for many future employees.

For the HR professionals this means having to guide line managers to structure the work according to the expectations of their most important future employees. This leads to new structures of the labour market too, and it provides future employees with new opportunities which have not been seen before. Countries such as Denmark, which in the future will be in even greater need of qualified candidates, should already be thinking of alternatives when looking for new employees. In Denmark this is done by looking, for example, at that section of the labour market with people between 50 and 65 years of age. Instead of retiring these people they can become valuable working capital for the companies.

Another way of getting newly qualified working capacity into the company is to use graduates from the various universities and business schools around the country. This thought is slowly emerging in Denmark, as there is currently much research in Danish universities into the competences of academics. Many companies prefer candidates with the right education combined with working experience. But the future small pool of young candidates may force the companies to hire more young graduates without practical experience and to develop them by work experience and learning on the job.

The HR business partner has overall responsibility for the recruitment process, which should be structured as follows:

1. The HR department receives a staff request from a particular line manager.
2. The recruitment process is discussed and designed with the relevant manager.
3. A job advertisement is compiled, which will be posted on job websites as well as the corporate website and intranet. In the case of strategic positions, the job advertisement could also be posted in relevant newspapers.
4. Applications are screened by an HR consultant; applicants receive confirmation on the receipt of their application.
5. Five to ten relevant candidates are invited for a first interview, typically with the line manager and/or a trusted employee.
6. One to three relevant candidates are invited for a second interview with both the line manager and the HR consultant and sometimes with future colleagues.
7. If relevant, the candidate is tested with a personal profile analysis and given feedback from a certified HR consultant.
8. An evaluation of the candidates is made by the line manager and the HR consultant.
9. An offer is made to the successful candidate; the negotiation of the remuneration package is carried out by the line manager and the HR consultant.
10. When the signed contract is received by HR, the recruitment process is finalised.

Introduction and integration of new employees

Many (mainly bigger) Danish companies have acquired considerable experience by building up a corps of tutors for the successful induction and integration of externally hired employees into the specific culture and working conditions of the company.

Tutors can play an important part in the induction and integration process, mainly by ensuring that all new employees are provided with a proper induction into their new job and also ensuring the learning and acceptance of the specific culture and history of the firm. In most companies, tutors have the important task of focusing on job security from day one, so that work accidents can be avoided.

A stronger focus on continuous learning, especially for the freshly hired employees, has expanded the need for new and various forms of training and education. Many companies still use external training, but more and more companies have seen the advantage in using a company's internal competences in staff training. Besides the fact that companies thereby make use of technical and personal competences, which are already in the company, the advantage with internal training is that the training managers also know the company personally, the history and – most important of all – the corporate culture. Training in corporate culture is one of the reasons why a lot of Danish companies involve employees in the induction process.

Many companies have worked out a tutor concept (mostly in cooperation with external consultants) which also includes a training part in order to prepare the tutors for their job. The tutors are mainly selected because of their knowledge and attitude towards the corporate culture, but naturally they are also chosen because of their communication skills. In an introduction phase many different people are involved. The overall role of the tutor is to be 'rope holder' (coordinator) in the process. Each company has developed a set of materials which precisely describes all the elements in the induction course regarding each person and the respective job. Therefore the job of the tutor is to make sure that all responsible persons in this process fulfil their roles.

Besides that, the tutor is also a personal adviser (mentor) for the new employee. Therefore the new employee is able to ask the tutor about all the practical things in the company, but he/she is also a person who can explain the more 'informal rules' within the company. Each tutor is chosen to cover a certain area. That means that all new employees are trained by an equal colleague. Even though the employees were positive towards this new project it was important to ensure that the tutors should not just be the manager's right hand. The tutor does not make decisions, such as whether the right person is in the right job or not. The tutor is only a collegial helper who has the task of getting the new employees properly introduced into the job and the company.

As it is the case for all new HR projects it is essential to have the full support and acceptance of top management. With the tutor corps it is also necessary to have acceptance from middle management, since providing the requisite resources is a precondition – both for the training of the tutors and also for the tasks the tutors have to fulfil when new employees begin their job. In the Danish model where unions and employers make agreements on payment and working conditions, the representative of the union often plays an important role in the day-to-day work. Therefore it makes sense for many Danish companies to include the union in such projects. It often leads to a many-faceted project, but it also ensures that the other employees support the project as their own representative has been involved in its development.

From the beginning, companies which implemented this kind of tutor project have experienced great support from their employees. The employees find it relevant and right to take the necessary time to introduce new employees to their job. Many companies have realised that it is fairly easy to recruit new tutors. Most tutors find it interesting to help new employees, and they often see it as a personal acknowledgement to be offered the assignment. But it is not only the tutors who are satisfied with the system; new employees are also made to feel positive and valued by the company.

In sum, the tutor concept provides a good result for the companies, as most people know that a good introduction is the first step towards successful retention.

Retention

Once the preferred candidate is employed and well integrated, the next challenge is to ensure that the employee is at all times satisfied, motivated and has the necessary skills to fulfil the tasks and responsibilities of the job. This has to be achieved both on a day-to-day basis but also in a more structured and formal way, since the following activities form part of the employee's continual improvement:

- day-to-day dialogue with colleagues;
- day-to-day dialogue with superiors and other managers;
- performance appraisals and feedback conversations;
- personal objectives and success criteria;
- personal development plan; and
- career plan.

All these activities can result in individual development measures, such as mentoring, coaching, formal or informal training (internal or external), job rotation and expatriate assignments.

Performance appraisal

It is most important that employees are always aware of the tasks and responsibilities of the job, and that they know exactly what is expected of them. The performance appraisal is invaluable.

During the performance appraisal process, employees and their superior managers agree upon the assessment of the employees' performance during any given period according to the objectives and success criteria that were defined for the employees either when they began with the company or from their previous appraisal. New objectives and success criteria will be set for employees for the following year and are agreed upon between employees and their superior managers, just as they agreed upon the employees' job description.

Rewards and benefits

The focus on reward management and benefits is currently topical within Danish HRM. Much debate is taking place over how to structure salaries to satisfy and retain employees.

When talking about reward management, the salary is merely the basis of a remuneration package. To this a number of various benefits can be added, negotiated in the sense that if the employee wants an MBA or a car the salary can be lowered in order to meet the personal needs and requirements of the employee. These individualised benefits are expected to have greater influence on the attitudes and motivation of employees than mere salary level. However, the costs for the company are equivalent to the 'normal' salary including the yearly adjustments and potential bonuses.

Future debate around remuneration will include:

– flexible working hours/holidays: the possibility of having flexible working hours – not necessarily implying fewer working hours a week, but working at different times, e.g. at home, when it fits into family plans;
– extra holidays instead of a pay rise;
– training and development possibilities: the possibility of taking a supplementary education paid for by the company. This could be an MBA or joining a management development programme or similar; and
– career opportunities: possible career opportunities not only in the sense of advancing in the company hierarchy, but also very focused on specialising within a certain area of interest.

Leaving the company

When employees leave the company it can be either their own decision to do so or that the company has dismissed them or asked them to resign. In all cases, certain rules apply to employees and companies alike.

In some cases the employee is offered an outplacement agreement as part of a dismissal remuneration package. This may help the employee to start a new career and to try to look at alternative possibilities for the future. An outplacement agreement may consist of any number of meetings with specially qualified consultants who will act as a personal mentor/coach for the dismissed employee for a certain time period.

The company in any case has to take into consideration that dismissed employees are still ambassadors and representatives of the company who can influence its image as an employer. It is therefore important to help the dismissed employees if this is possible and reasonable.

Future trends in Danish HRM

The future trends and challenges for Denmark's HRM sector can be summarised as follows:

- acceptance of a changed labour market structure and adjustment to these changes;
- more flexible and individually agreed contracts and remuneration packages;
- competitiveness as regards benefits and training and development opportunities;
- networking opportunities and competencies in order to share best-practice cases;
- creation of mutual learning and coaching environments in the process of work; and
- motivation and retention of skilled employees.

The HRM profession is challenged and is changing from its origins of being an administrative function to play a much more strategic role in the development of the companies.

Most characteristics of foreseeable future changes not only involve the HR department but the whole line management and the entire company in order to manage successfully organisational development. For some companies this might happen more or less automatically over the years as part of an already existing 'culture of change'; for others, hard work will be needed – especially by professional HR managers. In any case a developing work environment will be the focus in the future.

What are you and other Danish people extraordinarily proud of with respect to HRM?

In Denmark, we are known for having a very informal management structure, meaning that most Danish companies involve their employees in many company decisions. This means that the employees are an active part of the decision-making process and take responsibility for the company's image, success and social engagement. Several surveys by Arne Vesterdal, Direktør, Forskerpark Aarhus A/S show that Denmark has some of the most efficient and engaged employees in Europe.

The HR department must play a part in fostering and maintaining favourable employee commitment. Denmark is an economy made up of many smaller companies, but, as an example, 80 per cent of Danish companies conduct an appraisal. The reason for the high number – even in companies where there is no HR department – is due to the fact that HR development values have been focused upon in Denmark over the past ten years. Because of this recent employee development-oriented approach Denmark has experience with those policies. The authorities, the educational system and not least Danish managers have focused much upon values and the potential of HR. Furthermore, it has been emphasised that investment in HR must be visible, either through factors such as satisfied and responsible employees, reduction in absence (due to illness and so on), lower personnel turnover or a larger profit on the bottom line. Therefore managers at all levels have had to acknowledge the importance and value of HR. In Denmark HR has gained much respect and influence within companies, and many HR departments have been able to make themselves felt in the business, including at the strategic level.

EAPM AFFILIATE: PID – PERSONALECHEFER I DENMARK

BACKGROUND TO THE FOUNDATION

The members of PID (Personnel Managers in Denmark) have joined the organisation because they have a professional interest in HR. They need to be updated on news relative to the HR scene and to meet other HR managers with whom they can share knowledge and exchange experience.

Denmark is characterised by a business structure consisting of primarily small and medium-sized companies. Naturally there are also big companies like Lego, Gumlink, Carlsberg, Maersk and so on, but most Danish companies are smaller compared to other European countries. This means that although Denmark is a country with only 5.4 million inhabitants there are approximately 425,000 companies in the country. Having so many companies with such small numbers of employees, many of them are not in a position to have an HR manager. Most companies consider it necessary to have an HR manager when they have around 250 employees, while smaller companies solve HR problems by recourse to their managers and directors.

For these companies though, the HR 'department' often consists of only one person. This often leads to a lack of networking possibilities for the HR manager. Of course there are other managers in the company, but no sparring HR professional to discuss HR issues with. And no matter what size the HR department is, HR managers and the rest of their staff need to maintain and extend their knowledge and competences in HR.

The two purposes – networking and knowledge sharing – were the reasons behind the creation of the organisation PID in 1992.

KEY INFORMATION ON THE ORGANISATION

The members

All employees working with HR or with an interest in the subject are eligible for membership. PID has 860 company memberships most of which are private companies but about 15 per cent come from the public sector. That means that PID members differ in many ways. First there are members from many different organisational levels: from HR assistants to HR directors.

Educational backgrounds of the individual HR employee vary greatly: some of them have a high educational background within the area, while others have worked in a variety of environments, gaining experience and knowledge to provide an excellent HR grounding. Some have worked in HR for many years while others are new to the discipline.

Very often representatives of the organisation are asked whether it constitutes a union for HR managers, to which the answer is a clear 'no!'. PID is a trade organisation and all its members have joined because they have a private or professional interest in HR. They want to be kept abreast of news and issues in the field and want to meet other HR managers with whom they can learn, exchange experiences and develop further.

Activities

Publications

PID members have access to many activities. One thing that all members receive and which the organisation is perhaps best known for is its magazine *Personalechefen* ('HR Manager'). Articles in the magazine cover issues such as recruitment, retention, personnel politics, appraisal interviews, healthcare and so on.

Another newsletter *Human Resources News* is also published and distributed to members five times a year.

Networking

In order to create networks for members PID arranges three to four annual courses on different subjects. The courses keep the managers up to date and give them a valuable opportunity to meet other HR managers and consultants.

PID members can also participate in 'trade stories groups'. These groups meet five to six times a year and share knowledge and experience from their daily working life.

HR conference

In October 2006 PID held for the seventh time the yearly HR conference with six keynote speakers and fourteen workshops (Træfpunkt Human Resources) in Copenhagen. The exhibition had about 125 exhibitors and over 2,500 visitors. This might not be a large number for larger countries but for a small country like Denmark with perhaps only 3,000 HR departments the exhibition was well attended.

In a few words, what would you say is the one fundamental strategic competitive advantage your country offers compared to others?

To foreign companies the biggest advantage would be that the workforce consists of very independent employees. This spans the unskilled and highly educated alike. Besides this, Denmark is a country with a highly developed infrastructure and an efficient public sector. Denmark has probably the most flexible labour market in Europe which attracts foreign investors. Yet, as stated earlier, Denmark does have one of the highest tax rates in Europe. This said, the Danes are one of the most satisfied populations in Europe.

HR ACADEMIA: SCIENCE AND ACADEMIC EDUCATION IN HRM

INSTITUTIONAL FRAMEWORK

The Danish HR scene is heavily influenced by the institutional context character-ising society. Four significant issues deserve attention:

- high union density;
- flexicurity;
- national culture features illustrating Scandinavian management; and
- knowledge economy with a predominance of intangible production (know-ledge, service, public administration) while a decreasing proportion of the workforce is employed in manufacturing and agriculture.

These four characteristics will be described briefly below.

Union density

The proportion of the workforce being unionised in selected countries (in 1997, 1999 and 2000, depending on the data available) is presented in Table 4.2.

Table 4.2 Union density (Strøby 2004: 8)

Country	Proportion of the workforce unionised (in percentages)
Sweden	86
Finland	78
Denmark	76
Norway	55
Ireland	45
Austria	39
UK	29
Germany	27
The Netherlands	24
Japan	22
USA	14
France	10

Denmark clearly has a very high level of unionisation. Legislation and collec-tive agreements reflect this. However, also at company level, HR practice is usually characterised by close contact between management and representatives of staff.

Flexicurity

Despite the very strong societal pressure on Danish organisations to behave in (what is perceived to be) a socially responsible manner, there is a very interesting exception to this trend and pressure. This is found in Denmark where flexicurity is seen as an attractive monitoring device for the labour market. Flexicurity can be defined as:

> A policy strategy that attempts, synchronically and in a deliberate way, to enhance the flexibility of labour markets, the work organisation and labour relations on the one hand, and to enhance security – employment security and social security – notably for weaker groups in and outside the labour market on the other hand.
>
> (Flexicurity Research Program at Tilburg University)

Flexicurity rests on three pillars:

– the possibility for the individual employer to terminate employment contracts with employees;
– a financial safety net for individuals losing their job, typically provided by the government, municipality or other type of public funds; and
– a proactive labour market policy helping unemployed individuals back into the labour market.

This 'golden triangle', as it has been called, could actually be extended by a fourth dimension, i.e., the ways in which the employer can boost the employability (functional flexibility) of the individual in a particular job. This in itself increases the possibilities for keeping the individual in the labour market – and by doing so reduces the need for activating/testing flexicurity, as employees are less likely to leave their jobs.

It should be added that Denmark represents not only a high level of flexicurity, i.e. less red tape involved for the employer when firing employees, but also a perceived, and, possibly paradoxical, high level of job security as perceived by employees (documented in OEDC surveys), as well as a top-end growth in GNP.

The national culture

The two above-mentioned features (high union density and flexicurity) indirectly reflect the national culture. A vast range of studies has shown that the Danish business community and public sector are heavily influenced by what has been labelled Scandinavian management. According to Schramm-Nielsen/Lawrence/Sivesind (2004: 181), this can be defined as follows:

– a management style characterised by informality, equality and restraint;
– paralleled by generally flat hierarchies, compressed salary spreads and low fringe benefits;

- a consensual, participative and inclusive approach to decision-making and change implementation;
- a reluctance by most managers to articulate their power, an inclination to reasonableness and quiet persuasion rather than to charismatic dominance; and
- a market and/or customer focus tending to promote coordination across hierarchies and between departments.

Knowledge economy

The relative scarcity in Denmark of natural resources, apart from oil, combined with the fact that the Danish workforce is generally well educated, has made it attractive/necessary for the nation to focus on intangible, knowledge-intensive types of production, rather than relying on heavy manufacturing. In intangible production, the employer can benefit from having a competent and often committed workforce.

What would you like to teach foreign HR managers? What is important for them to know in your opinion?

To foreign companies the greatest challenge will be to master a Danish workforce which is straightforward but not particularly good at accepting authority. The Danes are hard-working and a very engaged nation, but they also make demands and like their voice to be heard. The Danes are known for working independently, and they relate to new processes and procedures in an open but critical way. They gladly contribute new ideas, and are not afraid to give their comments and ask questions.

Another important area is that the Danish labour market is made up equally of men and women. However, this is not the case when we look at managers and especially top management. Still, development in Denmark is heading towards more women getting training. Denmark is, in fact, the EU champion in training its staff. On average, Danish women get 55 hours of training per year, and men 31 hours per year according to Eurostat (http://epp.eurostat.ec.europa.eu).

If we look at the number of managers in HR departments, 50 per cent of them are women. Compared to the Danish labour market in general the proportion of female managers is only 25 per cent.

SCIENTIFIC APPROACHES TO HR

Current Danish research in HRM is not fundamentally different from mainstream HRM research in other European countries or the USA. HRM is seen as an interdisciplinary academic and practitioner-oriented field, focusing on the deployment of individuals in dynamic interaction with employment peers, managers and the organisational context.

In this sense, it is paradigmatically different from personnel management which has an individual-level focus (only) and is mainly concerned with the attraction, retention, development and departure of individuals. In contrast, HRM not only incorporates the organisational context, but also looks at the interaction and mutual dependency between the individual and organisational level. The synergy between individual learning and organisational learning is an example of this.

In addition to this, knowledge and service work (see the comment made earlier that Denmark is a knowledge–service economy) implies that the individual employee interfaces with the customer, user, client and so on. This is in contrast to manufacturing where the employee goes into the organisation (i.e. factory) and does not meet the customer.

Combining this, the difference between personnel management and HRM is illustrated in Figure 4.1 where the small circle is personnel management and the larger circle is HRM – crossing the two boundaries (i.e. the boundary to the organisation and the boundary to extra-organisational issues).

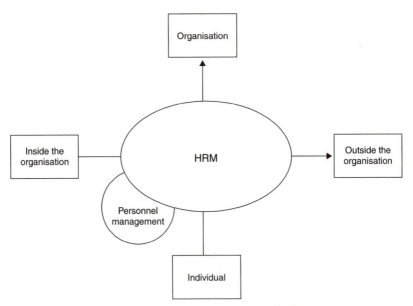

Figure 4.1 Difference between personnel management and HRM

A generic definition of HRM reflecting this approach is that HRM is the academic discipline and practitioner-oriented field which analyses the interaction and mutual dependency between individuals, their task/job and managers within an organisational context.

102

This definition assumes the following:

- there is a mutual dependency and interaction between the individual and the organisation;
- there is a mutual dependency between the organisational strategy and the HR strategy;
- there is a match (or if it does not work, mismatch) between the competence of the individual and the competence requirements of the organisation, reflecting what the person is able to do and what is required by the organisation;
- there is a broad-range psychological contract between the individual and organisation, reflecting expectations and demands from both sides, i.e. what they want;
- the employer demands not only physical presence and the ability to perform certain tasks during working hours, but also willingness and ability to develop competence and commitment;
- the employee expects not only compensation, but also challenge, development opportunities, meaningfulness, a socially responsible employer and flexible benefits;
- the actual responsibility for human resources is to a high extent assigned to the line manager; and
- the (possible) HR function plays the role of being a catalyst, a coordinator.

UNIVERSITY EDUCATION IN HRM

HRM is taught at most Danish universities at undergraduate, graduate and executive level. However, in most cases it appears as elective courses in programmes, the major focus of which is business, organisation, management, sociology and so on.

There are two exceptions to this. First, Aalborg University has a graduate programme in which personnel management and employment relations play a significant role. Second, Copenhagen Business School has two Master's programmes in HRM: (a) MSc in HRM (established in 1992); and (b) Master of Social Science in HRM (launched in 2007). These two degrees are two-year, full-time programmes, building on a social science Bachelor degree.

The programme is divided into a number of topics and subjects, each taught as modules over two to three weeks. Each topic combines insightful theoretical analysis and knowledge with a project in a real-world company. The company provides students with an assignment and feedback based on the students' report and conclusions. Further, the programme contains a ten-week internship in a private or public company, where students are challenged on the basis of their HRM knowledge of real problems in the business world.

The objective of the two degrees is not just to educate candidates for jobs in HR departments. Graduates are also prepared for undertaking jobs as consultants or in line management. As mentioned above, HR responsibility in Denmark is assigned to the line manager to a very high extent. Hence, a degree in HRM will prepare the student for a line manager job.

What would you say one ought not to do? What are the 'don'ts' in your country?

As mentioned before, Denmark used to be an agricultural country with a closed and very local culture. The challenge for most Danes is to accept that they are now part of an international community. This means that there has to be respect towards differences and an ability to take advantage of the cultural diversities.

Danes are also known to be people who love to discuss matters, and when a decision is made, everybody works to that end. The Danes are also quite sensitive; if management makes a decision concerning change without having first discussed it, this could have a negative impact on employees. Denmark is a country stemming from the writings of the Danish writer N.F.S. Grundtvig (born 1783), which means that the Danish society consists of various kinds of associations, where life and issues are up for discussion.

However, Denmark has not been good enough when it comes to the question of integration in the labour market, which makes this a top priority for many companies if they want continuing development for the country.

The Danes are also a people who care a lot about home and family. The phrase 'my home is my castle' is well suited to the Danes. They often prefer to invite friends and relatives home for dinner instead of going out to restaurants. Of course they also go to restaurants, but friendships are often built through private engagements in a homely atmosphere. Danish humour is known to be something of a challenge for foreigners, as Danes often use sarcasm and like to exchange remarks which may appear inappropriate. There is, however, no harm meant by this.

BEST-PRACTICE CASE: HRM IN A DANISH SUPERMARKET CHAIN

BRANDING WITH HUMOUR

Children who disappear into cardboard boxes, a wallet stuffed with coins, a cashier who says the whole barcode instead of using the scanner – all coupled with the slogan 'It only takes five minutes to shop in Fakta' (a Danish supermarket chain); combined with a very humorous advertising campaign, Fakta has put itself on the Danish map as one of the most famous brands within the retail trade.

Q.dk

It did not happen just by chance that Fakta infused its marketing campaign with humour. Obviously, one of the reasons is due to the fact that humour has a positive effect on people, and that funny ads make us remember and discuss them. Second, and importantly, is the fact that Fakta treats humour as one of the leading values of its organisation:

> In our vision we have written down that Fakta should be the favourite place to go shopping and the preferred workplace to be employed – and both parts must be fun to do. Retail trade is hard work, but it should not stop us from thinking that it is fun to do. Therefore customers must expect that we make a practical joke with them sometimes. There has to be room for doing these sorts of things.
>
> (Fakta HR manager Stig Loevstad)

With more than 4,000 employees, many of them under 18 years of age and the remainder also at the younger end, there has to be a culture which appeals to such young employees. Besides humorous campaigns, Fakta is also known for having a flat organisation with not a great deal between top and bottom levels of employees. This is also confirmed by the organisation being very open in its culture; here it is possible for all employees to be in contact with everyone else in the organisation. Young employees will often come up with positive ideas or raise issues that they want to discuss with the managing director.

What is your advice for a foreign firm entering your country's market? What should managers specially care about and, what is more, be aware of?

Compared to other European countries, the Danish labour market is very flexible. Denmark is currently experiencing a shortage of labour, and with an unemployment rate of only 4.4 per cent, most companies have a difficult time getting qualified employees.

However, it is quite easy to dismiss an employee. If an employer has good reason to dismiss an employee, this can be done fairly easily and with only a few months' notice.

Of course foreign companies in Denmark must become familiar with the laws and regulations of the country, and it is especially important to be aware of social obligations that companies must comply with in relation to their employees. The laws concerning sick pay, long maternity leave and extended holiday periods are among current issues in the Danish labour market. The labour market is less controlled by unions. A large part of the labour market regarding wages and working conditions is actually adjusted by local agreements between the employers and unions. Approximately 80 per cent of Danish employees are unionised, and there is a long tradition of this in Denmark.

If a foreign company buys or takes over a company in Denmark, it is important to give due consideration to all such agreements, which the company is already involved in, as the foreign company takes on all the obligations concerning company–union agreements. However, development is also leading in a new direction, which makes for less control and greater independence in this area. This results in the EU having more influence and in the harmonisation of rules and regulations for all European countries.

THE KEY SUCCESS FACTORS

Attraction

For most companies – also in relation to recruitment – the meaning of the brand has become very obvious. Whereas companies branded themselves for the benefit of their customers, most companies are now waking up to the fact that branding themselves for the benefit of attracting potential employees is necessary. With a shrinking pool of employees and a high rate of employment, it is certain that the need to brand and become known as an attractive employer will present itself as an even greater challenge in the years ahead.

A strong company brand will attract new employees, and Fakta has indeed witnessed increased interest from potential employees. At the moment, Fakta receives over 5,000 applications a year from people interested in joining the company.

'Real' people

In the mid-1990s Fakta had to downsize. Economically, and from a business perspective, this did not go down very well, and something very radical had to be done in order to help the chain to survive. A new managing director was appointed to turn the Fakta ship around, and a new vision and mission were drawn up for the organisation. At the same time an intensive marketing plan was put into effect, a plan that would see the Fakta shops as the favourite supermarket chain in Denmark.

In the attempt to make Fakta both Denmark's favourite supermarket chain and the most attractive employer in its field, the marketing plan was made very personal.

The weekly newspaper ads did not feature models, but rather real people who were actually employed by Fakta.

> When the decision was made that the new ads would be made with our own employees, our next job was to find suitable candidates. We discussed how to choose them, but we also agreed that it had to be voluntary, which is why we decided to use casting. Our employees signed up for casting and it is then decided who to use as models in the ads. The interest has been enormous, and besides the desire to be a model it also shows that our employees want to be 'known faces' within the company.
>
> (Stig Loevstad)

Q.dk

Competition

For a long time, retail trade has viewed employees in an impersonal way. This attitude – for many reasons – is on the wane, and the Fakta organisation has made its statement clear concerning this matter.

Besides letting employees speak in the ads, the company has benefited, as it is viewed as a great workplace. The humour is humanising and provides both customers and employees with a positive experience.

Another concept often used by Fakta is competition, which is highly engrained in the organisation. There has to be competition, but it cannot be aggressive. Among the 300 stores around the country, there are several which are more successful than others. Therefore it would be unfair to let the 'best' and the 'weakest' compete against each other. Stores are measured against stores that are alike, and by this it is not only the 'heroes' that are being celebrated, but also the stores who have achieved good or intermediate success.

> This special Fakta culture is part of our success, and it is also a main reason why we have achieved good businesslike results. When our analysis concerning job satisfaction shows that approx. 90 per cent of the employees are proud of working in Fakta, it is due to the fact that we have a positive name among the population, and it is more fun to be part of a businesslike success.
>
> (Stig Loevstad)

The good leader

The future offers big challenges when it comes to attracting and retaining employees. HR must continue to supply the organisation with the best employees, and Fakta believes that the solution is to focus on employees.

Younger employees are more demanding and companies must have attractive visions and values and, above all, they must do what they say, otherwise the new employees will seek employment elsewhere. Retaining a business like brand is as important for both potential and existing employees, as the employees of the future will choose jobs depending on the signals that each company sends.

In Stig Loevstad's opinion, the retail trade faces a special challenge when it comes to store managers. They are the ones who interface with both customers and employees, and in this respect are key to the business. He says: 'Earlier store managers were selected for their good, businesslike abilities. Today store managers must know a whole lot about business, but they also have to know a lot about how to motivate, engage and retain their personnel.'

HR image

Previously the company image was connected to the products and how companies were perceived by society. Nowadays we also talk about company image in terms of the workplace. It is not enough to be aware of the company's reputation in relation to customers but it also matters in relation to potential employees.

We now recognise that these two things should not be separated. The importance of sending the same signals to both groups is huge, and today HR is a part of the business, as business is part of HR.

Which people play key roles in your country? Which names should one know?

In Denmark there are only a few HR associations. The largest HR association in Denmark is PID (Personalechefer I Denmark), which has approximately 860 members and represents one-third of HR departments in the country. The Chair of PID is Mr Kim Staack Nielsen, who has been in that role since 1992. Besides PID there is the Centre for Ledelse and Human Consult.

From the world of education, Denmark has a number of prominent personalities within HR: Denmark's only professor in HR is Henrik Holt Larsen, Professor at Copenhagen Business School. Another well-known management professor and Ph.D. is Steen Hildebrandt, Aarhus School of Business. Of note, there is also Verner C. Petersen, Docent, Cand. Scient. and D. Phil. who is also from the Aarhus School of Business.

Other prominent persons within HR in Denmark are Lise Kingo, Executive Vice-President and Chief of Staff, Novo Nordisk A/S; Lars Stensgaard Mørch, Vice-President, Danske Bank; Maj Britt Andersen, HR Director, SAP Denmark; Henriette Fenger Ellekrog, Senior Vice-President Corporate HR, TDC A/S; Anders Thorup, Vice-President HR, IT and Communication, Aalborg Portland Group; Per Krogager, Vice-President HR, Tvilum Scanbirk; Lone Broberg, Vice-President HR, Aalborg Industries A/S; Lisbet Lollike, Director of State Employers' Authority, Ministry of Finance; Frank Høj, HRM Silkeborg Municipality.

References

Schramm-Nielsen, Jelle/Lawrence, Peter/Sivesind, Karl Henrik (2004): Management in Scandinavia: Culture, Context and Change, Cheltenham.

Strøby, Jensen C. (2004): Faglig organisering under forandring – komparative perspektiver på faglige organisationsgrader i Europa, in: Tidsskrift for Arbejdsliv, 6(3): 7–27.

.dk

The authors

Kim Staack Nielsen (ksn@pid.dk) is Chair of the Board of the Danish Personnel Managers' Association (PID). PID is a business organisation for Danish personnel managers. The organisation has approximately 860 company members and is the largest in its field in Denmark. He has been active within the area of personnel management and development both strategically and in practice for Danish companies since 1992. He has given more than 800 lectures in the field of personnel management and development to more than 17,000 persons from Danish as well as from foreign companies and institutions over the past fourteen years. Kim Staack Nielsen is the author of two HR books. He has a Bachelor's degree in business administration from Aarhus Business University of Economics and Business Administration. He has been teaching for more than fifteen years (from 1984 to 2001) at Aarhus Business College in Personnel Administration (evening courses at BBA level). He has been a member of the Executive Committee of the EAPM from 2005 to 2007.

Mette Nørlem (mn@pid.dk) is the Chief of Staff at the Danish Personnel Managers' Association (PID). She has a Master's degree in law from the University of Aarhus. She has been working in HR since 1993 and also teaches labour law at the Aarhus Business College.

Anja Agerlin Leschly (aal@novozymes.com) serves as a People and Organisation Partner at Novozymes' headquarters in Copenhagen. She was educated as a teacher at N. Zahles Teachers' College in Copenhagen (1996). Previously she had worked as Senior HR Business Partner, Microsoft Development Center, Copenhagen; Human Resource Manager, Ferring Pharmaceuticals, and Senior Management Consultant, HR Solutions, Ementor, Denmark. In June 2003 she was a speaker at the EAPM International Human Resource Congress, Rome and a participant in the EAPM Young HR Talents Programme.

Christina Grünbaum (christinagrunbaum@gmail.com) is working as an HR Development Consultant at Acergy – a Norwegian-based company. She holds a Master of Science degree in economics and business administration (HRM) from Copenhagen Business School (2001). During her study time she was an active member and chairman of the Danish Association of HRM, an association for students and graduates with an interest in HRM. Since her graduation she has held various positions within HR, all in an international as well as developmental capacity. She has worked for such companies as PricewaterhouseCoopers and Carlsberg Breweries. In 2003 she was a participant in the EAPM Young HR, Talents Programme, and gave presentations at two conferences in Milan and Rome.

Henrik Holt Larsen (hhl.ioa@cbs.dk) is Professor, Dr merc. of HRM at the Institute of Organisation, Copenhagen Business School. His major research interests are strategic and international HRM, careers, competence, organisation and management development, training and performance appraisal systems. He has written or contributed to approximately forty books and articles. He is heavily involved in international research programmes and serves as a consultant to corporations and public agencies in Denmark and abroad.

.dk

5 HRM in France: changes in the corpus

David Alis/Frank Bournois/Daniel Croquette/Pierre-Yves Poulain

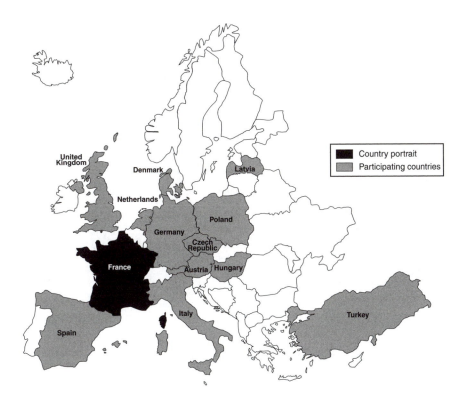

France: in a nutshell

In this chapter you will learn:

– that the state in France plays an active role in the economy and the society, although French HRM is influenced by governmental adjustment, e.g. the 35-hour week;

– that two important trends in French HR academia are a significant increase in research in the areas of HR tools and practices and a decrease in strategic HR research; and

– that Cegetel managed its extreme growth by implementing a developing management programme to sponsor managers during organisational changes and to build a corporate culture.

Capital:	Paris
Area (sq km):	547,030 (land 545,630; water 1,400)
EU membership:	since 1951 (founding member of the former so-called European Coal and Steel Community)
Population:	60,876,136
Languages:	French (official); regional dialects and languages (Provençal; Breton; Alsatian; Corsican; Catalan; Basque; Flemish)
Ethnic groups:	Celtic and Latin with Teutonic, Slavic, North African, Indochinese and Basque minorities
Gross domestic product:	1.871 trillion USD (2006)
Workforce (in percentages):	27.88 million (2006): agriculture 4.1; industry 24.4; services 71.5 (1999)
Export commodities:	machinery and transportation equipment, aircraft, plastics, chemicals, pharmaceutical products, iron and steel, beverages

BACKGROUND: HRM IN FRANCE: EXCEPTION AND PARADOX

LOOKING FOR STRATEGIC HRM WITH THE STATE AS FINAL ARBITER

France: from the personal function to strategic HRM

HRM really came into its own in France towards the end of the 1980s (Bournois 1997). Before this, one spoke of staff management, and the function of the personnel manager was essentially concerned with administration and social relations. It hardly existed as a discipline in management schools.

As time went by, the role of HR managers gained in importance, or at least lip-service was paid to it (Peretti 2006). In fact when strategic management developed in the 1980s in contrast to the traditional planning tendency and began to take into account environmental considerations, those involved tried to link up their staff management tools and techniques with corporate strategy, without always paying attention to its coherence with other aspects of the HRM function; hence the emergence of strategic recruiting, strategic training and strategic career management.

In 1987, at the same time that Tyson (1987) in the UK was writing about the strategic mutations of the function of staff management, the first book on strategic HRM appeared in France: business leaders should adapt their HRM practices to the type of strategy being adopted (Besseyre des Horts 1987). The role of HR managers grew progressively more important and an increasing number of them took their place on the board of directors.

But what does this motivation towards strategic management really indicate? Bournois/Derr (1994) published in the *Revue française de gestion* (the leading French management magazine) a provocatively entitled article 'Les DRH ont-ils un avenir?' ('Is there any future for HR Managers?'), which highlighted the giant strides that the function of HRM had made. In France, as in other countries, each in its own specific way, the role of the HR manager is developing from a functional role into a strategic-type role of which the main features are listed in Table 5.1.

However, HR managers should think about the different paths they could choose in the future. Several possibilities are open to them:

- allow HRM to become more and more integrated into line management which will lead to its losing its specialised organisational function;
- develop their competence in technical areas in which line management's expertise will never be very strong, for example, labour law; and
- seize the opportunity offered by internal and external transformations and concentrate their efforts in such areas as complex project management

115

where their regulation organisational skills will be appreciated. In this case, new types of work will be expected of them: HR managers will be entrusted with projects leading to change; they will have clearly defined assignments to be carried out within time limits. Having become internal consultants, their dependence on the company will continue to grow, and it may well come about, in certain cases where knowledge of the company is not essential, that HR managers will simply turn into external consultants for a number of companies.

It is important to stress the fact that these possibilities will not be identical in each European country. In countries where there is a strong tradition of negotiating with employees (in Germany and in the Scandinavian countries, for example), it is more likely that the traditional role of the HR manager will be maintained: compared to the English and German models, for instance, France is in an intermediary position.

Table 5.1 Developments noted in the roles of HR managers in the 1990s (adapted from Bournois/Derr 1994)

	The 'functional' HR manager	HRM incorporated into the supposedly 'strategic level'
Specific priority actions	Recruitment, training, compensation and benefits, industrial relations and so on	Corporate strategy, corporate culture, internationalisation, staffing adjustments
Focus	Control of resource costs	Flexibility of resources – but cost control at the profit centre level
Orientation	Tactical action at the micro-organisational level	Strategic action at the macro-organisational level
HRM customer	The employees and line management	Line managers and outside customers
Power/status	Rather weak	Rather strong (due to assimilation to top management)
Training background of the HRM	Specialised in HRM embracing other functions	General management-type HRM with operational experience or a line manager with significant experience in HRM
Profile	Specialist in management tools and systems	Generalist concerned with line management
Timescale of activities	Short term	Medium or long term
Management style based on	Transactions	Organisational change/ transformation

The state as the final arbiter

According to Sorge (1993: 67), the success story of France has consistently been based on the three following approaches:

- make the same institutional arrangements apply across the country;
- create an infrastructure to facilitate economic and social exchange; and
- use the best brains of the country in a technocratic civil service.

Government and companies are very centralised in France and most larger groups and companies have headquarters in Paris; the infrastructure was designed in such a way that major roads and railways invariably point towards Paris. The history is embodied in Paris. 'From Paris, standard systems of governance, law and education have been prescribed. From Paris, the State has reached out to become heavily involved in business, stimulating, protecting and owning it' (Hickson/Pugh 2001: 77).

So the state is important in France. It used to play and still plays a positive and active role in both economy and society.

From François 1er (1494–1547), Louis XIV (1638–1715), the Jacobins of the Revolution (1789), through to the civil code of Napoleon (1769–1821) and de Gaulle (1890–1970), the tradition of centralisation has been maintained in recent times.

Since the Second World War, the state has played a major role in financing the revitalisation of the company, with ownership of energy, transport, the main deposit banks and insurance companies, armaments, the car industry, among others. The presence of the state makes itself felt there largely through its being a shareholder, but also through the appointment of high-ranking public servants to posts of responsibility, even though changes of appointment corresponding to changes of government require a certain getting used to. In those companies which are in a competitive sector, HRM is by and large similar to what it is in private companies, where job security is fairly secure. Great public services such as EDF (the electricity company of France), the SNCF (the French national railway organisation) and La Poste (the post office with 270,000 employees) must be taken into account. In this second category of organisations, HRM is not well developed: cultural change is extremely difficult to bring about and there have been countless attempts at reform which have failed. The third category concerns state-administered organisations (the treasury, universities, defence and justice) as well as public hospitals (assimilated to the state). There are also local government bodies at regional, departmental and commune level.

HRM observes the tenets of public service statutes: job security, appointment by competitive examination, promotion by competitive examination and seniority; remuneration is hardly ever based on performance and for identical qualifications remuneration is considerably less than in the private sector. It must also be noted that public servants do not come under the standard labour law code. All these organisations linked directly or indirectly to the state must observe all the points of social legislation punctiliously and often serve as testing grounds for the government in office.

The state has also been used in France to protect against the extremes of a free market company, through major investment in industry, and has sought to ensure that companies invest in people through training. There is an obligation on companies to devote 1.4 per cent of their salary budget to training, and they are required to draw up a training scheme in consultation with work councils. The state is also involved in collective bargaining through legislation which, for example, requires all companies to prepare a 'plan de sauvegarde de l'emploi' before implementing layoffs.

Times are changing, but it is still 'the French exception'.

What is typical of your country in relation to the country itself (its culture, people, etc.) and its economy?

- The influence of the state and tradition, from Louis XIV, Colbert, Napoleon and de Gaulle: the state intervenes at several levels, not only in procedural matters, but also in relation to content.
- The role played by innovatory multinationals sets the pace for the implementation of dynamic policies in HRM (profit-sharing, participation, career management, among others).
- The difficulty of reaching a consensus for reform due to an often conflictual climate between trade unions and some employers. France is also characterised by nostalgia for its great empire and its revolutionary past. This nostalgia nourishes conservatism and the fear of change.

In spite of this, certain changes are worth noting. The law on vocational training, for example, as well as successful negotiations over working time, demonstrates the fruitfulness of social dialogue. SMEs are currently the authorities' focus of attention. The development of competitive poles linking enterprises, universities and research illustrates the French desire to achieve high economic standards and influence.

The 35-hour week: a 'statist' flexibility

The 35-hour week can be analysed as a result of the crucial role of the state.

In the industrialised countries, the 1980s and 1990s were periods of far-reaching transformations in the standards governing working hours and flexibility. Usually those initiatives come from the social partners (Alis/Karsten/Leopold 2006).

Yet France stood out during this period in that it maintained an interventionist state; the end result of public intervention came when the Aubry laws were passed introducing the 35-hour working week. It is his French exception.

This choice and this political determinism show the persistence of the French system of professional relations giving priority to the state. The Aubry law of 13 June 1998 was similar to the reductions in working hours decided on in an authoritarian way in the past: the 40-hour week in 1936 and the 39-hour week in 1982: once again, a left-wing government imposed a working-time reduction on a globally hostile management. But the *de facto* 35-hour working week has been, since 1997, affected by the working-time reduction (WTR) negotiated at company level, with wage moderation and working-time modulation, encouraged by public regulations (legal working time restricted to 35 weekly or 1,600 hours annually, exemptions conditioned by collective bargaining). The law provided for a twin schedule: a reduction in the legal working time to 35 hours per week as from 1 January 2000 for all companies with more than twenty employees, and from 1 January 2002 for all companies with twenty or fewer employees. The French civil service, to which this did not apply, was the object of specific (and conflictual) negotiations.

What assessment can we make of the evolution in French relations? The Aubry laws, like the Roman god Janus, present – at least – two faces (Freyssinet 2001; Alis 2003). On the one hand, these laws can be interpreted as an imperious state intervention, a return to centralising, interventionist logic at the expense of the autonomy of social partnership. The state remains the final arbiter. Statutory regulation is still the key element governing the use of employment conditions and the introduction of new working-time patterns. On the other hand, the law has considerably increased the room for manoeuvre for negotiators and the advantages they can gain through negotiation. The new legislation has encouraged social partners to seek agreement on the flexible implementation of reduced working time. As a result, negotiations concerning working hours at industry and company levels have shown remarkable growth. Over and above the increasing frequency of mandates and referendums, we find major changes in three domains (Brunhes *et al.* 2001: 71):

1. The law has introduced agreement and negotiation into themes from which they were absent, concerning work organisation and working hours in particular, a domain which was considered the exclusive responsibility of the management. The 35-hour agreement was new, mainly because it was global (involving wages, employment, work organisation), taking place in a period of three years.
2. It has led staff representatives to debate and negotiate on the conditions of individualised working conditions and no longer only on collective working hours.
3. At times it has brought to the negotiating table both management and employees who were not used to talking to one another.

119

While the state remains the main architect of change in the light of discord between French trade unions, as well as between trade unions and employers' organisations, Anxo and O'Reilly (2000) call this process of the creation of new working-time patterns 'statist flexibility'.

The laws governing society are in a perpetual state of change. This example illustrates both the reshuffling and readjustments necessitated by the unemployment crisis as well as the fact that these fairly considerable changes are well structured by law, while still permitting local negotiation and adaptation within the individual company. While emphasising the important role played by the regulations (the legal codes), we must insist upon the significance of the informal and instinctive lever of behaviour, which alone can provide the necessary flexibility when the regulations weigh too heavily: labour laws are legion, but firms rarely commit their HRM policies to paper (Brewster/Hegewisch 1994).

What is your advice for a foreign firm entering your country's market? What should managers especially care about and, what is more, be aware of?

A French paradox: France has a complex work regulation which seems to slow down initiative, yet France is rich in entrepreneurial spirit and knows how to accommodate foreign investors. A classic example is the Toyota installation at Valenciennes, where the authorities succeeded in squaring the legislation relating to working time with the time flexibility required by the company. It is thus advisable not to be discouraged, but, rather, to contact the authorities, the persons in charge. France is also the country where arrangements can be made: this is its 'Latin' side.

FRENCH PARADOXES: THE EQUALITY AND HIERARCHY BALANCE

Liberty, Equality, Fraternity as a motto

The motto of the French Republic is 'Liberty, Equality, Fraternity'; it is seen on every official document. These basic values mark indelibly the history of the nation; they are quoted when times are hard. But yet, as we shall see, there are certain snags that seem like contradictions to the foreign observer.

In the world of work, the value 'liberty' shows through clearly for the employers in their freedom to do business, to organise their company, to choose the management team; and for the employee there is freedom of expression, both individual and collective, with the employer through an elected representative group, without necessarily passing through the trade unions (due to the Auroux laws passed in 1982). The liberty and respect of one's private life is also assured by the law known as *Informatique et Liberté* (which could be glossed as IT and freedom),

120

passed in 1978, which makes it obligatory to declare all official files, computerised or not, to the Commission Nationale Informatique et Liberté (CNIL), including all personnel management files.

There are many examples of the value 'Equality' which shows up clearly in the life of the French people, be it in their free education system including university-level studies, or in their taxation system which deals with inequalities by means of tax duties on family fortunes.

The value 'Fraternity' which implies mutual support is also evident in the life of the firm. Very early on, General de Gaulle wanted employees to benefit from the profits made by their companies. So a law was passed, making profit-sharing schemes compulsory in all companies with more than fifty employees. This law typified the prevailing spirit of sharing in common the fruits of everyone's labour. Contractual optional profit-sharing schemes, a typically French phenomenon, may be signed at the local level by employers and representatives of the employees. These schemes allow the extra profits over and above the common participation to be shared out, and define the objectives which have been agreed upon and which will be renegotiated as time goes on. Such objectives are the improvement of productivity, product quality, reducing waste of raw materials and so on. These schemes, if well thought through and in keeping with the strategic objectives of the company, and if clearly explained to the employees, can prove to be an excellent means of motivation, above all in small and medium-sized companies. Statistics show that among companies with more than fifty employees where employee participation is obligatory, it is those that are the most productive, and that occupy the most confident places in their markets, that have the greatest chance of setting up contractual profit-sharing agreements. On the other hand, in companies where employee participation is not obligatory, such agreements tend to be set up in less productive companies whose competitive position is more risky.

This spirit of solidarity which militates against social exclusion is most evident in such measures as the common social service tax (*la contribution sociale généralisée*) which is levied on all salaries and wages in order to finance, among other things, unemployment benefits and a portion of the social security deficit.

High power distance and logic of honour

In spite of these sound values, French society also has certain characteristics that appear as almost contradictory. French companies are well known for being hierarchical and stratified, so where is the equality here? Authority is linked to the individual and to the post he or she holds but not necessarily to his or her competence. Laurent (1986) covers all this when he writes: 'Being an efficient executive in France means managing power relationships and playing the system.' According to Hofstede's analysis (2001), France is characterised by higher power distance and stronger uncertainty avoidance.

121

Power distance is the extent to which less powerful members of organisations accept that power is unequally distributed. In a large power distance culture, differences among people with different ranks are accepted, and an individual's societal or organisational position influences how he or she acts and how others treat him or her. A person in a high-level position treats those at lower levels with dignity, but the differences in rank are always clear. Delegating decision-making implies incompetence because the rank of a manager's position requires him or her to make decisions him- or herself.

Uncertainty avoidance is the preferred kind of structure. Strong uncertainty avoidance countries prefer more structure, resulting in explicit rules of behaviours, either written or unwritten. These nations have strict laws with heavy penalties for offenders, a high need for security and great respect for experts. Concern about doing things correctly is great, and people are not likely to start a new venture without very thorough research. Managers are risk-averse and likely to work for the same company for a long time.

France is also characterised by a contradictory combination of authority and freedom:

> There is a constant tension between the demand for strong authority, and individualistic assertion against it. France looks for a strong, authoritative lead. The conflict between individualism and authority sometimes leads to unpredictable and violent rebelliousness. The nationwide mass strike waves which occasionally sweep across France.
>
> (Sorge 1993: 80)

According to Hickson/Pugh (2001: 77), 'The authoritative lead begins at the top, represented in business organisation by the characteristically French figure of the PDG – *Président Directeur General* (of course, a man).' As Sorge points out (1993: 77): 'Even in the abbreviation PDG, the term loses little of its impressiveness, and is a good indicator of the weight of hierarchy and central responsibility rolled into one.'

France is one of the few countries which distinguish so clearly between the executive and the non-executive (Bournois 1991; 1992), to the extent that everyone can be placed precisely in one category or the other. The executive category corresponds to a kind of 'nobility'; for certain supervisory staff to reach executive status is a lifelong ambition.

The 'honour' of the businessperson, the engineer and the administrator is an important factor as D'Iribarne (1989) pointed out in his book *La logique de l'honneur* ('The Logic of Honour'). D'Iribarne conducted research based on in-depth interviews in three production plants of a French-owned aluminium company, one in France, one in the USA and one in the Netherlands. The plants are technically identical, but the ways in which they are managed differ dramatically. Three different kinds of logic – philosophies – control the interpersonal relationships: honour in France, the fair contract in the USA and consensus in the Netherlands.

According to Hofstede's comments on D'Irbarne's work, France is still a class society, like the caste society of India:

> There are at least three levels – the cadres (managers and professionals), the maîtrise (first-line supervisors) and the non-cadres (the levels below) – but within each of these there are further status distinction, such as between higher and lower cadres and between skilled craft workers and production personnel.
>
> (Hofstede 2001: 119)

An elitist education system

The education system is said to be elitist, inegalitarian, discriminatory and exclusive.

Management cadres are traditionally being recruited from the exclusive *'grandes écoles'*. This type of background has been more important than the results that individuals are able to achieve in the job. Self-made people are still not common in traditional French organisations.

As Sorge points out (1993: 80), 'Throughout the French educational system, there are omnipresent mechanisms to extract elites by competition on the basis of marks, in the so called concours. So "elite" is very much a relative notion. Elites are extracted from relative elites, and they in turn are in line for another process of elite extraction.' According, again, to Sorge (1993), a major step in this elite hierarchy is linked with the French *grandes écoles* which educate most of the future engineers, business specialists, administrators and managers of the country, whether in public administration or private companies. People, who later hold jobs that are rather different, go through courses of study which are rather similar. For instance, the top school for public administration, the Ecole Nationale d'Administration (l'ENA), will usually lead to its graduates being recruited by large, prestigious private companies.

Bournois/Roussillon (1998) highlight some characteristics of this elitist education system:

- the importance of the elitist education system which guarantees top posts for young graduates, with an established hierarchy of diplomas which contributes heavily to preconceived career patterns;
- highly responsible posts given very early on to young graduates from prestigious schools such as the national school of administration (ENA), the Hautes études commerciales (HEC), a major French business school, despite lack of practical experience;
- an emphasis on the theoretical, with young executives in 'consultancy' positions with strategic responsibility as opposed to operational;
- moving those from careers in government administration directly to top jobs in private enterprise. This practice of *pantouflage* allows top managers

to move back to their former positions in public administration if they desire; and

– exclusivity of 'old-boy networks' in French business life.

According to Hickson/Pugh (2001: 78), 'management is regarded more as an intellectual challenge with less of the driving commercialism than in the American image. So there is a taste for argument, and as much merit seen in defining the question as in giving an answer.'

Because of these inequalities in practice, the great national principles are called upon to justify and regulate the day-to-day situations: among the most obvious of these principles are honour (see the work of D'Iribarne), meritocracy and the exceptional-case principle (which only confirms the rule). For example, elitist, non-egalitarian practices are justified on the basis of merit, which is supported by the fact that competition assures an equality of opportunity. To deal with a sense of injustice that is sometimes felt, there is often a back way in for a certain limited number of borderline cases, which proves that the system is not as ruthless as it looks! A certain, very limited, number of places in the very prestigious, highly selective *grandes écoles*, such as l'ENA, Polytechnique, Sciences-Po, are reserved for a few extramural candidates. Thus at l'ENA certain trade union officials, heads of associations or elected representatives have a certain number of places allotted to them.

CONCLUSION

Sometimes the tensions built up between values (equality versus liberty, individualism versus hierarchy) can lead to serious public demonstrations when the basic principles seem threatened. The world of labour relations in France is built on a certain number of rules which must be respected. If these rules are ignored or tampered with, it can lead to increasing problems with the workforce. Furthermore, there are certain arguments that are unacceptable to society at large. If employees feel they are being cheated and deprived of their rights, workers can react more strongly and call upon the trade unions to defend them in spite of the very bleak economic situation. At the macro (national) level, the failure of a programme of social reform in 2006 called the *contrat première embauche* (CPE), a contract which obliged all new young employees to follow a two-year trial period while, at the same time offering them certain guarantees, shows the difficulty of reform and the risk of social conflict in France. At the micro (firm) level, before engaging in legal battles that always leave their mark on both parties concerned, it is so much more advisable to analyse the situation strategically and to do everything possible to inform and negotiate. Otherwise the whole of the workforce will become embittered and demotivated. We have seen that French firms are becoming more open to flexibility. But workers and executives are realising that they can be the victims of productivity propaganda for which they have sometimes made considerable sacrifices without reaping any rewards.

They have sometimes experienced any number of restructuring projects and are now no longer so keen to commit themselves unreservedly.

Finally, the role of the HR manager in France as 'business partner' and 'agent of change', and not only as an 'Administrative Expert' (Ulrich 1997) is becoming increasingly crucial.

What would you like to teach foreign HR managers? What is important for them to know in your opinion?

France encourages the development of intellectual and elitist training. It is a country strongly influenced by well-known business and engineering schools.

The social model and industrial relations play a key role: the typical model is one of consultation; it is absolutely essential for employers to inform, consult and negotiate with the different interested bodies, the works council, the trade union representatives, the staff delegates and so on. But they are not forced to arrive at an agreement. The legal requirements have been fulfilled when consultation has taken place.

The trade union influence has lessened considerably in the last few years and its membership rate has now reached a stable level of about 9 per cent, which represents the lowest rate in Europe. Five trade unions are said to be representative and employers are bound to recognise them as soon as an employee claims to be an official representative of one of them.

125

EAPM AFFILIATE: ASSOCIATION NATIONALE DES DIRECTEURS ET CADRES DE LA FONCTION PERSONNEL (ANDCP)

FOUNDATION AND HISTORY

At 90 rue d'Amsterdam in Paris, on 10 March 1947, some ten personnel directors from major companies were attending the last day of a training programme designed for them by Marcel Didier, founder of the Centre for Practical Studies and Psychological Training (CFP).

Over the past week, participants had listened with interest to the presentations, but, more importantly, they had learned a lot about each other by sharing their personal experiences, including their practices, the rationale behind their practices, their relationships with their superiors and with employee representatives, and the functioning of the then brand-new works councils. The group was far from having exhausted these topics of discussion and it was clear that the issues addressed would remain at the forefront of the profession for a long time to come. The group then decided to continue to meet. For them, the best way to do this was to create a formal structure, which later became the Association Nationale des Directeurs et Cadres de la Fonction Personnel (ANDCP) (national association of personnel directors and managers). The initial membership fees were paid immediately. Marcel Didier offered the use of his offices and secretarial staff in lieu of his membership fee.

In November, the first issue of the internal liaison bulletin was published. In 1948 the general assembly counted 75 voting members. In February 1949, a group was founded in Lyon, followed by another in March in Grenoble, and a third in April in Bordeaux. The ninth issue of the bulletin was thirty-eight pages long. By 1950, the association had 217 members. This number rose to 346 by 1953 and to 400 (of whom 75 per cent were from Paris) by 1955. The Normandy chapter created groups in Rouen and Le Havre in 1954.

After eight years in existence, the situation appeared to be satisfactory. This view was not shared, however, by a small group of members. They felt that the association had become too dependent on Didier's firm, that it suffered from inadequate administration (the actual number of paying members was not known), that the president and secretary-general behaved as though they owned the association, and that the work of the association was too limited in scope. One recent member, François Chérel, stood out because of his personality and he was approached to run for the presidency of the association. He was elected president in November 1955. He appointed Bertrand Hallé – who had served as personnel director for Olida for less than two years – as secretary-general.

From that point on, a new president was elected every three and a half years (the term was later reduced to three years, and then two years). The secretary-general is a necessary assistant to any president. However, the workload is just too great when both officials also have their own professional responsibilities, as was the case at the ANDCP for more than twenty years. Starting in 1965, the association instituted a paid administrative directorship. However, the person holding this position could not represent the president in relations with parties outside the association or with the regional groups. Then, in 1976, the association instituted a permanent paid position for its secretary-general. Finally, since 1985, the ANDCP has had a paid chief representative who attends to the needs of the association in terms of internal management and external relations.

What are you and other French people extraordinarily proud of with respect to HRM?

- The social ladder which has encouraged unprecedented economic development and the formation of elites.
- Educational obligation initiated by Jacques Delors, who was social adviser to Prime Minister Chaban Delmas in 1971. Education, long considered a 'burden', is now perceived as an investment which makes it possible to improve human capital.
- Birth rate: France has – along with Ireland – the highest fertility rate in Europe (1.9), which it combines with one of the highest ratios of working women (80 per cent for the 24 to 49 age group and mothers with a child under the age of 3). French women are thus professionally active, seductive and fertile.

EARLY YEARS AND CHALLENGES

Throughout its fifty-year history, the ANDCP has had two problems to which it has never found an adequate solution: the recruitment (or retainment) of HR directors from large-sized companies and the recruitment of sub-professional specialists in the fields of safety, social services, recruitment, training, apprenticeships, career management, legal affairs and disputes, research and statistics, and information and communication. HR directors from large-sized companies were among the ANDCP's members during the first fifteen to twenty years of the association's history. In some cases, reluctance to join was justified by the fact that there was more to contribute than to be gained from the association. However, there was – and still is – the very real issue of finding a common forum for professional exchange for executives with very diverse responsibilities. Personnel managers became more active when their group was to address administrative issues or when they were to exchange salary-related information for certain categories of employees, while personnel directors were more concerned with measures taken by their staff to control payroll costs, coming up with stimulating compensation packages, and issues such as merit pay and so on.

The ANDCP failed to recognise this specific need in time and did not find the appropriate structures to respond to it. The entire ANDCP organisation was based on geographical zones and, with rare exceptions, members were automatically affiliated with a regional group according to where they worked. It is easy to see the difficult situation this created for members, who, when they realised that there was a permanent gap between their own aspirations and those of their groups, were reluctant to say, 'I'm quitting. I'm going to play in the major league.' In addition to this refusal to discriminate, there was also (at least until around the 1970s) the idea that small and medium-sized companies should be allowed to benefit from the experience of large-sized companies (and vice versa) with regard to labour issues.

This advocacy-oriented choice on the part of the ANDCP, which was reiterated several times, implied mass recruitment and the refusal (at least implicitly) to organise and develop a parallel structure which could be perceived as elitist, at the risk of creating conflict between the major and minor players, a duality that echoed other, more traditional dualities between Paris and the provinces, between company headquarters and production centres, between service-sector managers and shop technicians, and between functional and operational staff.

Following the mass demonstrations that shook France in 1968 and that sparked the creation of new personnel positions in companies (and, correlatively, a rise in ANDCP membership), the association set a target of 2,000 members to be met mainly by the creation of new groups in previously unrepresented regions. The target of 2,000 members was reached by 1970, with the number rising to 3,000 by 1974. Since 1980, the ANDCP has counted around 4,000 members (the actual number has fluctuated between 3,800 and 4,200). The turnover rate is relatively high, mainly due to professional mobility but also due to budget cuts and time constraints, the latter covering both a true lack of time or a lack of freedom and autonomy vis-à-vis members' employers or perhaps obscuring dissatisfaction with the association.

In 1971, the ANDCP management committee put forward an estimate of the potential number of members according to its statutes. Using statistics on companies provided by the French national institute for research and statistics (INSEE), broken down by size of payroll, the association determined, based on the experiences of its members, the 'standard' personnel structure and number of personnel managers typically found in each type of company. The figure they came up with was 13,000. A new estimate was calculated in 1977 based on new statistics relative to companies with more than 200 employees and a reassessment of the 'standard' personnel department structures. The updated figure was between 9,000 and 10,000 personnel managers likely to meet ANDCP membership requirements. To give a general idea (based on active members only; that is to say those who fulfil all or a part of their duties), ANDCP members account for between 40 per cent and 45 per cent of personnel department managers.

What would you say one ought not to do? What are the 'don'ts' in your country?

The French love to be recognised and acknowledged for all work done. It is thus necessary to value and award appropriate compensation for work done. This is especially the case for qualified executives and technicians. The distinction between noble and ignoble activities is very vivid in the French mentality.

HR ACADEMIA: RESEARCH TOPICS AND METHODS

GROWING CORPUS WITH MOVING BORDERS

Definitions of HRM

Every society needs rituals. It was a French ethnographer and folklorist, Van Gennep (1994), who managed to demonstrate the importance of rituals in society (the thesis represents one of the rituals of passage to be analysed).

Analysing doctoral production for HRM presents an excellent opportunity to study the scientific field and analyse changes in the corpus: what are the most active areas for production, the preferred concepts, themes and theories, the methods used? In this way, we will be conducting a quantitative and qualitative analysis of changes in the production of theses on HRM over the period in question (1998–2001), while putting the results obtained into perspective.

To draw up an inventory of theses on HRM, it is necessary to define the content of this discipline beforehand. And yet there is no accepted definition among scientific researchers to date.

> The term 'Human Resource Management' can be understood from several points of view, from the most extensive to the most restrictive. Used in different conceptions, it has been considered as synonymous with personnel management, human relations, human resources, and even human and social development. The absence of a clearly defined and universally accepted terminology must be taken into consideration.
>
> (Amadieu/Rojot 1996: 1)

These two authors compare HRM with personnel management and labour relations, 'that is to say, the management of individual and collective working relations with all employees, groups of employees, organisations and their representatives'.

Other researchers focus more on the psychological dimension of HRM. In this way, Thévenet (1999: 11) argues for a new term: 'management of people at work in organisations'. According to this author, 'the management of people reflects the incorporation of the break-up of work standards and systems for representing workers, in addition to the need to manage the actual situation of people ... in organisations that are increasingly vague'. The approach is therefore more psychological.

The work of Brabet has led to a broader definition of HRM: 'A social sciences discipline for creating and mobilising various areas of knowledge useful for players and needed to understand, comprehend, negotiate and attempt to resolve problems linked to the regulation of human work in organisations' (1993: 224).

To avoid too wide an acceptance, we have chosen to define HRM based on its activities. In this way, Peretti (1997) describes the content of the function, while Bournois and Brabet (1997: 2733) propose the CORE model: 'C' for communication, including participatory management, internal marketing, labour relations; 'O' for organisation of work; 'R' for remuneration; 'E' for employment, from the individualised or collective management of careers to the more general management of the workforce and skills through recruitment and training approaches.

Can we establish a clear link between HRM and strategic management? Weiss (1999: 2) points to the close links between HRM and strategic HRM. According to this author, 'The HR system covers all the activities, missions and processes intended to attract, develop and maintain Human Resources. Strategic HRM explicitly links HRM with the company's strategic processes and highlights the coordination or congruence between the various HR practices.' We have chosen to incorporate this distinction between operational activities for HRM and strategic HRM.

We have also 'enlarged' the definition of HRM, by integrating strategic HRM. In the light of these trends, we have chosen to reference the theses submitted in the HRM field in France over a four-year period (January 1998 to December 2001).

We compared these 101 theses with those identified in previous reports. Table 5.2 presents the change in the number of theses submitted over a twelve-year period.

Table 5.2 Number of HR theses submitted over twelve years

HRM	1990/93	1994/97	1998/2001
Number of theses submitted	44	70	101

We can see a significant increase in the number of HRM theses submitted over these four-year periods, rising from 44 to 70, then to 101. In 1997, in the second edition of the *Management Encyclopaedia*, Simon and Joffre (1997:VIII) wrote: 'The space in this Encyclopaedia dedicated to HRM, in its radical version as reengineering, or in its more traditional dimension as the recruitment of executives, the classification of staff, the changing of organisational structures, negotiations and Human Resources, attests to the vitality of a discipline that is now fundamental for management sciences.' This development of the HR discipline is reflected in these figures.

EMPLOYMENT, SKILLS, WORKING HOURS AND LABOUR RELATIONS

The above topics come to the forefront in order to compare the research topics over time. We decided to use the grid created by our predecessors. We then transformed the data concerning the previous theses in order to set out the figures over four-year periods (1990/93, 1994/97 and 1998/2001).

The grid used (Table 5.3) makes a distinction between HR practices and the strategic aspects of HRM.

Table 5.3 Changes in HRM thesis topics (1990/2001)

Research topics	1990/93	1994/97	1998/2001
Number of theses defended	44	70	101
HR practices and tools			
1. Employment (recruitment, dismissal, personnel management, assessment)	2	9	14
2. Remuneration and profit-sharing	2	6	8
3. Personal development (training, skills, behaviour in the workplace, managing specific categories of employees)	7	14	25
4. Working conditions, reduced working hours and days in lieu, etc.	–	1	8
Subtotal 1	11	30	55
Strategic HRM			
5. Environment, industrial relations, company performance, etc.	5	7	14
6. Organisation, communication, etc.	12	13	13
7. Culture, innovation, quality, etc.	16	7	6
8. Other (ethics, cognition and decision-making, international, public sector HRM)	–	13	13
Subtotal 2	33	40	46

This enabled us to identify two major categories and eight topics as follows:

1. HR tools and practices: employment, remuneration, personal development and working conditions.
2. Strategic HRM: environment, organisation, culture and other topics.

What are the trends? A significant increase in research in the areas of HR tools and practices and a smaller increase in strategic HR research. Our goal was to conduct a more thorough analysis of these changes.

HR tools and practices

The 'HR tools and practices' category, which has seen a significant increase in terms of research, is marked by a particular increase in the fields of employment (upstream/recruitment as well as downstream/dismissal and redundancies), skills and working hours. The fourteen theses included in the 'employment' category may be broken down as follows: five theses focused on recruitment and integration; five examined staffing reductions and redundancy plans; four addressed career and management forecasts. So the theses submitted do echo the somewhat confusing times in terms of HRM, where redundancy plans are rampant while, at the same time, policies to improve recruitment and retainment ('the war for talents' as it is now being called) are developed. Management science theses provide food for thought concerning both of these issues.

The recruitment and integration of recent graduates was examined by three theses.

A number of theses addressed redundancy plans. These papers have raised the debate to a higher level and have sparked a thorough scientific investigation of the 'shareholder-driven redundancy plans' that have recently made headlines as well as the economic, financial, human and social consequences of these redundancies (Schmidt 2001). This research, which examines several aspects of the phenomenon, supports the accumulation of work that is the necessary basis for all scientific work.

The 'personal development' category has seen the most significant increase, going from fourteen to twenty-five theses submitted. This category is further broken down into several sub-categories. Eleven theses addressed skills management; four focused on management styles; four on motivation, involvement, and loyalty; and three on the management of certain types of employees (high-potential, top managers, engineers, and other management-level staff).

So the concept of skills has come to the forefront, despite the fact that 'it is a term without a clearly stabilised meaning' (Martin 2002). Certain thesis titles echo this issue: 'From job descriptions to the issue of skills' and 'From working conditions to skills management' are two such examples. Beyond the current popularity of these topics, the large number of theses that examined skills reveals profound changes within companies; changes that are part of the movement towards 'people management' as described by Thévenet (1999).

Finally, while the topic 'working conditions' has seen significant growth, this growth is linked to the increase in research on working hours. Of the eight theses submitted, three addressed flexible or reduced working hours, two focused on part-time work, two on health and safety, and one on the work environment. This increase in the number of theses on working hours is the result of changes in labour legislation in France (the 35-hour week), despite the fact that these laws are currently undergoing reform and other changes to increase flexibility. Beyond the changes in legislation, the increase in quantitative flexibility within European companies seen since the 1980s must also be taken into account. The reduction in working hours has been analysed from a number of viewpoints, including links with strategy, negotiation methods and organisational effects.

The increase in part-time work (which, we must not forget, concerned only around 12 per cent of the workforce in 1992 compared to nearly 18 per cent today) also requires further study. The issue of part-time employee involvement was thus addressed by two theses.

Topics that are still being researched but were not the subject of an increased number of theses during the period studied include remuneration and profit-sharing. Again, much of the research is transversal in nature, with work addressing the link between remuneration policy and strategy or the link between remuneration and skills management.

Strategic HRM

Unlike the other categories, the category 'Environment, industrial relations and company performance' has seen a considerable increase in the number of theses submitted.

The increase in the number of theses submitted in this category is related in particular to the increased importance given to labour relations. Of the thirteen theses submitted, six addressed labour relations, two focused on restructuring plans and strategy, and five examined the increase of flexibility and performance.

The topic of labour relations was thus a major area of research, with new topics resulting from the creation of new labour regulations such as European works councils or mediation. The fact that labour issues have continued to make head-lines should lead to additional research in areas such as the increase in negotiations within companies, which raises the issue of labour representation and the pronounced use of the referendum – related in part to the current labour union crisis in combination with commissioning within smaller organisations, seen, in particular, since the ratification of the Aubry laws.

The category 'Organisation, communication and social information systems' saw a wide variety of topics addressed by the thirteen theses submitted. New topics were also addressed in the field of communications, such as the contribution of labour observation projects or the use of psychoanalysis as an investigative tool.

Taylorism and other, much more recent, 'job redesign' and reticular organisation models were also examined. Theses on work groups, teamwork, project-based work and network-based work attempted to provide an understanding of these organisational shifts.

The category 'Culture, innovation and quality' inspired six theses. The topic of quality was a particular focus for theses addressing the hospital sector, with research on the organisational changes resulting from the development of accreditation. In terms of the relationship between culture and change, a paradox well known by theoreticians was revealed: consultants have brought the concepts of culture and identity to the forefront while trying to initiate changes within companies.

The international dimension was also taken into account in the research, either directly through international comparisons, or indirectly as part of studies carried out in organisations outside France.

In conclusion, this content analysis, despite its limitations, does demonstrate the increase in research on HR tools and practices, with increased importance given to certain topics such as employment (for recruitment as well as for dismissal), social development (from a skills management viewpoint), working hours and flexibility. Labour relations was another topic of significant interest.

This focus on operational HR activities must not, however, obscure the ever-increasing prevalence of 'strategic' HR models. Topics like organisational learning and change thus appeared in the background of a number of theses, including work on organisational learning, workplace health and safety, organisational change, management forecasts of jobs and skills, restructuring plans, and the reform and reduction of working hours.

Beyond putting forward a call for more research on the impact of flexible employment and new forms of organisation, we also wish to make certain recommendations concerning two very different topics: 'social and societal accounting' and its relationship to HRM and finance, and the international dimension.

Current issues have brought research carried out during the 1970s back to the centre of the debate, including work on 'social and societal accounting' and social audits, consideration of the interests of stakeholders, evaluating social performance and social management charts. There is thus a need to restart research appropriate to the current economic climate, with an examination of the optimisation of intangible investment, the development of socially responsible investment funds, and laws governing economic regulations that require companies to take into account the social and societal dimensions of their businesses.

Concerning research on international issues, we feel that there is a need to take into account the European and international dimensions of HRM. We are, of course, aware of the difficulties inherent in this task. Indeed, research that is international in scope requires extensive research resources, is costly, and suffers from a lack of funding. A policy that truly supports theses addressing the European and international dimensions is needed.

In order to promote academic exchanges within the European Community, the organisations concerned are ramping up their activities. Among them are the EIASM (European Institute for Advanced Studies in Management), the EGOS (European Group for Organisational Studies) and, more recently, the EURAM (European Academy of Management). Researchers, graduates with doctorates, and Ph.D. students have much to gain by working more closely with these organisations. The role played by events such as the EDAMBA (European Doctoral Programmes Association in Management and Business Administration) or CEFAG (Centre Européen de Formation Approfondie à la Gestion) conferences and the AGRH (Association francophone de Gestion des Ressources Humaines) – and its 'country ambassadors' programme in particular – should be emphasised. Research must also take care not to leave out the continents that drive economic growth, such as the Asia-Pacific zone or the Americas.

As regards research conducted in management sciences and HRM in developing countries, there is one risk that should be pointed out: the production of artefacts copying French research and inspired by North American research that do not take into account the realities of the countries studied. The development of contextualised approaches in management sciences should limit this risk and promote research that is better suited to its subject.

CONCLUSION: TENSIONS AND THE CRUCIAL ROLE OF THE ANDCP

Five tensions and controversies

This report on theses has enabled us to analyse changes in the corpus. It has also made it possible for us to identify five inherent tensions in the development of research on HRM.

Exploration/exploitation

March (1991), in his work on research practices, distinguishes between the exploration of new domains and exploitation. Exploration involves the search for new leads and the development of new theories. Exploitation involves taking an in-depth look at ideas for old leads and improving knowledge of known theories. This exploration can be particularly productive, as shown by the researchers Dogan and Pahre (1991) in their work on innovation in social sciences. These authors demonstrated the benefits of cross-fertilisation between theories, which represents a source of 'creative marginality' with a strong heuristic power. Malinvaud (2001) argues for exploitation in the economics field. The report on theses shows that both exploitation and exploration are taking place. These two movements appear to be necessary for the development of the scientific field.

Ideography/nomothesis

'Idiographic' researchers are interested in the narration and interpretation of unique historical events, while 'nomothetic' researchers look for generalisations and laws governing human behaviour. An analysis of management theses shows the development of qualitative approaches (based on idiographic approaches) and quantitative approaches (based on nomothetic approaches). Once again, there is a relentless tension between these two approaches. However, as recognised by certain epistemologists, if pure idiographs or pure nomothetes exist, there can be doubts about the seriousness of their work. This debate is reminiscent of the one between fundamental research and applied research, or the debate between theory and practice. In the words of Lewin (founder of social psychology), 'nothing is more practical than a good theory'.

Quantity/quality

Has the increase in the number of theses come about to the detriment of quality? We do not have any indicators to prove this. For us, the publication of research on methodologies and the maintaining of the demands in force seem to represent the means required to prevent a slackening off that would be harmful to the discipline. Debates about methodology and epistemology (for instance, the debate by the Centre de Recherche en Gestion (2000) on the criteria for a good management science thesis) seem to be fruitful.

Academic rigour/valuation

The success and valuation of Beaujolin's thesis (Beaujolin 1999) must not mask the ignorance in the specialised press about numerous works relating to the management of overstaffing (Schmidt 2001). The publication of theses allows the public – academic or other – to have access to quality theses (D'Arcimoles 1995; Neveu 1996; Roussel 1996; Perrot 2001). To a certain extent, to recall a well-turned expression from M. Thévenet, it is important for the 'Franciscans' of HRM research (rigorous and applied researchers, specialists in quantitative methods) to learn how to be 'Dominicans' too and value their work. This valuation work is also carried out by scientific associations. The AGRH (HR management association) or the recent SFM – *Société Française de Management* – are expected to contribute to this valuation work. However, we should not deny the tension that exists between these two objectives. Certain works written by renowned researchers often say little about the methods used (D'Iribarne 1989).

Current developments/historical perspective

Lastly, it is essential to respond to current developments (transformations in organisational structures, development and management of reduced working time, or the 'skills logic'), while also knowing how to put these changes into perspective. Looking back over old works of value is also useful. To take only a recent example in management sciences, the success of the Anglo-Saxon balanced scorecards popularised by Kaplan and Norton (1992) must not lead us to forget the relevance of French and European literature on management indicators, work carried out since the post-war period that should be rediscovered. The popularity of certain tools has more to do with linguistic arguments and rhetoric

137

than scientific reasons, which makes it even more necessary to be able to take a step back and evaluate trends critically.

THE CRUCIAL ROLE OF THE FRENCH-SPEAKING HUMAN RESOURCE MANAGEMENT ASSOCIATION

The development of academia is linked with the creation and development of the French-speaking Human Resource Management Association (AGRH). The Association was founded in 1989 to promote research and education in the field of HRM and to contribute to the development of the HRM function.

The French-speaking AGRH brings together faculty (professors and scholars) and Ph.D. students from universities and *grandes écoles*. Practitioners and institutional members are associated to its activities and publications.

The Association has around 500 members. Its activities include:

- Annual meeting (*congrès*): organised each year in France or in a French-speaking country, the annual meetings enable the presentation of 100 communications per year. The best papers relating to the topic of the meeting are published in the journal *Revue de gestion des ressources humaines*. The other papers are published in the meeting proceedings.
- Journal (*Revue de gestion des ressources humaines*): created nearly fifteen years ago, the *Revue* provides a scientific reference within the field of HRM. Its goal is to publish original papers, either theoretical or empirical, and to improve knowledge in HRM. Five to seven papers are issued four times a year. Papers are evaluated through anonymous reviews.
- Interest groups (*groupes thématiques de recherche*): members of the association are invited to participate in research groups dedicated to a specific theme, such as compensation, careers, work–life balance, new jobs and professional profiles, information communication technology and HRM, genders, humanism and HRM, HRM practices in SMEs, HRM in North Africa or research methods for HRM. These interest groups commit to publishing a state-of-the-art report covering their specific theme.
- Newsletter (*Lettre de l'AGRH*): to keep up to date with the HRM academic community, the AGRH publishes a newsletter twelve times a year. This newsletter provides useful information about colloquia, conferences and seminars, calls for papers, recent publications, activities of the association and its members and so on.
- Ambassadors (*ambassadeurs pays*): AGRH seeks to promote research and publications by French-speaking scholars beyond the borders of French-speaking regions. The role of ambassador has been created to facilitate exchanges between the HRM French-speaking community and other HRM communities throughout the world. The ambassadors' mission is to represent AGRH within other HRM academic associations, encourage participation of members of these academic associations in activities of the AGRH, and provide information about HRM activities and trends in different geographical areas.

In a few words, what would you say is the one fundamental strategic competitive advantage your country offers compared to others?
- a highly qualified and available workforce;
- the quality of infrastructures (universities, research);
- geographic location (at the heart of Europe); and
- art of living: cuisine and gastronomy, climate and weather, architecture (*'pays de Cocagne'*).

BEST-PRACTICE CASE: CEGETEL GROUP – A YOUNG TELECOMMUNICATION COMPANY MASTERING FAST GROWTH

HISTORY OF THE GROUP

Although Cegetel was created in September 1996, the interest of Compagnie Générale des Eaux (CGE) (to become Vivendi Universal) in telecommunications goes back to 1987.

CGE starting out in the telecom business (1987–95)

In December 1987, the radio broadcasting division of CGE won a licence to supply analogue-type services throughout France. Hence the launch of SFR (Société Française du Radiotéléphone). One of its first business achievements was the first subscription-free pocket pager, called Tam Tam.

Final adjustment (1996–7)

During a press conference on 4 September 1996, CGE disclosed its Group's new strategy in the telecom industry, having set as an objective: to become a global operator and the number one challenger of the historical operator (Barroux/Gadault 1996). In order to achieve this, all existing activities were grouped in a holding company, Cegetel, of which the newly appointed chairman was CGE's chairman, while Philippe Glotin acted as general manager.

The new global operator operated in three main areas: long-distance calls, mobiles and services to corporate customers. Its target for 2003 was 40 billion FRF turnover and a share of about 40 per cent of the mobile communication market, 20 per cent of the long-distance calls market and 10 per cent of the local loop segment. To this end, Cegetel invested 4 billion FRF between 1997 and 1999. Concerning the shareholding structure of Cegetel Group, the existing partners were invited to move to the level of the holding company, while it was specified that a strong international operator would become part of Cegetel's capital.

In 1996, an agreement in principle was concluded on the opening of Cegetel's capital: CGE was to remain the majority shareholder, while 'welcoming in' three partners: the German Mannesmann (already present through a number of stakes that added up to 15 per cent), the American SBC (also a shareholder) and British Telecom. The agreement included a new stake of 25 per cent (for 8.85 billion FRF) and a capital contribution from BT France (*La Tribune*, 27 September 1996). In the end, on 20 December, ATT bought the shares previously held by Générale des Eaux in Siris while Cegetel announced the creation of an entity dedicated to its business with corporate consumers: Cegetel Entreprises.

On 30 January 1997, after formal deliberations, the Board of Directors ratified the following shareholding interests: 25 per cent for British Telecom, 10 per cent for Mannesmann and 15 per cent for SBC. Meanwhile, the British Vodafone remained within SFR's capital (with less than 20 per cent of its capital).

In February 1997, Cegetel became a partner with SNCF in its subsidiary Telecom Development. This major partnership allowed the company access to its partner's 300,000 km of optical fibres. This was one of the largest networks on French territory, after that of France Telecom. At this time, Cegetel Group's most significant asset was SFR's mobile telephony service and its 600,000 clients. GSM technologies were then two years old and the opening of the telecom market to free competition was set to take place in January 1998.

The first corporate and enterprise-targeted communications and recruitment campaigns captured a great deal of attention and the number of unsolicited job applications sent to Cegetel increased from 800 to 4,000 a week.

A time of growth (1998–2000)

'Le 7', Cegetel's fixed telephony offering targeting consumers and professionals was launched in February 1998. This entailed a huge amount of work for Cegetel, which had to 'make its mark' in this new field. Its offer began with a certain amount of education, needed to promote the use of the prefix '7' chosen as the brand.

Meanwhile, SFR passed the 4 million client mark, while 'Le 7' subscriptions reached 600,000. SFR had thus doubled its number of clients in 1998. Cegetel Group's staffing levels increased by 80 per cent for the year 1998. The Cegetel Group began learning a new trade, after an agreement concluded at the beginning of the year between Cegetel, AOL, Bertelsmann and Canal+, which enabled Cegetel to support its internet developments through two brands: AOL for consumers and CompuServe for professionals.

In March 1999, mobile web services began, with WAP technology, which transforms an internet page into a format that can be read on the screen of a mobile phone. In April 1999, Cegetel passed the million fixed lines mark, and one-third of its clients in this segment were companies. In September 1999, Cegetel launched three major innovations for corporate consumers:

1. An offer to include all mobile phones in the company's telephony network. The mobile phone number of each employee is similar to his or her fixed phone number; people can work from anywhere with their portable computer, borders disappear and supposedly separate worlds suddenly converge.
2. An offer of Intranet access from a mobile phone. This offer enables any employee equipped with an SFR mobile to access his or her company's information from any place and at any time.

141

3. An offer of telephony via the internet which enables companies to make phone calls between their various sites using Internet protocol. In addition to the cost savings made, introducing this technology allows new developments such as a single answering service, videoconferencing and conferences calls, or call centres on the Internet.

In November 1999, SFR was recognised as the number one player, according to an ART survey (ART: Telecom Regulation Authority), for the quality of its network.

A new era (2000–2)

On 6 June 2000, Philippe Germond was promoted to chairman and Frank Esser was appointed general manager.

In July 2000, the Cegetel Group passed the ten-million-client mark. The number of clients had increased tenfold since 1996. The media pointed out that this old 'start up' had become France's top hiring company: from 2,000 employees in 1996, it had reached more than 8,000 by 1 January 2000.

In 2000, SFR was thus the first national operator to launch GPRS on its mobile network, the first step towards high-speed internet. This second generation of GSM norms makes it possible to send and receive huge amounts of data from a mobile phone at speeds comparable to those of present PCs.

The Group then decided to organise itself into client-focused business units. Cegetel Entreprises faded away. Two branches were set up: 'fixed telephony' under the Cegetel brand and 'mobile telephony' under the brand SFR.

In 2001, SFR was allocated a UMTS licence. In November 2002, SFR passed the 12.6 million client mark. In December 2002, Philippe Germond left the Cegetel Group to become the general manager of Alcatel. On 13 December 2002, the Board of Directors unanimously approved the appointment of Frank Esser as chairman.

CEGETEL'S HR DEPARTMENT AND ITS CORPORATE CULTURE

The HR Executive Committee is composed of seven members and is supervised by Jérôme Duval-Hamel, HR vice-president for the Cegetel Group. The HR structure replicates that of the Group's matrix organisation (Figure 5.1).

The HR Executive Committee has two HR experts and five HR directors (HRDs) belonging to each business within the Cegetel Group. Each HRD also manages all HR activities within his or her branch, in most cases, as a staff activity.

As the Cegetel Group is still young, it is difficult to identify a corporate culture.

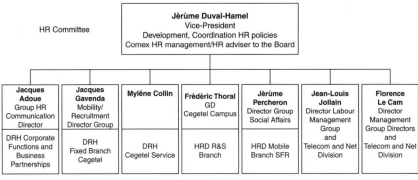

Figure 5.1 The Cegetel Group's HR and social affairs GD

In spite of this, several subcultures appear within the group:

– the top-level graduate school culture, identified by excellence and rationality;
– within the branch fixed telephony: sales culture and sales force;
– the 'start-up' culture, identified by creativity, pioneers, urgency, youth and the extreme growth levels experienced by the Cegetel Group; and
– an emerging culture based on good management counterbalancing the 'start-up' subculture.

> The Cegetel Group was built from scratch, by 'pioneers'. The sense of belonging within the Group is highly developed, particularly among those with the most seniority.

THE MAIN LINES OF ACTION WITHIN THE HR AND SOCIAL AFFAIRS DEPARTMENT

Industrial relations

The Cegetel Group took part in the drafting of the Telecom Collective Bargaining Agreement. Concluded on 2 December 1998, its aims are:

– promotion of labour dialogue;
– allowance for new working modes;
– optimisation of employee career path management;
– establishment of a continuous and single classification scheme; and
– establishment of a strong foundation for minimum contingency guarantees.

The Cegetel Group wishes to conduct an exemplary labour dialogue. As can be seen from the following list, agreements are numerous (Table 5.4).

Table 5.4 Importance of agreements concluded

Agreement type	Signature date	Related to
Framework agreement	23 April 1999	Organisation, flexibility and reduction of working hours within Cegetel's UES
Agreement	4 June 1999	Reduction and flexible working hours in the telecom sector
Cegetel Systèmes d'information site agreement	7 July 1999	Organisation, flexibility and reduction of working hours
Agreement	22 December 1999	Wages, organisation and working hours within Cegetel's UES for 2000
Agreement	20 December 2001	Wages, organisation and working hours within Cegetel's UES for 2002
Agreement	20 November 2002	Job entry for the handicapped

The Labour Dialogue Agreement concluded on 13 June 2002 was an important event in the Cegetel Group's history. The agreement sets the foundations and provides the means required for high-quality labour dialogue within Cegetel.

The agreement outlines labour dialogue concerning interpersonal, collective and institutional relationships at the level of management and the level of collective bargaining. It outlines the role of the players in this dialogue, in line with Cegetel's policies.

It modernises union practices and labour communications:

- The implementation of mediation within the Cegetel Group shows its willingness to prevent labour conflicts by looking for the most appropriate solution, as soon as tension is identified.
- Labour cyberspace is a specially designed area where listening and communication on labour issues can occur among employee representative bodies. This communication area includes: a permanent secretarial office, a video-conference room for regional site connections, a computer room and a press area with free access. Moreover, unions may use a communications area on the Cegetel Group's intranet.
- The Labour Training Institute provides economic, labour and institutional training to UES employee representatives seeking qualifications.

Employee representatives (of which there are 390), some of them holding several mandates concurrently, have been elected by employees or appointed by unions. The following chart offers an overview of current labour negotiations (Figure 5.2).

At the last professional elections, unions were divided as illustrated by Figure 5.3.

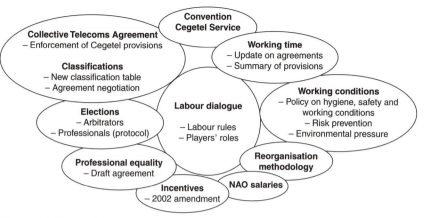

Figure 5.2 Current labour negotiations at Cegetel

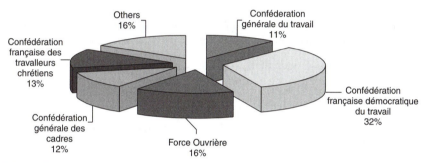

Figure 5.3 Unions at Cegetel

Developing people

The *Chorus* programme

This developing programme was created in 1998 during the extreme growth period experienced by the Cegetel Group. Its mission is:

– to train a population of professional young managers;
– to sponsor managers during organisational changes; and
– to build a corporate culture.

The Chorus programme is offered to managers of nearly all levels. It is composed of several courses, split up into a number of modules:

• Défi Chorus: a sixteen-day training programme with eight modules, each requiring two consecutive days (identify the manager's mission; contribute to creating value; motivate, delegate and empower; making oneself heard; discover and use HR tools; understand the way the Cegetel Group functions; prevent, face and demystify crises and conflicts, and change management).

- Chorus Plus: six à la carte sessions as an economic steering group, dealing with such issues as how to manage changes, lead, coach and mobilise a team, the manager's social dimension, how to prepare and conduct an appraisal interview (entretien d'appréciation et de développement, EAD), conducting a recruitment interview.
- Chorus Projet: a training programme for project management.
- Chorus Premium: four modules drafted specifically for the management of managerial functions (economic steering and creation of value, strategic analysis of organisations, leadership and authority, innovative management and communications).

Employee training

Employee training is a major HR activity in the development of the Cegetel Group. In 2001, almost 12 million EUR, or 4.24 per cent of payroll, was used for training. More than 80 per cent of employees have followed a training programme, which means, on average, three days of training sessions annually per employee.

As a main training actor of the Cegetel Group, Espace Campus offers 250 training courses geared to the telecom environment.

Key figures of 2001 include:

- the training budget of the Cegetel Group amounted to 11.6 million EUR;
- it accounted for 4.24 per cent of payroll (as compared to an average of 3.25 per cent for French companies) – the legal requirement is 1.5 per cent;
- access to training: more than 80 per cent of employees have attended at least one session during the year;
- average training expense per employee: 1,449 EUR;
- average training days per employee: three days;
- 213 Cegetel Group employees acted as in-house educators in 2002;
- 2003 priority areas: training policy is built around four axes;
- major investments in training programmes;
- employee skills achievement by planning real professional training sessions and managerial development through *Chorus* programmes;
- managing and supporting change; and
- optimisation of investments made, by using training discerningly and ensuring that its cost-effectiveness is satisfactory.

The development and assessment interview

This interview is meant to appraise an employee from two angles: (a) his or her global performance during the past year (mastery of job skills and achievement of objectives set previously); and (b) the development of his or her individual skills within his or her occupation.

This is a key moment of the year, a unique time for discussion, exchange and analysis between employees and their managers. This is also the opportunity to take stock of the work carried out.

The success of the interview depends on:

– its consistency with the management method and exchanges set throughout the year;
– the preparation of the interview itself; and
– follow-up after the interview, which will define the relationship thereafter.

It thus involves making an assessment of the actions, work and projects completed during the year, and appraising both the strong points and those to be improved. It stands as a useful tool for setting future objectives for the following year and for drawing up the necessary business plans. It also fits in with everyday team management practices; this is why the manager and his or her subordinate must hold regular updates during the year in order to take stock of the situation. This should allow them to reach an accurate, comprehensive and shared assessment at the end of the year, and define appropriate objectives for progress. In 2002, objective-based management was set up for all the Group's managers.

Recruitment and mobility

The Cegetel Group experienced an 'extreme' recruitment period from 1998 to 2000. It receives almost 60,000 job applications each year. The Cegetel Group's workforce has stabilised since 2000. Today, mobility therefore naturally remains a strong driver and a reality of Cegetel Group's HR development policy. Of all positions 37 per cent have been filled through in-house mobility. It is therefore possible to develop and establish employee loyalty, maintain motivation levels, encourage adaptation skills and increase team expertise.

In 2001, 15 per cent of Cegetel Group employees moved through in-house mobility at their own request. In some branches, the figure exceeded 20 per cent. This rate is all the more impressive given that average seniority in the Group is three years. In order to promote in-house mobility, most Cegetel Group positions are reserved for in-house requests before being offered on the outside market. Some positions are offered only to in-house staff.

When the employee masters his or her job and has held the position for more than two years, he or she may file a request to move. He or she is the prime mover when it comes to mobility. His or her task is to build a realistic project in respect of his or her expertise as well as of the Group's opportunities. He or she may move not only within the Cegetel Group, but also within the Vivendi Universal Group. A number of measures have been enacted to make geographical mobility within the Group easier.

Wages and the HR information system

The Cegetel Group's wage policy is built on two main criteria: individual and increasing rises in managers' variable pay (in 2003, all managers from a certain level upwards are entitled to variable pay).

Benchmarking studies are carried out on a regular basis by outside service providers (including Hewitt, Oberthur, Hay and Towers Perrin). As regards changes in wage levels, they are made within the Cegetel Group's employment classification. The incentive agreement is particularly attractive for employees (5.5 per cent of payroll). Salaries are managed in-house, using HR's software. The setting and hosting for the tool are subcontracted.

HR access is a constantly evolving tool. An in-house team is specifically devoted to it, with responsibility for providing technical support, consulting services and development. HR access covers many areas including: employee administrative management, wage management, training management, expertise management, recruitment management, group saving plan. Part of the information is entered by administration/wage employees, but can also be entered by other HR players. This software also enables employees to enter leave requests on their own and fill in their activity-monitoring sheet.

Moreover, a department dedicated to managing high potentials and executives was set up in 2000. The entity uses a tool-based approach to manage managerial potential. It defines and implements specific policies intended for executives in the areas of recruitment, mobility, training, career development, etc.

The Cegetel Group employs graduates of the following top-level schools (Table 5.5).

Table 5.5 Cegetel's graduates

School	Number of graduates
ESCP–EAP	33
Graduate schools in engineering (Polytechnique, ENST, Centrale)	35
IEP Paris	10
HEC, ESSEC	16
INSEAD	11

Which people play key roles in your country? Which names should one know?

Politicians play a vital role in France: Nicolas Sarkozy (right wing) and Ségolène Royal (left wing). The reform of the French social model is on the agenda, even if the content of the reform depends on the political process.

Business leaders also play a key role. It should be noted that France has, over the years, equipped itself with true 'captains of industry', capable of transforming small and medium-sized enterprises into great multinational corporations: François Dalle at l'Oréal, Claude Bebear at Axa, to name just a few examples. These businesspeople contribute to the evolution of ideas and practices. Claude Bebear has engaged in promoting diversity management practices and the former owner of Renault, Louis Schweitzer, heads the new authority charged with combating discrimination.

Ϙ.fr

References

Alis, David (2003): The 35-hour week in France: the French exception?, in: Personnel Review, 32(4): 510–25.

Alis, David/Karsten, Luchien/Leopold, John (2006): From gods to goddesses: Horai-management as an approach to coordinating working hours, in: Time and Society, 15(1): 81–104.

Amadieu, Jean-François/Rojot, Jacques (1996): Gestion des ressources humaines et relations professionnelles, Paris.

Anxo, Dominique/O'Reilly, Jacqueline (2000): Working-time Transition and Transitional Labour Markets, in: Günther Schmid/Bernard Gazier (eds): The Dynamic of Full Employment: Social Integration by Transitional Labour Market, Cheltenham, 339–46.

Barroux, David/Gadault, Thierry (1996): La Générale des Eaux se pose en rivale de France Télécom, in: La Tribune, 5 September.

Beaujolin, Rachel (1999): Les vertiges de l'emploi l'entreprise face aux réductions d'effectifs, Paris.

Besseyre des Horts, Charles-Henri (1987): Typologie des pratiques de gestion des ressources humaines, in: Revue Française de Gestion, novembre–décembre: 149–55.

Bournois, Frank (1991): La gestion des cadres en Europe, Paris.

—— (1992): The impact of 1993 on management development in Europe: in: Journal of International Studies of Management and Organisation, 22(1): 7–29.

—— (1997): Strategic human resources management: key issues, in: Shaun Tyson (ed.): The Practice of Human Resource Strategy, London, pp. 279–303.

Bournois, Frank/Brabet, Julienne (1997): Qu'est ce que la gestion des ressources humaines?, in: Yves Simon/Patrick Joffre (eds): Encyclopédie de gestion, 2nd edn, Paris.

Bournois, Frank/Derr, C. Brooklyn (1994): Les DRH ont-ils un avenir?, in: Revue Française de Gestion, mars–avril–mai: 64–78.

Bournois, Frank/Roussillon, Sylvie (1998): Préparer les dirigeants de demain, Paris.

Brabet, Julienne (1993): Repenser la gestion des ressources humaines, Paris.

Brewster, Chris/Hegewisch, Ariane (1994): Policy and Practice in European Human Resource Management – The Price Waterhouse Cranfield Survey, London.

Brunhes, Bernard/Clerc, Denis/Meda, Dominique/Perret, Bernard (2001): 35 heures: le temps du bilan, Paris.

Centre de Recherche en Gestion (2000): CRG: Débat autour de la thèse. http://crg.polytechnique.fr/Debats/index.html.

D'Arcimoles, Charles-Henri (1995): Diagnostic financier et gestion des ressources humaines: nécessité et pertinence du bilan social, Paris.

D'Iribarne, Philippe (1989): La logique de l'honneur: gestion des entreprises et traditions nationales, Paris.

Dogan, Mattei/Pahre, Robert (1991): L'innovation dans les sciences sociales: la marginalité créatrice, Paris.

Freyssinet, Jacques (2001): Politiques publiques et négociations collectives sur la durée du travail: la co-production de normes, in: Guy Groux (ed.): L'action publique négociée. Approches à partir des 35 heures – France-Europe, Paris.

Hickson, David J./Pugh, Derek S. (2001): Management Worldwide: Distinctive Styles amid Globalisation, 2nd edn, London.

Hofstede, Geert (2001): Culture's consequences: comparing values, behaviors, institutions and organisations across nations, 2nd edn, Thousand Oaks.

Kaplan, Robert S./Norton, David P. (1992): The balanced scorecard: measures that drive performance, Harvard Business Review, 70(1): 71–9.

Laurent, André (1986): The cross-cultural puzzle of international human resources management, in: Human Resource Management, 25(1): 91–102.

Malinvaud, Edmond (2001): Les échanges entre science économique et autres sciences sociales, in: L'économie politique, 11(3): 7–33.

March, James G. (1991): Exploration and exploitation in organisational learning, in: Organisational Science, 2: 71–87.

Martin, Dominique Philippe (2002): Relations d'objet et processus de transfert associés aux pratiques de GRH: propositions d'analyse et illustration à partir de la logique compétence, in: Gestion 2000, 3: 63–82.

Neveu, Jean-Pierre (1996): La démission du cadre d'entreprise: étude sur l'intention de départ volontaire, Paris.

Peretti, Jean-Marie (1997): Ressources Humaines, 4th edn, Paris.

—— (2006), Ressources Humaines, Vuibert.

Perrot, Serge (2001): L'entrée dans l'entreprise des jeunes diplomées, Paris.

Roussel, Patrick (1996): Rémunération, motivation et satisfaction au travail, Paris.

Schmidt, Géraldine (ed.) (2001): La gestion des sureffectifs, Paris.

Simon, Yves/Joffre, Patrick (1997): Encyclopédie de Gestion, 2nd edn, Paris.

Sorge, Arnt (1993): Management in France, in: David J. Hickson (ed.): Management in Western Europe: Society, Culture and Organisation in Twelve Nations, Berlin, New York.

Thévenet, Maurice (1999): Le retour du travail et la fin de la gestion des ressources humaines, in: Revue française de gestion, 126: 5–11.

Tyson, Shaun (1987): The management of the personnel function, in: Journal of Management Studies, 24(5): 523–32.

Ulrich, David O. (1997): Human Resources Champions, Boston.

van Gennep, Arnold (1994): Les rites de passage, Paris.

Weiss, Dimitri (1999): Les ressources humaines, Paris.

.fr

The authors

Dr David Alis (david.alis@univ-rennes1.fr), University Professor and Dean of the Institute of Business Administration at the University of Rennes 1 (IGR–IAE de Rennes), Researcher at the CNRS CREM Center for Research in Economics and Management. Main research: HRM, organisational behaviour, working time. Main publications: *Réduire et aménager le temps de travail. Pourquoi? Comment?* (2001); *Gestion des ressources humaines* (2001); *The 35-hour Week in France: the French Exception?* (2003).

Dr Frank Bournois (frank@bournois.com), Full Chair Professor of Management and Co-Director of the CIFFOP, Université de Paris II Panthéon-Assas, Affiliate Professor ESCP–EAP, Scientific Director of the Chair of Executive Governance. Main research: strategic HRM top teams, talent development, growing future leaders, high fliers, executive governance. Main publications: *Top Pay and Performance* (with S. Tyson, 2005); *Gestion des resources humaines* (with P. Leclair 2004); *Encyclopedie de dirigeance* (with J. Duval Hamel, 2005); *Pourquoi j'irais travailler?* (with J. Duval-Hamel, E. Albert, J. Rojot, S. Roussillon and R. Sainsaulieu, 2003); *Les meilleures pratiques des entreprises du CAC 40* (with J. Rojot and J-L. Scaringella, 2003); *Cross-cultural Approaches to Leadership Development* (with C.B. Derr and S. Roussillon, 2002); *L'intelligence économique et stratégique dans les grandes entreprises françaises* (with P-J. Romani, 2000); *Préparer les dirigeants de demain – une approche internationale de la gestion des hauts potentiels* (with S. Roussillon, 1998).

Daniel Croquette (Croquette.daniel@wanadoo.fr), past executive director of ANDCP (Association nationale des directeurs et cadres de la fonction personnel). Main research: HRM, skills management, vocational training.

Pierre-Yves Poulain (pypoulain@andcp.fr), Executive Director of ANDCP (Association nationale des directeurs et cadres de la fonction personnel).

6 HRM in Germany: mission (im)possible

Christian Scholz/Hans Böhm/Ingo Gensch

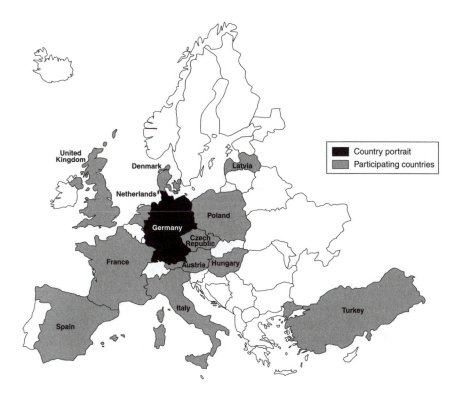

Germany: in a nutshell

In this chapter you will learn:

– that in Germany, many contradictory forces make it hard to manage human resources. Hence German HRM takes place in a very specific situation;

– that HR academia in Germany is influenced by three distinct academic institutions, each of which can be labelled with one of the three letters of 'HRM'; and

– that Dräger implemented some agreed HR instruments to ensure a consistent leadership framework and to coordinate the HR strategies within the company.

Capital:	Berlin
Area (sq km):	357,021 (land 349,223; water 7,798)
EU membership:	since 1951 (founding member of the former so-called European Coal and Steel Community)
Population:	82,422,299
Languages:	German
Ethnic groups (in percentages):	German 91.5, Turkish 2.4, other 6.1 (made up largely of Greek, Italian, Polish, Russian, Serbo-Croatian, Spanish)
Gross domestic product:	2.585 trillion USD (2006)
Workforce (in percentages):	43.66 million (2006): agriculture 2.8, industry 33.4, services 63.8 (1999)
Export commodities:	machinery, vehicles, chemicals, metals and manufactures, foodstuffs, textiles

BACKGROUND: THE FOUR CHANGING CORNERSTONES

HRM in Germany seems in various ways to be mission impossible. For outsiders it is hard to understand, and those aspects which seem to be understood present a rather frightening picture. Trade unions, codetermination, works councils and extremely high wages do not look very inviting to foreign investors. But even for insiders, HRM in Germany has become a rather strange system in recent years: short-term layoffs of employees as the dominating cost reduction strategy, but at the same time long-term efforts to secure the qualification level for the future; concentration on younger employees in spite of the expectation of a 'greying workforce'; a continuing lack of professionalism among HR managers and the need to economise affecting the HRM function. Many contradictory forces make it hard to manage the human resource and to anticipate the rules of the game in the future. However, there are signs that at least some of the changes might be pointing in the right direction. One example was *Time* magazine's cover story 'What's right with Germany' (Wallace 2004), telling us the economic challenges that are definitely a mission most likely to succeed, with HR as the key factor for success.

> HRM in Germany takes place in a very specific situation, which explains some of the strengths of 'HRM made in Germany'. However, HRM is not as easy as a few years ago, before the economic situation became tougher and it became obvious that competition and market principles would be the predominant coordination principles for the future.

FROM PERSONALVERWALTUNG TO AN INTERFUNCTIONAL PERSONALMANAGEMENT

The first step in the process of understanding the logic of a country's management styles and systems is to deal with its specific concepts and its specific terminology. In many cases, these terms are much more than interchangeable labels; they usually have distinct meanings and, when observed over time, also display changes in meaning as well as in focus.

Four different labels are used to talk about HRM in Germany, each representing a specific concept of HRM:

1. *Personalverwaltung* (personnel administration) is a term used mainly in HRM practice. It focuses on the head of the HR department (*Personalleiter*) and implies the efficient execution of the personnel administration (e.g. Goossens 1966).
2. In academia, the traditional term for HRM is *Personalwesen* (personnel affairs), which covers a wide range of activities, starting with the management

of the workforce (e.g. Gaugler/Weber 1976) and extending all the way to the more behavioural aspects of dealing with employees.

3. Also used in academia is the word *Personalwirtschaft* (e.g. Oechsler 1985; Drumm 1989), meaning the economically oriented administration of personnel. Similar to the German term *Betriebswirtschaft* – business management – it implies that employees can be thought of in terms of cost and benefit, profit and loss.

4. *Personalmanagement*, the fourth concept, is a term widely accepted and used at present among progressive HR managers and academics (e.g. Berthel 1979; Scholz 1989) to describe a management approach which considers the management of HR as an active part of the whole management process, combined with professionalism and strategic orientation.

Table 6.1 sums up these concepts. However, special attention must be paid to the terminology, which seems identical in English translation but which it is dangerous to confuse: in Anglo-American literature (e.g. Cascio/Awad 1981; Schuler/Jackson 1996), the shift of emphasis has been from personnel management to HRM, whereas in German literature, the shift – mainly due to the existing and continuously changing demands of practitioners – has been away from the traditional *Personalverwaltung* towards *Personalmanagement*. Still, both shifts reflect the same underlying idea.

At the beginning of the new millennium, we see movement on several different fronts, focusing on organisational matters as well as conceptual issues. One example for the former is the increased incidence of shared service centres and outsourcing activities. An important example for the latter is the move towards human capital management (e.g. Heidecker 2003; Deutsche Gesellschaft für Personalführung e.V. 2004; Scholz/Stein/Bechtel 2004). This reflects the new-economy experience that employees are a company's most important asset, which not only has to be acknowledged, however, but also substantially managed.

In a few words, what would you say is the one fundamental strategic competitive advantage your country offers compared to others?

Germany is one of the world's leading countries with an open society, social stability and an excellent infrastructure, a country which is optimally prepared to regain its status as one of the most attractive countries for high-quality, knowledge-intensive and reasonably priced research, development and production.

FROM 'CODETERMINATION' TO 'COOPERATION'

When foreign experts are asked about the characteristics of German HRM, the first concept they mention is *Mitbestimmung* (codetermination) as a typical German way to institutionalise industrial relations (e.g. Wächter/Stengelhofen 1995). At company level, employees are represented on an *Aufsichtsrat* (supervisory

Table 6.1 German concepts of HRM and its international equivalents

	Personalverwaltung	*Personalwesen*	*Personalwirtschaft*	*Personal-management*
When	starting in the 1950s	starting in the 1970s	starting in the 1970s	starting in the 1980s
Term used in	practice	academia (and practice)	academia	practice and academia
Central focus	personnel administration in companies	isolated function of personnel administration	personnel administration in a corporate context	professional management of HR in a corporate context
Equivalent in UK and USA	personnel	personnel management	personnel management	HRM

board), the control organ of all stock corporations. Being partly equivalent to the non-managing directors on a board of directors, the *Aufsichtsrat* is supposed to control the managing directors on the *Vorstand* (board of management). What is more, the board of management includes a so-called *Arbeitsdirektor* (labour director), who is usually not appointed against the will of the employees' representatives (Sadowski/Junkes/Lindenthal 2001). At operational level, a duly constituted *Betriebsrat* (works council) plays a valuable role in resolving a range of employment issues. Works councils may be established in any firms with more than five employees if employees are in favour of doing so. Council members are specially protected against dismissal. They have the right to be kept informed about the company's development; they must be consulted if someone is hired or dismissed, and their agreement is needed for regulating selection, assignment, leave and qualification issues. This means that they are involved in all decisions relating to individual workers. While there are usually non-company members in the *Aufsichtsrat*, the *Betriebsrat* consists only of employees of the company. This system is legally codified and plays a central role in industrial relations in Germany. Recently, the law has been changed to make it even easier to start a *Betriebsrat*.

However, it has proved to be increasingly difficult to manage at national unit level or even at production unit level when playing in the global economy. This became obvious in 2004 when companies such as DaimlerChrysler negotiated collective agreements in Germany, threatening to move production out of Germany, or when the (former German) car manufacturer Opel was hit hard in Germany by decisions by its parent company General Motors in Detroit and, as a result, lost its autonomy for bargaining with employees. Moreover, obvious managerial problems exist not only because of a lack of managerial expertise in a globalising world, but also because old internal structures have been retained for too long. In order to maintain 'corporate peace', management – supported by employee representatives and union representatives (who do not even need to belong to the company) in the *Aufsichtsrat* – has often retained inefficient structures. The implication: traditional codetermination no longer seems to function the way it used to. Critics point out that the consensual model often leads to situations in which 'capital' and 'labour' find solutions too fast and on a too low aspiration level.

In order to see the whole picture, it is important to understand the true logic behind codetermination. Codetermination is based upon the idea of *Betriebsverbundenheit* (the sense of belonging to a company). It has a long tradition, since 1922. Nicklisch (1922) was about the first to really address the notion of corporate culture and corporate communities (his term *Betriebsgemeinschaften*) in a systematic way: workers tend mostly to be proud of their companies, which in turn can be seen as an important source of motivation. *Betriebsverbundenheit* has been embedded in the German concept of *Partnerschaft* (partnership), which means constructive cooperation between different interest groups, such as trade unions and employers' associations. The idea of partnership was a historic necessity for post-war reconstruction and has also proved important for the reunification of East and West Germany. Partnership is also reflected in the educational system, where responsibilities are taken by several partners: besides a differentiated school and university system, there is also special pre-employment training in companies, mainly for those having completed basic secondary or intermediate schooling. These students chose a practical apprenticeship (*Lehre*) in conjunction with theory in vocational schools, which they attend part-time. Partnership also concerns the trade unions in Germany. Trade unions and employers' associations are free to negotiate collective agreements on wages and salaries (*Lohn- und Gehaltstarifvertrag*) and on working hours and leave entitlement (*Rahmentarifvertrag*).

Nowadays, owing to trends of individualism in German society, this cultural constant of partnership is beginning to change. Increasing pressure to reduce the headcount even in traditionally stable industries indicates that job guarantees across the board can no longer be given: the traditional social contract between companies and their employees, reflecting patterns of classic manufacturing industries is changing: two new movements are emerging as a result:

1. One is corporate Darwinism, according to which the principle of 'survival of the fittest' prevails in times of global competition. Employees with the skills that are needed most are the ones that survive in the market. Employees without distinct core competences are laid off as soon as they fail to contribute added value.

2. The other is employee opportunism. The first generation of employees with experience of a flexible work environment in times of economic boom have learned to take decisions which are in their own interest – even if the consequences for the company are negative. Instead of forging long-term career prospects with one company, they check out their market value by changing jobs. These new employees are self-motivated, ambitious and out to achieve their objectives.

The combination of the two movements is called 'Darwiportunism' (Scholz 2003). Its core question: given the behavioural assumptions of Darwinism and opportunism, what happens if companies play overt or covert Darwinism and employees look for overt or covert self-optimisation?

Although many companies think this phenomenon would not occur in their own work context, it is real and cannot be easily ignored. Darwiportunism is controversial, mostly because it is new and uncommon. But Darwiportunism is not necessarily bad; it also creates opportunities to develop the organisation. Combining both behavioural assumptions in different intensities, one receives different 'implicit contracts' for collaboration in companies. The advantage of the Darwiportunism concept lies in a realistic and differentiated view of the labour system: it means bidding farewell to the illusions of companies that love to care about their employees, and from employees who are totally loyal to their companies all the time. This can neither be ignored nor neglected, nor reversed. So companies have to come to terms with the new situation, which is mainly characterised by a dynamic interplay between companies' and employees' interests.

⊞.de

Nevertheless, the general idea of partnership has led to specific elements in German corporate culture which are perceived to be typical. German companies still show a specific German business culture with elements of partnership which is often overlooked from outside due to stereotypes, such as Germans being technically oriented or extremely bureaucratic.

💡.de

And partnership contributes to the Darwiportunism challenge in the sense that both sides seek win-win situations rather than unilateral dominance. This leads to the necessity of cooperation in the management–employees relationship, knowing about the limitations of codetermination on a global scale.

FROM 'EXPORT' TO 'EUROPEAN GLOBALISATION'

In the 1960s, the mental horizon of German companies was basically one of 'we in Germany and the rest of the world'. International business expansion meant exporting goods and services. It made no difference whether these were sold to France or to the USA. In both cases they were exports, and for Germany at least, selling goods to the USA was even a bit easier. In the 1970s, companies in Germany, as well as in much of the rest of the world, started pursuing some basic internationalisation strategies. Countries outside Germany were still considered similar, even though the European Common Market was just starting to play an important role. In the 1980s, Germany faced increased competition in most markets. In the battle of the 'triad', the three international regions, USA, Japan and Europe, saw themselves as competitors and acted accordingly. This situation increased the feeling in the European Common Market that its members should be protected. In the 1990s, Europe finalised the implementation of a Single Market and a political European Union. Today, the visible symbol is the euro, the currency adopted by almost all of the then members. The same period also saw the opening to eastern Europe and German reunification. European-centred management and global management began to coincide.

In 2000, Germany entered a phase, characterised by a totally new and hugely complex situation in Europe. The Common Market gradually attracted new countries and expanded to include twenty-five members of the European Union. Due to this, European companies became more powerful on a global scale. One example is Daimler-Benz, which merged with the US Chrysler Corporation. At present, we have a situation where companies in Europe are focusing to a large degree on Europe and are trying to find the right strategies to tackle the complex situation of an emerging mega-market. One of the strategies in addition to globalisation is regionalisation: focusing on regions within Europe which can attract capital and people and foster economic success. Gradually, the business climate in Germany has started to change. *Business Week* ran a cover story headlined 'Lean, mean, and …German?' (Miller/Woodruff 1997), in which key representatives of German companies were presented, along with their strategies to downsize their workforces and no longer be overly attentive to the needs of their employees – regardless of ongoing pay increases at top management level.

Furthermore, the HRM of globalising German companies has to organise the workforce not only in Germany itself, but also in countries where subsidiaries are located. First, an international HR strategy has to be defined; second, more operative support needs to be given, e.g. for the management of expatriates in foreign countries. The scope of activities that German HRM has to cover has thus broadened significantly.

What is your advice for a foreign firm entering your country's market? What should managers especially care about and, what is more, be aware of?

Entering the German labour market is quite easy because there is currently no shortage of labour. Entering the German sales market is more difficult because domestic demand has stagnated.

Foreign managers need to know the specificities of German social partnership, labour law, tax legislation and social insurance. Foreign companies can make mistakes which might cost them money and which present an obstacle to sustainable economic success if they fail to respect and adapt to the significant differences of culture and people in Germany and its regions. Regional differences in mentality, but also in local economic conditions, make it very important to consider 'soft' factors in any decision on location.

When entering the German economy and its markets, they should integrate experienced German managers and engineers in diverse management teams. Through good benchmarking, they should try to learn from the best German competitors.

FROM 'NICE TO HAVE' TO 'BADLY NEEDED'

From the 1970s through to the beginning of the year 2000, HR activities were instituted according to the principle 'get it because it is new and nice to have'. Like stamp collectors, HR departments became involved in various activities. Usually, these covered the core issues of a professional HRM, such as strategic HRM, personnel development, remuneration, personnel marketing or personnel controlling. But 'fashions' led to a situation where HR departments addressed topics which are far from HRM core issues, such as knowledge management, total quality management, internal consulting, networking management and health management. In spite of the fact that these issues contribute to the success of companies and of the workforce, it is questionable whether the formal HR function needs to concentrate on them – especially when these topics tend to become established in companies and it is usually easier to start them than to get rid of them. Another source of stimulus for the broad collection of HR issues in companies was the dawn of information technology. Nowadays, many HR departments seem to adopt an automatic 'must-have' strategy where shared services, employee self-service, e-learning, SAP/HR and other e-HRM issues are concerned, rather than assess the actual need for them in the context in question.

At the beginning of the development of a professional HR function, this collection strategy had, at any rate, the advantage of supporting the creation of many innovative ideas in HRM. For example, one of the most sophisticated working-time systems was developed by the German branch of Hewlett-Packard. Installed in 1984, it integrated flexitime, daily 'swing time', job sharing, transfer of holidays, long-term time accounts and compensation of overtime in money or time up to early retirement – all that in order to customise the working time and to fulfil specific needs of different employee groups.

From about the beginning of the year 2000, the HR activities perceived to be most important in German HRM focused on employee acquisition and retention. Companies worked very hard developing their own specific and unique employee value propositions. In spite of the Darwiportunism already discussed, scenario analysis indicates that the German workforce will lack qualified young employees in the future due to current demographic trends. This means that efforts to retain employees actually need to be intensified. Companies are starting to see the value of employees and to value their contributions to productivity and innovation.

Still, many companies have engaged in heavy layoffs and are trying to recover through HR cost-cutting programmes. The idea of lifelong employment, which some companies tried to create during the new economy hype, has disappeared. Instead, companies are trying to increase employee work time and thereby reduce labour costs to keep productivity and international competitiveness stable.

HRM now falls into the 'badly needed' category as a tool for executing the employee-related changes that are necessary. Interestingly, some HR departments are fighting at the same time for their own survival: they are threatened by outsourcing plans and recentralisation disguised as shared service centres.

What would you say one ought not to do? What are the 'don'ts' in your country?

Germans are still more formal in their daily business relationships than US or UK employees, for instance. Although most Germans are very adaptive in contact with US and UK partners, it is common in new social contacts and in cooperation between companies not to use first names but to address counterparts as Mr X or Mrs Y. The familiar *Du* form of address in German and the use of first names are still reserved for close friendly relationships.

If a German invites you to his or her home, it is a sign of friendship. Foreign managers should not accept such an invitation if they are not really interested in that person or if they are not ready to start a friendship.

EAPM AFFILIATE: DEUTSCHE GESELLSCHAFT FÜR PERSONALFÜHRUNG (DGFP)

HISTORY

The German association was founded on 7 January 1952 as Verein für sozial-wirtschaftliche Betriebsformen – Der Neue Betrieb (DNB – Society for Socio-economic Models for Firms – the New Company). The founders of DNB intended to contribute to a stable and successful development of the young post-war market economy and democracy in Germany. In order to coordinate and to stimulate various socio-political activities and programmes in the whole society, and especially in the economy, they thereby aimed to prove that the new *Soziale Marktwirtschaft* – social market economy – could be much more effective and successful than the socialist planned economy that was being implemented in the Soviet sector of post-war Germany – the part that later became the German Democratic Republic.

The stimulating impulse for the establishment of a society of this kind came mainly from Walter Scheel – later president of the Federal Republic of Germany – who was at that time a young Liberal Party (FDP) delegate in the regional Parliament of North Rhine-Westphalia. He received strong support from the scientific community, which was represented (among others) by the famous economist Prof. Dr Alfred Müller-Armack, University of Cologne (who in fact created the model and coined the phrase *Soziale Marktwirtschaft*), and a number of prominent entrepreneurs, such as Dr Erich Middelsten-Scheid, Vorwerck & Co., Dr Kurt Pentzlin, Bahlsen GmbH, and Dr Ludwig Vaubel, Vereinigte Glanzstoff Fabriken AG.

But DNB's founders and growing number of corporate members soon found that some of the most important and powerful socio-political organisations, especially the Federation of German Trade Unions (*Deutscher Gewerkschaftsbund, DGB*) and the Confederation of German Employers' Associations (*Bundesvereinigung Deutscher Arbeitgeberverbände, BDA*), neither supported nor accepted the idea of this new young society playing a steering and coordinating role in the area of social politics. The original founding idea of the association that later became the DGFP thus failed.

However, most of the company representatives in the DNB society were responsible for the management of employees and had already noticed how useful it was to share professional knowledge, pool practical problem-solving approaches and exchange experiences with colleagues from other companies. They therefore institutionalised the first experience exchange group, which came to play a central role in the successful and dynamic development of the organisation. A typical experience exchange group normally includes up to thirty HR managers from thirty different companies, meets three times a year and forms a very confidential network in which HR managers learn from each other.

Soon DNB organised the first conferences and seminars dedicated to topics like profit-sharing, compensation and benefits problems, and social partnership. These activities found broad acceptance and became very successful. Moreover, the first job descriptions and requirement profiles were developed for HR experts and managers, and seminars were devised and introduced to teach key skills and competences to representatives of the young HR profession.

Even in those days, HR professionals had a clear idea of what they needed to do to break out of their mainly administrative role and turn it into a challenging managerial profession. But it was not until January 1968 that an extraordinary general assembly – after long and heated debate – changed the name of the association to Deutsche Gesellschaft für Personalführung (DGFP: German Association for Human Resource Management and Leadership) and adopted a new constitution. According to this new constitution, the main purpose of the DGFP was now 'to support HRM in practice, scientific research, and academic teaching'. The main areas of activity were defined as:

- experience exchange groups for personnel managers;
- working groups formed by members from personnel management practice and academia to develop professional problem-solving recommendations;
- statistical inquiries into personnel management and social topics within DGFP member companies;
- empirical sociological research among members and the broader public in the area of personnel management; and
- examination of systems for personnel management policy and people leadership in practice.

Quite early on, the DGFP started to develop international links and cooperations. The first international experience exchange meeting was organised in 1959 with French HR colleagues. Other international experience exchange groups were formed with Germany's northern, western and southern neighbours. As there were quite a lot of US companies with German subsidiaries, study trips were organised to the USA to learn from HRM at US headquarters and from US companies in general.

In 1962, the DGFP got together with the ANDCP (Association Nationale des Directeurs et Cadres de la fonction Personnel) in France, the IPM (Institute for Personnel Management) in the UK and the SGP (Schweiser Gesellschaft für Personalmanagement) in Switzerland to found the European Association for Personnel Management (EAPM). The main objectives were to improve information flow and cooperation between European HR organisations, and to help to promote the successful development of the HR profession on a European level. In 2004, the EAPM affiliated twenty-six member organisations and the DGFP worked vigorously to secure the smooth and successful integration of the central and eastern European organisations into the European professional community.

As a founding member of the EAPM, the DGFP co-founded the World Federation of Personnel Management Associations (WFPMA) in 1976, which links together the continental HR federations of North and South America, the Asia Pacific Region and Europe, and which strongly supported the foundation of the new African Federation for Human Resource Management in 2004.

What are you and other German people extraordinarily proud of with respect to HRM?

Many Germans are proud of their country's system of social partnership, which used to make for a relatively harmonious culture and atmosphere in industrial relations, high stability and reliability of mutual relations, and a relatively low incidence of strikes. However, international competition demands new answers to make work systems more flexible and less costly.

Another strength Germans are proud of is the high average level of qualification. Germany is especially famous for its system of 'dual apprenticeship', in which state-led 'vocational schools' (*Berufsschulen*) cooperate closely with private companies and chambers of industry and commerce in educating, training and qualifying young apprentices in clearly defined commercial and technical occupations.

German HR specialists are proud of the level of professionalisation. Most companies have HR managers and perceive HRM as a task which contributes to corporate success. In line with this, activities are being initiated to develop professional standards for HRM in order to strengthen the position and value of HRM in companies.

DGFP has developed concrete professional standards and a corresponding system of education, training and certification.

PROGRAMMATIC BASICS

A working group of HR practitioners, scientists and consultants analysed the crucial challenges for HRM at present and in the future, and elaborated a scenario with the most significant environmental trends and developments which would influence HRM in the future.

Crucial challenges were identified: (a) value creation management; (b) competency management (including knowledge management); (c) management of HR instruments; and (d) management of change.

Future HRM will be influenced by different environmental areas, namely:

- the technological environment (i.e. basic innovations in natural and technological sciences, product and process innovations, innovations in information technology);

165

– the sociological environment (i.e. change of social and moral values, demographic development);
– the political environment (i.e. legal development and new laws, tax systems, economic and structural politics, labour market politics, educational politics and systems, parties, associations and organisations); and
– the market and competitive environment (i.e. globalisation, especially global competition, labour markets, capital markets, standards).

These environmental influences (Figure 6.1) were transferred to different areas of HR management (Figure 6.2) which are simultaneously different fields of education and training activities of the DGFP.

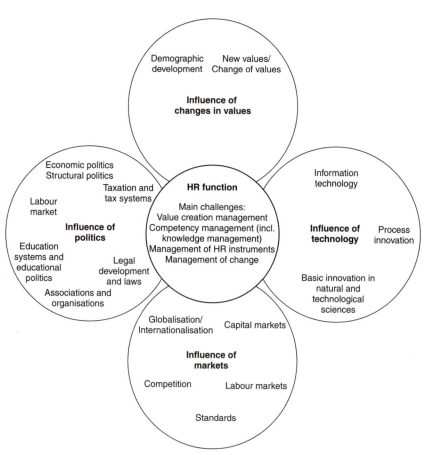

Figure 6.1 Current environmental trends and developments for HRM in Germany

166

Areas of HR management

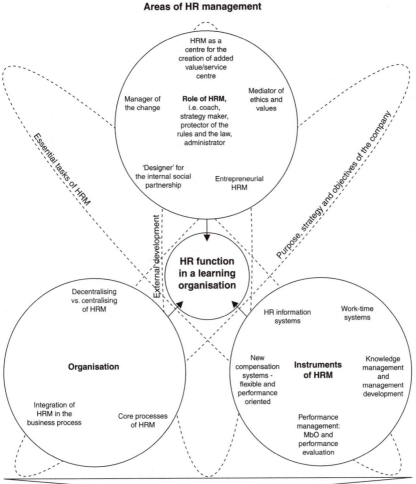

This leads to the requirement profile of HR manager

Figure 6.2 Different fields of DGFP activities

CURRENT ACTIVITIES AND PRODUCTS

Experience exchange network: for members only

In 2004, the DGFP had around 1,800 member companies and some 250 extraordinary individual members (mainly scientists and consultants). The corporate members send their HR managers and HR experts to the experience exchange network, which consists of 120 groups. This experience exchange and mutual learning network is still the DGFP's core activity and most highly regarded service for members. Approximately 4,500 HR managers cooperate in confidence within this network.

Academy for HRM

The DGFP Academy offers a broad programme of training courses and seminars in all HRM fields. The strategic approach is that HR people in the Academy find offers for learning everything they need to do an excellent, professional job. In addition to its seminars and training courses, the Academy organises the Annual DGFP congress, which regularly attracts 800 to 1,000 HR managers.

Five years ago, the Board of the DGFP set up a group of experts, drawn from universities, consulting companies and HRM teams in member companies, with a brief to develop professional standards for HR managers in Germany. The need was made obvious by the growing range of perceptions of what constitutes good, professional HRM in practice and what role it should play in company management. This group, internationally supported by UK and US colleagues, completed its work and published its results in 2002 (Deutsche Gesellschaft für Personalführung e.V. 2002a). The professional standards it developed formed the basis for an education and training programme for HR managers called 'ProPer' (from *Professionalisierung des Personalmanagements*). This certification programme covers eight modular learning fields: strategy, culture, social partnership, external relations, value creation management, competences management, instruments management and management of change. It also promotes the overall objective of developing socially competent, strong personalities as HR managers at three different levels:

1. Experts: qualified specialists in certain HR areas, lower management level.
2. Professionals: HR generalists at middle-management level. This level of professional standards also incorporates the DGFP recommendations for university and business-school education in HRM.
3. Executives: HR managers at top management level with comprehensive responsibility, board members.

The state of professionalisation is measured annually by the *PIX*, the DGFP professionalisation index for HRM.

Working groups

The DGFP brings together highly qualified experts from HRM practice, from universities and science, and from the world of consulting to develop practice-oriented approaches to the solution of unresolved HRM problems. The working groups are active for about two years and deliver their results to the professional HR community through articles in the DGFP journal and innovative contributions within the Academy programme, but mainly through the DGFP book series *Praxis-Edition*. Recent examples are books on personnel controlling (vol. 62, 2001), on HR tasks within mergers and acquisitions (vol. 67, 2002b) and on value-oriented people management (vol. 70, 2004). Normally, ten to fifteen of these working groups are active at the same time and the results they deliver are perceived as a major enrichment of practical and practice-oriented scientific HRM.

Personalführung journal and the dgfp.de Internet portal

The monthly DGFP journal *Personalführung* focuses clearly on HRM practice, regularly addressing one general topic and describing best-practice solutions to HRM problems. Readers confirm the high quality of the magazine and use it widely as a tool for self-initiated learning. The journal has a print-run of around 10,000.

The DGFP internet portal (www.dgfp.de) terms itself the 'Centre of competence for human resource management and leadership'. It presents a wide range of information and services, such as live expert talks, chat rooms, news groups, a large collection of problem-solving resources, examples from companies, a virtual library, etc. Only DGFP members have full access to all the documents of member companies. At present, the portal registers around 160,000 clicks a month.

Regional branches

In the 1980s, the DGFP developed the idea of offering its products and services in the closest possible proximity to its members and customers. The first regional office and training centre was opened in Munich in 1988 and named Bayerische Akademie – Regionalstelle München. In the following years, regional offices opened in Frankfurt, Leipzig, Düsseldorf, Hamburg, Stuttgart and Berlin.

The DGFP unit in the German capital Berlin, in particular, seeks to intensify cooperation with political institutions and offers HRM practitioners expertise for processes that pave the way for political decisions.

DGFP mbH

DGFP mbH is the profit-oriented branch of the DGFP. A complete spin-off of the non-profit DGFP e.V., it was founded in 1988 on the recommendation of the financial and fiscal authorities, who saw the continuation of certain activities in its programme as a risk for the non-profit, non-taxable status of DGFP e.V. DGFP mbH deals with all in-house training activities which are not designed to support the professional community as a whole but aim at helping to strengthen the competitive advantage of individual companies. It also conducts empirical inquiries on initial salaries for graduates, general compensation schemes and salary comparisons. The programme is rounded off by other comparative studies on key performance indicators of HRM, benchmark rounds among limited numbers of interested companies, a wide range of specific consultancy services and interim management services. Other tasks include securing and handling advertising for the journal *Personalführung* and organising the foremost exhibition of HR service providers at the annual DGFP congress; this also includes running a highly successful sponsorship programme.

The C.R. Poensgen Foundation

In 1998, the C. Rudolf Poensgen Foundation was integrated into the DGFP but, for strategic reasons, retained its own brand, programme and management. The Poensgen Foundation is intended to be the general management institute within the DGFP. Strategically this makes sense because it is becoming increasingly important to teach general management skills to HR professionals as well as to improve significantly the HR and social skills of general managers. The C. Rudolf Poensgen Foundation was founded in 1956 and is one of the oldest and most famous general management development institutes in Germany.

CONCLUSION: SUCCESSFUL GROWTH

The DGFP as a whole has enjoyed an extremely successful growth curve, and has monitored and significantly shaped the development of HRM in Germany. It is well respected and internationally recognised. The DGFP has developed professional standards for German HR managers and implemented a corresponding training and certification programme with regular monitoring of the degree for professionals in HRM. Additionally, DGFP mbH provides professional support for the HRM of single companies and the C. Rudolf Poensgen Foundation qualifies general managers in HRM. On the strength of all that, the DGFP sees itself as 'the driving force for the professionalisation of human resource management in Germany'.

> **What is typical of your country in relation to the country itself (its culture, people, etc.) and its economy?**
>
> With a population of 82.5 million people, Germany is the largest member of the EU. Although it was for decades the motor of economic development in Europe, Germany has been wrestling since reunification in 1990 with the financial burdens inherited from the socialist system of former East Germany.
>
> Germany has the reputation of being a country with a highly bureaucratic system. Compared to other countries, this is not so. However, its systems are under intense pressure to embrace radical reform in order to make administrative processes even leaner and faster.
>
> Germany is the world's foremost exporter – and not only because of big global players such as DaimlerChrysler, Siemens, Deutsche Bank, Volkswagen, BASF or BMW (to name but a few); its strong body of mid-sized and mostly family-owned companies also deserves some of the credit.
>
> Germany has a long tradition of trust-based cooperation between employers and employees, which worked well through crises such as post-war reconstruction and the collapse of the new economy. This social partnership – among other things – gives the works councils far-reaching rights at operational level.

HR ACADEMIA: THREE SCHOOLS OF HRM THOUGHT

HRM does not really have a long academic tradition in Germany. Unlike fields such as accounting, manufacturing and finance, HRM (or something closely resembling it) was for a long time unavailable as a specialisation option in universities' business administration programmes. It was not until 1963 that the University of Mannheim created the first chair of *Personalwirtschaft* in Germany. And it took until 1986 for the first chair of *Personalmanagement* in Germany to be inaugurated at Saarland University in Saarbrücken.

In the German Verband der Hochschullehrer für Betriebswirtschaft e.V. – the German association of university professors of business administration – a section for HRM was founded in 1973. Its mission statement underlines the relevance of employees as a factor of success, and the corporate challenge of treating them as such through responsible HRM. In times of changing employment structures and labour markets, the objective of the section is to broaden the theoretical base of HRM, to craft solutions to practical problems on the basis of scientific methods, and to create standards in education which will promote responsible conduct in future general managers with leadership functions and HR managers. From Eduard Gaugler's days as its first chairman, this section grew under his various successors, ultimately boasting 144 professorial members in late 2006. They form an active community. Each autumn, the annual meeting focuses on current topics reflecting developments in the field, such as:

- HRM as a field in business administration (1979/80);
- individualisation (1987/88);
- personnel development and labour market (1989/90);
- German unification (1991/92);
- restructuring and personnel reduction (1993/94);
- implications of new production and organisation concepts (1995/96);
- HRM and corporate change (1997/98);
- HRM and information technology (1999/2000);
- non-profit organisations (2001/02);
- HRM and corporate crisis (2003/04);
- diversity as a challenge for HRM (2005); and
- employment relations (2006).

They all reflect trends showing the initiative of the academic HR community leading to progress in the field of HRM both in research and in teaching.

The main publication for theoretical HRM topics in Germany is the *Zeitschrift für Personalforschung* (ZfP). Founded in 1987, it is a highly respected double-blind refereed journal. It has also English articles and special volumes. To multiply recent research results and to present the group out of which new researchers emerge, issues regularly present abstracts of university dissertations in the field of German HRM.

FOCUS ON 'H'(UMAN)

At the academic institutions currently addressing HRM in Germany, three distinct groups can be identified (Scholz 2004), each of which can be labelled with one of the three letters of 'HRM'. These schools of thought are broadly consistent with other analyses (Matiaske/Nienhüser 2004) which identify personnel economy (focus on 'r') as a clear-cut area of German HRM and, moreover, an area of personnel psychology/leadership (focus on 'h' in combination with a focus on 'm'). These approaches are proceeding along similar lines to the developments seen in the USA and UK, even though they have largely independent origins and different development paths. As to Germany, it can be stated that the approaches of the three schools of thought ('h', 'r', 'm') are slowly tending to get broader. Approaches which originally concentrated on the micro aspect of employee behaviour now tend to cover the resource aspect as well as the management aspect. The result is more integrative HRM as a whole.

This school of thought dates back – as mentioned earlier – to Nicklisch (1922) and notions such as *Betriebsverbundenheit* and *Betriebsgemeinschaften*. In them we see concepts similar to that of corporate culture (e.g. Schein 1985), and we see the basis for codetermination. Its research was initiated by Hax (1969), although not meant to be a specific HRM approach. Other roots of this school of thought come from the values of the Catholic doctrine of social morality (e.g. von Nell-Breuning 1950), which strongly influenced the normative aspects of HRM. Hasenack (1961) tried to initiate anthropological economics, and Fischer, interested in central issues of personnel affairs, created an 'ethical oriented corporate personnel and social policy' (1962).

The result of this is the first school of thought of German HRM, which works in a similar way to the Michigan approach in the USA (e.g. Tichy/Fombrun/Devanna 1982) as well as the 'soft HRM' with its focus on development in the UK (e.g. Legge 1995). In this 'h' school, the central topic of HRM is the behavioural component. So it concentrates on the description and regulation of people's behaviour in different environmental situations. Originating in Berlin (e.g. Staehle 1980) and developed in Hannover and Vienna (e.g. von Eckardstein/Schnellinger 1978), its focus is on training and development (e.g. Weber 1985) which are meant to integrate those tasks in the overall organisational development process. Employee-oriented approaches and topics are also discussed – e.g. micropolitics (e.g. Neuberger 1995), mobbing (e.g. Neuberger 1999) and diversity management (e.g. Krell 2003). This 'humanistic' school of thought is well reflected in practice, where several HRM 'gurus' stress related topics such as self-motivation and trust culture.

As to current 'h' school research, it seems that the 'humanistic factor' will be needed more and more to ensure the age structure and qualification structure within companies. Ageing German society and weaknesses in the German education system are forcing change in pension schemes and forecasts of what the workplace of the future will look like.

●.de

In the future, research with focus on 'h' has to deal with three issues.

The first is a major challenge that has emerged during the five stages is European cultural diversity, which translates into a workforce that is increasingly international and culturally much more diverse than ever before. Owing to the convergence of working systems and working structures across Europe, German HRM has to integrate, for example, employees from Spain and Portugal, who are influenced by the Mediterranean way of life, with people from Baltic states like Lithuania, as well as Sweden, Finland and Norway in the North. It has to cater for different religious backgrounds, especially the Islamic traditions of many Turkish and former Yugoslavian workers who came to Germany thirty to fifty years ago. And it has to integrate immigrant ethnic Germans from former German settle-ment areas in eastern Europe, who have another, completely different back-ground. All in all, cultural diversity is not only visible and interesting, but also significant in respect to H(RM) in Germany.

The second issue is the necessity to rewrite the social contract between employer and employee. We see highly profitable companies, which lay off people on a large scale. We also see a decrease in loyalty and the necessity of an increase in retention. We see – as it has been mentioned above in the context of Darwiportunism (Scholz 2003) – moves towards Darwinism and opportunism, which have to be combined with the well-established model of German social partnership.

The third issue derives from the fact that the leadership has to be adjusted. In the mid-1990s, CEOs of many large German companies changed to a manage-ment style, which followed the stereotypes of US management and moved even further (e.g. Miller/Woodruff 1997); their compensation shot upwards, and there was much public criticism. After ten years, it seems that we are in need of a calmer and more people-oriented style – which could turn out to be an important research issue, both descriptive and prescriptive.

FOCUS ON 'R'(ESOURCE)

The second German school of thought is strongly oriented towards planning. Its reference points are company resources and corporate strategy. The focus on 'r' is associated with researchers in Stuttgart (e.g. Macharzina/Oechsler 1977; Ackermann 1987). One central issue is the integration of social and technocratic leadership. HR policies are combined with corporate policies through planning systems which tie both sectors together. Another important issue in that field is control of HR (e.g. Potthoff/Trescher 1986), which forms a link with the account-ing and finance functions of a company.

One prominent branch of this school of thought is personnel economy, which has its centre in Trier and stresses resource efficiency in respect of remuneration and also incentive models for functioning labour markets (e.g. Sadowski 2002). Other German-speaking centres of the personnel economy school are

Bonn – where the tournament theory, for example, is applied to HRM (Kräkel 2000), especially to career systems – and Zurich, where topics discussed include HR decisions at risk (e.g. Backes-Gellner/Lazear/Wolff 2001). This 'hard' approach to HRM sees itself close to microeconomics, but bears no direct resemblance to HRM categories in the UK or the USA.

♥.de As to current 'r' school research, the discussion of human resources and their value will become more and more intense, not only among institutional economists. Research will have to look for substantive methods of measuring the 'value' of human resources.

In the future, a crucial issue for academic research with the focus on 'r'(esource) will be the search for the value of human capital. Currently, slogans such as 'our people are our most important asset' are merely verbal statements with limited impact. Employees are in many cases considered as cost drivers, not as a real value. Therefore transparent human capital valuation is needed, which allows companies to state and to monitor their human capital. As a first step, human capital management research has recently led to proposals like the Saarbrücker Formel ('Saarbruecken formula', see Scholz/Stein/Bechtel 2004), which uses a standard procedure to express the company workforce in monetary terms. However, much more research is needed in order to understand the true nature of human capital as the key driver for the success of the company.

FOCUS ON 'M'(ANAGEMENT)

Like the New York approach in the USA (e.g. Huselid/Jackson/Schuler 1997) but with no equivalent in the UK, this third school of thought in Germany originated in value-added orientation (e.g. Wunderer 1992) and strategic HR planning combined with a focus on strategic fit targeted in Saarbrücken (e.g. Scholz 1982).

Accordingly, successful HRM has to address central fields of activity, levels and orientations, which together form a consistent framework for systematic HRM (e.g. Gaugler/Huber/Rummel 1974; Scholz 2000; Drumm 2005). Recent developments of the strategic management approach in HRM broaden the perspective to current corporate challenges such as the concordance of explicit and implicit contracts between employees and organisation (e.g. Scholz 2003; Wunderer/Küpers 2003) since at this point, strategic decisions are needed.

♥.de As to current 'm' school research, HRM requires competent, professional HR experts. Perhaps the solution will be found in the German education and research system. But regardless of who answers the following question, it is important for German HRM research to ask: what should professional HRM in practice look like?

As to the future of the focus on 'm'(anagement), that issue of professional HR managers will lead to interesting questions: on the one hand, we have the popular concept of HR as a business partner which definitely calls for a strict management perspective. On the other hand, we still do not see an impressive increase in strategic HR. Therefore, academia has to stress the 'm' in HRM, both in research and in teaching.

What would you like to teach foreign HR managers? What is important for them to know in your opinion?

Foreign HR managers will find instruments in Germany similar to those in the rest of the world's leading countries. For instance, job evaluation, HR development, leadership and organisational development function the same way as anywhere else.

However, there are two differences. While some countries tend to concentrate on a few, but widespread HRM instruments (in the USA, for example, on the balanced scorecard), HR instruments in Germany are more diverse. On the other hand, German companies tend to be fairly monocultural as far as IT solutions in HRM are concerned. Most companies use SAP or Peoplesoft standard business software, ignoring home-grown IT solutions.

Language is important. Where foreign HR managers need to communicate and cooperate with blue-collar employees and their representatives, knowledge of German is extremely helpful.

BEST-PRACTICE CASE: DRÄGER GROUP – 'TECHNOLOGY FOR LIFE' SUPPORTED BY A STRONG COOPERATION CULTURE

The Dräger Group (Dräger-Gruppe), with around 10,000 employees, is one of the world's leading enterprises of its kind. Founded in 1889, Drägerwerk AG of Lübeck in Germany grew from a small company manufacturing valves and fittings, the first pressure reducers and pressure gauges. In recent years, Dräger has resolutely broadened its scope, evolving from a mere supplier of products and systems to a provider of solutions and services. Dräger Medical develops, manufactures and markets medical engineering products and system solutions and provides services all over the world in the acute clinical care and home care sectors along the entire patient-processing chain. The company's objective is to improve the quality of patient care and, at the same time, help to cut costs in the healthcare sector by improving clinical processes. Dräger Safety is engaged in the worldwide development, manufacture and marketing of equipment, applications, system solutions and services for all areas of hazard management. The systems and equipment supplied by Dräger Safety warn human beings of contamination in the air and protect them by enabling them to breathe properly even in extreme conditions. In their core business, Dräger Medical and Dräger Safety are represented in more than 190 countries across all continents and operate their own companies in more than forty countries. In addition to sales and services outlets, Dräger companies engage in the production and development of products from Dräger Medical and Dräger Safety in Germany, the USA, Sweden, the UK, the Netherlands, South Africa and China.

STRUCTURE OF THE DRÄGER GROUP

The Dräger Group today consists of a management holding company, Drägerwerk AG, the two independent subgroups Dräger Medical and Dräger Safety and the service companies Dräger Interservices GmbH and Dräger InTek GmbH. A transparent, efficient, market-oriented organisational structure is thus ensured. This clearly defined organisational structure requires a very high degree of responsibility, promotes more efficient competitiveness, results in clear-cut competences and, at the same time, enhances the company's flexibility. The particular advantages of this group structure lie in the utilisation of joint services and the swift and secure transfer of know-how. Within the Dräger Group, the holding company acts as group manager.

The subsidiary companies assume full responsibility for operational activities (including financial control) within the subgroups Dräger Medical and Dräger Safety. To cement close ties between holding company and subsidiaries, the appointment or removal from office of, for example, a subsidiary's general manager is undertaken by the relevant bodies of the subsidiary with the participation of the holding company.

DRÄGER'S HR DEPARTMENTS

The organisational structure of the Dräger Group is aimed at providing a rigorous subgroup structure to improve overall earning power. Against this backdrop, the holding company and the two subgroups have their own independent personnel departments geared to suit their particular needs and requirements. At the heart of the group structure, the holding company's personnel department assumes responsibility for basic functions that need to be performed for the entire Group. These include central management training. The subgroups, together with the holding company, are jointly responsible for devising management development activities. Over and above these, management and cooperation principles are defined and uniform personnel policies on fundamental matters specified in the HR strategies (HRSs) for all group companies, for which the valid requisite benchmarks have been established. Also included in this is coordination of personnel management efforts within the company as well as matters involving worker participation, trade unions and collective agreements.

The personnel departments of the two subsidiary companies Dräger Medical and Dräger Safety are responsible for HRM and personnel development. Among other things, this includes personnel strategy, responsibility for personnel joining or leaving the company, training and further education programmes, training in management skills and all operational personnel functions up to and including pay and time accounting.

COOPERATION AND MANAGEMENT: THE HR INSTRUMENTS

Strategic level: HR strategies, leadership framework, employee survey

At all levels in all its companies, the Dräger Group requires staff to embody Dräger corporate culture. Whatever the assignment, the customer always comes first. Consequently, Dräger staff act not only for the customer but also for the company and thus for themselves. This is a goal pursued and achieved by promoting skills and employee advancement on the basis of a few benchmarks:

- identification with the company, its culture and its objectives;
- partnership through cooperation and management by joint planning, joint decisions and joint responsibility;
- a culture of trust with predictability, reliability, open communication and the courage to take the initiative;
- recognition of personal performance, joint attainment of objectives and constant improvement;
- decentralised structures demanding a high level of economic efficiency and closeness to the customer as well as allowing as few interfaces as possible;
- untrammelled freedom in daily routine work;
- room to manoeuvre for staff and managers;

- moving decision-making to the lowest level possible;
- entrepreneurial thinking and action by all staff; and
- all staff sharing in profits.

With regard to its leadership framework, Dräger employs management concepts in many regions of the world. However, different criteria are applied in different regions for the selection, development and performance standards of management staff, which makes cross-border identification and development of potential managers difficult. Promoting first-class management calls for a world-wide, uniform understanding of management criteria based on common standards. At Dräger, these standards need to be geared to business success, be implementable on a global scale and yet still be simple. They must also be seen to make sense, be fair, acceptable to managerial staff and, of course, allow representation in some measurable form irrespective of the cultures prevailing in the countries in question.

Dräger believes the advantages of its leadership framework lie in the fact that it forms a basis for trust and worldwide identification and also facilitates the selection and advancement of potential managers. Furthermore, it permits standardised management training and international transfers of managerial staff. Managerial staff members themselves are given an orientation frame, i.e. the opportunity to discover for themselves where they stand at present and which management qualities they need to develop for the future. Another aim of the leadership framework is to boost the attractiveness of Dräger as a company to work for. All over the world, Dräger wants to be an attractive company for the best people, which means it needs to be able to find and retain the best people.

A survey of Dräger employees, conducted worldwide, has been further developed to provide a strategic management instrument. As an enterprise facing international competition, the motivation and performance of its employees play a vital role in implementing the objectives and strategies that Dräger aims to achieve. This is the starting point for the employee survey: it is intended to support the Executive Board and senior and executive managers in the task of creating preliminary conditions for employee performance and satisfaction. That is why the questionnaire's primary gearing is to strategically relevant topics. It is also why a comprehensive presentation of the results is made first to the Executive Board when the survey has been concluded. The results are analysed against the background of future corporate objectives and, where action is required, strategically important fields of measures are mapped out. Proposals for improvements in these fields of action then have to be drawn up and implemented at all levels and in all sectors within a specified time frame. The tangible benefit of the employee survey is found in the reliable and differentiated data it produces on human factors important for success at Dräger. The enterprise receives very concrete answers to questions such as: do employees have a decent working environment? Do they possess the requisite abilities and skills for their spheres of responsibility, or can they acquire these skills at Dräger? In addition, employees can state whether they receive feedback or recognition from their supervisors and whether cooperation between them is functioning properly. These are just a few examples of aspects which are of crucial importance for creating conditions in which performance and satisfaction can develop in an optimum manner.

An employee survey is not a one-off act but an important part of a permanent process of change and improvement. Innovation and change are a permanent item on the agenda, especially for a global player such as Dräger driven by technology and innovation.

Operational level: staff dialogue, compensation, profit sharing, working time

At least once a year, line managers enter into a personal dialogue with each individual member of staff in a face-to-face interview. Away from the hectic day job, a confidential discussion can take place between the two of them to address matters relating to the task in hand, its performance, the degree to which goals have been achieved, employees' interest in further education, their development within the company, their opinions on their daily work, how they rate themselves, their own aims and concerns. Subjects can also include, for example, the way the department is organised, whether the allocation of assignments is clear or unclear, individual work organisation or team-building/team-hampering factors affecting cooperation with colleagues.

Together with its subgroups, Dräger, as a major industrial employer, is bound by the terms of the collective agreement with *IG Metall*, the German metalworkers' union, so there is little leeway for individual remuneration. That is why additional remuneration for payments outside the collective wage agreement is geared, among other things, to how successful an employee has been. Employee premiums are mostly based on group success because it is often impossible to identify the personal success of the individual, e.g. in manufacturing operations.

Moreover, Dräger allows its employees to share in the company's economic success, recognising their active contribution to the company's performance. This also serves to implement Dräger's philosophy and its HR strategies: 'Dräger is an attractive company for employees and gives them a share of its profits.' Economic success means that the Dräger Group, the subgroup or the company in question is generating sustainable and reasonable earnings, has attained the goals set for the year in question and has recorded a satisfactory profit:

– As long ago as 1900, the company gave its employees a non-predetermined share of its profit for the year.
– In 1904, a performance bonus of 4.8 to 6.5 pfennigs per working hour was awarded at Dräger. This was the equivalent of 25 per cent of the hourly rate of pay, which at that time was between 30 and 46 pfennigs. Even in 1904, the introduction of this bonus system resulted in exceptional output growth.

179

- In 1982, Dräger demonstrated a pioneering spirit in the field of working-time scheme models. For decades now, working-time rules have had to meet two requirements: on the one hand, they needed to be economically advantageous for the company; on the other hand, they had to be attractive for employees.
- From 1983 to 2002, every year employees were given certificates of beneficial interest. Like company shares, these certificates entitled the bearer of the certificate to a share of the Group's profits every year. After a lock-up period of six years, they could be sold on the stock exchange at any time. The idea of issuing certificates of beneficial interest combined direct employee participation with effective wealth formation for employees.
- In 1995, management profit-sharing (MPS) was introduced for senior and executive management staff. The aim of MPS is to provide rewards for the attainment of the requisite results and agreed targets, if the Dräger Group or the subgroups Medical and Safety achieve a minimum earnings figure in the year in question. The targets for managerial staff have to fulfil certain criteria: they must be objective and logical, they must always be measurable and the senior or executive manager in question must be able to exert a direct influence. To ensure managerial efficiency and ensure that activities can be focused, no more than three targets may be agreed for personal spheres of responsibility. The criteria for measurement must be communicated regularly through the reporting system.
- In 1996, Dräger enlarged its working-time scheme models by introducing a scheme allowing flexible working time at the employee's own discretion, called in German *Eigenverantwortliche flexible Arbeitszeit* (EFA). The aim is to achieve greater independence and a higher degree of work satisfaction for the individual employee. For Dräger, the EFA scheme has the advantage that targets can be met on time, and with the customer in mind, after consultation with staff. On top of this, huge sections of the old time-recording procedures have been transformed into a working-time on trust basis, dispensing with all physical forms of recording the times worked.
- Since 2005, the idea of issuing certificates has become an earnings/performance-related top-up contribution for the company pension scheme.

FOSTERING ABILITIES, ADVANCEMENT AND PROMOTION: HR DEVELOPMENT

Drägerwerk AG has developed a corporate culture which gives due consideration to the decisive role of the staff for the company's success. For Dräger, the continuous development of staff qualifications and continuing education for employees is of strategic importance. Management development is secured in close cooperation with the member companies of the group under the leadership of HR at Drägerwerk AG. Here, knowledge and information in respect of the demands made on managerial staff, and their selection and promotion of next-generation staff skills are embodied in the principles of the management development scheme. This could be said to reflect the statements concerning employees, managerial staff and their advancement under the principles for cooperation and management. It is important to specify the selection criteria, the demands made on managerial staff and the manner in which next-generation candidates displaying exceptional commitment, performance and potential can be identified and fostered. The management development scheme at Dräger also contains an injunction to review the manning of all senior management positions worldwide once a year.

The management development programme pursues two main objectives: on the one hand, a common pool is to be established within the Dräger Group for future managerial staff. On the other, their knowledge of management matters should be aligned with potential assessment throughout the Group.

To attain these goals, central management development is carried by two supporting pillars: on the one hand, there is the management development (MD) scheme for executives and, on the other hand, the Dräger career advancement (DCA) scheme for the selection and systematic development of next-generation management staff. The leadership framework provides the common basis for the criteria.

Fostering management skills

To ensure uniform understanding of the knowledge of management methods among top managers within the Dräger Group, two leading business schools (IMD of Lausanne and SMP of St Gallen) were chosen to conduct management training courses within the Group worldwide. The aim is to achieve a largely uniform method of imparting knowledge to middle and top management. MD for executives is a course of training based on the strategies of the Dräger Group and the subgroups. Knowledge of modern management methods is conveyed in annual application-ready modules, ensuring practical implementation. Here, the emphasis is on the subjects of strategy, change management, process management, marketing, HR and financial management.

The second supporting pillar for management development is the identification and advancement of next-generation management staff candidates. The DCA programme is a systematic and modular development programme for the next generation of managerial staff and an instrument in tune with business requirements adapted to the needs of Dräger. The increasingly global orientation of the business units has forced Dräger to engage fully in advancing the individuals with core competencies in the companies abroad. In addition, the advancement of employees is considerably more effective when this can be implemented as individually as possible and in line with the prevailing circumstances. The DCA also has as one of its objectives the critical manner in which the participants regard themselves. Maximum transparency, frank and open communication and fairness are of prime significance here. Entry into the DCA scheme takes place on the proposal of the line manager in question and joint processing of the

181

'potential check' questionnaire, a pragmatic appraisal system along the lines of the criteria contained in the leadership framework.

Training and continuing education

Dräger's greatest strength lies in the commitment and qualifications of its employees. Their knowledge, motivation and initiative are indispensable for corporate success. Here, Dräger lays great emphasis on quality. This applies not only to the products but also to the qualifications of its most junior employees. That is why Dräger offers next-generation staff well-founded and interesting training courses in the form of a wide variety of professional buildup seminars and training courses under qualified course leaders. Included in the range of apprenticeship courses at Dräger are those leading to qualifications as chemical laboratory assistant, mechatronics specialist, industrial craftsman or forwarding craftsman. In addition, there is the possibility at Dräger of entering into a dual course of studies in three different subjects. Access to professional life through the combination of practical training and courses of higher education studies gives the student in question the status of a sought-after specialist. To be able to view functions from two points of view is one of the salient aims of this course of studies. When this is combined with a technical or also a commercial orientation, vocational qualification with know-how is assured. The course of studies concludes with the submission of a thesis.

Skill management can identify and foster the requisite supplementary measures needed to enhance the job-related qualification profile of the employees. This involves functions which are within the responsibility of the manager and/or the employee. This is never an exclusively management function. It is rather the case that it has to be ensured that all employees are in possession of the right knowledge and abilities to be able to fulfil their function. Support for these subjects and functions is available from the skill management sector: it provides the appropriate general conditions, instruments and processes, makes the offer of suitable training courses and gives advice on the choice of qualification measures. In addition to attending seminars, this continuing education can also be addressed by a large number of other measures, e.g. extending terms of reference or project targets. Moreover, skill management develops training course concepts and is responsible for project training worldwide or is a participant in such projects. This includes, for example, introducing management feedback, improving qualification potentials, implementing the management development concept, international trainee programmes and a great deal more. In an international working group made up of HR managers from Germany, the Netherlands, France and the USA, Dräger has developed a short-term exchange programme (STEP). Within the scope of this programme, employees are intensively deployed on project-related assignments in subsidiary companies outside Germany for periods of up to three months.

Success at Dräger depends on its employees. They are the company's strength. For that reason, it is of decisive importance that good employees also have the resolve to do their best for the company. This motivation is not merely a function of components such as profit-sharing, career advancement measures and proper management but also from life in the company apart from work. Against this backdrop, Dräger has provided its employees with a wide-ranging leisure activities programme called LUNA (in German: *Lust Und Neugier Auf...*). Dräger finances the activities, the employees invest their leisure time and none of this involves having to ask anyone in authority for permission. The reasons for a programme of this kind are many and varied: outside work, at events transcending the boundaries between the various departments and divisions of the company, cross-unit communication and cooperation are promoted and faces can be put on names in other departments and companies, and employee motivation and health consciousness are given a boost. Anything a company also makes available for the leisure-time activities of its employees over and above what is customary in that branch of industry makes the company employing them more attractive.

Q.de

Corporate culture

All communities, whether they are states, religious groupings or other special interest groups (military, associations, clubs), have always developed their own collective cultures. These cultures consist of the special interests, values and standards, rituals, signs and symbols that give each culture its own peculiar identity. The members of such a community stand by the purpose for which it was founded, are committed to its objectives, believe in its values and represent them outwardly. In the process, the members acquire a feeling of trust and security because everything is foreseeable and calculable. As a result, the end product generated by such a feeling of solidarity is strength. To develop this kind of trust and confidence at Dräger, HRM maintains an assortment of integration measures, training courses and activities to foster and enhance the joint experiences of staff. In this way, a feeling of togetherness, of solidarity can be built up among colleagues.

'Wilderness experience' is a seminar concept opening up new and very promising perspectives in personnel development. This is because it affects more than just the professional and private environments of the participants. What is involved in the case of experiences in the wilderness is leadership, self-assessment and assessment of others, the ability to accept criticism and the willingness to engage in introspection. For managerial staff, the object is to intensify communication skills above and beyond hierarchical and business unit limitations. That is why the groups are mixed: from head of group through to the Executive Board director, managerial staff have to face up to an extreme situation together in untamed nature. Hierarchical thinking is diminished by being mutually dependent on each other and through experiencing the differing strengths and weaknesses of the other team partners in stressful situations. It has been shown that the lessons learned in the training courses continue to have an effect back in the participants' daily routine, and communication at work is considerably improved.

The participants in wilderness experience courses retain their ties for years and even decades, and thus intensify the benefits of the networking needed in the company.

Towards the end of their first year of apprenticeship, Dräger takes its apprentices into the mountains of the Klein Walsertal valley on the border between Germany and Austria. In the two weeks they are there, they get to know what teamwork really means and how strong the individual is in the group. During their outdoor activities each participant has the opportunity to get to know his or her limits and either accept them or do something about it. Safety and confidence are always given top priority here. 'Outward bound' is an important module for each apprentice in personality formation.

There have been sporting activities at Dräger since as long ago as 1937. It started at that time with football and athletics and today there are twenty-five sporting activities to choose from, with 1,050 people signed up. In-house sporting activities have many positive effects on the working climate: barricades and barriers between colleagues are broken down, communications within units and even across departmental, hierarchical and subgroup divides are improved. In addition, they are good for the health of staff and forge powerful 'networks'.

Dräger also looks after retired and long-service staff. There is a group made up of former Dräger employees, the Dräger Seniors, who meet regularly for various activities. In this way, the bonds between them and Drägerwerk are kept alive and the social structure is strengthened: information is exchanged about work at Dräger, new friendships can be easily made and loneliness in old age can be countered. In addition, Dräger employees who have worked for the company for particularly long periods of time are honoured when they celebrate their twenty-fifth or fortieth anniversary.

Business excellence system: comprehensive quality management

Total quality management (TQM) represents the idea that quality control cannot be limited to installing a 'quality controller' at the end of the production chain to check the quality of the end result. What is needed is for the concept of quality to permeate the entire organisation – from the second the raw materials are delivered to the moment the final product leaves the plant. To implement this idea at Dräger, there is the business excellence system, better known by its acronym *BEST. BEST* promotes the continuous improvement of all products, services and processes, including all staff and employees, and leads to growing customer satisfaction and improved business results. *BEST* is Dräger's road to TQM. The degree of maturity of the units under review is assessed by *BEST* reviews analysing business excellence and highlighting scope for improvement. Experienced managers from the upper level of management and from all sectors within the business units and companies of the Dräger Group at home and abroad are employed as reviewers. Crucially important here is the fact that reviewers not only conduct interviews in their own departments but also write reviews across business unit boundaries. This permits an exchange of experience between the companies and all sectors of the business units worldwide as well as benchmarking within the Group. By virtue of the Dräger Group's gearing to the European Business Excellence Model of the European Foundation for Quality Management (EFQM), it is also possible to establish benchmarks with other European companies. In addition, more detailed assessment can be attained thanks to the EFQM model: a holistic analysis of all processes and improvement activities can be made.

SOCIAL PARTNERSHIP

As well as flexible working-time schemes, childcare is an important factor in striking the right work–life balance – between the need to earn a living and the desire to have a family – to retain highly qualified mothers, for example, in the service of the company. This is one of the reasons why the Executive Board at Dräger has actively supported an all-day, all-year-round facility near the Dräger plant to look after children aged 1 to 6. The company kindergarten, called Kunterbunte Kinderkiste e.V., which celebrated its tenth anniversary in 2003, is a model project initiated by a Dräger working group – consisting mostly of women – seeking to achieve a better work–life balance. This women's group was brought into being by the chief personnel officer with the aim of developing measures for an improved work–life balance.

In addition to the state pension, Dräger pays its staff a company pension after a certain number of years' service – at the latest from the age of 65. Over and above this, Dräger gives its staff the opportunity to make their own personal contribution towards their retirement pension.

From 2005 each employee will receive the promise of an annual contribution payment from the company: to implement this, a personal 'pension account' will be opened for each employee with an annual statement of account. These payments will depend upon the income of the employee and will be index-linked. Employers' contributions and any extra voluntary contributions by the employee will flow into this pension account. The capital thus accumulated will earn interest. When the time comes, a disability pension, retirement pension or surviving dependants' pension will be calculated on the basis of the accumulated capital. Special one-off payments into this pension account can also be made (without deductions for taxes and social security contributions) to boost the provision for a retirement pension. To make this considerable improvement to the retirement pension possible, the EPS, a voluntary profit-sharing payment, was made for the last time in 2005 for 2004, and after the financial year 2005 this was transformed into the company's contribution to the employee's pension account.

Which people play key roles in your country? Which names should one know?

The following people play an important role in German HRM: Ludwig Georg Braun, President of the Deutscher Industrie- und Handelskammertag (German association of chambers of commerce and industry); Dr Dieter Hundt, President of the Bundesverband der Deutschen Arbeitgeberverbände (BDA) (Confederation of German employers' associations); Michael Sommer, chairman of the Deutscher Gewerkschaftsbund (DGB) (Federation of German trade unions).

Last but not least we should mention the board members of DGFP: Günter Fleig (DaimlerChrysler AG), Stefan Lauer (Deutsche Lufthansa AG), Dr Juliane Wiemerslage (Deutsche Bank AG), Dr Peter Lütke-Bornefeld (GenRe Kölnische Rückversicherungs-Gesellschaft AG), Prof. Heinz Fischer (Fachhochschule Pforzheim), Stefan Dräger (DrägerWerk AG), Prof. Dr Claus E. Heinrich (SAP AG), Wulf Meier (Allianz Versicherungs AG, Dresdner Bank AG), Zygmunt Mierdorf (Metro AG), Dr Gerhard Rübling (TRUMPF Werkzeugmaschinen GmbH und Co. KG), Prof. Dr Christian Scholz (University of Saarland).

References

Ackermann, Karl-Friedrich (1987): Konzeptionen des strategischen Personalmanagements für die Unternehmenspraxis, in: Helmut Glaubrecht/ Ernst Zander (eds): Humanität in Personalpolitik und Personalführung, Freiburg, pp. 39–68.

Backes-Gellner, Uschi/Lazear, Edward/Wolff, Birgitta (2001): Personalökonomie. Fortgeschrittene Anwendungen für das Management, Stuttgart.

Berthel, Jürgen (1979): Personal-management. Grundzüge für Konzeptionen betrieblicher Personalarbeit, Stuttgart.

Cascio, Wayne F./Awad, Elias M. (1981): Human Resource Management, Reston, Va.

Deutsche Gesellschaft für Personalführung e.V. (ed.) (2001): Personalcontrolling in der Praxis, Schriftenreihe der DGFP, 62, Stuttgart.

—— (ed.) (2002a): Herausforderung Personalmanagement. Auf dem Weg zu professionellen Standards. Ergebnisse des Arbeitskreises "Personalfunktion der Zukunft", Schriftenreihe der DGFP, 65, Frankfurt/Main.

—— (ed.) (2002b): Erfolgreiches Personalmanagement im M&A-Prozess, Schriftenreihe der DGFP, 67, Bielefeld.

—— (ed.) (2004): Wertorientiertes Personalmanagement. Ein Beitrag zum Unternehmenserfolg. Konzeption – Durchführung – Unternehmensbeispiele, Schriftenreihe der DGFP, 70, Bielefeld.

Drumm, Hans Jürgen (1989): Personalwirtschaftslehre, Berlin.

—— (2005): Personalwirtschaft, 5th edn, Berlin, Heidelberg.

Fischer, Guido (1962): Politik der Betriebsführung, Stuttgart.

Gaugler, Eduard/Huber, Karl H./Rummel, Christoph (1974): Betriebliche Personalplanung. Eine Literaturanalyse, Göttingen.

Gaugler, Eduard/Weber, Wolfgang (1976): Einführung in das betriebliche Personalwesen: Grundlagen der Personalarbeit, Wiesbaden.

Goossens, Franz (1966): Personalleiter-Handbuch. Kompendium des betrieblichen Personal- und Sozialwesens, 4th edn, München.

Hasenack, Wilhelm (1961): Mensch im Betrieb. Inwieweit kann oder muss die Betriebswirtschaftslehre den Menschen in ihre Untersuchungen einbeziehen?, in: Zeitschrift für Betriebswirtschaft, 31: 577–96.

Hax, Karl (1969): Personalpolitik und Mitbestimmung, Köln, Opladen.

Heidecker, Michael (2003): Wertorientiertes Human Capital Management. Zur Steigerung des Unternehmenswertes durch die Personalarbeit, Wiesbaden.

Huselid, Mark A./Jackson, Susan E./Schuler, Randall S. (1997): Technical and strategic human resource management effectiveness as determinants of firm performance, in: Academy of Management Journal, 40(1): 171–88.

Kräkel, Matthias (2000): Delegation and strategic compensation in tournaments, discussion paper 17/2000, University of Bonn.

Krell, Gertraude (2003): Die Ordnung der 'Humanressourcen' als Ordnung der Geschlechter, in: Richard Weiskopf (ed.): Menschenregierungskünste. Anwendungen poststrukturalistischer Analyse auf Management und Organisation, Opladen, pp. 65–90.

Legge, Karen (1995): Human Resource Management, Basingstoke.

Macharzina, Klaus/Oechsler, Walter A. (1977): Personalmanagement, 1, Wiesbaden.

.de

Matiaske, Wenzel/Nienhüser, Werner (2004): Sinnprovinzen in der Personalwissenschaft – Befunde einer empirischen Untersuchung, in: Zeitschrift für Personalforschung 18(2): 117–38.

Miller, Karen L./Woodruff, David (1997): Lean, mean: and …German? Hard-driving managers are forging a new business culture, in: Business Week, 6/1997: 22–3.

Nell-Breuning, Oswald von (1950): Der Mensch im Betrieb, in: Zeitschrift für Betriebswirtschaft, 20: 257–66.

Neuberger, Oswald (1995): Mikropolitik: Der alltägliche Aufbau und Einsatz von Macht in Organisationen, Stuttgart.

—— (1999): Mobbing, 3th edn, München, Mering.

Nicklisch, Heinrich (1922): Wirtschaftliche Betriebslehre, Stuttgart.

Oechsler, Walter A. (1985): Personal und Arbeit. Einführung in die Personalwirtschaft, München.

Potthoff, Erich/Trescher, Karl (1986): Controlling in der Personalwirtschaft, Berlin, New York.

Sadowski, Dieter (2002): Personalökonomie und Arbeitspolitik, Stuttgart.

Sadowski, Dieter/Junkes, Joachim/Lindenthal, Sabine (2001): Labour Co-determination and Corporate Governance in Germany, Trier.

Schein, Edgar H. (1985): Organisational Culture and Leadership. A Dynamic View, San Francisco, etc.

Scholz, Christian (1982): Zur Konzeption einer strategischen Personalplanung, in: Zeitschrift für betriebliche Forschung, 34: 979–94.

—— (1989): Personalmanagement – Informationsorientierte und verhaltenstheoretische Grundlagen, München.

—— (2000): Personalmanagement. Informationsorientierte und verhaltenstheoretische Grundlagen, 5th edn, München.

—— (2003): Spieler ohne Stammplatzgarantie. Darwiportunismus in der neuen Arbeitswelt, Weinheim.

—— (2004): Human Ressourcen Management, in: Georg Schreyögg/Axel von Werder (eds): Handwörterbuch Unternehmensführung und Organisation, 4th edn, Stuttgart, pp. 428–40.

Scholz, Christian/Stein, Volker/Bechtel, Roman (2004): Human Capital Management. Wege aus der Unverbindlichkeit, München, Unterschleißheim.

Schuler, Randall S./Jackson, Susan E. (1996): Human Resource Management, 6th edn, St Paul.

Staehle, Wolfgang H. (1980): Management. Eine verhaltenswissenschaftliche Perspektive, München.

Tichy, Noel M./Fombrun, Charles J./Devanna, Mary A. (1982): Strategic human resource management, in: Sloan Management Review, 23(2): 47–61.

Von Eckardstein, Dudo/Schnellinger, Franz (1978): Betriebliche Personalpolitik, 3rd edn, München.

Wächter, Hartmund/Stengelhofen, Theo (1995): Germany, in: Ingrid Brunstein (ed.): Human Resource Management in Western Europe, Berlin, New York, pp. 89–112.

Wallace, Charles P. (2004): What's right with Germany, in: Time Europe, 26 July.

Weber, Wolfgang (1985): Betriebliche Weiterbildung. Empirische Analyse betrieblicher und individueller Entscheidungen über Weiterbildung, Stuttgart.

Wunderer, Rolf (1992): Von der Personaladministration zum Wertschöpfungs-Center. Vision, Konzeption, Realisierung unternehmerischer Personalarbeit, in: Die Betriebswirtschaft, 52: 201–15.

Wunderer, Rolf/Küpers, Wendelin (2003): Demotivation – Remotivation: Wie Leistungspotenziale freigesetzt und reaktiviert werden können, Neuwied.

.de

The authors

Dr Christian Scholz (scholz@orga.uni-sb.de), full Chair Professor of Business Administration since 1986, specialising in organisational behaviour, HRM, and information science, Saarland University, Saarbrücken, Germany. Director of the Saarland University MBA School Europa-Institut; Honorary Professor in HRM at the University of Vienna. Research focus on strategic HRM, virtual corporations, internationalisation research. Major publications: *Personalmanagement* (5th edn 2000); *Spieler ohne Stammplatzgarantie. Darwiportunismus in der neuen Arbeitswelt* (2003), *Human Capital Management* (2004).

Dr Hans Böhm (boehm@dgfp.de), Deutsche Gesellschaft für Personalführung e.V., Executive Director since 1992. Member of the Executive Committee (1992–2007), President (1995–7), and Secretary General (2003–7) of the European Association for Personnel Management (EAPM), member of the Board of the World Federation of Personnel Management Associations (WFPMA) until 2007. Author, co-author and editor of several books on HRM. Executive director of the C.R. Poensgen Foundation (2004–6).

Ingo Gensch (info@dräger.com), Drägerwerk AG (1982–2005), Executive Board member responsible for HR at Drägerwerk AG (1984–2005). Chairman of the supervisory boards of Dräger Aerospace, Dräger Interservices, Dräger Synematic, Dräger Pro Tech and Dräger Electronics (1995–2003). Since 1992, member of the executive boards of NORDMETALL and Berufsgenossenschaft FuE and, since 2000, member of the supervisory board of the private University Nordakademie. Several publications on HRM.

The authors wish to thank Univ.-Prof. Dr Volker Stein (University of Siegen) for his valuable comments.

7 HRM in Hungary: from party functionaries to business managers

György Kővári/Pál Bóday/János Bogdán

Hungary: in a nutshell

In this chapter you will learn:

- that the labour market processes, the globalisation of competition and the characteristics of micro-level adaptation processes are some of the most important environmental challenges;

- that HR academia in Hungary was influenced by the transformation of the social, economic and political system which diversified the demands on specialists and organisations; and

- that to implement Borsodi's strategy, to have the best people in all positions at all levels, many integrated policies and procedures have been developed throughout the company.

Capital:	Budapest
Area (sq km):	93,030 (land 92,340; water 690)
EU membership:	since 2004
Population:	9,981,334
Languages:	Hungarian
Ethnic groups (in percentages):	Hungarian 92.3, Roma 1.9, other or unknown 5.8 (2001)
Gross domestic product:	172.7 billion USD (2006)
Workforce (in percentages):	4.2 million: agriculture and forestry 5.5, industry 33.3, services 61.2 (2003)
Export commodities:	machinery and equipment, other manufactures, food products, raw materials, fuels and electricity

1 BACKGROUND: THE PERSPECTIVES OF HRM

This chapter relies on theoretical considerations and research findings as well as on practical experience, while placing emphasis upon the main trend in the development of HRM. What it sets out to show is the strategic role of HRM and the redefinition of the philosophy of management, which are major tools for securing and maintaining competitive advantage and limiting operational risks.

In the nearly two decades since it was introduced, strategic HRM has given rise to heated disputes both in scientific journals and among practising professionals. Even those who do not treat strategic HRM as a trendy synonym for traditional personnel management (PM) have clashed with others, depending on whether they emphasise the 'resource' side or the 'human factor' side of the expression.

Supporters of the 'resource' theory take the view that, like other resources, human resources must be obtained at the cheapest possible price, harnessed efficiently and developed and utilised profitably. This approach can be linked to the stratification of the labour market (primary and secondary markets) and to the typology of flexibility (training, mobility, organisation, wages). This kind of approach to flexibility is a strategic answer to the difficulties that management is faced with in hiring or laying off staff. The 'resource-oriented' approach can be connected to theories of organisational strategy, 'product lifecycle' or organisational growth.

Conversely, in the approach emphasising the 'human factor', the human resource is assigned an exceptional role due to its ability to create wealth. Without it, no other resource is able to generate assets. It thus follows that the key to strategic initiatives lies in the knowledge, commitment and creativity of human beings. This approach can be linked to an interpretation of the organisation as a unified team in competition with other teams, where the most important 'factor of success' is the self-fulfilment of 'players' in the organisation, the development of people's knowledge and abilities. Behind this approach are the theories of organisational development rooted in behavioural science.

Regardless of whether the human factor's outstanding role is based on the paradigm of human capital as a strategic resource or on people's ability to create wealth through their knowledge, commitment and creativity, HR experts now have more responsibilities than in the past and different responsibilities in terms of planning, decision-making and management.

In the field of planning, the emphasis is increasingly laid on reducing market uncertainties, establishing alternative strategies and supervising the implementation of policies and action programmes. In the fields of decision-making and action, the yardsticks of competence are not only time and strategic thinking but also the performance and coordination of the roles of the specialist and the internal service provider and adviser. Ultimately, the effectiveness of HRM depends on organisational assets being increased, the systemic relations used to serve strategy being strengthened and the synergic effect of HR systems being harnessed.

The economic appreciation of human factors, and hence the strategy-forming, system-developing and system-maintaining function of those factors and their function as internal service provider and adviser, is accompanied, on the one hand, by the renewal of management philosophy and, on the other hand, by a shift in the role of HR managers.

What is typical of your country regarding the country itself (its culture, people, etc.) and its economy?

Because of accession to the European Union in 2005 there has been a sharp rise in wages and living standards since 2001.

As to culture, Hungarian hospitality is legendary. Nevertheless, certain rules should be observed when building (business) relationships with Hungarian people. In Hungary, a firm handshake is customary upon greeting one another. When addressing business partners (and adults in general) titles and surnames should be used. Closer friends use first names. Where a man and a woman are involved, it is the woman who decides on the use of first names.

It is customary for Hungarians to celebrate 'saints' days' or name days in a big way with colleagues and friends. A card and a small gift are common for name days.

Because Hungary used to belong to the Austro-Hungarian Empire, there are many shared traditions. For example, Hungarians listen to Austrian folk music, celebrate Christmas in the same way as Austrians, and have assimilated German or Austrian words into their language. In the other direction, Hungarian words have found their way into the Austrian language and the Austrian *Palatschinken* (*palacsinta* in Hungarian, 'pancakes' in English) originally stems from Hungary.

ENVIRONMENTAL CHALLENGES: ORGANISATIONAL RESPONSES

As far as environmental factors are concerned, we will look at labour market processes, the globalisation of competition and the characteristics of micro-level adaptation processes. Then we will tackle the productivity of intellectual work as the engine of economic growth.

Our postulate is that organisational phenomena can only be interpreted in the context of interaction between the organisation and the environment. The economic appreciation of human factors and the advance of transformative technologies and knowledge-intensive sectors open up new perspectives for strategic initiative and competitiveness.

Labour market processes

One of the characteristic features of the current and future equilibrium of the Hungarian labour market, one which distinguishes it from the labour markets of the advanced market economies, is that employment and unemployment do not change in inverse proportion to one another (Timár 1994; István 1997). Paradoxically, the number of persons registered unemployed and the number of those employed can decrease simultaneously. In the 1990s, after the political transition, a wide range of jobs were lost and employers and employees left the labour market en masse, significantly swelling the ranks of the economically inactive population. As a result, the rate of dependants per 100 income earners rose from 98 in 1989 to 157 in 1998. The low rate of employment – in other words, the unfavourable income earner–dependant ratio – has been an obstacle to higher living standards ever since, and undermined the government's efforts to meet welfare and social commitments.

Another characteristic of our labour market is that, in spite of the economic recession, productivity has risen dynamically since as long ago as 1992. Although this counter-cyclical development in productivity has improved the domestic and international competitiveness of viable companies, a price has had to be paid in terms of a further deterioration in the chances of a rise in employment.

Finally, there are the alarmingly high ratios of long-term and juvenile unemployed. This labour market trend is in line with trends in western Europe, with the significant difference that the stream of people returning from unemployment to employment in the domestic labour market is a great deal smaller. Among employees who lose their job, those with the worst chances mostly leave the labour market and stop 'distorting' the jobless figures.

The keys to widening employment are economic growth stimulating more demand for labour and institutional changes encouraging and enhancing labour market flexibility.

As far as labour market forecasts are concerned, while 200,000 of today's 600,000 professionals will leave the labour market by 2010, the fast quantitative growth of higher education means that 500,000 fresh graduates can be expected to take their place. To prevent erosion of the higher education reserve base, bearing in mind that it has already diminished to just over half its former size, two-thirds of secondary school-leavers will need to pass their school-leaving examinations. This is the greatest challenge facing primary and secondary education in the forthcoming years. Returning the focus to higher education, the virtual

195

deficits and surpluses anticipated will be particularly marked in college education. This is a result of outdated educational structures. Unless conditions change, there is a risk that the efficiency of college education, the utilisation of human capital and the employment prospects of certain groups of professionals will worsen.

Globalisation of competition

One of the main factors fuelling uncertainty over the future is the globalisation of competition (Lauter 1998). Essentially, globalisation is the fast, cross-border spread of production, financial, sales and R&D operations, obeying solely the logic of competition and seeking only the highest possible return on the capital invested. In other words, corporations thinking in worldwide strategic terms will take value-chain functions to wherever they can be performed with maximum efficiency to produce the best possible results. Although globalisation of competition as yet concerns only a small minority of companies, those companies determine the way the global economy works. While new and promising development prospects are opening up for related sectors and enterprises, globalisation is accompanied by painful economic (think of regional financial crises), social and environmental shocks. Rapid technological development will, on the one hand, trigger mechanisms that will level out wages in global competition; on the other, as more labour markets enter the international arena, it will widen the economic and income gap between regions and countries and at the same time maintain structural unemployment.

In the context of ever more globalised competition, heightened productivity remains the engine of economic growth, but the productivity of intellectual work is increasingly becoming the key to growth. This is where countries like Hungary, which is relatively poor in natural resources, fuels and physical capital, have a chance to catch up, finding comparative advantages if they can link up with the mainstream of the world economy, develop their human capital effectively and utilise it sensibly.

Technology and market competition require new forms of work, and management organisation and a new corporate philosophy. This is the reason why more and more attention today is devoted to the problem of corporate governance, expressing the institutionalisation of the relationship between owners and management, embodying the general endeavours and interests of corporate management. The different models of corporate governance characterise not only the ownership structure, but also the motivation structure, the mechanism of communication, the code of patterns of business behaviour and the relationship between organisation and environment.

.hu

As the advancement of Anglo-American capital plays a decisive part in the globalisation of competition, the spread of Anglo-American-style corporate governance is more and more conspicuous.

The main protagonist of the Anglo-American type of corporate governance is the stockholder, whose objective function is the maximisation of return on equity. In contrast to this, in the European (German) model, the expectations of the different stakeholders penetrate corporate governance, which makes the European model more rigid when restructuring but at the same time more socially sensitive. The dilemma, well known to many companies operating in the Hungarian market, arises when the Anglo-American type of corporate governance tries to make progress in a German-style legal and institutional environment. Essentially, the challenge lies in combining the advantages of the two models while maintaining the ability to operate and minimizing unfavourable side effects.

Micro-level adaptation

The problem discussed in the previous section can be amply illustrated by micro-level adaptation processes and their consequences for the labour market. The ultimate reason for micro-level adaptation processes is that anticipated costs are always much easier to predict reliably than future income. One time-honoured method used to cut costs and applied in all other operations vital for survival is downsizing, a form of streamlining which always involves mass layoffs. 'Re-engineering', by contrast, which seeks to transform processes in a sensible way, results in renewed competitive strength and a vigorous upswing, despite all the conflicts implied in the accompanying layoffs.

> The Anglo-American model of corporate governance is characterised by large-scale layoffs and large-scale job creation. In the European model, on the other hand, the labour market is regulated by strict rules and social constraints.

In circumstances where companies do not lay off employees and job creation remains low, so those with a stable job receive decent pay and fringe benefits but, when unemployment rates are high, then the long-term unemployed and career starters will make up a high proportion of those out of work. Provision for the unemployed is mainly considered the responsibility of the welfare state. The service providers of the welfare system, even in our country, are financed by relatively high taxes. On the other hand, taxes increase labour costs and weaken the international competitiveness of companies, further worsening labour market performance. In Japan, the corporate governance model is also interwoven with various syndicates. Large corporations postpone layoffs as long as they can, preferring to finance the cost of internal labour reserves at the expense of profits.

From an analysis of strategic responses to the necessity to compete, it can be concluded that adapting viable companies builds on two pillars: on structural and cultural changes and on the development of human capital. This can be observed in Figure 7.1.

197

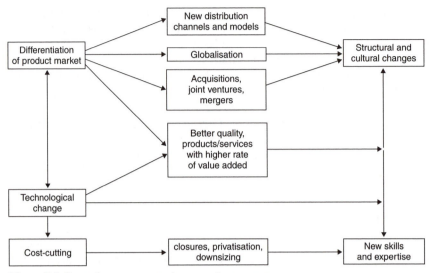

Figure 7.1 Strategic responses to the necessity to compete

COST–BENEFIT-BASED DECISION-MAKING

All this seems to confirm our paradigm that knowledge, experience and skills are a form of capital, part of an organisation's assets, one of an organisation's strategic resources. The development and maintenance of that resource are costly, requiring investments by both the individual and the organisation. Managing these human resources calls for cost–benefit-based decisions. Comparing expenditures and gains is necessary because it helps managers to plan and reach decisions. Moreover, it serves to assist management in appraising how efficiently the different parts of the organisation have been developing and utilising human resources.

Human resource planning may be useful to an executive management in various ways in the process of creating a strategy as well as implementing it: (a) exploring the opportunities and hazards in the environment; (b) analysing organisational characteristics – strengths and weaknesses; and (c) action programmes and strategic operations.

From a budgetary viewpoint, it makes a real difference what kind of recruitment and induction policy is applied in staffing a company; what cost-effective alternatives exist to meet current and anticipated labour requirements, how internal (training) costs compare with external (recruitment) costs. And an organisation faced with several possible candidates will want to choose the candidate who will be of the greatest economic value to the company in the future. The planning, recruitment, training, performance appraisal and compensation system embedded in the business strategy impacts on human capital as an asset and thus on the value of the organisation as a whole. Without economic appraisal of human resources, incentives to encourage attainment of strategic goals and the promotion of staff within the organisational hierarchy would be 'working blind'. It must not be forgotten that a person's economic value to the organisation lies in his/her productivity and promotability.

In the cost-calculation system of cost–benefit analysis, a distinction can be made between the investment costs (recruitment, selection, induction, training) and current costs (wages, fringe benefits) of employment. As regards the recouping of investment costs, the job stability of workers is a factor of key importance. The wastage rate shows the number of persons quitting the company compared with the current staff, regardless of whether they will be replaced or not. The wastage rate can be used to compute the length of time a recruit can be expected to stay with the company. Wastage analysis is also necessary to determine the rate at which investment costs need to be written down. The average length of time recruits are expected to stay with the company can be taken as the lifespan of the 'asset' embodied in the investments. The analysis has a dual objective: on the one hand, numerical quantification of the action alternatives, on the other, assessment of the efficiency of HR activities or supervision of budgetary activities. Investment cost is the sum total of actual past expenses. 'Replacement cost' is the gain sacrifice that replacing staff would currently cost. 'Opportunity cost' is what the same labour capacity could have achieved if it had been put to the most profitable alternative use.

⊞ .hu

The essential difference between traditional personnel management and strategic HRM is a matter of approach. In the latter, HRM is the duty and responsibility of every single manager, not just of the HR unit.

HR activities such as training, motivation, recruitment and selection are not appraised as service for production or updating methods; they are based on achieving goals laid down in the business strategy.

💡.hu

FROM TRADITIONAL ORGANISATION TOWARDS KNOWLEDGE ORGANISATION

Transformative technologies like informatics and other state-of-the-art techniques and methods increasingly found in business practice, such as controlling, process re-engineering or benchmarking, have also restructured and redefined the functions of HRM. HR activities are supported by expert systems, and jobs formerly done by specialists are today performed by modern computers using fantastic algorithms. Furthermore, they provide interactive solutions that make some service and consultancy functions accessible to employees and business partners in a self-service system. Expert systems supporting HRM and 'digitalisation of paperwork' (correspondence, tendering, completing questionnaires, newsletters, etc.) increase efficiency and reinforce the earlier tendency for HR experts with a sense for business to belong increasingly to the group of persons shaping organisational strategy and to become key figures in crisis management. On the other hand, organisational innovation is driven more and more by the trainability of staff, organisational learning and the collection, distribution and sensible utilisation of knowledge.

The essence of the new paradigm shift is as follows: in 'knowledge capital', the emphasis shifts to 'know-how' and human capital encompasses trainability and competences as well as technical expertise and experience.

In the knowledge organisation, the success of management is measured by the increase of not only 'tangible' assets but also 'intangible' assets. Decisions are governed jointly by the cost–benefit principle and the principle of competences. The development of human capital and the efficiency of management turn mainly on how successfully the company is able to collect, disseminate, store and utilise knowledge. At the same time, human economic value is determined not by productivity and promotability potential alone, but also by trainability and competence (asset-creating ability). In line with the shift in focus of HRM, strategy formation is now joined by change management and competence development. Strategy, of course, focuses on value-added factors, and in doing so, pursues one of the most important aims of value-based management: to make knowledge transfer fast and efficient. The significance and professional authority of HRM is secured by the extent to which it can contribute to strategic initiatives and to the acquisition and maintenance of competitive advantages. So the question that arises is as follows: What are the major tasks and environmental challenges that organisations need to face? What are we doing to address them? What can we do to address them? What initiatives can we come up with to find the solution?

Managers need a new approach to enable them to shift from convention to adaptation, from long-term planning to problem-solving, from programme orientation to holistic attitude. Strategic HRM transforms the management system. It does not mean, however, that everything needs to be changed. Many things that exist are rational, efficient and may be suitable for the organisation. Attention must be paid to it lest 'the more changes the better' attitude gets as destructive as the attitude characterised by obstinate resistance to change. Systems are in a constant process of transformation, like clay's ever-changing shape in the potter's hands. What makes the situation different is that, unlike the potter, masters of management do not need to bake the clay to make it solid; on the contrary, they are supposed to keep it soft and malleable. Such are 'open' systems: they are in a direct mutual relationship with their environment.

Auditing of HRM has developed in recent years. In the early days, efficiency indicators (fluctuation, wages, fringe benefits, training costs) were examined separately, but later top managers of companies seeking to improve their competitiveness began showing an ever more intense interest in the processes and relationships behind research findings. They were no longer satisfied with counting the costs of recruitment and selection or training, they also wanted to know whether these were only expenditure or whether they could also be seen as investment, likely to produce a yield. Eventually, the problem of auditing HRM was solved by the headway made in HR control, and especially the strategic 'balanced scorecard' (Kaplan/Norton 1992), an ever more indispensable means of forming and implementing a strategy: the quantitative and qualitative aspects of knowledge capital and competences have been organically incorporated into 'management accountancy' and into the strategic thinking of executive management.

It was not until half-way through the 1990s that there began an acceleration of the process which resulted in traditional personnel and labour functions being replaced by an integrated organisation with an empowered and competent leadership capable of HRM. Within barely a decade, the application of state-of-the-art methods led to spectacular results in the private sector, mainly due to the large-scale influx of foreign capital. In the public sector, however, the breakthrough has still not happened.

The overview of the shift in roles and its implications cannot be complete without a review of HR manager competence requirements. It is obvious that, compared with the earlier situation, proficiency in change management methods and the techniques for measuring the return rates of different types of capital, as well as the role of general business and international or multicultural knowledge, preparedness and experience, will grow in significance. If the development of organisations 'grows out' of the traditional assortment of personnel managers' roles, the environment will force the emergence of managers equipped with the competences necessary for strategic HRM, while on the other hand organisations will be able to produce them.

What are you and other Hungarian people extraordinarily proud of with respect to HRM?

Appreciation of the human factor in the economy and the increased significance of education as an investment in human capital have a common root: human resources mean innovation. Nevertheless, they also mean the highest operational risk.

EAPM AFFILIATE: ORSZÁGOS HUMÁNPOLITIKAI EGYESÜLET

In the wake of the economic, political and social regime change set in motion in the late 1980s and early 1990s, personnel management in Hungary has undergone a substantive change in virtually every respect. In the period since that time – with some credit due, perhaps, to the Hungarian Association for Human Resource Management (Országos Humánpolitikai Egyesület (OHE)) founded in 1990 – we have succeeded in reaching the point where a significant proportion of companies are already engaging in a level of activity on a par with that of Europe. Naturally, the economy itself has played the largest role in this achievement. Specifically, much is owed to the fact that a significant proportion of Hungary's economy is in the hands of international business organisations whose HR staff have brought their own system of professional requirements.

HISTORICAL ANTECEDENTS

Unless they are given a brief introduction to the past, professionals who have always worked in a context of market economy conditions cannot possibly grasp the present state of HRM in Hungary.

In the initial phase of the socialist economy, political factors played a clearly dominant role in the grooming of party functionaries. The main task was to assess the reliability of non-manual workers – specifically, this applied primarily to those in leadership positions – as well as their commitment to party policy (manual labourers were dealt with by the labour affairs section – thus the origin of a several-decades-long division in what is now an essentially integrated field). As this task was essentially carried out without the benefit of any objective criteria, no professional requirements were ever drawn up for those carrying out this activity. The sole requirement was that they should be politically reliable. This meant, at the same time, that this stratum was generally recruited from among unqualified people with good connections in the party and the home affairs ministry. As a result, functionaries were mistrustful of everyone else, while virtually everyone else lived in fear of them. This fear was perpetuated by the early destruction of careers. Another feature of this period was that, although the personnel director's superior in the hierarchy was the company director, for the most part he or she was actually required to report to the party and the organs of the home affairs ministry – sometimes even at the company director's expense.

After the 1956 revolution was crushed, the political situation was very much consolidated, and the role of the functionaries changed very little. This was reinforced by the fact that with the dissolution of the State Defence Authority a large number of staff gained leadership positions in personnel.

A more conspicuous change resulted from the New Economic Mechanism introduced in 1968, which increased the economic independence of state companies (the key sign of this being that it ended compulsory compliance with central planning at company level). As part of this change, certain professional components were already beginning to appear in personnel work, but the political component still remained – though doubtless with less emphasis. This was reflected in the fact that personnel work remained centrally regulated as late as 1990 (until the eve of the political regime change). A characteristic two-tier system took root during this regulation from the centre. From time to time, the party would draw up guidelines for its functionary-grooming policy (1967, 1973 and 1986) and these were more or less slavishly followed in resolutions on state personnel work passed by the Council of Ministers (1968, 1974 and 1987), which in turn were no less slavishly interpreted in the relevant 'executive' orders issued by the individual ministries. Although the regulations made a strong substantive shift towards professional components, the inspectorial role held by party organisations at various levels and their right to a voice in these matters were both continually asserted until the summer of 1990.

Significant among the professional components were selection, qualification, training and, as of 1987, evaluation of individual performance. The appearance and strengthening of these professional factors had a dual effect on personnel work. First, it drew continually on concepts from certain academic disciplines (e.g. psychology, labour law and andragogy). Second, workers in this field were beginning to receive institutionalised professional training as well as further training. As of 1985, the National Management Training Centre also launched a ten-week (300-hour) course on a trial basis replacing the former three-week courses. It concluded with students writing a dissertation. Based on experience from this experiment, training for personnel work was launched on a national scale in 1987, at both the secondary and tertiary levels. This was necessary in part because the resolution on this subject passed by the Council of Ministers in 1987 tied the filling of posts in personnel work to educational qualifications and the completion of such courses. In expanding professional training opportunities, universities opened up a new stage of development in which students could master the theoretical foundations underlying the field of human resources on both undergraduate and postgraduate courses.

There was spectacular development in terms of substance as well. Whereas knowledge of politics and related areas played a serious role early on, with professional knowledge being only of secondary importance, the tide turned in 1985, and as of 1987 the former was entirely excluded from the training. Naturally, the actual carrying out of personnel activity was not depoliticised to this extent, but for the most part acquiring professional knowledge based on western models greatly assisted students in deciding on their professional future.

As mentioned previously, the other part of human resources, manual labour, came within the purview of the apparatus for labour affairs, and proceeding from a power position of sorts, wage issues for all staff fell within their competence as well. As professional knowledge was necessary for those working in this field from the outset, the Labour Ministry had dealt with their training from the 1960s. The main emphasis in that training was placed on certain methodological subjects (e.g. statistics, work organisation, wage-setting techniques and labour management techniques), as well as more general knowledge subjects (e.g. sociology, psychology and management). Labour affairs enjoyed far greater prestige among companies (and thus among the general public) on a professional level, primarily due to its system of training, which had developed much earlier. However, the area of personnel enjoyed a more privileged position in the organisational structure. This is because central regulations placed the personnel director directly under the company director (general director), whereas the area of labour affairs fell under the deputy director for business affairs.

In 1987, the Council of Ministers passed a resolution in which the integration of the two areas – personnel work and labour affairs – was recommended. This sparked an unprecedented battle between the two fields. Although there were no doubt numerous positive examples as well, in the largest proportion of cases it was the personnel directors themselves who represented the main obstacles to integration since they believed that following a merger it would be workers in the area of labour affairs who would enjoy the greater prestige (one of the main components of which being the professional course they had completed). It was owing to these battles that integration proceeded very slowly indeed. The process was accelerated by the resolution passed by the Council of Ministers in 1990, which stated that the law on personnel work would no longer apply to the private sector. It should be noted that, as a result, a substantial number of business organisations believed that personnel work needed to be done away with. Significantly, this belief was fuelled in part by views shaped by the practice of the 1950s, which established personnel work as a sort of damaging, politically loaded activity. Managers who viewed the situation in its proper perspective naturally saw their task as combining personnel work with that of labour affairs, not as putting an end to the former.

In a few words, what would you say is the one fundamental strategic competitive advantage your country offers compared to others?

Because of its geographical location in central Europe, Hungary forms a hub between East and West. As such, it is currently becoming a logistics centre for international companies delivering products to neighbouring countries. Apart from logistics, we also note that international companies are relocating their research and development operations to Hungary.

THE CURRENT SITUATION

Training

From what has already been said, it is clear that Hungary has seen many years of ever expanding opportunities for those involved in human resources to receive professional training. If, in addition to this, we consider that the professional content of those training options was always based on US and western European practice, then it becomes apparent that there are numerous professionals working in the field today in Hungary whose theoretical training has provided a suitable foundation – even under real market economy conditions – for high-quality activity facilitating effective management. Naturally, we should also point out that training represents only one part of this bright picture – although it is, without a doubt, a very important one. At least as significant, certainly, is the fact that nearly one and a half decades have elapsed since the start of the regime change and this has provided an opportunity for a significant proportion of practitioners in this field to be replaced. Some earlier actors whose approach had ossified with time and who were unable to adjust to the changes simply left their posts (indeed left the labour market altogether) for demographic reasons, while others found their niche in other fields. A large proportion of those stepping into the outgoing practitioners' shoes have been young, comparatively recent graduates, often with a good knowledge of languages.

Aside from the educational opportunities accredited by the state, other professional forums have also facilitated such training – and will continue to do so in the future. Four types of event should be highlighted: conferences, special short courses, round table forums and international exchanges of expertise.

Conferences

Organised regularly since the second half of the 1980s, conferences first consisted primarily of lectures at which participants became familiar with specific interpretations of requirements from the centre as well as with the experiences of others. It was thus in 1991 that the OHE broke with tradition by organising a conference based on exchanges of expertise, where sufficient time was allotted to discussions following the individual lectures as well as to opportunities to learn about other participants' experiences. The association has followed this practice at national conferences it has staged since that time and continues to do so today. This probably explains why the conferences have been considered key events in the domestic HR field virtually since the beginning.

HR professionals receive their official training at universities. At the same time, in increasing professional skills it must always be borne in mind that lasting results can only be provided by practice-oriented forms built on firm foundations of principle and theory. Any extreme that leans in either direction does damage to this process. An overly academic approach produces professionals who are constantly thinking things over and generally incapable of reaching a decision,

205

while a narrowly practical approach without theoretical foundations or a logical system for support hinders recognition of a given situation, reduces flexibility, renders creativity impossible and ultimately represents the main stumbling-block to badly needed change.

Hungary boasts a number of training and consulting firms capable of arranging special events which achieve this goal. However, it should be noted that there are a number of HR consultants who feel that this process runs counter to their interests because they believe that a well-trained professional will have less need of professional advice. Looking at the situation from another angle, we must acknowledge, however, that, although a professional without know-how certainly needs expert advice, there is only a very slim chance that he or she would recognise this need, owing to this very lack of knowledge, and thus an equally slim chance that the need for consulting would even come to light. In contrast, a professionally well-prepared HR manager is fully aware of the fact that in order to do his or her work effectively he or she must make use of consulting services in the greatest variety of areas.

💡.hu

> It cannot be a goal of professional training to learn DIY. Instead, participants must be encouraged both to develop an outlook and to establish a foundation of knowledge and skills that enable them to strike a harmonious balance between tasks which may be carried out by themselves, by staff at their departments and by consultants.

This is the goal that the OHE set for itself when it founded the OHE Academy of Human Resource Management in 1998. This series of events provides participants with training which does not attempt to compete with the many hundreds of hours of courses offered at the various higher education institutions. On the contrary, its goal is to provide direct practical knowledge – something which higher education institutions can do only in an extremely restricted manner if at all – and to do so in such a way that it can be applied in everyday HR activity, adjusted for local conditions.

The series of events aims to achieve this goal by taking into consideration several aspects in combination: one general area is covered during each one-day event, which, in addition to a brief presentation and subsequent consultation and discussion, facilitates the practical introduction of the knowledge gained through the use of group problem-solving and situation exercises as well as through the completion of questionnaires. In order to guarantee interactivity, group size is restricted to twenty-five participants. Trainers for the individual events are noted members of the field: practitioners as well as consultants with a great deal of practical experience. They use course books and extracts from the professional literature as required to treat subject areas in the greatest possible depth and perspective. The Academy syllabus can be covered in four terms, treating five areas each term. Individual events are organised once every three weeks in Budapest. The OHE issues a certification of attendance to those who participate regularly throughout a term and a certificate of completion to those who finish the entire course.

Round table forums

The practice of holding round table forums (or round table conferences) is not a new one. The first such series of events was organised by the National Management Training Centre in 1985. Serving participants for over ten years until 1996, these forums featured brief introductory talks by experts on a given current topic, followed by an informal exchange of views on the topic, which also drew participants in.

These kinds of events are held by several firms today; however, interest in them appears to have dropped off. There are many who think that the main reason for this is that they cover only a single topic at a time and that, given the nature of this approach, such training is fundamentally unstructured. The time commitment for local residents exceeds half a day, while those who need to travel to the venue for the event must devote an entire day. Ever fewer people can spare the time for this kind of activity.

International exchanges of expertise

Interchanges were launched in 1984 by the National Management Training Centre in cooperation with the Deutsche Gesellschaft für Personalführung (DGFP, the German Association for Personnel Management). At the beginning, these annual gatherings saw ten German and ten Hungarian experts participating at alternating venues, where in addition to discussing general current issues they had the opportunity to learn about each other's specific practical work. While it was clear at the first gatherings that Hungarian participants were in much greater need of information, this became increasingly balanced at forums by the early 1990s – by then we were able to supply our German partners with useful information directly. In the second half of the 1990s, we took the decision with our German colleagues to expand the field of participants. We continue to alternate with them on the organisation and arrangement of venues, but each year since that time we have invited colleagues from Bulgaria, the Czech Republic, Poland, Slovakia and Slovenia. At the last event in autumn 2004 in Berlin, we also had Latvian guests.

These events have been arranged (and continue to be arranged) in numerous forms and at a variety of venues under the aegis of an increasing number of organisations. Those early years clearly proved that, in order to raise the level to an international standard as soon as possible in Hungary as well, it was necessary to establish an organisation with professional foundations, free from political and governmental influence, and it was in recognising this that the OHE was formed in May 1990. It is not the aim of the association to provide guidance from the centre for organisations carrying out such activities, but it does endeavour (and has managed in its work thus far) to be an authoritative organisation providing the field with service of the highest quality. From the very beginning, it received a great deal of assistance from the DGFP and, following its admission to the EAPM (European Association for Personal Management, June 1991), from organisations in numerous countries, in particular the British Institute of Personnel Management (IPM, now the CIPD) and the Austrian ÖPWZ.

Internet portals

In addition to this, HR professionals also receive assistance in other areas so that they may perform work of the highest possible standard. The latest channels include internet portals which provide a glimpse of the various areas of HR activity. There are also the conventional forms of assistance, such as company visits for exchanges of expertise, consulting provided by a variety of service providers (such as the OHE), as well as trade journals and magazines.

CONCLUSION: OPTIONS AND CHANCES

HR professionals avail themselves of these options to varying degrees. Some nearly always take advantage of the opportunities available, others never do. This partly explains why such a heterogeneous situation has developed in the Hungarian economy to date.

This is reflected in the fact that there are numerous enterprises applying HRM practices whose activity is clearly on a par with that of Europe, while elsewhere this work not only lacks strategic approaches, but cannot even really be described as professional work: the activity is limited to the simplest form of administration prescribed by law. The first group consists primarily of foreign-owned companies, though there are also a number of Hungarian companies that fit this description. At the other extreme are mostly small enterprises – though mid-sized enterprises are not rare either – where personnel issues are dealt with by the head of the firm, based on instinct, of course, with almost no professional foundation, and related administrative tasks are generally handled by underqualified staff.

In summary, it is clear that in the nearly one and a half decades since the political, economic and social regime change, what was once personnel work/grooming of functionaries with no small amount of politics in the background has been replaced by HRM built on professional foundations. It is safe to say that no other field has undergone such major changes in this period. These extremely significant substantive changes were naturally accompanied by key personnel changes as well. Practitioners in the field were only able to satisfy the fundamentally new requirements brought about by these changes if their training was also radically revised in both substance and form. This was greatly pushed forward by the international firms that entered the Hungarian economy and brought know-how and new expectations with them. What must also be acknowledged is the role of the OHE, which is as old as the regime change and which with its conferences, training, exchanges of expertise and trade journals – and in so many other ways as well – has endeavoured to provide assistance to help turn the Hungarian personnel work of the 1990s into HRM for the dawn of the twenty-first century fully in line with European standards.

What is your advice for a foreign firm entering your country's market? What should managers especially care about and, what is more, be aware of?

One thing that should be noted, especially by companies that are highly customer oriented or those that are 'customers' themselves and depend on local supplier companies is that, for most Hungarian companies, customer acquisition is far more important than customer service.

.hu

HR ACADEMIA: A REVIEW OF HR RESEARCH AND TRAINING

The economic significance of human resources has been emerging in economic thinking for a century now.

Under the impact of the big oil crisis and the stagflation of the 1980s there was growing awareness of the fact that development and utilisation of human resources were the most important conditions for continuous adaptation.

Scientific management versus behavioural sciences

Research results and practical experience both show that the rationalist perceptions of 'scientific management' as well as the human concepts of behavioural sciences are unduly abstract and one-sided. Empirical studies indicate that 'scientific management' has been entrapped by overspecialisation, strict control of standardised working methods and omnipotent prestige patterns. The meticulous and continuous improvement of a centralised formal organisation is expected to result in better performance and emphasised incentives for performance by keeping in mind the instrumental nature of the employee role.

Excessive reliance on specialisation and standardisation tends to restrain performance growth and often meets with resistance from workers. As a consequence, it reduces the problem-solving and innovative abilities of organisations while mobilising but a fraction of available 'skills' for solving non-routine tasks.

The tendency of 'human relations' led to the inclusion of human needs into the 'programme for transforming the working environment and jobs'. It separated fulfilment of work expectations not only from technological organisational conditions, potentialities and the market environment, but also from the varying aspirations of different employee groups. However, it called attention to the motivating role of decentralisation, job enrichment and participation.

As well as making use of the achievements of the 'two schools' above, the 'human capital' concept has aggregated the basic principles of human resource management. For the time being, the key to improving efficiency lies in high-quality, reasonably allocated resources (including human resources), which obviously assume proportional returns on investment in these resources.

The Hungarian labour market

In developed market economies the main force driving the adaptation of the labour market to the changing environment and the structural changes of demand is the flexibility of companies themselves. The ways companies adapt are by:

- reducing cost levels, including specific labour costs;
- adjusting staffing level and hirings to growth patterns;

- making more use of external labour market competition and unequal opportunities for the sake of internal labour markets;
- making greater use of flexible and part-time forms of employment and business partnership relations;
- defining job descriptions less rigidly and restructuring value-creating processes;
- innovation, organisational and personnel development; and
- decentralisation of collective bargaining.

Before the systemic transformation in Hungary took place, the behaviour of enterprises in the labour market and their wage policies were characterised by accumulated labour reserves and competition in the acquisition of additional workforce. The main tools included efforts (a) to raise corporate wage levels at the highest rates possible; (b) to increase staff by integrating smaller economic organisations operating in their environment; and (c) to stabilise informal bargaining processes with key employees and to win their loyalty.

Comparative analyses have revealed that the 1980s saw no essential change in the basic features that had distinguished the labour market policies of Hungarian enterprises from those of the market economies before.

- The labour demands of enterprises were not sensitive to wages. Wages were primarily regarded not as cost factors but as a means of attracting and keeping the workforce.
- It fell to macro-economic management to raise the wage levels of enterprises lagging behind in the wage competition, even at the expense of anti-inflation policy.
- Employment policy centred on easing the labour shortage and cushioning its consequences, with the economic actors unprepared for coping with structural unemployment and the frictions it causes.

In the wake of the systemic transformation, the need to strengthen the adaptability of society, including business, called for an accelerated 'learning process'. It became essential to radically alter the educational and training systems, to assimilate new values and models of socialisation, and to develop abilities and attitudes that could improve chances of mobility and facilitate the shaping or modifying of individual life strategies.

Research into economic transformation

During the past decade, research workers – in addition to exploring the ways and means of HRM – have studied the impact of economic transformation on the revaluation of human capital as well as on employment, unemployment and wages.

One of the studies (Kertesi/Köllő 2002) analysed tendencies between 1986 and 1999, looking at market appraisal and the productivity of groups of employees at different levels of education and in different age groups. A considerable quantity of wage data and data on estimated production functions at large enterprises were used in that study. The wage data suggested a general rise in return to education for all age groups between 1989 and 1992. However, after the recessive period of transformation, overall appreciation of schooling stopped as market systems and institutions developed and new technologies appeared. Only the wages of young and skilled workers (and their relative productivity) continued to increase, first at foreign companies using modern technologies and then at Hungarian-owned firms as well. In contrast, the productivity and wage returns on previously acquired skills and experience ceased to increase after 1992. The appreciation of knowledge base and skills was confined to the younger age groups during the period of technological renewal.

Another study (Kőrösi/Surányi 2002) analysed the characteristics of the parallel and concurrent processes of corporate job creation and destruction after the recessive transformation period. Dynamic firms created new jobs at an internationally quite exceptional speed before 1996, but downsizing companies destroyed jobs with a similar intensity. The high intensity of job creation and destruction processes coincided with a very stable employment situation at the aggregate level. The stability of the macroeconomic indicator and intensive job reallocation at companies was the result of extremely rapid and deep restructuring of the corporate sector.

A third study (Fazekas 2000) examined the impact of foreign working capital investments in regional labour markets and attempted to find, by regressive estimates, the factors influencing the regional distribution of employment at foreign-owned companies. It looked into the historical changes in the effects of the major underlying variables and into the impact of the expansion of employment by foreign-owned companies on the regional differences in unemployment rates. Finally, the paper summarised the development policy conclusions that are significant from the companies' and local labour markets' point of view.

Other papers (Galasi/Lázár/Nagy 1999) studied the effectiveness of four active labour market programmes (training, wage subsidy, start-up support and community service) by using follow-up questionnaire survey results. For the survey – which covered the period subsequent to the completion of the programmes – data were collected on the labour market careers of some 6,000 job losers who had left the active programmes in 1996. The effectiveness of the programmes was measured by the probability of finding jobs either in unsupported job openings or in entrepreneurship. The papers analysed the ways in which the effectiveness of the different programmes was influenced by the characteristics of the particular programme, the characteristics of participants and the conditions of local labour markets.

The sudden expansion of Hungarian higher education in the 1990s gave cause for some concern. Was the expansion going to result in massive overeducation – notably in a growing rate of unemployment among young graduates or in groups of employees displaced by them – and/or was it going to reduce the return on education, i.e. the higher earnings related to diplomas? The paper dealing with this problem (Kertesi/Köllő 2005) used data breakdowns by cohorts and occupations, and examined symptoms of eventual overeducation between 1995 and 2004. The market values of newly obtained college or university diplomas had grown enormously up until the year 2000 but the growth slowed down afterwards, with a narrower earning margin awarded to graduates starting on their careers. At the same time the data did not bear out the concerns of previously mentioned graduate unemployment and displacement impacts.

The past fifteen years have seen a growing number of publications covering HRM. A few comprehensive works have appeared; also specialised textbooks and handbooks methodically dealing with all areas of HRM (Bakacsi *et al.* 2000; Elbert *et al.* 2001). In addition, the HRM systems – from recruitment and selection through performance appraisal, remuneration, fringe benefits and new terminology to personnel development, training and career-path design – have been analysed by many journals.

HRM: development

Up until the 1970s there was no significant achievement in HRM research or higher education. The start of research and the training of highly qualified professionals lagged two to three decades behind the developed market economies.

Budapest University of Economics has played a leading role in both research and the modernisation of higher education. The academic management of the university has lent support to the two fundamental principles of the development concept: (a) high-standard education is conditional upon the development of scientific workshops assisting the professional development of professors and staff members by enabling the HRM-related disciplines in Hungary to catch up with international achievements that hold the lead in this field; and (b) our primary task in higher education is to impart professional knowledge relating to general economic, business and management cultures, and knowledge that is required for the beginning of careers and, in postgraduate courses, providing high standards of occupational specialisation.

In the mid-1980s the introduction of the integrated professional academic programme of labour and personnel set an important benchmark in streamlining postgraduate courses.

Our aim was to impart theoretical and methodological knowledge newly acquired in human resource economics – together with related expertise in economics and labour economics, management and organisation, sociology, psychology and law – in order to help to lay the groundwork for formulating policies of, and creating the institutional conditions for, furthering a more efficient utilisation of manpower and a more effective discharge of management responsibilities.

We were open in other fields, too, allowing the enrolment of not only economists but also specialists with technical, legal and other high-level qualifications and with experience in personnel and labour administration and policies.

Rigid and excessive specialisation at graduate level inevitably tends to impede convertibility of skills, adaptability to changing conditions and requirements in the course of professional careers, and the chances of desirable career modification. All these factors often cause social losses and personal disappointments.

The transformation of the social, economic and political systems – which started and was largely completed in the late 1980s and early 1990s – placed substantially changed demands on specialists and organisations dealing with human resources. At the beginning of the period, special courses were the dominant form of training. At the same time, efforts were expended in embarking upon the renewal of corporations formerly divided and sometimes doomed to decay, as well as upon the integration of social, labour-related and personnel activities. The acceleration of this process was often hindered by shortages of suitable specialists. The Budapest University of Economics met the processes to improve business half-way when it launched the previously mentioned postgraduate courses for personnel officers and HR managers.

Unemployment was unknown to the Hungarian economy and society for decades. In the absence of need, specialists did not learn how to deal with situations in which internal and external circumstances forced them to resort to downsizing or reductions in staff. The evolving reconciliation of conflicting interests between employers and employees called for new skills. Not only did the knowledge of specialists active in different firms need to be enlarged; there was also a need to prepare specialists for new functions. The fresh challenges compelled several colleges and universities to launch educational programmes designed to meet one or other of the demands for skilled personnel. Unfortunately, the mass training provided, especially in philosophy departments, was sometimes not adequate.

Graduate programmes at the Budapest University of Economics were geared to occupational trends in daytime courses. These courses were designed to impart theoretical, methodological and factual knowledge relating to economics and management culture and promoting the starts of careers, whereas skills continued to be improved by postgraduate courses.

Since autumn 2000, a diploma in the only accredited postgraduate training course can be obtained only by students with a certificate of proficiency in a foreign language. Accession to the European Union and the incorporation of recent years' research results into curricula brought the need to streamline teaching material in most subjects of study. The question of higher education can be settled satisfactorily by the 'Bolognese process'. We have joined the European Higher Education Area and have introduced the system of multi-cycle programmes. The Bachelor degree programme in HRM is one of six business faculties in the field of economic science. Under the new system, HRM BA was launched at six colleges/universities in September 2006. The Bachelor programme runs for three years (180 credits) and provides an economist qualification in human resource management. The purpose of HRM BA is to prepare specialists who are able to develop and utilise human resources, to analyse the structure and operation of labour markets, and to coordinate conciliation processes. With the manifold knowledge they acquire in economics and behavioural science and the use of analytical methods, our students will be able to continue their studies in either business or economics faculties offering Master's degree courses.

It is obvious that Master's programmes will only be open to the most capable students who have achieved the best results. Even so, the opportunity to improve special skills and to become familiar with new scientific achievements as well as with international practice will continue to be offered by postgraduate courses for people with work experience.

What would you like to teach foreign HR managers? What is important for them to know in your opinion?

Foreign companies find highly qualified staff in the country because young managers are open-minded, have excellent language skills, especially in English and German, and know foreign cultures.

BEST-PRACTICE CASE: BORSODI SÖRGYÁR – A BREWERY INTEGRATING ITSELF INTO AN INTERNATIONAL GROUP

BACKGROUND

Borsodi Sörgyár is one of Hungary's leading beer companies. There are three major players in the beer market: Brau AG (Heineken), SAB-Miller (Dreher) and Borsodi. Each of them has a market share of over 30 per cent and it is difficult to say which is market leader at any particular point in time. Nevertheless, there is no doubt that during the past three to four years Borsodi has shown far better operational and business results than its competitors. Volume and market share have grown continuously, profitability has improved, and average annual EBIT growth has exceeded 30 per cent.

This marvellous growth and success has happened in a market environment which has not really been favourable for breweries. During the 1990s the Hungarian beer market underwent major restructuring. In 1990 the total volume of the market was over ten million hectolitres. In 1996 the figure was less than seven million, due to changing drinking habits (mineral water and non-alcoholic segments were the winners) and the weak purchasing power of the population. Now, the market has returned to a very slow growth curve (2 to 4 per cent/year), but since accession to the EU a new and unfavourable structural change has been seen. This is due to the very rapid growth of cheap, canned beer (mostly imported from Germany because of strict environmental regulations). As a result, the sales volumes of local core brands have dropped dramatically. All the breweries face the same new challenge: how to compete with the cheap and popular brands and at the same time remain profitable.

Before we take a closer look at the company, we should mention that the privatisation of the beer industry was completed relatively soon after the political and economic turnaround and an era of strong market competition started among the newly privatised beer companies. The privatisation of Borsodi was the first to take place, in 1991. The majority of the shares owned by the State Property Agency were bought by one of the leading European beer companies, the Belgian Interbrew. At that time Borsodi was a small, regional brewery operating almost exclusively in the north-east of Hungary. This acquisition opened up new opportunities for the brewery and now it is no longer a regional operator but one of the strongest players in the country. Borsodi owns the biggest local core brand – *Borsodi Sör* – which commands almost 20 per cent of the whole market.

Borsodi produces and sells over 2.3 million hl of beer. Major brands, aside from the above core product, are the locally brewed international premium brands, Interbrew, Stella Artois and Beck's, plus the local amber beer, *Borostyán*.

Since it was established in 1973, Borsodi has always been known as a leading innovator in the beer industry. The first locally brewed non-alcoholic beer (*Borsodi Póló*) and the first 501 keg (a stainless-steel barrel) were introduced into the market by Borsodi. Since 1991, Borsodi has continued to be the leading innovator, with a number of new packaging solutions, such as the first locally canned brand, multipack, high-quality PET (polyethylene terephthalate) bottles, etc., to its credit. Borsodi was the first among the breweries to be ISO 9001 and ISO 14001 certified.

What is the secret? How did Borsodi manage to become a leader in the beer market? A number of journalists put these questions to Borsodi's general manager at the celebrations marking the brewer's thirtieth anniversary in 2003. The answer was clear and straightforward:

- a strong and experienced parent company – Interbrew – and the support provided by it;
- a winning brand portfolio and very conscious brand-building; and
- people who are experienced and committed.

Q.hu

The focus now is really on people. So let us take a closer look at people management practices at one of the foremost players in the Hungarian beverage industry. What is the role of HRM at this company, what are the people-related strategies and practices? How are these contributing to business results?

What would you say one ought not to do? What are the 'don'ts' in your country?

If you have a drink with your Hungarian business partner, do not clink beer glasses in a toast because many Hungarians consider this bad luck. This fear dates back to a failed Hungarian rebellion against the Habsburg Empire in 1849. The Austrian generals toasted the demise of the Hungarians with beer while their counterparts were executed for the attempted coup.

THE ROLE OF HRM AT BORSODI

Before privatisation, as in any other state-owned company, the role of HRM at Borsodi was mainly administrative, with an element of (partly political) control over the employees. Almost all aspects of employment were centrally defined and regulated, and the administrative function meant local implementation and supervision of regulations. The function itself was called the personnel department and was a subfunction of finance. The personnel manager normally reported to the finance director and was not a member of the top management team.

It is irrelevant to say that companies at that time had their own HR strategy as part of their business strategy. There was only one dominant employment strategy – full employment as the core element of the socialist economy – which had to be observed locally. Everything was subordinated to this political aim.

Major HRM functions were compensation and benefits, staffing, labour administration and career management (called 'cadre development'):

- Compensation and benefits management was very often handled by the finance department and encompassed only payroll matters. Job classifications were fixed by the industry-level tariff system, wages and salaries were centrally determined, and there was no real scope for local solutions.
- Staffing was an interesting function, because of the Hungarian situation. Hungary was the only country of the traditional socialist bloc where, after the economic reforms of the late 1960s, the concept of a 'socialist market economy' was introduced. This meant that the political establishment accepted that the market also played a role in the socialist economy, although its role was 'special'. As a consequence, Hungary did not deny the role of the labour market or the fact that companies were competing for employees in that market. Staffing departments were not just there to administer employee movements in and out; their brief also included looking for appropriate personnel. As a matter of fact, fundamental labour market institutions were missing. Although unemployment existed (but was not officially accepted), there was no nationwide network of employment offices, no headhunting companies. The search for new employees was conducted mainly through advertising or networking.
- Career management (cadre development) was the most politicised function. Both the local communist party organisation and the regional bureau played an important role in assessing potential and developing and placing candidates in new, managerial positions. A major part of the assessment process focused on loyalty to socialist values but managerial capabilities and professional skills and experience were also appraised.

The political and economic turnaround of 1989–90 and privatisation in 1991 brought rapid transformation to Borsodi, in the course of which the role of HRM and HRM practices underwent fundamental change.

As competitiveness became the most important objective, the rationalisation started at company level. The company headcount was reduced dramatically – from a total of over 2,000 to 700 now. Most of the reduction was achieved by outsourcing non-core activities (e.g. cleaning services, canteen, some maintenance-related activities, depots, transportation, malting, etc.). The rest came from automation, better organisation and improved productivity ('world-class manufacturing').

HRM acquired strategic importance. The most visible sign was that the HR manager (now called 'director') became a member of the senior management team, reporting directly to the general manager of the company. The senior management team (known as the 'committee of directors' (CDs)) is the highest-level decision-making and executive body of the company.

HR ORGANISATION

The new HR organisation is based on three main functional units as shown in Figure 7.2.

Figure 7.2 HR organisation

Responsibilities are distributed between the parties involved. The HR director is responsible for HR strategy development, internal communication content definition, employee satisfaction survey and action plans, recruitment and selection above middle-management level, representation of company interests in dealings with employee organisations (trade union, works council), and collective bargaining and salary negotiations.

The personnel manager is responsible for recruitment and selection below middle-management level, succession planning, the performance management process, and career management (organisation and people review).

The compensation and benefits manager is responsible for compensation strategy definition and development, reward and recognition programme management, headcount and salary planning (budget, strategic plan), job evaluations (Hay), labour administration, and employee relations.

The development manager is responsible for learning and development, strategy definition and development, competence and knowledge management, identification of training and development needs, development programme management, job descriptions, and organisation design and development.

Facility management (housekeeping) also reports to the HR director and is concerned almost exclusively with managing third-party service providers, such as canteen, cleaning, office material supply, gardening, office building refurbishment and managing investment projects to improve physical working conditions, etc.

HR STRATEGY AND POLICIES AS PART OF THE COMPANY'S STRATEGY

Borsodi's strategic objective, as defined in its vision, is to be not only the best brewer but the best beverage company in Hungary. All subsequent function strategies are defined according to this vision.

The Borsodi HR vision is to be the best employer in the industry, one of the most attractive employers of choice in Hungary.

The HR mission statement is to provide high-quality HR services to management and employees to facilitate the realisation of Borsodi's vision and mission: they are now in full compliance with Interbrew's core values and code of conduct.

What are the strategic implications of the above for different HRM subfunctions? Because the volume of this case study is limited there is no room for discussing all the elements of HR activity at Borsodi. We shall therefore focus on certain key areas, including staffing, compensation and benefits, job evaluation, competences and knowledge management, performance management, succession planning and career management, employee relations and internal communication.

The declared strategic objective is to have the best people in all positions at all levels.

♥.hu

> Policies and procedures have been developed to make sure this strategy is implemented in recruitment and selection, internal promotions, transfers, performance management, competence assessment, learning and development, succession planning and career management.

The key question focuses on a reliable and realistic profile of requirements for each position. A competence model, encompassing both behavioural and technical (professional) competences, has been developed by an expert team of HR professionals, functional experts and external consultants to define the key competences and levels of competence needed for all positions so that it is possible to measure how external or internal candidates meet the requirements. Competence gaps can then easily be assessed, development needs identified and development programmes set up.

It is the role and responsibility of the managers to assess competences with the active support and assistance of HR. A detailed handbook on the competence models helps them to do so. Under certain circumstances, an assessment centre or development centre is organised and operated with external consultants.

Competences and knowledge management are closely connected with performance management and learning and development.

For key – mostly managerial – positions there is a competence model developed on the basis of the corporate Global Leadership Competence Model.

The six core leadership competences and their assessment and grading criteria were elaborated by a multicultural team of Interbrew HR professionals (including one of the authors). These competences are used for the CDs and above to define development needs in order to fill existing and assessed competence gaps.

For levels below the CDs, an adapted local version of the model has been introduced. The series of workshops at which local interpretation of the behavioural indicators and their measurement criteria were defined was attended by all managers. The workshops provided an opportunity for all managers to understand the core competences, relate them to their own area of activity and define behavioural patterns which are relevant to that area, which are observable and which make the model operational.

ACTIVITIES IN HRM

The performance management cycle

Assessment of leadership and technical competences (defined by functions) is an integral part of the performance management process. Borsodi has fully adopted the corporate standard: performance management is equally focused on the 'what' and the 'how'. 'What' means the business results and 'how' means the way the business results are achieved, i.e. the behavioural competences.

An annual performance management cycle has been implemented, and an interim goal achievement review, which makes it possible to modify objectives if there is a reason to do so.

The HR function plays a leading role in the performance management process as the owner of the process. Initiation, timing, control and advising/consulting also form part of this role. Assessments are made by line managers together with incumbents.

The results of the competence assessment are used to plan learning and development programmes at both company and personal level, but this is not connected to the bonus system. Each employee who takes part in the performance management process has an annual personal development plan. How well an annual plan is accomplished impacts on assessment at the beginning of the next year.

The results of performance assessment (the extent to which business objectives are met) are used for calculating annual bonuses for groups and individuals.

Compensation and benefits

The basic principle aligned with Borsodi's corporate values is that the company pays for performance. Its compensation policy sets out the basic rules for job evaluation and grading (using the Hay system), for positioning in relation to the market (median base salary) and for selecting market competitors to define that positioning.

Variable payment is designed to reward group performance (in most cases this is the company result), but there is room for personal achievement bonuses up to a maximum of 25 per cent of the total bonus. In all sales functions, there is a results-based monthly or quarterly bonus, plus a collective bonus depending on the year-end result of the company.

Now, all employees of Borsodi are entitled to an annual bonus depending on the company result for the year. The bonus criteria for different employee groups are announced at the beginning of the year. Actual performance figures are reported regularly during the year.

A wide range of benefits in kind are provided for the employees. One of the benefits is the cafeteria system, where at the beginning of the year each employee can select the most appropriate combination of benefits (different tax options and implications can be taken into account). A pension fund and health fund are also available and subsidised by the company.

Organisation and people review (OPR)

It is vital not only for the local organisation but also for the corporation as a whole to ensure that key positions are staffed by talented, high-performing internal candidates.

- Organisational structure is aligned to the business objectives and organisational capabilities are present.
- The right people are in the positions and development needs are met.
- There is a pool of talent (at both local and international level) to make succession easy.
- Individual career objectives are known and harmonised with company needs.
- Key performers are successfully retained.

The OPR process is closely connected with performance management, using data and information acquired when performance, competences and potential are assessed.

Every year there are two OPR runs, one in spring and one in autumn. The first is focused on organisation to ensure maximum organisational alignment with the yearly business plan. The second is focused on people: the performance, competences and development potential of key people is assessed for their recent position and possible career move. International mobility is also appraised.

The process starts at country level and then goes to regional, zone and corporate level to identify potential successors for different positions.

Learning and development

Local and corporate-level learning and development programmes are in place for those identified as local or corporate talent pool members (called high potentials (HiPots)). The local management training course is set up with the Business School of Miskolc University. The Miskolc University Borsodi Business Academy is for young talent with management potential. This is a four-semester mini-MBA programme teaching the basics of business management. Students receive a credit for each completed subject and those credits can be used later if they want to complete the official MBA course of the university. The full programme is paid for by the company.

HiPots at corporate level can attend the Insead–Wharton Programme, a special management training course designed for Interbrew.

Learning and development budgets for each function are planned parallel to the annual budgeting process with the active participation of HR. Competency gaps are assessed and analysed and the learning and development manager helps the functional heads identify the most appropriate development programmes. This may be a training course, but other options, such as job rotation, temporary placement, project assignment and job enlargement, are also available.

Employee relations and internal communication

Being the best calls for a continuous dialogue with employees. Internal communication is one of the key HR responsibilities (shared with the communication department) at Borsodi. The quarterly company magazine *Borsodi Sörlevél* and the intranet site 'Sörnet' are the most popular communication channels.

Every two years, an employee satisfaction survey is conducted by an independent company to measure satisfaction with:

– work;
– management;
– working conditions;
– internal communication;
– compensation and benefits;
– training and development;
– career; and
– HR support.

The questionnaire is almost the same on every occasion, so changes can be seen and analysed. All employees are directly involved in the processing of the results, and focus groups define action plans and monitor the implementation of any action.

Borsodi attaches great importance to employee involvement and participation. The most recent evidence of this is the new corporate strategy communication process. The communication tool that was selected by the corporate HR is a unique one and specially designed to involve all employees in the discussion of the new strategy and its strategic pillars and to mobilise them to identify their respective role in the implementation of the strategy. The *Insight Map* was a large book containing nothing but situational pictures (no text) relating to the brewing industry (e.g. points of consumption, production, delivery, competitors, etc.). Local facilitators were trained to lead small employee teams (with a maximum of fifteen people in each group) through the world of brewing reflected in our strategy and values. Group discussions on the strategy lasted for between three and three and a half hours, and every employee participated. A huge number of suggestions, proposals and, of course, criticisms were collected, and action plans set up. Feedback on implementation is also provided to all employees.

It is the HR director who represents the company in dealings with the works council and the Trade Unions Board of Representatives. Annual information sessions are held at least twice a year to provide information on business results and other issues impacting on major groups of employees. Negotiations take place on annual salary increases and on collective agreements. In general, the relationship is cooperative and so far both parties have been able to avoid conflicts.

Why Borsodi is an example of cutting-edge HR practice in Hungary

It is very difficult to assess what is cutting-edge in HR. Is it the usage of the most up-to-date HR techniques or methodology? Is it having systems that are extremely sophisticated and supported by a complicated IT infrastructure?

The way we see it, cutting-edge means providing the best support for business and ensuring that people are satisfied.

At Borsodi, HRM is really close to business. HR strategies are defined as integral parts of business strategy. As a result, people are considered core to business success. The whole edifice of competence and business result-based performance management is designed to ensure maximum alignment.

HRM is not just a function performed by HR managers; it is becoming more and more an integral part of all managers' leadership practices.

There are no doubt companies in Hungary employing more up-to-date HR techniques than Borsodi. One can also find much more sophisticated IT support systems. What makes Borsodi unique is the way it has integrated all aspects and elements of HR into a complex HR management system. As a result, there is a very good, cooperative and supportive working atmosphere where people like to work and be together. Business results and employee satisfaction survey scores (compared to international benchmarks) are the best indicators of that.

.hu

This is not just because of HR. HR itself, without the real support of the whole management team, would not be able to achieve the results. Building a culture of performance, quality, human focus, respect and trust calls for teamwork, where HR is just one of the players.

Which people play key roles in your country? Which names should one know?

One should naturally know the names of the political leaders mentioned in the introductory table of this chapter.

In addition, Hungary can be proud of numerous inventors, musicians and artists, such as (to name only a few of those whose inventions and work attracted worldwide attention) Oszkár Asbóth (inventor of the helicopter), László József Bíró (inventor of the ballpen), János Irinyi (inventor of the match), Béla Bartók (renovator of classical music), Tony Curtis (actor), Zsazsa Gabor (actress), György Konrad (author).

References

Bakacsi, Gyula *et al.* (2000): Strategic Human Resources Management. Akadémiai Kiadó, Budapest, pp. 1–254.

Elbert, Norbert F./Mártonné, Karoliny/Farkas, Ferenc/Poór, Jószef (2001): Personnel Human Resource Management Handbook, Budapest.

Fazekas, Károly (2000): The Impact of Foreign Direct Investment Inflows on Regional Labour Markets in Hungary. Budapest Working Papers on the Labour Market (BWP) 8/2000, Institute of Economics, Hungarian Academy of Sciences, Department of Human Resources, Budapest University of Economics and Public Administration.

Galasi, Péter/Lázár, György/Nagy, Gyula (1999): Factors Underlying the Effectiveness of Active Employment Programmes. Budapest Working Papers on the Labour Market (BWP) 3/1999, Institute of Economics, Hungarian Academy of Sciences, Department of Human Resources, Budapest University of Economics and Public Administration.

István, Gábor R. (1997): Belso versus foglalkoztatási munkaeröpiac, in: Közgazdasági Szemle, 6.

Kaplan, Robert S./Norton, David P. (1992): The balanced scorecard – measures that drive performance, in: Harvard Business Review, 70(1): 165–70.

Kertesi, Gábor/Köllő, János (2002): Economic transformation and the revaluation of human capital – Hungary 1986-99, in: Andries de Grip/Jasper van Loo/Ken Mayhew (eds): The Economics of Skills Obsolescence. Research of Labour Economics, 21: 235–73.

—— (2005): The Expansion of Higher Education, High-skilled Unemployment and Returns to College/University Diploma. Budapest Working Papers on the Labour Market (BWP) 3/2005, Institute of Economics, Hungarian Academy of Sciences, Department of Human Resources, Budapest University of Economics and Public Administration.

Kőrösi, Gábor/Surányi, Éva (2002): Job Creation and Destruction. Budapest Working Papers on the Labour Market (BWP) 8/2002, Institute of Economics, Hungarian Academy of Sciences, Department of Human Resources, Budapest University of Economics and Public Administration.

Lauter, Peter G. (1998): Világgazdasági kihívások az ezredfordulón, Európa Fórum, 1/1998.

Timár, János (1994): A foglalkoztatás és munkanélküliség sajátosságai a posztszocialista országokban, Közgazdasági Szemle, 7–8.

The authors

György Kővári, University Professor at the Department of Human Resources, Corvinus University of Budapest. Main research: strategic HRM, industrial relations, labour market policies, corporate governance, mechanism of wage determination and incentives. Main publications: *Old and New Forms of Wage Bargaining on the Shop Floor* (1986, ed. P. Galasi and G. Sziráczki); *Hungary Faces Unemployment* (1991); *Wage Trends in Hungary* (1991); and *Models of Strategic Human Resource Management* (2003).

Dr Pál Bóday (boday.pal@ohe.hu), Hungarian Association for Human Resources Management (OHE), Executive President. Bóday is responsible for managing OHE, which includes organising national and international conferences, experience exchange meetings, seminars and other courses, editing OHE's monthly magazine *Személyügyi Hírlevél*, and representing the association in international bodies (EAPM, IFTDO).

Dr János Bogdán (janos.bogdan@borsodi.hu), Borsodi Sörgyár Rt., Director of Human Resources, responsible for managing the 'people function' at national level. This includes HR strategy and implementation, recruitment, rewarding, performance management, industrial relations, competence and knowledge management, people development and all other subfunctions of HRM.

8 HRM in Italy: the evolution of a profession

Massimo Delucchi/Massimo Roascio/Barbara Parmeggiani/Massimo Lanzanò/
Valerio Salone/Giulio Carè/Mario D'Ambrosio/Filippo Abramo

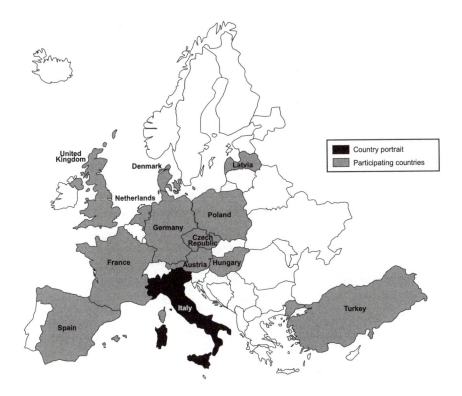

Italy: in a nutshell

In this chapter you will learn:

- that HR in Italy has become a real success factor with a competitive edge. Therefore, HR managers are managers of processes connected to strategic resources and structures;

- that Italian HR academia is in a phase of transition. Mainly in HR theory, the role of HR managers as business partners is becoming more important; and

- that a transformation of personnel managers into business service providers can succeed by realising that guided role development is necessary in order to be effectual.

Capital:	Rome
Area (sq km):	301,230
EU membership:	since 1951 (founding member of the former so-called European Coal and Steel Community)
Population:	58,133,509
Languages:	Italian (official), German, French, Slovene
Ethnic groups:	Italian (includes small clusters of German-, French-, and Slovene-Italians in the north and Albanian-Italians and Greek-Italians in the south)
Gross domestic product:	1.727 trillion USD (2006)
Workforce (in percentages):	24.63 million (2006): agriculture 5; industry 32; services 63 (2001)
Export commodities:	engineering products, textiles and clothing, production machinery, motor vehicles, transport equipment, chemicals; food, beverages and tobacco; minerals, and nonferrous metals

BACKGROUND: EVOLUTION OF THE ROLE OF PERSONNEL MANAGEMENT IN ITALY

THE HISTORY OF HRM IN ITALY: FROM THE 1990s INTO THE FUTURE

The economic trend has showed signs of recovery albeit against a backdrop of great competition due to the effect of technological innovation and greater opening up of markets. Information technology has started to cancel out the advantages of geographical proximity and the market has moved closer to going global. In this competitive development framework, companies are definitely out to recover any efficiency margin by singling out and pursuing all solutions capable of cutting costs, such as focusing on core business, using the service industry, downsizing, rationalizing, and selecting goods and markets.

There was a marked development of small and medium-sized companies. Streamlined companies in the north-east, which exported Italian goods, were more successful than bigger companies at grasping growth opportunities in new markets. Even state holdings (characteristic of Italy, where the state-owned companies are present in many sectors where profit is not necessarily an objective) espoused the trend towards efficiency and the state/business owner started the privatisation process.

This process of reorientation and repositioning companies in the market also entailed an organisational re-examination, in which the buzzwords were decentralisation of responsibilities, result centres, responsibility for processes, cross-party committees and collective management. This led to a reduction in hierarchical levels, a focus on process management rather than on just functional structures, identification of business units, protection of strategic functions such as technological innovation and planning. 'Bosses' were required to take on the role of managers, meaning executives capable of managing all variables of complex processes, not only technical and functional but also managerial.

The regulations of the 1990s were rich and meaningful in their attention to trade unions (Protocol 23/7/1993, Rassegna online 1993), which for the first time had defined rules and criteria for renewing national and company collective agreements, and aspects of labour law. We should remember regulations on collective redundancy, new forms of employment flexibility, known as the *Pacchetto Treu* (Treu package) and employment reform.

The new legislation, receptive to greater flexibility while not breaking with the past, was geared to fostering and encouraging company reorganisation processes and a new approach to relations with trade unions open to forms of fully responsible concerted action. Together with the evolution of the business world, they have created an opportunity for personnel management to become a landmark of the cultural, organisational and management change stage.

Even the role of the personnel manager came to rely more on management skills and evolved vigorously. As an agent of change, the facilitator and director on the manager's team acted in full agreement with senior management. The personnel manager focused on organisational change project management, manager training plans, internal communications plans, service evaluation programmes, and consistency with the company's value system. The personnel manager found self-justification in authoritativeness and focused on the growth of the management culture.

> **What is typical of your country in relation to the country itself (its culture, people, etc.) and its economy?**
>
> It is difficult to describe the culture of a country in a few words; what we can just say is that, on the positive side, creativity and flexibility are certainly typical of Italians. On the negative side, lack of collective consciousness and lack of respect for rules are also typical. For the economy, this means a highly individualistic approach to business problems (small enterprises account for more than 90 per cent of Italian economic output).
>
> The following sections examine the changes brought about in recent years, from the 1990s onwards, when the authority of personnel managers started to grow as a result of their role as change facilitators and HR enhancers. The breadth of that evolution merits special emphasis: it turned out to be so decisive that it transformed the nature of the function from regulatory and disciplinary to strategic. The phase we are going through now threatens to restrict the strategic functions of the HR manager once again.

The post-1990s period

Macroeconomic challenges, which highlight limits to the growth capacity of markets, fall in demand, obsolescence of traditional sectors and moments of hardships in the new economy alternated with stages of tumultuous growth. All this brought keener competition and narrower margins for companies.

Companies making traditional goods downsized even further, while those producing innovative goods enjoyed growth opportunities but not certainties. There were concentrations at international level with internal repercussions. Companies made their organisations simple and lean. They emphasised the strategic and orientation roles of holdings by decentralising full responsibility for results to functions and functional processes and giving them the authority to handle functional levers in every field, including the field relating to HR and organisational and functional structures.

> By completing the evolutionary process, the personnel manager turned him- or herself into a manager of processes connected to strategic resources and structures in close coordination with top management. The personnel manager became a qualified and competitive supplier of professional services, an authoritative consultant to managers of operational functions in their role as managers of resources and organisations.

The role of HR managers in the future

In recent years, personnel management in Italy has gone from a purely administrative and regulatory role to a strategic role. This means that the function today plays a role in developing company strategies on the strength of a recognised centrality of HR. It has become a real success factor and competitive edge for a company.

Companies' renewed interest in greater use of the service industry – as well as a range of 'atypical' employment contracts and flexible forms of employment made possible by labour market reforms – seems to question the fundamental role of personnel managers as agents of HR enhancement. On the one hand, staff are lost to outsourcing initiatives; on the other, they are either hired temporarily or hired through supply contracts with third parties.

From this standpoint, one cannot theoretically exclude a new business model in which business owners, rather than directly managing (and therefore enhancing) the personnel required for carrying on their business, acquire services rendered by people with whom they can establish a mere service–supply relationship (through supply contracts, project contracts and other contracts).

Personnel managers are required to deal with this threat to their role, which they have been able to help to evolve so positively, but certainly not without ongoing qualified professional commitment. The actions and initiatives they need to develop and pursue these aims must not cause them to back away from the processes of promoting the service industry and legislative progress; otherwise they would be putting themselves out of the game. Rather, personnel managers must propel themselves back into the role of leading players and anticipators of strategic company choices in the field of HR.

Faced with the combined effects of the development of regulations and the market environment, the personnel manager must convince top management to take options that guarantee long-term sustainability of the highest levels of efficiency and efficacy, both in the policy of harnessing the service industry and in a company personnel policy that provides adequate motivation for employees.

Thus the processes of promoting the service industry should be implemented in pursuit of the goal of achieving real added value for the company (the people involved should be appropriately motivated to make a real contribution to that value increase), and flexible and atypical forms of labour contracts should be used only to meet special strategic requirements, thereby avoiding the generalisation of practices that are supported only because they make for short-term reductions in costs.

By safeguarding the real centrality of HR in a company, the role of HRM can continue its positive evolution towards more and more approach and orientation functions rather than functional ones.

231

What would you like to teach foreign HR managers? What is important for them to know in your opinion?

Our advice for a foreign manager would be to understand local culture without any preconceived idea about Italians. Trying to impose external methods without open discussion could be very dangerous. Another word of advice: be interested in more than just sun, food and the arts. Read Italian writers; a lot can be learned from them about Italian culture and mentality.

THE ROLES FOR HRM IN ITALY: HR MANAGER AND HR BUSINESS PARTNER

Whatever role is recognised for HRM, it is the interpretation of the role itself which shapes the way that other company players see the HR manager, and which influences and conditions the internal value system by helping to maintain the relevance assumed by the organisational position:

- The HR manager who looks for justification for him- or herself and handles internal relations by using levers the company institutionally entrusts to him for his own personal ends, helps create a sort of ambiguous gratitude and secures indulgence for functional initiatives on the strength of an irregular reward–penalty mechanism.
- The HR manager who looks for justification for him- or herself in a thorough knowledge of laws, contractual regulations and resource development and management techniques is not on the same team as his or her colleagues. He or she is not bringing innovation into the field of organisational behaviour, and is not enhancing resources, not even with his or her collaborators.
- The HR manager who makes a pact with top management based on the affirmation and maintenance of a value system of organisational behaviour is backing and managing evaluation, pay rise, career and organisational plans and programmes consistent with the framework of company values in a shared and transparent climate. Such an HR manager is an agent of change, a balancing element in internal relations, a motor of the internal communication process. This type of HR manager justifies him- or herself by authoritativeness and becomes an informal adviser to colleagues in finding solutions to management problems.

The latter interpretation of the role enhances the function and guarantees, in the evolution of organisational forms and methodologies of companies, retaining the level of relevance acquired on the company's internal value scale in the long term.

The recent evolution of the competitive scenario and the organisational and business models is also forcing personnel departments to rethink the model they have used up until now. This has driven the definition of policy and actions towards people. The most successful experiences are characterised by an evolution of the

HR function towards a partnership model with line management. This is considered new as it is based on the sharing of common goals and the overall redefinition of mission, role and competence between HR functions and management roles. These experiences have some characteristics in common:

- the HR function is oriented towards satisfying the needs of line management and of the other business units;
- HR strategy is strongly integrated with business strategy;
- the introduction of an 'internal marketing' logic for HR services, in line with a segmentation of the services offered; and
- radical revision of organisational set-up and processes to take full advantage of new technologies and platforms.

In the most significant experiences carried out by companies that adopted such an approach, attention has generally been paid to three main areas: (a) more attention to the outcome of a real HR strategy; (b) redefinition of organisation and competences in relation to new technologies and systems; and (c) rethinking of function positioning and of the professional culture that has to characterise it.

Contexts, objectives and business priorities strongly determine HR function requirements as well as the impacts on both the new managerial and leadership roles and on the employee value proposition (EVP). It is then possible to identify the principles that should drive HR action and the related service model.

In the different contexts, choices made on vision, mission and service model determine the choice of a certain function position and the tradeoff between strategic orientation and operative orientation. The emerging organisational asset needed to control the three main service frameworks is going to be designed around three main points:

1. Competence poles to plan and manage high-content professional services (compensation, performance, talent management, managerial development).
2. Service centres including administration processes and activities, payroll, HR information services, budget and reporting.
3. HR business partners mainly geared to managing the relationship with both line management and employees.

This transformation also requires a significant professional adaptation: management and development professionals are increasingly qualified as 'business partners', able to support staff, executives and directors in all organisational and managerial needs. Information technology systems provide people and management with all the information and knowledge relating to job relations and managerial data management. 'Project' functions (training, compensation, development, etc.) are able to provide paradigmatic solutions for specific challenges.

EAPM AFFILIATE: ASSOCIAZIONE ITALIANA PER LA DIREZIONE DEL PERSONALE (AIDP)

The AIDP, which is Italy's personnel management association, is an association of people who are professionally active in the field of HR, working in organisations of every size and description in both the private and public sector, involved in services and consulting activities, in management positions or positions entailing functional responsibilities, including people who deal with issues regarding the relationship between people and work in a scholarly, research or academic capacity.

Established in 1960, the AIDP is a non-political, non-profit association composed of members who joined on an individual and voluntary basis. Its goal is to enhance the professionalism of its members and, within the wider context of the social evolution of the country, to serve as an active component in the process of developing HR in the workplace with the aim of promoting the primary inalienable importance of the individual, and human dignity in the workplace and society at large.

Boasting some 3,000 members, the AIDP has fourteen regional and inter-regional chapters and is an active member of the EAPM (European Association for Personnel Management) and the WFPMA (World Federation of Personnel Management Associations). In 2001, the AIDP created the Mediterranean Federation for the study and diffusion of issues regarding the HRM in collaboration with the governments of France, Spain, Portugal, Algeria, Morocco and Tunisia.

It regularly publishes two journals addressing all its members: *Direzione del Personale* (on a quarterly basis) and *Hamlet* (on a bimonthly basis) – which are available on news-stands with *L'Impresa* – and has produced a series of books on HRM published by Guerini e Associati Editore. Each year, the AIDP organises a national congress focusing on issues of special cultural and social relevance.

The association also focuses a great deal on young people in search of employment and professional orientation, promoting important educational initiatives such as Master's programmes, seminars teaching key job-hunting skills (creating a CV, job interview skills, self-assessment, how to respond to job advertisements, etc.), internship opportunities, general employment information, scholarships and so on.

The AIDP promotes a number of initiatives involving a high degree of social and civil commitment such as the Aziende Attive award in collaboration with AIRC (Italy's cancer research association), recognised by the President of the Republic, honouring the most outstanding projects designed to safeguard health in the workplace. AIDP and ALI (the association of Italian booksellers) have signed a convention for the promotion of reading and books in the context of Italian companies.

The roster of AIDP members includes such prominent names as Alenia, Alitalia, BNL, BMW, Capitalia, Colgate-Palmolive, COTRAL, Daimler-Chrysler, ENEL, ENI, EXXON MOBIL, Ferrari, FIAT, FS, Generali, Glaxo, Gucci, IBM, Lottomatica, Microsoft, Poste Italiane, Procter&Gamble and Telecom.

.it

HR ACADEMIA: ITALIAN UNIVERSITIES AND TRAINING IN HRM

In the late 1990s, Italian universities underwent a process of restructuring aimed at bringing them into line with other European countries. One of the objectives focused on by the law was to create a bridge between academic study and professional life by implementing periods of internship in private or public organisations at the end of study courses, and projects whose results are presented by the student at the degree stage.

With this new scenario, the old academic culture started to face the big changes emerging in the workplace with the globalisation of markets, the ICT revolution and the knowledge economy. Within this framework, a very important role is played by HR, with the intangible capital of competences and know-how. Among the consequences of this changing situation are (a) the growing presence of HR managers among teachers of organisation, training, communication and HRM; and (b) the growing number of faculties addressing HRM. This phenomenon has more to do with MBAs than with 'traditional' university programmes.

As far as universities are concerned, HRM plays an important role in economics and political science courses, mainly in Milan, Padua and Rome – La Sapienza Universities. One can find many Masters in HRM both at Universities (Luiss – Rome, Bocconi – Milan) and at private organisations.

The theoretical thinking on HRM has changed a great deal since the 1970s: from a conflict-based approach linked to industrial relations, typical in the 1970s, we have moved in the 1990s to a psychological approach (Novara, Spaltro), to a sociological one (De Masi and others), to an organisational development one (U. Capucci). Developments in the current century present HRM as a well-established profession with a set of common techniques and methodologies published in well-known handbooks (Paneforte 1999; Boldizzoni 2000; Auteri 2001; Costa 2005, and many others).

In recent years, people management has started to be considered as a valuable part of business strategy in the framework of knowledge economy, so HR managers are increasingly considered as business managers in charge of people, seen more as human capital than as employees. Both theory and practice increasingly look at HR professionals as business partners who have to contribute to the creation of added value to the company. The last two national conferences of the AIDP have focused on these issues. Looking to the future, HRM in Italy has to achieve a certification scheme process, similar to that of the UK, which should be necessary for all young people seeking to enter the profession. This will require close cooperation with universities, business schools and HR associations.

What would you say one ought not to do? What are the 'don'ts' in your country?

'Don'ts' in our country have mainly to do with respect for other people. Never show a sense of superiority in any way (management methods, culture and so on); such an attitude will only create enemies.

BEST-PRACTICE CASE: UNICREDITO ITALIANO – PRACTISING BUSINESS PARTNERSHIP

THE CONTEXT

In January 2003 Unicredito Italiano launched the S3 project, which aimed to redesign the organisational asset of the entire group to enable the bank to benefit from the emerging competitive dynamics and become a multi-specialist banking group on a European level. The S3 project sought to enhance the evolution of Unicredito from a federal model, based on specialisation of the different banks of the group on a geographical basis, to a model based on control of different customer segments (customer-driven specialisation).

The crucial step was the 'unbundling' of the configuration used up until that point by Italian banking, which had seven banks focused on specific areas (Credito Italiano, Rolo Banca, Cariverona, Banca CRT, Cassamarca, Cassa di Risparmio di Trieste, Caritro), transforming it into a model based on three main market segments: private, corporate and retail banking. The conditions achieved within the group and in the market suggested the usefulness of this project, aiming to obtain a competitive advantage in coherence with certain internal and marketing variables:

- same technological platform for all banks belonging to the group;
- critical mass in all three market segments;
- heightened needs of a dedicated service market;
- service quality more important than brand and 'logistics'; and
- competitors engaged in restructuring activities already completed within the group.

The S3 project made possible the creation of three banks specialised in each segment:

- The Retail Bank, based in Bologna, focused on segments of mass-market customers, affluent ones and small businesses, 23,000 employees, about 2,800 branches and with a mission to become the largest local Italian bank, committed to helping households and small businesses realise their life projects.
- The corporate bank, based in Verona, focused on corporate customers, served about 250 branches and 4,000 employees, with the aim of setting the standard for a new banking relationship through excellence in design and delivery of products, and services and customer selection, so as to be recognised as the key partner in managing clients' risks.
- The private bank, based in Turin, focused on high net-worth customers, with 150 branches, 1,600 employees, about 750 relationship managers and with a mission to become the leading Italian wealth management provider focusing on preserving and increasing the wealth of private clients through a holistic approach, superior services and innovative solutions.

The three banks refer to three segment departments which include: Clarima (consumer credit), Unicredit banca per la casa (retail customer loans), Locat (leasing) and Xelion (network of financial advisers). The group macro-picture is completed by support companies such as UPA (centralised productions), USI (information technology) and URE (real estate).

What is your advice for a foreign firm entering your country's market? What should managers especially care about and, what is more, be aware of?

Managers of foreign firms entering our country should know that a person-to-person approach is needed to avoid making mistakes. Individuals in Italy want to be treated as such and a foreign manager should behave accordingly. Creativity is not a problem in this country, but it must be organised in a team spirit and that is not an easy task.

IMPACTS ON HR DIRECTORATE AND HR MANAGER ROLES

The HR directorate has been one of those most intensely involved in the huge effort of guaranteeing that the new configuration of the group is supported by adequate resources from the point of view of both professional skills and geographical positioning. The effort made by the HR directorate throughout the period of the S3 project aimed at ensuring the best allocation of resources from the seven regional banks.

After the phase during which it was necessary to support the launch of the new organisational model, an analysis was initiated of the new model's impacts on the role of HR managers.

At the beginning of 2004, a project called 'Being a new HR manager' got underway; taking as its basis the topics highlighted in 2003 as critical issues for the function of HR managers (the first year of management based on the S3 model), the aim was to define the new role of this function and the development guidelines to be monitored. A spotlight was trained on the role of HR managers, i.e. personnel managers in charge of resources management and development in the different territories into which the three banks were segmented and the personnel executives of the companies providing products or services.

That role was considered critical because it represented the function in its direct relationship with line management and it was responsible for leading business management towards change. The way the role was interpreted up to that point was mainly 'operative' and was aimed at providing assistance to management, which consisted in helping them to face their 'problems' (not only those relating to personnel management) and focus on achieving business targets.

The challenges that HR managers faced were: elasticity, adaptability, pragmatism and common sense as well as company processes and mechanisms. On the other hand, considering the strong focus on the short-term period, there was some orientation towards medium- to long-term staff planning. There was concern that the HR manager's role was not evolving according to the role intended for the HR function and the type of HR–line management relationship that the group had intended to pursue to support the business segment strategies.

THE PROJECT GOALS AND THE PROJECT PHASES

The project had the following goals:

- identifying and setting the new profile of the HR manager role;
- enhancing HR managers' role so that they could understand the new profile required as well as what they could develop to comply with it (also providing them with a personal path);
- involving and making HR managers responsible in an active role needed for the ongoing change;
- letting HR managers test ways to lead their structures towards a new HR model, supporting development and reorientation; and
- increasing coordination and cooperation among HR managers and within HR central structures.

The project was divided into three phases as illustrated by Figure 8.1: (a) identifying the new elements of the HR manager profile; (b) sharing the role profile with HR managers and setting priorities in action change; and (c) implementing the HR manager profile, identifying guidelines – after an analysis also carried out at individual level – for the development of the competences and knowledge necessary to meet fully this new role, and asking HR managers to contribute to the innovation of HR managerial practices in line with the evolutionary path undertaken by the function of HR managers.

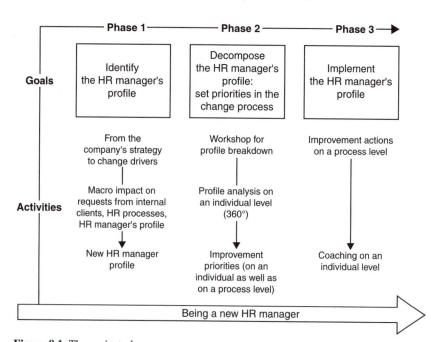

Figure 8.1 The project phases

Phase 1: defining the new HR manager profile – the referral model

To achieve the project goals it was fundamental to identify a referral model in phase 1 to guide the analysis on the HR directorate role and, as a consequence, on the guidelines for the development of the role of HR managers.

To reach the definition of the new profile through a structured itinerary, the referral model, as described in Figure 8.2, was adopted. This suggested defining the new role only after investigating:

– the HR vision and mission, which, based on contexts, objectives and priorities, makes it possible to define the managerial and leadership role and the EVP; and
– the HR model, aiming to identify (in close connection with what the vision and mission analysis showed) the principles and policies that need to inspire the HR action, its roles and competences, and the consistent service model.

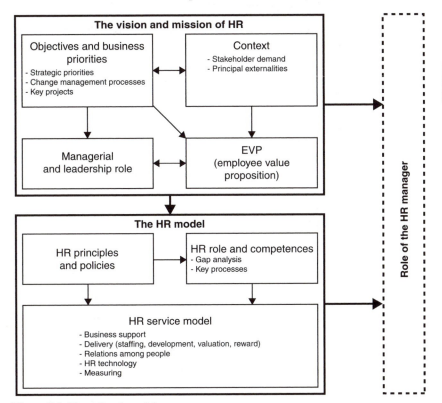

Figure 8.2 The referral model

The model described above had been submitted to Unicredito after being applied to support analysis of the evolution of HR functions in companies operating in many different areas but having in common the need to redesign their mission, service, model and role to make them equal to the emerging requests.

In order to collect data needed to build the HR manager profile on the basis of the model described above, interviews were conducted with:

– a number of business line managers to further the evolution of company strategy, staff expectations and the state of the art of HR service processes from the internal client's point of view; and
– a number of HR function referees to conduct an initial analysis of the drivers of function change, the managerial philosophy to be adopted on change drivers, the state-of-the-art of service processes from the HR viewpoint and, as a consequence, the evolution expected as far as the HR manager profile is concerned.

The aim was to define the new profile not on the basis of theoretical presuppositions out of context, but on the basis of a consideration which, starting from strategic and organisational evolution, was able to identify the areas that need to be examined to empower both the function and HR managers to provide the support required by the new organisational context.

The analysis confirmed that the HR directorate was gradually changing to control three main contexts with different service models, goals, competences and role profiles (Figure 8.3): (a) HR shared services (which involve administration processes and activities, payroll, HR information technology, budget and reporting) aim primarily to ensure the integrity of data, to guarantee swift and reliable information for the management relating to phenomena relevant to the HR field of interest and to ensure HR reliability for administration processes; (b) professional services (HR excellence) involving development processes and activities, training, organisation and selection and aimed primarily at guaranteeing high-quality professional service, policy and systems and supporting their application and implementation; and (c) HR business partners (which involve the local personnel units which focus on service to the line managers, are able to transfer policy and apply management systems and criteria developed in other HR contexts.

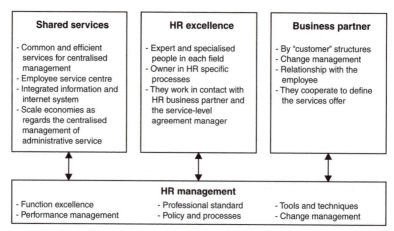

Figure 8.3 The new HR configuration

Starting from the evolutionary configuration of the directorate and seeking to correlate the three contexts to HR service requests (Figure 8.4), it appeared clear that HR managers, thanks to their knowledge of business problems, were the crucial link making it possible to address HR services to the line management and to guarantee the contextual application of HR methods and instruments.

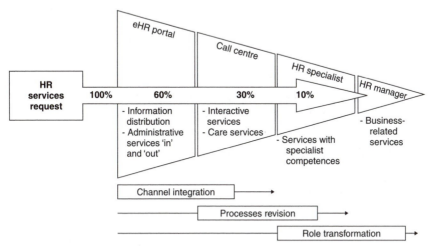

Figure 8.4 HR service request

Nevertheless, it was also clear that any attempt to move towards such a model affecting only HR roles and competences would have risked failing if it had been unable, on the one hand, to provide HR managers with effective tools (relevant to 'HR excellence' structures), and, on the other, to free them from all time-consuming commitments and activities for the line management which can be better carried out by shared services.

In short, the full implementation of the new model requested not only interventions aiming at a role transformation and development of new competences, but also process review interventions and interventions designed to improve HR tools.

The limits of the project did not make it possible to act on all areas of competence. Nevertheless, the chance was taken to analyse the service model in general and the HR manager role in order to exploit HR business partner (HRBP) confrontation moments and identify (in a bottom-up logic) which managerial and management tools and processes were necessary to allow the full implementation of the model and full entitlement to the new role that was about to emerge.

Through the analysis carried out using the model mentioned above, it was possible not only to give consideration to the configuration of the project but also to detect some other interesting details, which proved very useful for identifying the profile needed as a reference to guide the evolution of the HRBP role in the new context.

243

In brief, the arrival point for the new HR manager role consisted in identifying it more and more as the central organisational entity among the various line management activities and the whole coherence of the group HR policies:

- knowing the reference business as key driver of credibility and accreditation with the line;
- people's medium- to long-term planning skills;
- not just direct management tools but also advanced managerial sensitivity development among managers; and
- not just elasticity, adaptability, pragmatism and common sense, but also strong managerial and on-the-job competences together with the ability to guide line management during change.

These elements have become the main subjects of the analysis, sharing and assessment carried out in phase 2 of the project.

Phase 2: sharing the HR manager profile

Once the emerging profile was identified, an effort was made in phase 2 to share it with all the HR managers by taking the following steps:

- Initial workshop to share the change drivers and the new profile with HR managers and to evaluate the consequent impacts at individual, process and function levels with the aim of achieving a shared description of a common vision.
- Self-assessment and complete feedback on the components characterising the HR manager profile.
- Final workshop to deliver the results obtained during the self-assessment and the personal development plan and to launch the process improvement plan.

The complete feedback meant that each HR manager was able to receive feedback on development, competences and organisational behaviour from a large number of people with whom they had institutional work contacts, which differ in terms of goals and relationship model. The involvement of a number of key witnesses made it possible to analyse the HR business partner from various 'angles', on the basis of predefined criteria and competences and in accordance with the analysis carried out during the profile identification phase, in which the correct balance was sought between HR, line management and internal client viewpoints.

The list of privileged witnesses who made and detailed the complete feedback was drawn up by:

- bosses (the direct boss or, in the case of a matrix structure, the hierarchical and functional referent);
- peer colleagues (at least three clients and internal providers: at least one market/branch manager for the banks, at least one operational unit manager); and
- direct collaborators on the first organisational reporting level (between about three and five).

The results contributed to the development of HRBP competences, guaranteeing the possibility of activating coherent and tailored development/self-development, coaching and valorisation support interventions.

Phase 3: improving the HR manager profile

From an individual-level development action viewpoint, a path acting on two levels was set:

1. Improvement actions initiated directly by people, after reflection on the complete feedback results (which go beyond a diagnostic tool and thus become an individual development tool), after discussion with those responsible and after receiving coaching.
2. Support initiatives for individual development and for better role coverage, enacted by the company in line with the outcomes of the discussion on the new role profile and the needs expressed by the HRBPs.

IMPROVEMENT ACTIONS ON TOOLS, METHODOLOGIES AND PROCESSES

Following the shared opinions about the profile, six work groups were activated, formed by the same HRBPs with the goal of making improvement proposals coherent with the evolution of the evolutionary reference model, and focused on:

- the contribution that the HR function in general and the other HRBPs in particular can make to improving the processes of the different realities of the group; and
- the contribution in terms of improving: management system and knowledge development, reporting system and cost analysis, mobility and career path.

The logic presuppositions suggested including an analysis on HR processes and practices as follows:

1. The consideration that the new interpretation of the role of the HR manager also requires a positive contribution to the improvement of the level of service delivered to the lines through intervention of HR.
2. The consideration that it is not possible to imagine full coverage of the new role unless action is also taken on the relationship with the central HR (HR excellence and shared services), based on the availability of updated development tools and information sets for HRBPs.

Further added value from the insertion of HR practice and process analysis in the process was delivered by the circumstance that, contrary to what normally takes place in similar experiences, the intervention areas were not dictated from above; they were chosen by the HRBPs from the areas considered most critical in their specific context (Figure 8.5).

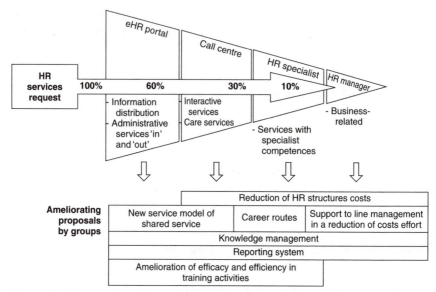

Figure 8.5 Work carried out by coherence groups according to the evolutionary reference model

Work sessions – even though they were limited to two or three and had to be carried out within a limited time frame (one month) – resulted in the selection of a number of improvement proposals interesting enough to go along with the evolution designed for the role. Such proposals looked at three main areas:

1. Rationalisation of HR processes to reduce costs, enhance efficacy and focus attention on activities with added value.
2. Work on methodologies supporting HR activities to improve them and make them more popular and more widely used by HR business partners.
3. Provision of HR services to line management according to a new logic.

Among the proposals put forward, some have become particularly important for their double adaptability – to the coverage of the new role and to the evolution of the function towards the new model. They are relevant to the subject of new ways of sharing and developing new knowledge along the whole cycle of HR activities and to the subject of the new logic needed to guide HR process report production.

KNOWLEDGE MANAGEMENT SYSTEMS SUPPORTING THE NEW HR ASSET

The ongoing change needed to be supported by tools able to help the function – as a professional community – to rationalise, share and provide access to knowledge for people and in particular for HR managers as a step in the process of acting efficiently on processes and on competent professional practices.

The knowledge workshops with HR business partners were meant to identify practical ways to give common ground to individual knowledge, acting both on support instruments and on culture and management suggestions.

From the very beginning, it was clear that the problem was the availability and usability of information of interest, rather than its existence. The primary goal was not so much to develop new knowledge, but rather to guarantee full access to the information set pertinent to the job in a structured and diffused way which was not based on informal networks.

The new tool configuration proposal keeps the following three items, in particular, in the frame:

1. Thinking about knowledge systems not only in terms of information technology tools but, most of all, in terms of systems capable of institutionalising the way knowledge is acquired, developed, systematised and shared.
2. Structuring a process beginning with knowledge needs and community competences and only then planning technological solutions and correct channels for sharing information.
3. Involving members of the community represented by HR business partners in designing the model used (feeding, filling, data input, etc.), creating, as a consequence, a strong feeling of involvement among future users of the 'system'.

The team developed its work along the following guidelines:

- agreement on the approach to the systematisation, consolidation and development of the knowledge of the HR function;
- individuation (for two test processes: professional management and development) of the technical and professional knowledge relevant for the activities performed and for the relevant sources of knowledge, as a first step in the building of tools (including IT tools) needed to support and share information within the function; and
- initial identification of the areas of knowledge of interest (HR field/territory, governance/coordination and business) to be presented, and possible instruments and initiatives to support their consolidation and development (in addition to traditional ones, such as job rotation, training, etc.).

In a few words, what would you say is the one fundamental strategic competitive advantage your country offers compared to others?

The one fundamental competitive advantage of this country is creativity in almost every field (food, machinery, fashion, design, etc.).

CONCLUSION: THE NEW RATIO OF HR MANAGERIAL REPORTING

Other subjects relevant for the way the new roles are interpreted – both for the HR function itself and for line management – was the configuration of the information system and the HR data outcome throughout the entire process. The anticipated goal was inspired by the assumption that it was necessary to integrate considerations of the structure of HR reporting (already initiated in Unicredito) and IT tools with thought on the procedures required to ensure that production and distribution of information were harnessed to provide real support for interpretation of the new role.

No more reports to be produced following set traditions but reports to be addressed in accordance with the events to be monitored and organised in a service logic oriented towards the same HR business partners and line management. The conclusions reached showed the fundamental characteristics that HR process report production must have if there is a strong will to achieve the goal of convergence towards the HRBP model:

- flexible reporting system, able to dynamically satisfy emerging information needs, focused on the monitoring of predefined phenomena;
- need to satisfy information requirements diversified according to the recipients (HR, line management, etc.);
- different level of aggregation and detail depending on managerial needs and the visibility level of the final recipient;
- different views on the macro-categories of information for in-depth analysis of phenomena; and
- report access modalities, with availability of standard reports to satisfy the need of a large number of users, and ad hoc personalised reports on request.

The project, thanks to the different actions that have been undertaken, has achieved the goal of making the HRBPs' role evolve in line with the role identified for the HR function as a whole and with the HR–line management kind of relationship that the group intended to pursue to support the strategies of the business segments. Thanks to this, both the function and the HRBPs have maintained an operative response to the short-term needs of the individual departments into which the group has been subdivided, without losing the common basis of managerial views and HR competences.

Moreover, reflection has led the HRBPs to stick substantially to the proposed model and to realise that only guided role development (reinforced by supporting and aiding actions) can enable them (and the whole function) to drive the ongoing changes in trends.

The path started at the beginning of 2004 was completed by the end of the year when the Unicredito group declared new strategic development guidelines that ask all functions which are not front end (which includes HR) to further emphasise the convergence between a service profile both to line management and to business.

The evolution profile individuated for the function, the characterisation of the role of the HR manager as HRBP and the effort to improve the reading and understanding of the organisation variables are coherent (and in a way anticipatory) results of the company's requests.

Which people play key roles in your country? Which names should one know?

Apart from political leaders, such as Mr Berlusconi, Mr Prodi and so on, a major role is played by bankers (Mr Profumo, CEO Unicredit, Mr Passera, CEO Intesa Group), by the President of the Italian employers' association Mr Cordero di Montezemolo and by certain economists (Mario Monti, Padoa Schioppa).

Q.it

References

Rassegna online (1993): Il testo dell'accordo tra governo, Confindustria e sindacati sulle nuovi relazioni sindacali (protocol from 23 July 1993); available at: www.rassegna.it/2003/speciali/concertazione/protocollo.htm.

The authors

Massimo Delucchi (aidp@aidp.it), Gruppo Ligure AIDP, Consultant and Vice-President.

Massimo Roascio (www.telecomitalia.it), Telecom Italia Group, Head of Human Resources Professional Services.

Barbara Parmeggiani (rso@rso.it), RSO partner, manager of RSO Corporate Education and CEO of ICUS FRANCE (RSO Group), works mainly in HR assessment and development, executive coaching, training and communication (also web-based), culture/morale surveying. She is a consultant for development systems design, advanced training, managerial communication, blended learning and knowledge management.

Massimo Lanzanò (rso@rso.it), RSO consultancy company, Head of the Telecommunication business unit.

Valerio Salone (rso@rso.it), RSO, Head of Bank, Insurance and Financial Services business unit. He is in charge of organisational review and change management and is responsible for planning and implementation of competence systems, innovative training and development paths, knowledge management systems and e-HR services.

Giulio Carè (rso@rso.it), RSO, Senior Consultant since 1998 and partner since 2001. He is in charge of several projects relating to organisational change, people valorisation and development, and planning and implementation of competence systems.

Mario D'Ambrosio (aidp@aidp.it), AIDP (Italian Association of Personnel Management), President. Vice Dean at European University of Rome, responsible for organisation, marketing and promotion activities. Visiting Professor of human resources and communication at the universities of Pescara, La Sapienza (Rome) and LUMSA (Rome). Partner of consultancy companies in HRM. Personnel director of major Italian companies.

Filippo Abramo (filippo_abramo@bancosardegna.it), Banco Sardegna, Human and Technical Resources Director. President of FMRH (Fédération Mediterranéen des Ressources Humaines).

.it

9 HRM in Latvia: show respect and get results

Aivars Kalniņš/Anita Sāne/Sandra Zariņa

Latvia: in a nutshell

In this chapter you will learn:

- that HRM in Latvia is embedded into a new context due to the enlargement of the European Union. Therefore new exigencies, e.g. regarding the labour market, have to be challenged;

- that Latvian HR academia is at an early stage. The focus is on developing practical applications for individual companies which will lead to world-class HR service for business; and

- that Lattelekom has an irrational corporate culture: the most effective way to run its business is by combining an autocratic management style with commensurate corporate culture.

Capital:	Riga
Area (sq km):	64,589 (land 63,589; water 1,000)
EU membership:	since 2004
Population:	2,278,500
Languages:	Latvian (official), Lithuanian, Russian, other
Ethnic groups (in percentages):	Latvian 59.0, Russian 28.5, Belarusian 3.8, Ukrainian 2.5, Polish 2.4, Lithuanian 1.4, other 2.4 (2006)
Gross domestic product:	35.08 billion USD (2006)
Workforce (in percentages):	1.173 million (2006): agriculture 10.8; industry 15.6; services 63.0 (2006)
Export commodity:	wood and wood products, machinery and equipment, metals, textiles, foodstuffs

BACKGROUND: HRM AS A CHALLENGE

THE NEW CONTEXT

The year 2004 brought significant changes throughout Europe. The enlargement of the EU gave a new flavour to the old Europe. Ten new countries became members of a large and wealthy community. One of these was Latvia, a small country in eastern Europe.

Year by year, since the Independent State of Latvia was re-established, improvements have taken place in the entrepreneurial environment. The Latvian Parliament has passed many new laws. Step by step, the rules of the open market game are entering the culture. The differences in competitive advantages are beginning to shrink. The marked advantages for some in the first years after privatisation are beginning to disappear in many areas of the economy. We are coming to a time when enterprises of the same type or the same profile might have the same resources (money, equipment, etc.), the same technologies, the same knowledge and the same calibre of specialists available – even within a very small labour market in such a small country.

Government policy is strongly inclined towards continued integration into the economic life of Europe and improving economic relations with Russia. Although living standards have improved over the last few years, poverty levels remain high in comparison to other European countries. Most former state-owned enterprises are now in private hands and account for more than 65 per cent of GDP and over 66 per cent of all jobs.

⊞ .lv

Because of its location on the famous trade route from the Vikings to the Greeks, transport and transit trade account for more than 15 per cent of Latvia's GDP. Latvia has three major ports, one of which, Ventspils, is among the leading European ports in terms of cargo turnover. The best-performing economic sectors are mechanical engineering, timber and construction, textiles, food processing, chemicals and pharmaceuticals. Latvia's largest trading partner is the EU.

Considerable growth has taken place in the IT sector, and the software industry has an annual growth rate of 150 per cent. The government is promoting Latvia as a favoured location for high-tech industries, and support for the IT sector in its bid to become an eastern European leader in the export of software development services.

According to government sources, Latvia has a significant pool of skilled, relatively low-cost labour.

> **What is typical of your country in relation to the country itself (its culture, people, etc.) and its economy?**
>
> Latvian people are hard-working, do not follow rules literally and are quite reticent in early stages of communication. They have respect for westerners and

imported goods except for food. They are not polite when driving. The economy is one of the fastest growing among the new EU members: around 10 per cent GDP growth per year. 'Latvia is one of the most successful countries in the Post-Soviet Union area' (B. Karlson, USA Ambassador, December 2004, Riga). Latvia's national culture is based on a Christian understanding of the world, strong working traditions, geographical positioning at the crossroads between East and West, and the experience of two World Wars which destroyed everything.

THE WORKFORCE

The total size of the Latvian labour market is 1.8 million persons, including 1.2 million active in the labour market. The majority of them are concentrated in the largest cities – Riga, Daugavpils, Liepaja and Jelgava. The unemployment rate on 1 January 2007 was 6.5 per cent. The overall unemployment rate is moderate yet stable, but there are significant regional differences. Currently the greatest number of people work in manufacturing, which accounts for 15.6 per cent of total employment; 15.6 per cent are in the wholesale and retail trade and the automobile, motorcycle, personal and household appliance repair sector; 10.8 per cent are in agriculture, hunting and forestry.

Lately, there has been a tendency for employment to grow in forestry, construction, transport and communications, health and social care.

The education system

Along with location, the key economic asset of Latvia is its people, who have benefited historically from a sound education system, even under different ruling powers. With the first technical university having been established in 1862, Latvia currently boasts a modern three-level education system, which has achieved international recognition through good average standards and outstanding results in international competitions for students.

Because Latvia has the second highest per capita ratio of students in Europe (after Finland), it maintains the inflow and availability of new specialists in its labour and intellectual markets. As a result of an underestimation of needs for some social science subjects, like business and law during the Soviet period, and the resulting shortages in specialists, these subjects have become the most popular with students in recent times. However, the natural sciences and technology, particularly IT and applied technologies, are currently experiencing increased demand as a direct result of the need for these skills in the expanding industrial sector.

Vocational education institutions throughout the country provide a variety of programmes for the industrial (such as metalworking, forestry/woodworking and construction) and service sectors. These also function as centres for the further qualification of persons already in the labour market.

The labour market

Latvia offers significant labour cost advantages across virtually all industries and positions, within a short distance of western Europe. Although rising steadily, labour cost increases remain lower than advances in productivity, which means that current labour costs in a variety of positions, from factory worker to software engineer, amount to only 20 to 30 per cent of those in western Europe (Table 9.1). It should be noted that regional differences in labour costs are considerable – as much as 40 per cent between the city of Riga and the remote Latgale region, a significant additional advantage when choosing locations for highly labour-intensive operations.

Table 9.1 Medium gross monthly wages/salaries in selected positions, 2006 (Fontes R&I compensation survey)

Area of activity	Indicative position/qualification	EUR/month
Management	Director of a medium-sized company	4,269
IT&T	Network administrator of a small/medium-sized company	839
	Programmer–analyst	1,238
	Call centre operator	441
Logistics	Truck driver	626
	Warehouse worker	484
Manufacturing	Engineer, CAD design	911
	Engineer, manufacturing equipment	854
	Qualified worker	740

The main challenge for Latvian labour market policy is to react to changes in the economy and to foresee the fields and activities in which labour will be needed.

Undeclared work has attracted attention in connection with Latvia's joining the EU and the difficult budgetary situation has led the government to seek to exploit sources of public income as fully as possible.

Clandestine employment of both Latvian citizens and foreign nationals is thought to be common in sectors such as construction, trade, industry, agriculture and sport. According to experts, the problem is complex and arises for a number of underlying reasons. Undeclared work takes a number of forms, such as: unpaid overtime, fully or partly concealed paid work (whereby the employee receives payment in cash, off the record), and employment without employment contracts or with invalid contracts. Moreover, this clandestine activity distorts competition among businesses and leads people knowingly to agree to be employed illegally.

Many employers argue that in the current situation, when starting or modernising a business requires intensive investment, their businesses would be impossible without illegal work. They would hope to switch to legal employment as soon as the main problems of setting up and expanding their businesses are solved.

Another factor is that social security contributions are high in Latvia, mainly due to an extremely unfavourable demographic situation. For every 1,000 people of working age, there are 603 people either above (347) or below (256) working age.

The labour law

The labour law of Latvia came into force on 1 June 2002. Before this law, employment issues were regulated by a Code of Labour Laws, adopted in 1972 by the Supreme Council of the Soviet Republic of Latvia. The Labour Law includes provisions transposing many EU employment and social policy directives, such as those relating to equal treatment, collective redundancies, working time and rest, the protection of young workers and posting employees to work abroad. The law also incorporates principles of the Council of Europe's European Social Charter and various International Labour Organisation (ILO) conventions. Hence, there has been no need for further major changes since Latvia joined the EU in May 2004.

Employment relations in Latvia are essentially based on the employment contract. A set of legal acts provide for mutual employment relations between an employer and an employee established by such a contract. These include the Latvian Constitution (*Satversme*); the Labour Law (*Darba likums*) – the main law regulating individual and collective employment and industrial relations; international laws applicable to Latvia; other national legal acts; collective agreements; and procedural work rules.

What would you say one ought not to do? What are the 'don'ts' in your country?

It is important to appreciate that Latvians are well educated, hard-working and not stupid. See and treat them as partners. Do not regard Latvians as poor labourers from eastern Europe – show respect and get results!

THE SOCIAL DIALOGUE

Latvia has long-standing trade union traditions; the first unions were formed in 1905. The unions were established on sector lines. After Latvia's independence at the beginning of the 1990s, trade unions experienced a sharp fall in influence and membership. Sector and large enterprise unions survived, while in newly established enterprises, unions were established reluctantly, if at all. The number of union members fell after independence, not only because many enterprises went bankrupt, but also because workers left en masse as they did not see the importance of unions and did not want to pay membership fees. However, unions are gradually regaining their importance, and they now act as meaningful social partners, although they still represent only 20 per cent of the total workforce.

In April 2007, 151 trade unions were registered. There is one national centre, the Free Trade Union Confederation of Latvia (LBAS). The LBAS groups twenty-four trade unions or professional employees' associations in various sectors, which themselves represent 2,900 union organisations in state and municipal institutions and private enterprises, with over 165,000 members.

Company attitudes towards the establishment of unions vary. Those companies that care about introducing good management practices not only do not object to them, they actually facilitate the formation of unions. However, smaller firms are more reluctant to see unions established. Furthermore, unions have not yet been established in several sectors (e.g. among road transport workers), while in some sectors several unions are active (e.g. in the metalworking and machinery construction sectors).

Unions today seek to act as sector and occupational unions for the common defence of employment, economic and social rights. They conduct social dialogues with the government and employers' organisations.

LBAS is a member of the International Confederation of Free Trade Unions (ICFTU), the European Trade Union Confederation (ETUC) and the Baltic Trade Union Council (BTUC). It also prioritises cooperation with the ILO and the Baltic Sea Trade Union Network (BASTUN). LBAS members cooperate with international trade union organisations for their sectors and similar union organisations in other countries.

From the point of view of HR work, this means that there are companies where dialogue with trade unions is an important part of HR work, while there are others that have no unions and no such types of work.

The Latvian Employers' Confederation (LEC) is the only employers' association, which in conformity with the Law on Employers' Organisations and their Associations represents employers' interests at the National Tripartite Cooperation Council. The LEC was established in 1993.

LEC membership is currently as follows: thirty-five regional and industry (sector) associations in various fields of economic activity. At present, about 30 per cent of all Latvian employers are members of the LEC. The LEC joined the International Organisation of Employers (IOE) in June 1994 and has participated in ILO activities since it was founded in 1993.

259

NEW BEHAVIOUR FOR A NEW CONTEXT

Most businesses are already well aware of some of the sales and customer service strategies that attract new clients, provide more new services to existing customers, guarantee services of high quality and maintain existing customers.

Imagine: products and services offered by your company are excellent, and your marketing and sales people are well educated. However, you are not always happy with the results achieved. What else can you do? Have you ever thought that we very often think of selling as just 'receiving orders' and fielding top-class products and services? Do you think about the parties involved at the moment of sale (they are not just the salesperson and the client)? What are the selling dilemmas? Does your company really understand what factors are motivating sellers, and do you, as the seller, know what is really meant by excellent job delivery? Does the fact that you are regularly being informed about the new products and general company developments mean that you are directly involved in company processes and that you have good business understanding? What determines good or bad luck in selling? What do the words 'client understanding' mean? And there are many more well-known minor questions, the deeper meaning of which remains ambiguous.

Taking all these questions into account, we can say that many companies are starting to look for new competitive advantages. Companies are looking for new and very advanced customer bases, getting good insight into every more or less significant customer for a small country. Very specific customer satisfaction programmes can now be launched in a very narrow marketplace. New quality improvement systems are under development or being introduced (EFQM-type activities, for example). Some companies are entering highly complicated technological areas and trying to put into place some of the most advanced ideas and organisational development theories from the continent.

Many of these competitive advantages are in areas where the possibilities are easily described. It is relatively simple to describe on paper or on the web how the new advanced customer database of a new 'delivery-by-post' company functions; the result is that its competitors very easily copy it. The initial conclusion is very strange: competitive advantages are fleeting. A company would lose them immediately after a competitor imitated them. So a look at corporate culture provides some possible answers.

What is your advice for a foreign firm entering your country's market? What should managers especially care about and, what is more, be aware of?

Latvians are Europeans but some things work differently in this country. Please check that your ideas are viable in Latvia. We do not follow rules literally; it is good to know that. For foreign companies entering the Latvian market we would suggest: first, gain some understanding of local culture;

second, learn some basics about the history of Latvia; and third, do not think you are 'automatically better coming from the West'. Westerners need to be informed about the grey economy and probably the national differences between groups of people in Latvia.

UNDERSTANDING CORPORATE CULTURE

The cultural system may be the basis for a competitive advantage in markets because it could prove so difficult to imitate. Historically, because of the persistent Soviet influence on the country, corporate culture issues stood somewhat apart among the range of competitive advantages possible. Looking at the examples of local companies established from zero with relatively 'old histories' (Kalnozols, Parex, Reaton and Latvian Mobile Telephone), we could conclude even as ordinary customers that changes are happening within their corporate culture. Despite these changes, the well-established corporate cultures are more stable, and as such create a competitive advantage in this very small and narrow marketplace. For the customer, that fact is still significant at the moment of decision about the next purchase of services or goods.

EAPM AFFILIATE: LATVIJAS PERSONĀLA VADĪŠANAS ASOCIĀCIJA

HRM IN THE COMPANIES

There were already personnel departments in larger companies in Latvia during the period of the Soviet occupation. Their main function was to maintain employees' records, including job contracts, employment register books and orders about employee recruitment, discipline and dismissal. Things started to change slowly after 1990. Western companies establishing branches in Latvia introduced their HR practices. MBA programme students acquired western HR management knowledge. The Latvian Association of Personnel Managers (Latvijas Personāla vadīšanas asociācija (LPVA)) also played a role in spreading HR knowledge and sharing best experiences.

Most large companies in Latvia today have HR departments, but the level and duties performed still vary a great deal from one company to another. Some privatised businesses, and also state organisations, that kept most of their staff and management from Soviet times, have made variously paced transitions from Soviet-style personnel departments. Newly established companies, at some stage in their development, recognised the need for personnel managers and/or departments. Most Latvian HR managers are women (about 90 per cent) between the ages of 25 and 35. There is no statistical data available about the exact number of personnel managers and personnel department staff employed in Latvia at present. According to the data of the Enterprise Register, HR managers constituted 4 per cent of the board members of the top 300 Latvian companies (mostly based on foreign capital) in 2002. Thus there is still room for improvement in the HR manager's role in Latvia.

As to available HR services, an employer can either carry out all recruitment and staff selection alone or use the services of recruitment companies. There are regular recruitment companies, others offering web-based recruitment services, and a few offering headhunting and executive searches. Other HR-related services available include management assessment, organisational structure audits, HR procedure improvement, performance improvement, motivation, internal communication, job satisfaction assessment and employee training/retraining. The most common reasons for the need for these types of service in an increasingly dynamic economy are: company take-overs, mergers and acquisitions, privatisation, strategic change and restructuring, revitalisation and repositioning of companies, benchmarking or structuring of organisational effectiveness (downsizing). These services can provide key decision-makers with professional expertise about the competencies of individual team members, the functioning of the whole team/organisation, as well as bottom-line recommendations on improving the efficiency of organisations for the future.

What would you like to teach foreign HR managers? What is important for them to know in your opinion?

We would like to teach foreign HR managers how to work very hard, how to make transitions and reorganisations and how to work in a small country where everybody knows everybody.

THE LATVIAN ASSOCIATION OF PERSONNEL MANAGERS

The Latvian Association of Personnel Managers was established in 1996 to promote best HR practices in Latvia. The organisation grew slowly until 2000, when twenty new members joined the Association, making it a visible force in Latvian HR development. In April 2007, the Association had 205 members, most of them companies (legal entities), represented in the Association by their HR managers. There are also businesses, government agencies and HR service companies represented in the Association. Members are mostly located in Riga, but lately companies from Valmiera and Ventspils have also joined the Association. One of the goals of the Association was to become a member of the European Association for Personnel Management (EAPM). That was achieved in June 2001 during the Association Congress in Geneva.

The Association organises training seminars on current HR topics, visiting member companies and disseminating their best practices. It also has collaboration agreements with the Latvian Employers' Confederation and the Latvian Chamber of Trade and Commerce. The Association has collaborated with the Latvian Business School in organising annual personnel management conferences since 1997. The Baltic Conference of Personnel Management was planned for 2005 in cooperation with the Estonian Conference Centre.

Eva Selga chaired the working group on 'Professional standards for personnel specialists', which was approved by the Latvian Ministry of Education on 10 July 2002.

An annual award for the best achievements in the field of HR was established by the Association in 2000. The aim of the award is to raise the competence and prestige of HR professionals and show the positive influence of HR practices for company development. The award winners were the Latvian Savings Bank, the IT company Dati, Latvian Mobile Telephone Company and the Latvian State Forest Organisation.

The Association supported the establishment of the Master's programme in HR that started in September 2003 at the Riga School of Economics and Business Administration.

Future tasks for the Association among others would be the promotion of research in the HR field and encouragement of cooperation with institutions of higher education.

HR ACADEMIA: THEORY AND PRACTICE

Many aspects of HR science have been applied and widely used in organisations in Latvia. However, there is almost no general research in this field that would influence its local development and practical solution to overall problems. All research is confined to very practical applications for individual companies; it is not geared to developing the field.

There are almost no original books on HR theories. Most work is directly translated from English, or local associated professors issue collections of well-known HRM theories and authors in the local language. The first attempt to depict the current HR situation in Latvia is *Practical Human Resource Management* by Inese Esenvalde (2004). She has managed successfully to tie together HRM, leadership and change theories with her observations on real company practices. It could be the beginning of further publications and discussions on this theme that might lead to true scientific development in the field.

Because of the influence on HRM development, it is worth noting that a couple of original books have been published on social and organisational psychology, with the aim of introducing these subjects to the general public in Latvia. Silvija Omārova (2001) and Viesturs Reņģe (1999a; 1999b; 2003) are outstanding professors, whose work is promoting these fields.

Mostly, HRM is taught only as a separate course in management and/or psychology programmes. The specialisation of organisation psychology did not appear at the University of Latvia (Reņģe 2003) until 1997, and only in autumn 2003 did the first fifty students embark on studies in personnel management to get a Master's degree in three years.

Currently, two educational establishments present information on HRM as part of full programmes and not just as separate courses.

One state school makes it possible for students to acquire a first-level professional degree acknowledged by the Latvia Higher Education Quality Evaluation Centre. However, only a little more than one-third of the course is devoted to HR. The rest covers general education subjects such as information systems, economics, entrepreneurship, foreign languages, etc.

The second establishment is the Riga International School of Economics and Business Administration. As can be seen from the name, the school provides a higher professional education. The graduates of the HR programme receive a professional Master's degree in HRM. It is hoped that this programme will lead to new advances in HR development. However, it is not yet accredited. For the time being, the students of the programme are mostly practising HR managers, who at last see the opportunity in Latvia to receive academic status for the knowledge they possess. The hope is that in the future it will grow into an HR research centre. This programme is built from a combination of business and sociology courses on the basis that HRM is an interdisciplinary science. The programme includes modules on economics and entrepreneurship, social sciences, IT and systems, research and management sciences. The following courses are integrated in the module on HR theory and practice:

– HRM;
– business relations;
– job safety;
– documentation;
– professional ethics;
– organisational marketing; and
– training and career development.

It is apparent that many HR aspects (e.g. job design, compensation, motivation, retention, and so on) will be treated only briefly, because they are incorporated into the programme not as separate courses but only as parts of other courses.

The science of HRM is obviously at an early stage of development in Latvia. In practice, HRM works very well here, with outstanding HR managers who have developed remarkable skills through self-study and education abroad – creating a unique situation with little local HR scientific development but world-class HR service for businesses.

.lv

.lv

What are you and other Latvian people extraordinarily proud of with respect to HRM?

We are proud of our ability to switch to a market economy quite quickly, and without too much investment from outside. We are proud to see real results of continuing change in the shape of new and renovated buildings including shopping centres, theatres and hotels. In the HR area, we are proud of our smooth transition to the modern type of HR strategies, policies and procedures in a very short time.

BEST-PRACTICE CASE: LATTELEKOM – LEARNING FROM AN IRRATIONAL CORPORATE CULTURE

LOOKING AT THE TIMETABLE

We will use the culture web of one relatively large Latvian telecommunications company, SIA Lattelekom, to illustrate deeper insights into the mix of corporate cultures with Latvian elements. SIA Lattelekom is a fixed telecommunications network operator. The company was established in 1994. The shareholding structure is as follows: Latvian state 51 per cent, TILTS Communications consortium 49 per cent. TILTS Communications is owned by a subsidiary of Sonera Corporation, Sonera Holdings B.V.; Telia Sonera has a 99.4 per cent holding in Sonera Corporation. During the ten-year period analysed, total investment in the telecommunications network ran to 470 billion LVL (the national currency is the *lat*). The digital network owned by Lattelekom may be seen as a national asset because of direct or indirect involvement of every Latvian citizen in the project development.

To describe the present culture of the company, we will first look at seven areas. The managers of the company made comments which can be assigned to them. The areas and comments were as follows:

1. The company's politics: typical comments by the employees referring to their salaries or the company's politics were 'good benefits system', 'nice salary, especially for jobs outside the capital', 'one man cannot change anything in the company (at least, I can't)', 'manager X is a hero (meaning in reality that he is good at intrigue)', 'impossible to lose one's job', 'office politics is legitimised in established top management laws for somebody's personal benefit', and 'secure, long-term positions'.

2. Symbols: the comments made here were 'artefacts support democratic environment', 'informal interpersonal communication', 'substitution of the language of office politics for a legitimate business language (inside company management, "political games" are described in everyday business language or slang)'.

3. Rituals and routines: comments in this area were 'many meetings', 'decisions made by boards not by individuals', 'outside consultants usual change-makers', 'no vertical communication in the whole company', 'no acknowledgement of real problems', 'typical old-fashioned "highest award" ceremony in company as example of the old culture'.

4. The paradigm: employees stated 'competence in intrigues as the key to success within the company', 'core business – technical modernisation according to a big plan', 'overall decrease in spending on training combined with development slogans'.

5. Power structure: employees commented on 'interpersonal networks', 'based on politics and intrigue – top management accepts such', 'many small kings and their small kingdoms', 'individual power depends on the president,

i.e. whether he likes you or not', 'personal benefits for the kings and their access to the distribution of funds is the basis for power'.

6. Control systems: comments included: 'individual targets in some units in place', 'feedback–reward system not linked with targets', 'volume targets as a key', 'targets not clearly communicated in the company as a whole', 'clear CAPEX [capital expenditure planning, budgeting and controlling] procedure'.

7. Organisational architecture: the subjects identified in this area are 'unclear responsibilities', 'complex matrix structure', 'customer segment-based organisation', 'competition among business units', 'unclear BU/HQ roles'.

There are in fact many options for analysing corporate cultures. To present a critical review of the subject, we have looked at some of the most popular corporate culture classifications and have drawn some conclusions about their possible application in real cases. What we are actually looking for is a model in which culture specifics might be presented in a more visible form.

BASIC CULTURE APPLYING MANFRED KETS DE VRIES

It is important to keep in mind the personality of the leader and the specific circumstances in Latvia in the post-Soviet period. According to Manfred F.R. Kets de Vries (2001), a leader has a critical role in creating a corporate culture. The way in which a manager or leader acquires and interprets information from inside and outside the organisation can influence employees and become the basis of an irrational corporate culture.

Kets de Vries would say that we have a real example of an irrational corporate culture. The case described above shows the situation where a company; has experienced a period of dysfunctional management at higher levels; that is to say where internal and external environment requirements have been underestimated or in some cases overvalued. The company management's reaction to the inside and outside signals has been inconsequential or inadequate. It seems that, where a situation is underestimated, not enough resources are allocated to address the real issues. There is also evidence of insufficient response to internal and external signals, including response to only one part of the problems (the control system, for example), leaving solutions to other parts of the problems unexamined.

Some comments in the example provide insights into the development of social defence mechanisms within the company. There are indicators of fatalism in the behaviour of the employees, manifested in unrealistic fears or unreal fantasies. Such a circumstance is very typical in post-Soviet countries, especially among the generation that has real work experience of the previous era. It makes it even harder to break out of the destructive closed loop.

According to Kets de Vries' classification there are five possible types of irrational corporate cultures:

– bureaucratic corporate culture;
– political corporate culture;

  – charismatic corporate culture;
  – evasive corporate culture; and
  – suspicious corporate culture.

The characterisations of different irrational cultures by Kets de Vries leads to the conclusion that, in the case of the company in the example, we are dealing with a suspicious organisational culture. The culture of an organisation is usually closely connected with its effectiveness. From examples and personal experience we can characterise weak organisational cultures in Latvia with these five key features: (a) there is no clear system of values in the company, no clear understanding of how to create success in the working place; (b) employees do not agree on the ways to achieve corporate targets; (c) different parts of the organisation have different understandings about corporate goals and values; (d) leaders of the organisation are destructive and do not support the development of a common understanding; and (e) traditional ceremonies and rituals are not connected with corporate targets, causing disorientation.

Conclusions may be drawn on the basis of examples from the service organisation of the company – there are similarities between the results of analysis of the company's corporate culture web and the weak culture described by Kets de Vries. Our conclusion is that, in the case of the service organisation, we are dealing with a suspicious corporate culture. That type of organisation is pervasively suspicious in dealings with people, customers and processes throughout the company. A suspicious company is too sensitive to the outside world, which also makes it difficult for it to deal with customers. The strategy of the company taken as an example is passive and conservative. In reality, the strategy of that company was unknown to employees and customers and not even accessible for deeper analysis by specialists. There is an increasing possibility of failure in the future. As a result, competitive advantage could be affected in some areas. From our point of view in the post-Soviet era, this could be one of the reasons for relatively low standards of customer service in companies, resulting in low competitiveness for the country as a whole.

APPLYING CHARLES HANDY

Applying Charles Handy's (2000) four types of corporate culture from *Gods of Management*, we come to similar conclusions. According to Handy, the four gods of management reflect four cultures (Table 9.2).

Table 9.2 Corporate cultures (based on Handy 2000)

The culture	The god
Club	Zeus
Role	Apollo
Task	Athena
Existential	Dionysius

The example that we are using for analysis fits more with the role culture or Apollo:

> Apollonian thinking is logical, sequential and analytical. Apollonians would like to believe in a formal scientific world, where events move according to predetermined formulae. They like to proceed from problem definition to the identification of the appropriate solution mechanism. On the whole, the more of these mechanisms you know, and can use, the more problems you are likely to be able to deal with. Efficiency tends to mean simplification, getting things down to the bare but essential figures.
>
> (Handy 2000: 53)

The more we examine the results of the culture web analysis, the more confident one can be that there is a role-type culture in that company:

> Power in the role cultures stems from one's role or position or title. Written into that role is a list of rights as well as responsibilities. The organisational chart is a diagrammatic way of showing who can give orders to whom or via whom. If you don't have the title you can only ask, not tell. The authority of your position not only entitles you to tell someone to do something, it also allows you to create a complex of rules, procedures and systems for your own domain. These rules, procedures and systems are railways of the steady state. They direct and steer the flow of information and activities which turn inputs into outputs.
>
> (Handy 2000: 55)

The key features of that kind of corporate culture also come from the Soviet era, when everything was prescribed by rules and regulations. And as we see in a real example, such attitudes are still alive in the corporate cultures of big companies with relatively old cultures.

Taking the same company as an example, we will look at its strategy or where it would like to be in the future. Its future is painted by the same middle managers of the company cited above. It shows in some ways just how far in the future they will be able to go and how real the changes are that they could make if their top management would support them. For simplicity's sake we will use the same culture web format as was used for the original interviews.

- (Desired) comments by employees: intrigue-makers are villains, heroes are innovative teams, common experiences of teams are important, anyone can change anything for the better, good benefits system, secure, long-term position, fraud is severely punished, more satisfied customers are reported, nice place to work, veterans learn new things.
- Symbols: fluent business language is used, informal personal communication, artefacts support democratic environment.
- Rituals and routines: teamwork, two-way vertical communication, recruitment process, visible, clear promotion and assessment process, all meetings prepared, only a few boards with clear responsibilities, one united HQ.

- The paradigm: client focus, core business–customer understanding, promotion of ideas, motto: 'To change for the better'.
- Power structure: based on expertise, interpersonal network as part of the structure.
- Control systems: team-based control mechanism, continuous feedback, oriented to long-term development, promise-keeping and customer satisfaction versus meeting procedural requirements, unit rewards based on how well they cooperate with other units.
- Organisational architecture: flat hierarchy, business units responsible for business, structure encourages collaboration among divisions.

Surprisingly, there is no mention of national culture as basic to the corporate culture; perhaps it is so ingrained that they fail to notice it.

How might one motivate those people to think and act differently? They value order and predictability in their lives. Things need to fit into place, with contracts precise and honoured, roles prescribed and adhered to. It is not easy to describe the motivation of those people without making them seem dull. Our judgement is simply that it will help to break the closed loop and move to a new culture in the future. This should include adopting the notion that it will help to break away from the experiences of the past years.

The results of the analysis of the data certainly indicate some connections between an organisational culture and the effectiveness of the organisation. At the same time, because of the small amount of data available, the results do not show with absolute clarity that the influence of national culture is a factor in a 'smooth result'.

The telecommunications sector is one of the most advanced in the country and displays a very high level of competition. Top management in these companies sometimes take very radical steps to improve the effectiveness of the organisations.

CONCLUSION

Local specifics: the managers and the owners

The examples above highlight a few facts about relatively big companies with different ownership structures – those which are locally owned and those owned by foreigners from both East and West.

However, these examples apply only to certain business sectors, mainly major manufacturing, the banking sector and the communications industry. Typical enterprises are still small or medium-sized companies owned by local people. Usually, the owners are also the top managers of the companies. Where we speak about one- or two-owner companies in which the owners are the top managers of the company, we are touching on leadership issues. The influence of leadership on corporate culture seems more significant in those enterprises than in others.

Key characteristics of entrepreneurs and managers

For the more visible differentiations, we will look at key characteristics of the entrepreneur and manager and a description of their impact on culture. Characteristics of the typical regional manager include:

- needs to work really hard to reach the top manager's position;
- manages on the basis of a budget and approved business plan;
- frequently uses outside consultants (sometimes very expensive);
- invests very little or no personal money in the development of the company;
- usually recruited for top position when company is already strong;
- very much likes the position, role and functions in the company;
- trusts in the theories and concepts (sometimes no flexible attitude towards theories);
- struggles with discipline, clear management processes and structures;
- usually believes him- or herself to be a guru in the relevant sector;
- accepts market influence as a disturbing factor and does not like it;
- usually claims to manage something which is difficult to oversee;
- often blames rules and regulations when something goes wrong; and
- strongly believes that in the worst times he or she can easily leave the company.

In organisations under the leadership of such managers, it is very common to find predominantly hierarchical cultures as defined by Cameron and Quinn (1999). It is also typical for those in top management positions to tend to spend shorter periods in the office. From the analysis of characteristics in the example, we can draw certain parallels with statements about corporate cultures:

> The relation between strategy and dominant culture is usually self-perpetuating. So not only does a defender culture match well with a 'commodity' positioning, but also it is likely to seek out those parts of the market which secure such positioning. Moreover, the organisational routines – for example, selection and recruitment – are likely to perpetuate the dominant culture by not selecting individuals who will 'rock the boat'.
>
> (Johnson/Scholes 2001: 67)

That description fits very well with local realities. It leads to a situation where in the biggest companies, in specific areas such as transit business, top managers keep their positions for long periods of time and recruit people with the same cultural experiences as their own.

In May 2004, during a conference on the competitive advantage of the Baltic states, there was a great deal of discussion about leaders' roles in activities geared to the development of corporate culture. The conference was organised by CEEMAN (Central and Eastern European Management Development Association).

An autocratic management style

Scandinavian managers offered one of the main conclusions: coming to Latvia, they discovered that an autocratic style of management was still highly popular,

271

and it was a great surprise to find that local employees expected the same, even where top managers were Scandinavians. Local managers agreed theoretically that a more democratic management style and a different company culture would be great. At the same time they mentioned during discussions that, in the real world, the most effective way to run a business was with an autocratic management style and commensurate corporate culture. The dilemma for expatriate managers is how to work towards a more democratic management style and company culture, still understanding that it will not always be effective enough to achieve the targets.

In the Latvian labour market there are opportunities for advancement for employees with a good education and strong motivation. The fact that local managers still adopt an autocratic style of management is due to the existing situation; many people live with the idea that they hate the work they are doing but very much love the money they receive. Changing the methods of motivation and boosting interest in the final outcome of the work done can lead to a possible change both in management style and corporate culture.

Philip Weckherlin from Competitive Edge Services (Switzerland) has painted a very pessimistic picture. Some top managers can cause big problems by taking the whole risk for company operations but not taking corporate risk seriously as a personal risk. He felt that for businesses in this region the most effective way to run a business was by combining the role of manager and entrepreneur in one person (CEEMAN 2004).

Combining the role of manager and entrepreneur

It is worth highlighting the typical characteristics of entrepreneurs in the region, stressing the differences between them and previously mentioned managers. The characteristics are highlighted using the same reference points:

- has a clear vision for the company;
- believes (but not always correctly) that he or she knows precisely when business is going well;
- invests significant amounts of personal money in the business;
- has usually been involved in the difficult start-up of the business;
- has a very good sense of the market and the customers' needs;
- has a deep understanding of the company's needs;
- enjoys business like a hobby;
- has company and business problems in mind all the time;
- sometimes makes chaotic decisions;
- can create something from nothing;
- struggles for improvements in the company;
- deeply involved in real problem-solving;
- believes and knows that the company can survive if he or she can do more than is probably possible; and
- during hard times for the business, stays with the enterprise until the very last.

Many local enterprises have gone through different developmental stages, scaling and descending from peaks of success. The entrepreneurs' presence is most important during the start-up phase of the business, when their involvement in putting the company on a solid footing is enormous. In some enterprises, managers might later be recruited from outside; however, many local entrepreneurs have a strong belief that they need to be close to the company's operations all the time. Where successful businesses are growing and expanding rapidly, operating under such conditions can actually be very difficult.

Historically, this club culture is found more frequently in small business entities. In the cases analysed, a club culture is typically excellent for rapid decisions. Of course, speed does not always guarantee quality. It depends on the calibre of entrepreneurs and their inner circle; incompetent, ageing or disinterested managers will probably quickly contaminate and slowly destroy their own club.

In a club culture, it is control of resources and personal charisma that count. If you own a club, you can tell people what to do. If you have a good track record, you have an aura of success, which is called charisma. From the power bases of resources and charisma, club culture effects change by exchanging people. Individuals are pieces in these cultures. If a link fails, it is replaced. We see the process in local companies every day.

In a few words, what would you say is the one fundamental strategic competitive advantage your country offers compared to others?

Q.lv

Our advantage is that we can find solutions in complicated situations by relying on our own resources alone and can make the necessary changes quickly. We are a small (rapidly adaptable) country between Russia and the West (transit location).

National differences

A common feature of the Latvian economy at present is the coexistence of very successful companies alongside very unsuccessful companies that seem to have done little over the past ten years. In terms of HR, some companies manage their people in an entirely modern way, differing in their practices only slightly from companies in mature western markets. On the other hand, some companies still use practices that are virtually the same (differing perhaps only formally) as those of a centrally planned economy. It is quite difficult to discuss key issues of people and organisational development in such a context.

Different types of companies

In the group of the most developed companies we find those that were established by strong international companies from 1991 to 1996. They usually invested enormous efforts in restructuring an existing state-owned company in a joint venture or by building an entirely new one. They could invest on a large scale, using expatriate managers for medium- to long-term work assignments, providing extensive fast-track training- to local managers. Enormous investments in the latest technologies also accompanied investment in organisational and HR development. These companies have clearly finished the initial phase of building their human resources; their managers and specialists, who joined the company in its start-up phase, now have six to eight years of experience. Such companies typically have highly skilled labour forces; however, their strong market position and stability have certain negative effects. Some of those companies can no longer offer sufficient professional motivation to their best people, who enjoyed the challenge of building the company from the start. Such companies have therefore developed a variety of tools to motivate and retain qualified people – starting with complex systems of employee benefits and ending with long-term, customised, western-style motivational plans. These companies realise that money is not the only motivator for qualified employees, and they have shown a willingness to adjust their entire management style in order to retain them.

This group often includes companies in the area of fast-moving consumer goods, pharmaceutical supplies, many manufacturers and service providers. In several of the sectors, however, companies are still in the phase of developing new local operations, subsidiaries of international companies.

In strong contrast to the above group are the companies that for various reasons managed to survive the past ten years without restructuring and without changes in their organisational development and HR practices. In these companies, the major problem remains overemployment. Typical are administrative and technical functions oriented to one narrow, repeated operation with no flexibility and low added value. This low qualification can also extend to managerial positions. Paradoxically, these companies do not face some of the problems that more developed companies do. They usually have a low turnover of employees and few problems with retention. Nonetheless, the know-how deficit and overemployment are problems so big that they can only be overcome by dramatic restructuring. The restructuring process is naturally accompanied by many negative implications, from the need to totally change well-adopted working habits to mass layoffs. Former employees often have little or no chance to find another job, owing to their low level of qualifications and to narrow experience.

The above cases represent two extremes – each showing a specific problem in the market. Between these extremes we also find many other cases. Indeed, there are a number of small and medium-sized Latvian companies which successfully overcame all the inevitable growing pains. Their managers – and usually owners – gained the necessary experience. Even though they do not share the ambitions of the large international companies, they are developing in very promising ways. Those who had problems with overemployment solved them in previous years. Although they are not fully comparable with international companies, they are healthy from both a financial and a personnel standpoint. In such companies there is usually pressure on salaries to rise as employees realise that their skills are useful in international companies as well, allowing them the option to search for more lucrative offers. Such companies often feel the need for gradual implementation of managerial tools and systems which they did not need in the past and therefore did not use. The necessity for training and employee development becomes clear and requires a more systematic approach than just introductory instruction. These companies are usually developing their HR systems from scratch.

One of the more troublesome groups of companies is those that are not managed by their owners, local or international. While some of the companies bring in substantial revenues, it is usually not the result of substantial management practices. Rather it is often due to factors rooted in the planned economy, such as a monopoly market position or unique international relations in various parts of the world. They usually experience little or no development in personnel management as positive financial results have insulated them from the push for change.

Historical development of corporate culture

Many management theories are coming to Latvia from the USA. In US-owned companies the characteristics are:

- a bias towards action;
- autonomy and entrepreneurship;
- productivity through people; and
- simple form and lean staff.

Where to put Latvia in that sense? For centuries we have had a large German influence. Like Austrians and Germans, our people dislike uncertainty, want equality but not individualism, and espouse masculine and material values. They are asking for Apollonian institutions tempered by formal democratic procedures.

The fifty years of Soviet rule only increased the desire for equality. At the same time, a culture developed in which people would not be responsible for the outcome of activities because somebody somewhere decided everything. There was no visible ownership of values and goods; there was common property for the whole country. This was a time with strong masculine management and direct power everywhere. The generation of people aged 35 to 55 who are still working have the cultural experience of that earlier time deep within them.

Existing salary is rarely motivational. And if it is unfair (internally a typical situation in Latvia), out of line with similar jobs elsewhere or otherwise open to real criticism, then it is a major demotivational factor. In one company we know, salaries are regarded as completely open: anyone can go into the accountant's office and ask what anyone else earns and be told. The main effect of this is to act as a control on how salaries are set; there is neither unfairness nor griping there.

In the early 1990s the majority of Baltic people could hardly speak any foreign languages. It was a nightmare meeting decent intelligent people and not being able to have any discussions or exchanges of information. Translators and interpreters were used, and we can only admire the patience of our Nordic colleagues when they were trying to understand what was being said.

Even the approaches to communication were different. An adult from the Baltic initially saw no need for a long discussion about what needed to be done and how it should be tackled; he/she wanted immediate action. But Nordic colleagues only gradually started to understand that a deficit of resources changes all action plans; none of the 'ready-made recipes' could be used straight away in the Baltic countries. Local companies with western, shareholding, expatriate managers – especially in top positions – have been typical up until the present time. Examples of the kinds of strong individualists produced in Anglo-Saxon countries are found in Latvia. The Scandinavians are usually more collectivist, which can be a polite word for conformist. Germans in Latvia might be hard-working, efficient and egalitarian; however, they are also conformist and with notable exceptions not particularly adventurous.

As a result the most important existing barriers to change in the Baltic region are:

– language;
– culture;
– history;
– distance;
– money; and
– differences in experience.

As a further result, the following conclusions can be made about corporate culture specifics in the country and the region:

1. The dominant type of corporate culture in companies that have been in the Latvian market for a long time is the autocratic, or hierarchical role (depending on classification model).
2. In the companies with local ownership and management (entrepreneurs), club culture elements are dominant.
3. Under certain circumstances, examples of suspicious culture development are found in the local market.
4. The most influential factor among the factors specifically impacting on culture is the Soviet-period experience.

Which people play key roles in your country? Which names should one know?

Our president Vaira Vike-Freiberga and those with big money: Andris Škele, Aivars Lembergs, Valerijs Kargins.

References

Cameron, Kim S./Quinn, Robert E. (1999): Diagnosing and Changing Organisational Culture, London.

CEEMAN (Central and East European Management Development Association) (2004): CEEMAN News 34, December.

Consultancy Company Fontes 'R & I' (2006): Fontes R&I compensation survey, Riga.

Esenvalde, Inese (2004): Praktiskā personāla vadība, Riga.

Handy, Charles (2000): Gods of Management, London.

Johnson, Gerry/Scholes, Kevan (2001): Exploring Corporate Strategy, London.

Kets de Vries, Manfred F.R. (2001): The Leadership Mystique, London.

Omārova, Silvija (2001): Cilvēks Dzīvo Grupā, Riga.

Par darbaspēka apsekojuma rezultātiem (2006): online; www.csb.lv (accessed 22 March 2007).

Reņģe, Viesturs (1999a): Organizāciju psiholoģija, Riga.

——(1999b): Sociālā psiholoģija, Riga.

——(2003): Organizāciju psiholoģija, Riga.

.lv

The authors

Aivars Kalniņš (aivars.kalnins@pasts.lv), Lattelekom from 1994 to 2004, HR Strategy Director from 2002 to 2004. Since 2004 Vice-President of SIA Reaton Ltd. President of LPVA (Latvian Association of Personnel Management) until 2005.

Anita Sāne (anita.sane@falck.lv), MBA, HR Director, member of the Board of Falck Apsargs JSC, group of Securicor Company since 2006. Before joining Falck, Personnel Manager, BSW Latvia SIA, Head of Department at Vidzeme University College and from 2000 to 2003 Assistant Professor and lecturer.

Sandra Zariņa (info@lv.abb.com), ABB SIA, Vice-President, HR manager responsible for Latvia, Lithuania and Estonia.

10 HRM in the Netherlands: economics of personnel policies

Lo Tigchelaar/Pieter Haen/Lucas van Wees

The Netherlands: in a nutshell

In this chapter you will learn:

- that HRM in the Netherlands is largely influenced by Anglo-American HRM traditions. Nevertheless, four lines of thought are important which underline the accomplishments needed by HR managers;

- that HR academia in the Netherlands is mostly dominated by Tilburg University. The Tilburg HR programme is implicitly acting as a Dutch prototype for HR education on the university level; and

- that it is important for companies to alter their orientation in respect of the dual ladder system.

Capital:	Amsterdam
Area (sq km):	41,526 (land 33,883; water 7,643)
EU membership:	since 1951 (founding member of the former so-called European Coal and Steel Community)
Population:	16,491,461
Languages:	Dutch, Frisian
Ethnic groups (in percentages):	Dutch 83, other 17 (of which 9 are of non-western origin, mainly Turks, Moroccans, Antilleans, Surinamese, Indonesians) (1999)
Gross domestic product:	512 billion USD (2006)
Workforce (in percentages):	7.6 million (2006): agriculture 2; industry 19; services 79 (2004)
Export commodities:	machinery and equipment, chemicals, fuels, foodstuffs

BACKGROUND: FROM DISCOURSE TOWARDS INNOVATIVE DEVELOPMENT?

What drives renewal and innovation in the personnel policies of organisations? Managerial and organisational need? Or a legal imperative of wider society? Or is it the academic community of professionals in university and service firms, offering carefully designed and evaluated products ready for application? The answer must be disappointing and disenchanting. During the last decade, the frequency of challenging opportunities for research and development in HR has been slowing down. Currently some organisations have reopened their gates to allow field research, enabling university staff and consultants to carry out innovative projects beyond mere 'desk' research and the provision of short-term solutions. This may lead to an increase of future-oriented and innovative demand, and to a reduction of silent unemployment on the supply side.

How can this cynical picture be changed? In an optimistic scenario we may try to reinforce the supply side, keeping in mind that in the 1960s and 1970s there was a mainstream of good ideas stemming from psychology and sociology and adopted by (top) managers, although they had not initially asked for them. We propose a virtual research agenda, stressing the importance of four promising lines of thought, in which many salient accomplishments can already be observed.

What is typical of your country relating to country itself (its culture, people, etc.) and its economy?

.nl

* open economy;
* multilingualism;
* high financial reserves (cumulating in a unique structure of pension funds, building on the huge savings of the Dutch) making it possibele for the Dutch to be heavy investors in other countries (the USA, eastern Europe, etc.) as well; and
* a relatively large number of multinational companies (Royal Dutch Shell, Unilver, Philips, Heineken, etc.) building on the first multinational company in world history, the VOC (*Verenigde Oost-Indië Compagnie*: Unified East-Indian Company) established in 1602.

GENERAL CHARACTERISTICS OF HRM

Essentially HRM is the economics of personnel policies. Labour, historically considered as a difficult factor to control, is supposed to be managed much better by economic means, and our respected employees will be driven by psychological means towards economic objectives. After machines, technical equipment, supply chains and logistics have been honed to a high degree of perfection, the unpredictable behaviours of employees will be the last hurdle to be overcome by 'managerial control' (Guest 1989).

Many authors and professionals want to avoid the cynical connotation of this definition, because they see the objective of HRM as personal development of the employees, through training and coaching, through improvement of the educational value of jobs and the working environment – and all this closely related to the higher needs of the individual. In this concept, the term HR is underlined much more strongly than management.

This developmental philosophy runs counter to economic and selective views on managerial decisions to invest only in specific employees, i.e. healthy employees, or potential managers eligible for higher responsibilities, and other staff meeting the specific requirements of the organisation. From this view we deduct the importance of calculations and basic economic choice by management. In strategic and business planning, cost as well as return on investment in people are taken into account. This investment philosophy has given rise to some new lines of thought, theory and practical application. Employability and mobility, organisational change and innovation, and the structure and quality of the HR function are just a few examples.

In the landscape of HRM we recognise many interdisciplinary strands: the problem of productivity improvement relates not only to the psychology of pay and motivation but also to the technical and organisational characteristics of the workplace, the freedom workers perceive and their consequent commitment, the planning, goal-setting and control cycle prevalent in the organisation, etc. (Algera 2001). In this respect HRM is clearly beyond psychology as such. Incidentally, it is already well known that the problem of 'utility' and 'applied value' of tests and other selection techniques may be addressed very well by a microeconomic decision model (Roe 1983).

Finally, we will clarify the definition of HRM by using a threefold meaning of integration:

1. Integration of subjects: a combination of previously separate aspects of personnel policy, i.e. reinforcing mobility by financial rewards or removing hurdles in the benefits package by communicating the similarity between jobs (Tigchelaar 2003).
2. Integration of HR aspects in managerial decision-making (Dyer 1983; Kouwenhoven/Hooft 1990).
3. Integration of social-political expectations from external stakeholders (unions, government) and the managerial agenda. The distinction or even gap between managerial and social determinants of HR priorities, and essentially between HRM and 'social policy', as well as the question of whether the social-political environment of the organisation belongs to strategic planning, are still subject to a continuing debate, in this country at any rate (Paauwe/Huijgen 1996;

Dalen/Gründemann/Vries 2003). However, as many HR professionals and directors obviously choose the economic approach of HRM, leaving the difficult and poorly regarded task of negotiations with unions to specialised negotiators (Tigchelaar 2003), we do not expect a conflict of interest.

What are you and other Dutch people extraordinarily proud of with respect to HRM?

- high level of education;
- dualism in employee relations, significant roles for the labour unions and works councils, dialogue ('Polder model');
- flexibility that has created huge specialised world-class firms (Randstad);
- flexibility in forms of labour contracts, e.g. for temporary workers, interim managers, part-time jobs; and
- skilled labour force, solid social climate, stable work climate.

HR ASPECTS OF STRATEGY: STRATEGY OF HR?

The economic approach of HRM has already given rise to an in-depth cost–benefit analysis of many diverse policies. What have been the critical variables and levers of change in a programme aimed at reduction of absenteeism? Did absenteeism rates really decrease in a statistically significant sense to a sustainable lower level? Next, what is the magnitude of the consequent improvement in productivity? How do we estimate this result in financial terms?

What is known about the cost of implementation, the cost of maintenance, and the positive effects of a new salary system? Questions of this kind, prompted by HR managers and their superiors, presuppose quantitative measures and financial indices (Kaplan/Norton 1996). Moreover, this approach requires a continuous cycle of goal-setting, evaluation and feedback, imposed by the HR function itself, or agreed upon with management, so the need for a relevant budget is self-evident. Specific goal-setting, combined with a neat specification of requirements and expectations regarding new HR systems and procedures, will make modern HR departments less vulnerable to criticism and questions concerning the applied value of their tasks and services. This potential vulnerability is considered one of the driving forces of the growing attention paid to benchmarking, quantification, utility of selection and other personnel decisions as well as, recently, to 'human capital evaluation' (Evers 2004).

The request for added value in our view also refers to the process of consultancy to management and to other parties in and around organisations. How can influence be measured? Of course opportunities to do so depend on the subject matter involved. We feel, however, that if HRM is really to reflect a profession, many HR aspects may/should be brought into the decision-making process in addition to manpower planning, recruitment and remuneration. Supported by (applied) research, this is a challenging but realistic mission for the HR function. This implies a plea for:

– detecting 'niches' for new HR policies; in fact this is the marketing role of HR;
– developing new products and services; and
– convincing management and other judges, after careful evaluation, of the applied value and contributions to organisational effectiveness.

There is naturally much risk involved in this approach. It will be more difficult than planning an organisational change project within the frame of an agreed budget. Risk may be reduced, however, by developing new ideas and concepts and designing new policies, while at the same time integrating HR tasks in the responsibility of line management (appraisal rounds, control of absenteeism) and/or outsourcing certified specialist activities like safety–health–environment (SHE) and services for appropriate workplace conditions (ARBO).

Where priorities need to be established within a limited budget, designing a new salary system with a view to reinforcing desired behaviours in different work processes and sectors (supply chain, sales, R&D) may be a more promising solution than increasing services for individual counselling. But again, much depends on value judgement: HRM or social policy!

The active, strategic orientation of the HR function is the opposite of the passive attitude reflected in traditional routines and procedures. We refer to the well-known yearly appraisal and salary reviews and to regular potential assessments and career inventories, which form part of the culture of many (multinational) companies. It is feared that the origins and objectives of these procedures have been lost from sight and the existence of such policies will turn out to be 'irreflexive' and 'algorithmic' by nature (Gomez-Mejia/Balkin 1992).

So nobody is questioning the strategic objectives, contingencies on work and organisational outcomes, and the positive effects and possible negative side-effects of such procedures. In the typical case the only managerial concerns may be control of wage cost and timely identification of successors. This algorithmic approach should not be confused with higher level HRM, as this requires more insight and research on the relationship between pay and organisational effectiveness, and between personal qualities and the successful performance in a higher level job. Although everybody will admit that a correct and transparent set of basic 'personnel administration' systems is an important cornerstone for a more complicated composite of psychological and economic variables. Basics precede innovation!

.nl

What 'niches' may be fulfilled by modern HRM and applied research? What hitherto silent needs of management may be satisfied? We propose a virtual research agenda, future-oriented, mindful of the accomplishments of prominent researchers and consultants but still with the old adage in mind that 'more research is needed'.

What would you like to teach foreign HR managers? What is important for them to know in your opinion?

The Dutch are very egalitarian. They are both easy and difficult: easy in the sense that they are hungry for information and good ideas, difficult because they are very experienced and not open to much persuasion by others. They tend to 'know it all', but will in fact accept and seize viable plans and projects which are presented vigorously and backed up with convincing evidence. Ideas are objective and independent of the people presenting them.

Leadership is based on merit, competence and achievement. Managers are vigorous and decisive, but consensus is mandatory, as there are many players in the decision-making process.

Long debates lead to action, taken at the top, but with constant reference to the 'ranks'. Ideas from low levels are allowed to filter freely upwards in the hierarchy.

Structure, design and quality of the HR function

In an attempt to describe the tasks and problems of the personnel function, we have already made a distinction between tasks that relate to the strategic managerial agenda and tasks that relate to the social-political environment. We will use this distinction as a basis for a classification of tasks. In addition, we distinguish an active strategic attitude and a passive administrative one. In this way, two positions on two dimensions result in a specific four-cell matrix (Figure 10.1).

We will clarify the meaning of the cells following Born/Nollen (1998):

1. Actively anticipating strategic and entrepreneurial problems. Formulating strategic objectives and means, among them HR. This is what we call HRM.
2. Passively complying with the requirements of the organisation, and maintaining and repairing existing systems and procedures. Applying regular ('algorithmic') reviews of manpower needs, appraisal outcomes, salary increases and training needs within the framework of an agreed budget. This is what we call personnel administration.
3. Actively anticipating developments in society, the outcomes of the 'three party consultations' between government, employer federations and unions typical of the continental model of industrial relations, attitude changes of unions and their members, changes in social security and other relevant legislation, i.e. equal opportunities. This may be referred to as the social policy of the firm.
4. Complying with the needs of the workers, groups and their direct supervision. Prevention of absenteeism, personal help and counselling, grievance and conflict handling, and controlling for good working conditions to meet the legal imperatives and judgements of outside experts. This is what we call services and care.

We indicated above that it will be impossible – or at any rate very difficult – for the personnel function to develop towards HRM if the basic cells of our

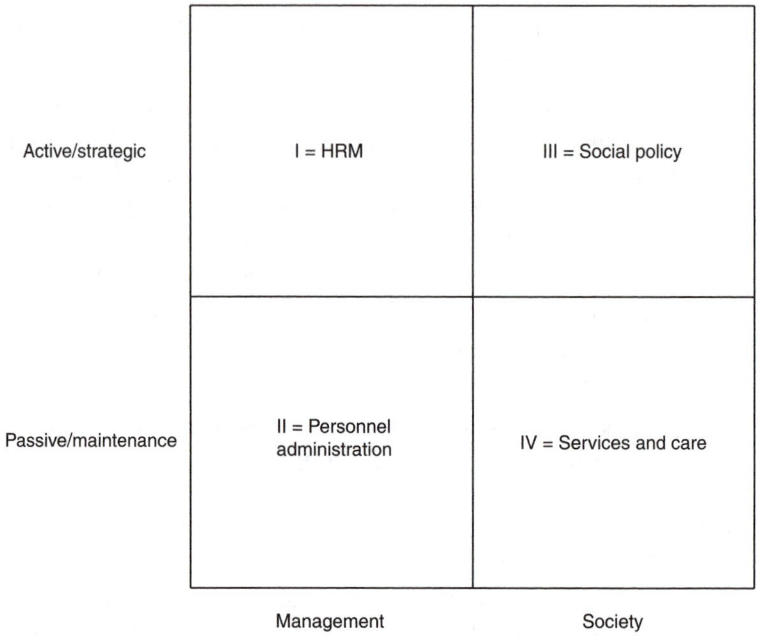

	Management	Society
Active/strategic	I = HRM	III = Social policy
Passive/maintenance	II = Personnel administration	IV = Services and care

Figure 10.1 Tasks of personnel management (based on Born/Nollen 1998)

matrix, personnel administration and services, are not satisfactorily filled. This means that where expectations of basic systems and services are not adequately met, according to the scores assigned on employee rating scales, the increasing emphasis on 'strategic contributions' currently favoured by many HR professionals does not make sense and is very unlikely to succeed. In several thesis projects conducted by Ph.D. students, but also in consultancy projects aimed at evaluation and quality improvement of HR departments, it is shown that employee satisfaction with the process and outcomes of basic procedures and services is often low, and in some surveys is related to low transparency and equity, i.e. regarding salary increases and differentials, and lack of commitment towards the organisation (Tigchelaar 2003). These findings underline the need for maintenance and repair activities in the area of personnel administration.

What factors may be considered determinants of the development of the personnel function towards higher level HRM?

In the first place, personal characteristics. This means that personal attitudes of (top) managers do play an important role. Managers' view and vision of the way that strategic options and decisions are related to consequences for human resources should perhaps be called a conceptual factor, an aspect of processing and combining information.

In the second place, structural characteristics of the organisation which make for a stronger embeddedness in strategic decision-making. A good way to further this is through official representation of HR in the management team. The assumption is that the team has the discretionary power to make decisions that are significant for a rounded organisational unit, at any rate on growth and downsizing, product range, cooperation with third parties, survival and continuity. And all this with an eye on profitability and profit. It has been observed that only a modest part of so-called management teams has been assigned this financial responsibility and authority. This is not even the rule in so-called business units (Ruyter 1992).

As a general rule, decentralisation and delegation do not give rise to a higher level of responsibility and authority for locally operating teams. So there are many reasons to describe and define autonomous business units (BUs) more exclusively.

One possible proposal: a BU is an autonomous part of an organisation (company), the management of which has been assigned the discretionary power to make strategic and tactical decisions relating to a time frame of several years. In view of these decisions, information stemming from all relevant organisational functions is combined.

This definition may be considered very strict and exclusive from a practical point of view. But it should be noted that some BUs have nothing but commercial significance as they are sales offices coupled with one or two support functions. In other cases, we have observed doubts about the real strategic and integral nature of decisions. Frequently, risky financial decisions and combined budgets for financial and human resources are functionally controlled by a higher level authority in headquarters or overseas.

In the ideal case, a BU consists of six to seven functions: (a) three primary functions: marketing, production and R&D; and (b) three to four supporting functions: finance and accounting in relation to the money stream (M1); logistics in relation to movement of materials (M2); recently we have observed the growing importance of information management; and last but not least the movement of manpower (M3), which is the nucleus of the HR function.

A general management role or position may be added on top of these functions. An essential characteristic of this picture, however, is the exclusive and dedicated nature of every support function's position towards the BU. In principle, there are no 'double binds' to other BUs. This condition underlines the integration of support functions in the managerial structure and process.

This is true for the HR function as well. HR will provide services and information exclusively for one BU. It is expected that this information is specific for the BU in question. The HR manager will report to the general manager of the BU, and in close cooperation with other team members, plan and formulate specific projects and challenges, i.e. reinforcing the sales force by recruitment, training for a new account approach, and group payment. This way of positioning HR is called 'decentralisation in line-management' (Kouwenhoven/Hooft 1990) as opposed to 'delegation from central staff'. In that case an HR official who hierarchically belongs to the central HR department is delegated to the local site or business. This example should not be confused with real decentralisation. In the BU-specific role, the HR function may develop to 'business partner'. Of course, there will be functional consultations with HR managers elsewhere in the company on similar business positions. Moreover, if the BU and its functions have a large number of staff, the business partner HR manager may supervise a group of HR professionals.

The BU-related positioning of HR is said to be observed in 30 to 40 per cent of cases and is expected to increase rapidly. This expectation is confirmed by many pilot studies and thesis projects (Vermeulen 1997; Tigchelaar 2003). As the restructuring and decentralisation of complex (multinational) companies proceeds, the HR function will change, but only after a time-lag of several years. So the dedicated position of HR in a business will not be immediately clear from the organisation chart. It is a matter of gradual advancement. Management may feel uncertain about the description and personal requirements of this new HR role. This may inhibit the search for suitable candidates to adopt this role.

A second nuance is that the already mentioned 40 per cent refers to private industrial, commercial and financial organisations and will reflect an overestimate if applied to all organisations, including public governmental and health-care organisations.

A third nuance is that the majority of HR departments are embedded in conventional organisational structures, defined by:

- category of staff, i.e. craftsmen, college graduates, senior staff, nursing practitioners;
- site or location, regardless of the parts of the business located at that site; and
- region, in the case of financial services, banks and public services companies, and manufacturing facilities grouped together at some point in the past. In these cases, the need for a comparable social-political policy is very strong.

A fourth nuance relates to the existence of specialist HR jobs, i.e. for compensation and benefits, for staffing and management development, for training. Moreover, at the higher managerial levels of some companies a distinction is made between the HR director of a BU and the director of social affairs in view of the industrial relations of the country.

From additional interviews in our inventories we may conclude with some hesitation that the BU-related position and the decentralisation of HR have been welcomed by (general) management (Tigchelaar 2003). This position enables HR aspects to be incorporated into the decision-making process, which means that investment decisions in R&D are combined with HR contributions to innovation, that merger and acquisition planning takes account of the typical HR policies of both organisations (due diligence), and that appropriate manpower planning takes place before a new sales organisation is built up in a new country.

These examples sound very optimistic. However, the BU-related position is perceived by management as effective, as adding value to the previous practice of making decisions without HR input in spite of the nuances mentioned above and some conflicting tendencies.

EAPM AFFILIATE: DE NETHERLANDSE VERENIGING VOOR PERSONEELSMANAGEMENT EN ORGANISATIEONTWIKKELING

The Dutch Association for Personnel Management and Organisation (De Nederlandse Vereniging voor Personeelsmanagement en Organisatieontwikkeling (NVP)) is the network for HR professionals who are engaged in issues such as HR strategy, employment relationships, recruitment and selection, rewards systems, conditions of employment and training plans. It was founded on 28 January 1965. Current membership stands at 6,500.

The NVP's main objectives are to help to determine and defend values and standards in the field of HR, to have an important say in the development of new social legislation, to set codes of conduct regarding HR, to meet professional training needs and to improve industrial relations in general. Basic education and training in HR are offered in the Netherlands in full-time and part-time programmes by several colleges and universities. The NVP offers refresher courses, organises seminars and workshops on new or reborn topics and provides a platform for discussion on all aspects of HR and new developments in the field.

Such discussions are often 'held publicly' through articles in the NVP's monthly publication *Personeelbeleid*. This full-size magazine also keeps all members and subscribers informed of all the important developments in HR.

The Dutch are internationally orientated by nature. Holland boasts many international or multinational companies. It is therefore not surprising that European developments in social legislation, industrial relations and anything else that relates to international HR are of great interest to NVP members. The NVP therefore organises international meetings with sister institutes in Europe and participates in the EAPM, the European umbrella body of national HR organisations.

The association comprises the nine interest sections and nine regional branches presented below, each with their own board of management. Each board of management draws up an annual plan and stages regular meetings.

At national level, the organisation is run by a National Board of Management and a Members Council. Fifteen staff are employed at the head office in Nieuwegein to service the organisation. From this location, the association also lobbies government and political institutions on HR-related issues.

THE WORKING ENVIRONMENT

The working environment refers to the totality of work-related factors which affect the health, safety and well-being of employees, which in the Netherlands is under the control of the so-called ARBO service (services for appropriate working place conditions). ARBO policy may be seen on the one hand as having much in common with personnel and organisation (P&O) policy and on the other as being a subset thereof, e.g. work and organisation expertise of in-house or external ARBO services.

The rights and obligations of employers and employees are laid down in ARBO law. However, creating good working conditions goes much further than mere compliance with these laws. Employers and employees are jointly responsible for giving real substance to this legislation.

The goals for this section are to keep association members up to date on the latest developments in this area – especially ARBO legislation – to improve professionalism and stimulate exchange of practical experiences.

TERMS AND CONDITIONS OF EMPLOYMENT

The Board of Management has concluded, on the basis of research, that the Netherlands is moving from a macrosocial welfare state to a mesosocial welfare state, with far-reaching consequences for social stability, work organisations, employers and most of all for P&O people.

The four goals of this section are:

1. To translate developments on the social, societal and socio-economic fronts at macro level to the meso level (organisations) and the micro level (P&O) and to offer advice on these developments.
2. To make an inventory of appropriate instruments for the implementation of the aforementioned changes and, where they do not currently exist, to play a role in their development and offer advice about them.
3. To develop, both proactively and reactively, as a reliable and professional sparring partner for (non-)governmental bodies and to offer advice, whether solicited or unsolicited, to such organisations.
4. The section stresses the importance of an interdisciplinary and fully integrated approach to employment issues.

The mission is as follows: the terms of employment section is committed to realising a return on investment, with regard to this area of responsibility, for the work organisations in which P&O personnel are held accountable for this subject. In the pursuit of its mission, the section intends to become the authoritative resource on terms of employment and the partner and platform of choice for P&Oers and their work organisation.

HUMAN RESOURCE DEVELOPMENT (HRD)

This section was formed in 1999. Since then it has grown very rapidly to 1,500 members, making it the largest section in the association. The section brings together members in work organisations who are responsible for the development of the organisation and its staff.

The section's engagement may best be described as follows: the section does not concentrate on HRD as a specialist topic but on the contribution it can make to all developments within a company. It deals with all forms of competences required by companies. The section works to clarify all developments in economic, societal and (information) technological subjects and to apply them to the HRD sphere of activity. One of the section's objectives is to create conditions within which companies can stimulate learning.

Four meetings are held a year, on topics selected in conjunction with members.

The section distinguishes four main objectives:

1. The development and establishment of a vision of the relationship between developments in companies and HRM on the one hand and HRD activities and policy on the other.
2. Recognition and discussion of concrete developments in companies and their environment which influence the organisation and HRD.
3. Recognition and discussion of visions and methods of working within HRD.
4. The creation of a platform for the exchange of experiences.

e-HRM

The Board of Management found the previous terms 'social policy information' very old-fashioned and no longer appropriate for the topics we find interesting. This section focuses on the area between personnel policy and IT.

A personnel information system is no longer the exclusive province of the P&O department. With the increasing devolution of personnel issues, line management needs to be provided with the tools to carry out these tasks and needs assistance as well. Getting rid of administrative burdens, managing personnel information in an international environment, adapting to internet for P&O and carrying out e-HR functions are all new challenges for association members.

Lengthy written monthly reports (which still contain policy information) are no longer required. Personnel information must always be accessible in an attractive format, combined with other information about the organisation and always open to other viewpoints. These are the points forming this section's agenda. The objective of the e-HRM section is to spread knowledge of information and communication technologies in P&O areas in general and to encourage better use of personnel information systems in particular.

INTERNATIONAL

This section organises lecture cycles, conferences and meetings to promote the transfer of knowledge to and between members and creates opportunities for exchanging experiences. The subjects are chosen on the basis of interest shown, spontaneous suggestions and the contribution of Board members who all have experience of international HR policy. The subjects are chosen in such a way that not only policy and strategic aspects but also practical implementation issues are reviewed.

The target group consists of experienced international HR managers and association members who work in small or medium-sized organisations and, as activities become internationalised, are confronted with both policy and practical issues. These HR job-holders often have to work on their own and under time pressure to achieve results. Experience shows that they often pay too much attention to technical details and not enough to aspects of policy. The section therefore offers members the opportunity during meetings to exchange experiences and discuss new developments.

Standard solutions to problems in the field of internationalisation and HR policy are not often available, but the lectures and accompanying discussions generally lead to improved awareness of the difficulties. This helps to avoid over-hasty decisions and mistakes. Learning from each other is therefore of critical importance.

The international section aims to create a meetingplace for association members who are interested or actively involved in international aspects of HRM.

MANAGEMENT DEVELOPMENT

Management development (MD) is a classic instrument within HR policy, one which is really proving its worth in the current climate. Shorter employment periods, flexible personnel and employees who put personal development before loyalty to their employer are forcing organisations to nurture and support key managers and experts.

MD supports this through a planned and systematic process of evaluating the needs and possibilities of these (potentially) key employees. The objective is to achieve continuity in filling important positions with high-quality personnel and to stimulate personal development in accordance with the needs of the organisation.

The MD section seeks to improve the professionalism of its members in the field of MD in the following ways:

- Organising plenary sessions for members. Subjects discussed can include topics such as competency management, MD within professional organisations, career development and MD.
- Project groups are formed to further develop specific topics in plenary sessions, for publication or scientific research.

The section maintains contact with other groups operating in associated fields and regularly keeps members abreast of developments. These groups include the Dutch Institute of Psychology, the European Federation for Management Development and the Dutch Foundation for Management Development.

GOVERNMENT

The differences between the operational methods of government and the market-oriented external world are getting smaller – they are growing towards each other. The government wishes to be more commercial, so it attaches more importance to client service and cost awareness. The commercial players feel they have much to contribute on issues of public interest (the environment and ethics, for instance) and political priorities (such as integration, rehabilitation of employees and the question of integrity). In other words, each can learn from the other.

This is an important fact. However, there are still many purely governmental-related issues that need to be considered. P&Oers working within government are concerned with these issues, and the government section concentrates on them.

STRATEGIC RECRUITMENT

This section's mission is to provide an innovative platform to facilitate strategic recruitment by its members. This results in the following objectives: (a) to improve organisation performance through strategic recruitment; (b) to develop a strategic recruitment plan; and (c) to create a platform for recruitment.

In order to achieve this, the section focuses on the issues: employer branding, strategic manpower planning, positioning strategic recruitment within the organisation, labour market research, tactical recruitment – tools, initiatives, innovation and development, as well as on Recruiter-Online.

The strategic recruitment section is a founding partner of Recruiter-Online (www.recruiter-online.nl), an internet platform created to keep HR professionals up to date on all the aspects of this area of expertise.

SELF-EMPLOYMENT

This section focuses on association members who work independently to bring products and/or services to the marketplace. Self-employment can take many forms, such as researcher, consultant, interim manager and trainer, actively operating in the field of people, work and organisations.

A number of work groups have been formed by members sharing a common interest. These groups develop specific themes and report back regularly to plenary sessions. The following groups are currently active:

• Interest protection: examining ways to offer an attractive choice of insurances against incapacity for work, sickness costs, corporate and personal liability, and legal expenses.
• Collective support: this group concentrates on issues such as offering assistance, help and advice in the (personal) performance of professional activities. It is also engaged in promoting the section on the internet.

- Professional entrepreneurship: the focus here is on ways of further professionalising entrepreneurial activities.
- Code of behaviour: this group is in the process of being formed.

As well as functioning as a network, the objectives are: (a) to offer a platform for the exchange of knowledge and experience in the various fields; (b) to act as a sounding-board for advisers working solo and needing to consult a fellow adviser; (c) to offer opportunities to engage in projects which are too large to be undertaken individually; (d) to offer opportunities to pass on projects to colleagues with more appropriate skills or expertise; and (e) to create items of common interest, such as insurances. Regular meetings are arranged to achieve these objectives.

HR ACADEMIA: BEST PRACTICE AT TILBURG UNIVERSITY

In 1986 a new graduate (Ph.D.) course was launched called *Personeelweten-schappen* ('personnel sciences'). This educational programme and an outline for supporting research had been prepared, from 1983, by a working party established and coordinated by Professor Jules Van Dijck (organisational sociology), in which quite different faculties and departments were represented.

The general objective was to provide an orientation towards personnel and social problems occurring in the management and administration of organisations, in industry as well as in government, and in the growing non-profit sector, i.e. healthcare. New courses to be developed would be grounded on the integrated application of insights and knowledge from economics, psychology, sociology and law, which are the basic sciences from the point of view of the initiators and designers of the curriculum. The interrelatedness of problems of work and organisation gave rise to an additional point of view, although not a basic discipline: the development of technology as a determinant of work processes in organisations.

The new course should be a good blend of scientific and professional orientation. Scientific refers to cycles of theories and hypotheses testing in the relevant basics; professional may refer to another cycle of change and evaluation, of policies and ways of organising, and a problem-solving attitude. The scientific as well as the professional side of the curriculum are characterised by the interplay between personnel, internal organisational, cultural and social-political factors, which ultimately determine organisational effectiveness.

DISTINCTIVE COMPETENCES

On the occasion of the foundation of the new curriculum, strategic points of view then played an important role. In comparison with the courses offered by professional colleges – at that time at any rate – they might be considered 'distinctive competences'.

- An integrated and multi- if not interdisciplinary approach. This implies the provision of courses like 'strategy and HRM' or 'industrial relations and union policies', in which the monodisciplines are not easily recognised, after a thorough introduction in the basic sciences. This approach is reflected in and supported by the development of 'cases' in which real-life complex problems derived from managerial practice are analysed and solved by small groups of students.
- An orientation towards diagnosis and action. This means that careful analysis and knowledge-creating precedes the development of new policies, proposals for change and consultancy.

- A strong strategic dimension. Attention should be paid to managerial planning and decision-making and to the way HR may contribute to the strategic process and may be brought into the managerial agenda. Finally, action refers to the development of skills. In so-called 'skill-labs', the writing of policy papers, effective consultancy and negotiating behaviours are trained.
- Keeping an eye upon transformations in society and changes in the social-political environment. This implies that one-sided 'managerialism' should be prevented, taking into account changing values and norms (on being a good employer, a good organisational citizen, etc.), anticipated changes in labour law and the social security system, trends in the outcomes of collective bargaining with unions. The curriculum should comprise HRM as well as industrial relations (IR).
- An emphasis on quantitative methods and models in most courses of the curriculum. After a number of years, the emphasis on statistical methods has increased to a level where statistical skills are on a par with those of sociology and psychology research students in the same faculty.

AN OUTLINE OF THE PROGRAMME

At the outset (1986–7), the personnel sciences programme consisted of four phases: (a) an introductory year (*propeadeuse*); (b) an introduction to basic sciences; (c) the integrated courses and cases on five problem and policy areas; and (d) a thesis project. The introductory year comprises courses in economics, psychology, sociology or law.

The introduction to basic sciences is composed of: business economics/accounting, macroeconomics (growth, conjuncture, labour market and wages), microeconomics (including institutional economics, transaction cost and agency), technical production systems (two courses), work and organisational psychology, organisational sociology, labour law, several courses in statistics and a general introduction to HRM. In addition, students undertake supporting studies (i.e. philosophy, social security) which are optional.

The integrated courses and cases ('mainstream') cover the areas that are described in the following sections.

HR systems and procedures

Labour contract and employment relationship, the contract portfolio, legal aspects of dismissal, job evaluation and wage structure, recruitment and selection, performance appraisal, other techniques and objectives of appraisal, design of salary systems, career path design and predictability, and the outcomes of these policies: good performance, motivated employees, satisfaction and commitment.

Leadership and organisation

Leadership theories and models, criteria for leadership effectiveness, conflict and cooperation, power and coalitions, communication within and between groups, as well as applications to project management, organisational change and management of professionals.

Technology and the worker

Decision-making on technological developments in products and services (e.g. from products to systems) and production processes, its impact on jobs and on the demand and supply of qualifications, safeguarding skill variety and learning in the workplace, planning and change of production systems and the consequences for the quality of working life (QWL), working-time arrangements.

Industrial relations and labour market

Main developments and prognoses concerning the labour market and its relevant segments, the structure and rules of collective bargaining, legal aspects of collective labour agreements, levels of participation on the shop floor, participative decision-making, workers' councils, company and branch-level bargaining, legal imperatives on the social policies of organisations.

Strategy and HRM

From strategic planning to strategic behaviour, the relationship between strategic issues and HR, strategic choice in staffing and personnel planning, in compensation and salary systems, in career and management development systems, HR contribution to productivity improvement, to innovation in R&D and faster times to market, HR aspects of acquisitions and mergers (due diligence), the (re)design and quality of the HR function.

In addition, a SKILL-LAB runs more or less parallel to these courses.

The thesis project is a project of six to eight months' duration, pursued by students individually, almost without exception in an industrial, commercial, governmental or healthcare organisation (outside university anyway). It leads, after presentation and public defence of the thesis, to the award of the DR's degree (*doctorandus*), equivalent to the current Master of Arts (MA) degree.

The programme can, of course, be seen as a living organism. Through continuous evaluation and feedback, many elements have been revised, replaced and extended. In the current programme, nevertheless, the core structure described here can be easily recognised. Obviously, it may be considered a prototype for further development. In the 1990s, some capita selecta were added on age-related factors in HRM, equal opportunity and minority groups, and personnel planning. Recently, since 2003, new and very relevant courses have been developed under the headings of human capital evaluation, human resource development and health management.

It should be pointed out that students originally started on the introductory year (*propeaedeuse*) of another curriculum, i.e. economics. This situation changed in 1993. Since then, there has also been a direct pathway for students from secondary education to personnel sciences and an immediate acquaintance with HRM.

The legally imposed BA–MA structure (2003) in which every four-year university programme is split into two phases – three years, then one – has not led to significant changes in the subject matter involved. With the implementation of the BA–MA structure, the attention paid to research methods and statistics in the Master phase (fourth year of study) has been reinforced. Moreover, at the end of the third year a new milestone has been erected: the so-called Bachelor thesis, leading to the BA degree. In contrast to the objective of the legislation, this BA degree is not generally considered the quality assurance stamp of a rounded-off, accomplished programme. Thus it is not an optional finish, but primarily a milestone or stepping stone towards further personal development, in which scientific approaches will be dominant. The same conception is observed in other faculties and departments.

What would you say one ought not to do? What are the 'don'ts' in your country?

- don't tell stories, the Dutch prefer facts, facts, facts;
- no extravagance;
- do not forget to recognise Dutch internationalism and solid economic achievements;
- show the way to mutual profit (win-win for all parties involved); and
- no sarcasm, only a few jokes.

EVALUATION AND SOME CRITICISM

After the first graduates in 1989, the number of students has increased rapidly. Many cohorts exceeded 100 students. In 2005 the number of alumni was close to 900. The accomplishment of the objectives, of course, goes beyond numerical success!

As far as the position in the labour market is concerned, it has been observed that alumni from the first cohorts generally acquired interdisciplinary integrated HRM-like jobs, close to management as a business partner – in their second career step, at any rate, if not in the first. During the past ten years, however, the number of graduates starting in a specialist position, like recruitment, compensation and benefits, reintegration of the disabled or unemployed, has increased steeply. The number of jobs acquired, involving applied research and development of new policies, is very poor, probably due to the current lack of demand for innovative input for HR policies. These observations are evidently in contrast to the profile of the curriculum. Nevertheless, we may conclude that many employers and top HR managers have welcomed this new type of graduate because of his/her broad education, distinctive competence in comparison to monodisciplinary candidates, and potential employability in the HR sector and (general) management jobs. Moreover, the Tilburg initiative has been considered an appropriate response to HR trends in business and society.

In 1987, one year after the start of the programme, an autonomous, separate personnel sciences department was allocated to the faculty of social sciences. This may have led to the remarkable tensions between the new and the adjacent departments of sociology and psychology. For (work and organisational) psychologists in particular, the new programme must have been a threat, because they claimed the HR domain for themselves and stated implicitly that HRM was largely if not entirely covered by applied psychology. Initially, the attitude of psychologists towards the new department and curriculum has been sceptical and negative, and has sometimes led to overt aggressive behaviour.

Some of the lessons learned from the process of organising this programme may be important in view of similar initiatives in HR academia.

Tensions within the faculty must be well managed. This requires a well-balanced attitude on the faculty board, meaning the successive deans and administrative directors. Their attitude towards interdisciplinary programmes has shown a lack of stability, predictability and continuity. On many occasions they have been in favour of the traditional disciplines.

Debates between adherents of 'fundamental science' and 'professional application' should be prevented, as they have already led to an undesirable polarisation of attitudes, which is a barrier to the development of innovative HR projects. This has also led to critical questions about the allocation of personnel sciences in the context of the faculty of social sciences. The programme and department might be better embedded in a faculty of management and organisation or in a faculty of economics.

The faculty has not been very successful in attracting and retaining dedicated staff members. Factors that explain this result are certainly: poor HR policy, temporary short-term contracts, compensation and benefits below equity, poor student–staff ratio due to the overwhelming number of students, and as a consequence only a small margin of time for research and publications. With some minor exceptions, it has been very difficult to attract senior staff members with a background in economics and/or with experience in innovative development of HR policies in an industrial environment. In addition, a shifting, fluctuating attitude towards part-time staff members may be observed. In some periods they were favoured, in view of the ideas streaming from the professional HR world into lecturing and course development; in other periods, however, they were less appreciated because they did not contribute to the scientific profile of the faculty.

Staffing problems, a dominance of staff with a psychology background, and changes in the view and vision of the strategy of the programme, in the 1990s, gave rise to a series of step-by-step decisions to abolish two semester courses on technical production systems, and to diminish the economic aspects of the programme. These decisions were heavily criticised by alumni and HR managers in the outside world. Even looking back many years, we find that only one general introduction to economics tailored for HR students was offered! Of course, this has caused doubts about the breadth of mind of the students, the employability of the graduates, and the promising profile. In the end, what is at stake is the distinctive competence. Fortunately, since 2003, the approach from economics has been saliently reinforced by a newly developed course on human capital evaluation (Prof. Gerard Evers).

With the appointment of Prof. Jaap Paauwe in November 2005, a new era has been ushered in for human resource sciences in Tilburg. Because of his background in economics, his previous role as professor of business economics and organisation at Rotterdam's Erasmus University, his view and vision of HRM in relation to industrial relations, there are high expectations regarding the future of research and practice in the field of HRM.

In retrospect, it may be concluded that the original Tilburg programme was implicitly acting as a prototype for HR education at the university level. In at least four faculties of management and organisation, programmes and courses have been redesigned in order to offer a specialisation in HRM and/or a secondary option (minor) in some relevant aspects like management development or industrial relations. In at least seven universities, students of organisational sociology and psychology are recommended to follow additional HRM courses, while the number of (part-time) chairs and professors in HRM has been increased significantly. In the meantime many ideas stemming from the Tilburg experience have been applied in postgraduate and post-experience HR education, offered by commercial institutes as well as by universities. Professional colleges now offer many more interdisciplinary programmes, leading to a professional BA degree, stressing much more the importance of compulsory introductions in economics, management and strategy than they did in the past.

BEST-PRACTICE CASE: ROYAL PHILIPS ELECTRONICS, SHELL AND THE DUAL LADDER – A TRUE BALANCING ACT?

Many employing organisations make a more or less structured distinction between two career ladders: one for managers, the other for (top-level) specialists. With a dual ladder of this nature, the technical/scientific professional essentially dominates the specialist/top specialist ladder, while other categories of staff are on the management ladder (van Assen/Keijzers 1992).

The dual ladder system has worked satisfactorily up to a certain level. There has been and still is a degree of staff mobility between the two ladders. However, there are indications that there will be a change in the 'natural' career progression in the near future (Bardwick 1986). These developments lead on to the formulation of the following questions, which will be considered in detail in this section (van Wees/Jansen 1994):

1. What are the possible consequences for the social status of management jobs as opposed to specialist jobs?
2. How can attractive career prospects be offered to a large number of people in spite of the reduced opportunities for upward mobility?
3. How can the selection and identification of managers and/or top specialists be improved?
4. What are the consequences of the development outlined above as regards the social status of management jobs as opposed to specialist jobs?
5. Will expertise and management talent be valued equally in terms of money and status, now or in the future?

$\mathbf{Q}$.nl

> If such change actually occurs, it means that various occupational groups will have to alter their orientation vis-à-vis the world of organisations and businesses (Katz 1988).

$\mathbf{\Psi}$.nl

The average educational level of the working population has risen steadily since the Second World War. The decentralisation of knowledge, power and income has meant that unprecedented numbers of people, from right across the social spectrum, have had the benefit of a higher education. Uptake of highly educated personnel was no problem, since many organisations and businesses needed a growing level of expertise to cope with the speed of technological development and increasing complexity.

Even now, we see a continuing shift in populations within employing organisations towards the highly educated. In the not-too-distant future, for example, far more workers in many companies in the Netherlands will be undergraduates or university graduates. Not only in large organisations, but also in small and medium-sized businesses, it is becoming routine practice to recruit highly educated staff. These developments fit in with the transition towards a more knowledge-based society, striving to compete in the global arena (Dyer 1983).

It is not the uptake of highly educated staff within employing organisations that is causing concern so much as the career orientation of those staff. Many of them have expectations of reaching top-level positions, or of becoming a manager.

> **What is your advice for a foreign firm entering your country's market? What should managers especially care about and, what is more, be aware of?**
>
> In the Netherlands there is a dual consultation structure, both with the unions and with the (obligatory) workers' council. The laws concerning job protection are strong.
>
> Although the law, on the surface, seems rather rigid and rigorous in its protection for labour contracts, the flexibility in forms of labour contracts and the right to part-time work has consolidated labour participation and employment.
>
> In business, it is good to know that the pragmatic Dutch, though mainly concerned with facts and figures, are also great talkers and rarely make final decisions without a long 'Dutch' debate, sometimes running the risk of over-analysing. Foreign counterparts are also subjected to this and routinely tested for bluffing, as Dutch people with their long international experience in business hate to think of themselves as being in any way gullible.

CAREER ORIENTATION: SOME EMPIRICAL EVIDENCE

Although demand for managers can be expected to increase in the future, the prediction is that demand for top jobs will outstrip supply. A survey conducted among polytechnic and university graduates who had joined Philips showed that 47 per cent wished to develop further within their own specialist area, 11 per cent outside their specialist area and 38 per cent in management. Polytechnic graduates showed a pronounced preference for remaining in their specialist areas, while university graduates mainly wanted to develop in a management direction (Klep 1987).

Assuming that the promotion policy within organisations remains unchanged, while the number of highly educated staff within the organisations gradually increases, it seems appropriate to ask whether in the long term there will be sufficient jobs to satisfy the current level of aspirations of the highly educated. Unlike in the decades just after the Second World War, when graduates were a relative rarity in many companies and quickly reached the top, the present and future will see a sharp increase in competition between highly educated staff within employing organisations.

A sound HR development policy will aim to direct this competition in such a way that many people will modify their aspirations without losing their motivation and creativity. An open and businesslike approach to these employees can avoid conflict and demotivation in the future.

Only a small proportion of highly educated staff will be able to fill top jobs, after careful selection and identification. Most of these jobs are to be found at the top of the management ladder. Others will find a suitable position at middle management level. Many will have to continue their careers on the technical/scientific professional ladder. This ladder generally has fewer rungs and does not reach as high as the management ladder. This is one of the reasons why many ambitious, highly educated people endeavour to move as soon as possible from a technical starting position to the bottom rungs of the management ladder.

On the other hand, there are some highly educated people who have an aversion to management jobs and, for reasons of professional interest (and sometimes also for an easy life), would prefer to stay on the professional ladder. The choice of a career, be it in management or a profession, is partly determined by the fact that the two ladders are not of equal status: vital decisions are still taken by managers, not by technical specialists. In the decision-making process, the input derived from the professional side is often only one of the variables which have to be taken into account by the manager. This sometimes leaves the specialist, who is often not accustomed to thinking in terms of political strategy, feeling misunderstood and powerless.

All in all, there is a real risk that expert, talented, highly educated staff, for which the organisation had envisaged a professional career, will opt for the management ladder for career reasons. On the professional ladder, on the other hand, there may be workers with a very high management potential who opt for a career on the professional ladder for reasons of professional interest.

This all leads on to the finding that in practice there are at least two problems, which have been mentioned above, concerning the existence and relationship between the two career ladders: (a) how can the selection and identification of managers and/or top specialists be improved?; (b) how can attractive career prospects be offered to a large number of people in spite of the reduced opportunities for upward mobility?; and (c) in a number of large organisations, studies have been carried out to discover what characteristics are essential to good management and/or good managers.

TWO BUSINESS CASES

This has led to clusters of management characteristics, which are sometimes difficult to distinguish from personal style characteristics. We should like to talk briefly about the approach adopted by two organisations, Philips and Shell.

Royal Philips Electronics in the Netherlands is one of the world's biggest electronics companies, as well as the largest in Europe, with 161,500 employees in over sixty countries and sales of 30.3 billion EUR in 2004, activities in over sixty businesses and more than 100,000 registered patents. Philips is currently number one in the global markets for lighting, electronic shavers and DVD recording equipment and number two in medical diagnostics worldwide. Within the cyclical goods market, Dow Jones recently ranked Philips the global leader in sustainability.

Shell is a global group of energy and petrochemical companies, operating in more than 145 countries and employing over 119,000 staff. Most people know Shell for its retail stations and for exploring and producing oil and natural gas. Shell's activities also include:

- marketing, transporting and trading oil and gas;
- providing oil products for industrial uses including fuel and lubricant for ships and aircraft;
- generating electricity, including wind power, and producing solar panels;
- producing petrochemicals that are used for plastics, coating and detergents;
- developing technology for hydrogen vehicles; and
- no production of coal or nuclear power.

At the end of the 1960s Shell had a large-scale survey carried out, under the chairmanship of Prof. van Lennep, among managers and other members of the organisation, aimed at identifying factors which help to predict career potential. The survey revealed that one quality above all had the greatest predictive value. This quality, called 'helicopter', refers to the capacity to distance oneself, to look at problems from a higher vantage point, while seeing the connections between things, i.e. recognising which things are connected and thus being able to distinguish between what is of major and what of minor importance. Van Lennep himself called this 'common sense', the capacity for looking objectively at situations in which one is involved. At Shell, helicopter quality was found to be closely linked with three other qualities required in managers:

1. Power of analysis: the capacity to break down complex problems into manageable component parts.
2. Imagination: the capacity to think in terms of alternative solutions.
3. Sense of reality: having a pragmatic attitude; the 'both feet on the ground' approach.

In later years a fourth aspect was added, i.e. effective leadership. This aspect is closely related to the possession of complementary qualities such as self-confidence and modesty. The absence of such complementarity will soon lead to overestimation of one's own abilities or a failure to influence others.

Later, the appraisal processes Shell used for its senior staff were reviewed and brought in line with senior management opinion on the present and future management of the human resource. This led to a redesign of the processes, which, after extensive trials, were introduced at Shell worldwide from 1989. One of the renewals was that a broader set of qualities was introduced in which more attention was given to operational and leadership qualities.

In the early 1970s a survey was conducted under the chairmanship of Prof. L. Tigchelaar among a large number of managers at Philips, who were asked what they saw as the criteria which had determined success or failure in their own careers. This revealed four essential main characteristics:

1. Conceptual effectiveness is concerned with matters such as vision, seeing problems in context, having a perspective of the future, seeing new opportunities and their consequences, etc.
2. Operational effectiveness has to do with result motivation, the ability to work independently, the capacity to establish priorities, and the willingness to take risks.
3. Interpersonal effectiveness relates to the capacity to cooperate and to lead, the ability to inspire and convince.
4. Achievement motivation focuses mainly on the capacity to take risks and to work under pressure, and also on whether the person concerned is ambitious.

Effectiveness is a recurrent theme. The decisive factor is not whether people have management qualities, but how they handle them and what they produce. Having good social contacts, for example, is naturally welcome, but a far more interesting question is whether these contacts can be activated for the benefit of the management task.

💡.nl

In spite of the existence of the above-mentioned methods of identification in large organisations, the questions of whether highly educated specialists can also perform non-technical tasks or jobs remains unanswered.

Q.nl

A PROFESSIONAL CATEGORY: 'ENGINEERS'

As an illustration, let us consider the professional category 'engineers' (Dutch: *Ingenieur*, which is used here, generally refers only to graduate/chartered engineers) which is becoming established in employing organisations.

Is an engineer after graduation someone who has only mastered the technical sciences, or has his education already begun to lead him in the direction of a management job?

A survey of members of the Royal Dutch Institution of Engineers (KIVI) carried out by Eindhoven University of Technology showed that an engineer is trained in technical subjects and at the start of his career does mainly technical/scientific work and is not required to perform many management tasks (van Vonderen/Vaags 1985). As the engineer gets older, however, the number of non-technical tasks increases. Various surveys have shown that engineers feel poorly prepared for 'management jobs' – 'management' here meaning a wide range of tasks which are of a non-technical nature but are necessary for the progress of a project, for the performance of a department or organisation or for the care of its staff.

Engineers do not automatically make 'good managers'. Depending on their personality, education or training, they often experience difficulties in switching from the certainty and predictability of physical problems to the uncertainty of management problems and responsibility for them.

The most difficult aspects of the work are internal coordination and general leadership tasks. Engineers rarely mention a 'technical' task as the most difficult aspect. It is the management aspects which make their work most difficult. It appears that management jobs require more emotional (e.g. contacts with people) and behavioural skills (e.g. decision-making and target-setting), whereas direct technical work requires greater symbolic (e.g. testing theories and ideas) and perceptual skills (e.g. collecting information).

This has specific implications for professional engineers who take on a management role. The transition to such roles will frequently be marked by a number of characteristic problems (Krembs 1983; Osterman 1984; Pelz/ Andrews 1975):

- Strong self-identification with technical skills: many highly educated people still consider themselves specialists and have a high level of professional loyalty, which they find difficult to put aside. Once they become managers, they endeavour to be both specialists and managers.
- Strong achievement motivation: the opportunity to solve technical problems is attractive to achievement-motivated employees. Those with the highest achievement motivation have often been identified for the management ladder. The achievement job influencing others is often far more important than the manager's own individual achievements.
- Failure to focus on maintaining relationships: technical specialists too often prefer to work alone. Generally they are task oriented. Where they enter into relationships, these are often confined to fellow professionals.
- Failure to focus on strategic/organisational questions: many professionals have difficulties with questions of political strategy within an organisation. They are strongly oriented towards tasks and targets and forget how important it is to obtain assistance and support from others.

Organisations can assist specialists in their transition from the professional to the management ladder. A number of tools can be suggested for this: (a) develop instruments to make specialists aware of the characteristics of management jobs before they are faced with the decision whether to become a manager; (b) help the new managers to acquire the new values and standards needed to perform management tasks; and (c) top management must feel responsible for creating the right balance between managers' and specialists' skills.

It is to this last aspect that we should now like to devote a few words: how can attractive career prospects be offered to a large number of people in spite of the reduced opportunities for upward mobility?

In a few words, what would you say is the one fundamental strategic competitive advantage your country offers compared to others?

A skilled, highly educated, multilingual, flexible and motivated workforce with high work ethos and high performance.

WHERE WE STAND AND LESSONS LEARNED

The impression is that too many specialists make the move to the management ladder too early in their careers (Thijssen 1996). In many organisations there is little or no mobility between the two ladders at the higher levels. This means that managers have little opportunity to 'top up' their technical know-how and are often inadequately equipped to evaluate decisions on 'technical' merits.

Innovation is becoming less and less the monopoly of industrial laboratories. The speed of industrial innovation is partly determined by the quality of the cooperation between research, work preparation, production and marketing. Suggestions for improvement are often generated not by the scientific/experimental approach but as a result of suggestions from production staff.

Managers with a business school mentality are often less conscious of the fact that production innovation has become a formidable weapon in international competition. They are therefore deprived of technical reserves which are necessary for the organisation of innovation activities. The Japanese have taken a different view: a high-technology company cannot permit itself to employ promising students in 'unproductive' staff jobs.

There may be a lesson to be learned here. In an era where highly educated people will find little opportunity for upward mobility, this may provide scope for alternative inspiration and a new career direction. In a situation in which promotions will be in short supply, top management has a choice between extending existing promotion policy by increasing the number of jobs and career stages, and reducing the importance of promotion by reducing the number of levels in the hierarchy. In the latter case upward mobility will be low, with the result that many people will focus on job opportunities with challenging aspects. In the former case, many will still be on the lookout for promotion. But there is little to be achieved by a pseudo-promotion, in which the job title changes but there is no increase in responsibility.

On the other hand, in an organisation with a small number of levels in the hierarchy, people can be profoundly valued without reaching a higher level. Essentially, promotion policy is linked with the way in which organisations are structured. In a more horizontally structured organisation, the power of decision-making will be more decentralised and there will be a larger number of jobs involving considerable responsibility.

Increasing the number of autonomous and semi-autonomous groups may be a means of allowing many people to participate at varying and increasing levels of responsibility. Early delegation of powers, special project assignments to employees from different disciplines, widespread availability of courses in business studies and other junior management courses may be used as a means for broadening highly educated staff, not merely as an introduction. The formulation of concrete career paths within and between the professional and management ladders will provide opportunities for breaking out of the rigidity which exists within many dual ladders.

.nl

If organisations want to remain sufficiently in touch with the various occupational groups of their highly educated staff, they have no option but to look for creative solutions through which they can provide an HRD perspective for their management and specialist talent.

Which people play key roles in your country? Which names should one know?

- economy: Tinbergen;
- HR: Hofstede, Trompenaars, Kets de Vries;
- unions: Jongerius;
- finance: Zalm;
- politics: Balkenende, De Hoop Scheffer; and
- of course, Erasmus, Van Gogh, Rembrandt, Copernicus, Huygens, Spinoza.

References

Algera, Jen A. (2001): Human performance management in de 21- ste eeuw, concurrentievoordeel door mensen?, in: Nico van Bleichrodt *et al.* (eds): Werken en laten werken, Houten.

Bardwick, Judy M. (1986): The Plateauing Trap, New York.

Born, Hans/Nollen, Marcel (1998): De kwaliteit van de personele functie, Ph.D. thesis, University of Tilburg.

de Ruyter, Henk (ed.) (1992): Integrerend leiding geven en unitvorming. Van concept tot realiteit, Zeist.

Dyer, Lee (1983): Bringing human resources into the strategy formulation process, in: Human Resource Management, 22(3): 257–71.

Evers, Gerard (2004): De economische waarde van werknemers, University of Tilburg, Tilburg Institute for Social Policy Research and Consultancy (IVA).

Gomez-Mejia, Luis/Balkin, David B. (1992): Compensation, Organisational Strategy and Firm Performance, Cincinnati, South-Western.

Guest, David E. (1989): Human resource management: its implication for industrial relations and trade unions, in John Storey (ed.): New Perspectives on HRM, London, pp. 41–55.

Kaplan, Robert S./Norton, David P. (1996): The Balanced Score Card: Translating Strategy into Action, Boston.

Katz, Ralph (ed.) (1988): Managing Professionals in Innovative Organisations, Cambridge.

Klep, Marten P.L. (1987): Opinie-onderzoek HBO-ers en Academici 1987, Philips.

Kouwenhoven, Cees/van Hooft, P.L.R.M. (1990): De praktijk van strategisch personeelsmanagement, Deventer.

Krembs, Peter K. (1983): Making managers of technical gurus, in: Training and Development Journal, 37(9): 36–41.

Osterman, Paul (ed.) (1984): Internal Labour Markets, London.

Paauwe, Jaap/Huijgen, J.H. (1996) Personeelsmanagement in bedrijf, Alphen a/d Rijn.

Pelz, Donald C./Andrews, Frank M. (eds) (1975): Scientists and organisations, Ann Arbor.

Roe, Robert A. (1983): Grondslagen der personeelsselektie, Assen.

Thijssen, Jos (1996): Leren, leeftijd en loopbaanperspectief, Deventer.

Tigchelaar, Lo S. (2003): De ontwikkeling van de P-functie naar HRM, in: Tijdschrift voor HRM, 3: 95–116.

van Assen, Albert/Keijzers, F.J. (1992): Loopbaanontwikkeling en inzetbaarheid van kenniswerkers, in: Gedrag & Organisatie, 5(6): 417–27.

van Dalen, Erik J./Gründemann, Rob de Vries, Sjiera (2003): Onderweg naar morgen: Ontwikkelingen en hun betekenis voor toekomstig HRM, in: Tijdschrift voor HRM, 3: 63–90.

van Dam, Karen/Thierry, Hendrik (2000): Mobiliteit in perspectief. Een overzicht van onderzoek rond de mobiliteit van personeel, in: Gedrag & Organisatie, 13(1): 29–49.

.nl

van Vonderen, Marijke L./Vaags, D.W. (1985): Ingenieurs hikken aan tegen niettechnische vakken, in: De Ingenieur, 11 November.

Vermeulen, S. (1997): De competenties van de business unit personeelsmanager, University of Tilburg: Doctoral thesis dept. of HR-studies.

Wees, Lucas van/Jansen, Paul (1994): Dual ladder in balance, in: International Journal of Career Management, 6(3): 11–19.

The authors

Dr L.S. Lo Tigchelaar (cubic.lt@dataserve.nl). In 1987 he was appointed Professor of Personnel Sciences at Tilburg University. From 1996 he has been a part-time professor and is currently an external consultant and interim manager with high-tech organisations. He has been founder and president of the Management Development and International sections of NVP.

Dr P.W.M. Pieter Haen (pieterhaen@duurstedegroep.com) is Vice-President of the European Association for Personnel Management (EAPM) and Board Member of the Dutch Association for Personnel Management and Organisational Development (NVP). Since 1992 he has been President/Founder of Duurstede Groep Management Consultants Search & Selection.

Dr L.L.G.M. Lucas van Wees MBA MBT (l.van.wees@wxs.nl). Since 1985 he has worked for Shell, Philips and KPN, and since 2001 he has been Vice-President of HR Commercial and Global for KLM which merged mid-2004 with Air France. He has written three books, is co-author of four books and published in various (international) articles, including for *Personnel Journal*, the *International Journal of Career Management* and the *Journal of Management Development*.

.nl

11 HRM in Poland: integrate to develop people

Tina Sobocińska/Antoni Ludwiczyński/Ryszard Michalczyk/Renata Trochimiuk/
Joanna Górska

Poland: in a nutshell

In this chapter you will learn:

- that in Poland the requirements due to the political change in 1989 could have only be met by the changes in the personnel function. HRM thus underwent a qualitative change to ensure the necessary resources;

- that the Polish economy aims at acquiring a knowledge base. Therefore lifelong learning is one of the most important research fields in HRM academia; and

- that by implementing and adapting Japanese HRM practices, Polska Wytwórnia Papierów Wartościowych S.A. (PWPW) achieved an improvement in the employees' work quality which led to greater value in products and services.

Capital:	Warsaw
Area (sq km):	312,685 (land 304,465; water 8,220)
EU membership:	since 2004
Population:	38,536,869
Languages:	Polish
Ethnic groups (in percentages):	Polish 96.7, German 0.4, Belarussian 0.1, Ukrainian 0.1, other 2.7 (2002)
Gross domestic product:	542.6 billion USD (2006)
Workforce (in percentages):	17.26 million (2006): agriculture 16.1; industry 29; services 54.9 (2002)
Export commodities:	machinery and transport equipment, intermediate manufactured goods, miscellaneous manufactured goods, food and live animals

BACKGROUND: DEVELOPMENT OF THE HRM CONCEPT IN POLAND

FROM PERSONNEL ADMINISTRATION TO HUMAN CAPITAL MANAGEMENT

The year 1989 is undoubtedly one of the most important dates in Polish post-war history – if not the most important date. To be able to exist in the conditions of a market economy, Polish companies had to adapt to its rules, deal with global competition and become increasingly aware of the unavoidability and dynamics of the changes in the environment and organisations themselves. It is only through changes in the personnel function that these requirements could be met. It can thus be claimed that the transition which started fifteen years ago was connected with transformations in management, including people management.

It is no exaggeration to say that the changes in people management in Poland constituted a crucial stage in a qualitative transformation. Generally speaking, they were similar in direction and nature to the earlier changes in the USA and western Europe; however, they had specifically Polish features stemming from more than their inclusion in the transition (Pocztowski 2003a: 20–1). Here in Poland with our difficult experiences, we faced a clash between the challenges of modern times and burdens from the past. These burdens made the personnel function political and central but failed to provide systematic solutions. Thus the personnel group had to undergo a 'qualitative' change to be able to ensure the necessary support and resources (which were increasingly, and more importantly, people) for companies learning to function in a changing environment.

An important factor in Polish transformations was the popularity of HR knowledge, which was spread simultaneously in two ways: through the development of HR practices and through the activities of universities and publishing houses. Western companies played a significant role in the former. They contributed their experiences, their know-how and the opportunities to use consulting companies, first foreign, then Polish. Universities gave access to theoretical knowledge, conducted research, taught subjects focused on people's behaviour in organisational contexts, and publishing houses supplied first translations from English and then Polish publications.

The stages seen in the development of the personnel function in Poland resemble those described in the world literature. They are: personnel administration, personnel management, human resource management (HRM) and human capital management (HCM). These transformations have taken place on the theoretical front, but in practice all stages coexist, with the earlier ones dominant. The specifically Polish feature of the changes the personnel function has undergone is the forced accelerated pace and now huge disproportions and differences in the quality of HRM. If the level of HRM was ranked on a scale covering:

- unawareness of the problem;
- underestimation of HR;
- declaration of the significance of HR; and
- actions focusing on rational use of HR,

most Polish companies would be placed somewhere between the phases of underestimation and declaration. Few organisations truly appreciate the significance of employees and follow this line of thinking, seeing them as their most valuable asset. Most numerous is the group of companies where personnel are still cost drivers.

What is typical of your country in relation to the country itself (its culture, people, etc.) and its economy?

- Polish people have a perception of the strong position and importance of their country in different respects – historical, geographical, economic, cultural.
- With the economic surge of the 1990s, Poland became the economic tiger of central eastern Europe, building on the massive surge in living standards between the beginning of the twentieth century and the 1980s.
- They are a conservative society in some ways, with a lot of respect for tradition, culture, history.
- Polish people have a different perception of themselves: they are a very open, modern and democratic society and treat everyone as a close friend and with the traditional hospitality for which their country is known worldwide.
- 'Poles can do it – we are Jacks of all trades.' They are proud of their capacity to adapt and ability to handle even very difficult problems; new challenges are their driving force.

MAIN THEORETICAL AND EMPIRICAL TRENDS IN HRM

No coherent theory

This text is an overview and an attempt to characterise academic approaches to HRM in Poland. The basic hypothesis is: there is no coherent theory; there are theoretical and empirical trends in the realm of HRM in Poland. This is a fundamental problem, an Achilles' heel both in our country and others. Theoretical considerations often focus on the question of behaviour, and fail to explain why certain phenomena occur and when they occur. Without the explanation of the reasons and mechanisms of the HR phenomena we are destined to use the trial-and-error method and therefore rely on its consequences. This simplified situational approach has so far exerted a strong influence on the way some practitioners, consultants and HR researchers think. Some theoreticians claim that HRM is not a fully developed academic discipline, that what we have now is the process of its development (Listwan 2002: 9–11) and that 'some scientific approaches to HRM theory nowadays are starting to refer to the trends in academic research' (Ulrich 2001: 254).

Main trends

The main theoretical and empirical trends in HRM in Poland are as follows:

- strategic HRM covering the architecture of HRM;
- HRM in the context of restructuring in the company, competence management, and measurement and development of human capital;
- flexible working and reward patterns; and
- knowledge management, including the balance between private and professional life.

These trends focus on selected themes. They differ in the way they approach HRM and in the terminology used. They are also present in different academic centres, such as Warsaw with the Warsaw School of Economy, the Leon Koźmiński Academy of Entrepreneurship and Management (WSPIZ), the Institute of Labour and Social Studies, Cracow with its University of Economics and University of Science and Technology, Wroclaw with its University of Economics, Katowice with its University of Economics and Lodz with its university.

It is impossible to present all the trends here. For this reason the authors focus on presenting the main assumptions and empirical research within the dominant problem areas. Using criteria such as the amount of research done on a given subject, the number of publications and the extent to which they are reflected in the educational programmes of universities, and consulting and training companies, the dominant areas have been identified as strategic HRM, flexible working patterns and knowledge management.

 .pl

Strategic HRM

The concept of strategic HRM was developed in the USA and the countries of western Europe, notably in the UK, in the early 1980s. It was claimed at that time that the strategic resources for building competitive advantage for a company were competent, highly motivated employees, who were innovation oriented and ready to act in changing conditions. In Poland, the concept of strategic HRM appeared in 1997–8, and the first publications (except for the earlier translations from English) came out in 2000–1 (Juchnowicz 2004; Rybak 2003). According to most of the authors, formulating HR strategy should be preceded by answering two basic questions:

1. What is the value of human capital in the context of the opportunity to solve strategic problems and build a competitive advantage?
2. Are there any employees in the company with unique skills essential for distinguishing the company in its sector and market?

The determination to formulate HR strategy is not invariably accompanied by the consequences of its implementation. The main problem is rather an inadequate coordination of HR strategy with other strategic areas of the company: both theoreticians and practitioners believe that the responsibility for implementing HRM resides with all managers, according to the mission and strategy of the company. It means that every manager should also be a HR manager. That is the only way for HRM to support the whole chain of values by means of recruitment, employment, training, development and rewards.

The methods of strategic HRM should contribute to the integration of actions at personnel management level and to the integration of the overall strategy of the company with HR strategy. SWOT analysis, personnel audit, social balance, benchmarking, outplacement, assessment centre, career plans, remuneration package, long-term incentives and managerial contracts (Ludwiczyński 2001) are examples of potential methods. But companies often look for effective action in an intuitive way without considering a strategic approach by using the methods mentioned. Moreover, the company and HR strategies should be particularly supported by a rewards strategy (Borkowska 2001).

The current focus of strategic HRM in Poland is on developing holistic systems of competence management. This area is studied by the theoreticians (Oleksyn 1999; Juchnowicz/Rostkowski 2003) and consulting firms such as Deloitte, HAY Group and Mercer HRC, adapting their experience to Polish circumstances, as well as by the Polish companies ProFirma and HRK Partners.

Strategic HRM has become the subject of much research in Poland. The most significant studies have been undertaken by the team from the Cracow University of Economy, and covering the 101 biggest companies (Pocztowski *et al.* 2001), and another one conducted on 261 firms by the Warsaw School of Economics (Rybak 2003).

> Despite declared high awareness of the personnel function, few companies formulate a HR strategy and even fewer implement it. Implementing personnel strategy requires consistency but also high organisational culture with strategic HRM as its value.

The fact that strategic HRM is important in Poland is confirmed by its presence as a subject in the curriculum of many universities and business schools for managers and personnel specialists and a separate postgraduate study programme.

Flexible working patterns

In the 1980s, academics in the USA and western Europe became interested in the area of flexible organisational structures and employment. The research undertaken at that time contributed to the reduction in the number of full-time workers and the increase in less stable forms of employment. In Poland, interest in flexible working patterns appeared in the mid-1990s – when the first temporary employment agencies (subsidiaries of foreign companies) were set up – and reached its peak in the late 1990s. It was reflected in the literature (Borkowska 1998), but a thorough understanding of the problems of flexible work was not covered in publications until after 2001 (Kryńska 2003). Borkowska and Kryńska are the best-known experts in this area in Poland.

Key dilemma: stability or flexibility

Polish authors emphasise that the key dilemma nowadays is the choice between stability and flexibility of work because, for a company to operate effectively, these two contradictory requirements need to be met simultaneously (Borkowska 1998: 45). Stability of labour is a condition and at the same time a guarantee of the development of human capital in the organisation. Flexibility of labour, on the other hand, enables a company to react to changes in the environment effectively and to be cost-competitive. In order to meet this challenge, companies introduce innovations in the form of employment, working time and rewards policy so that flexibility is maintained in 'legal, functional, quantitative, financial and time and space-based working conditions' (Pocztowski 2003a: 127).

Polish companies have introduced changes in the status and the structure of working patterns. Despite the dominance of traditional employment (full-time and permanent jobs) there are more non-typical patterns in the market. Numerous companies are tending to reduce permanent jobs and base employment on specific campaigns and assignment projects (Borkowska 1998: 42).

The Institute of Labour and Social Studies conducted wide-ranging representative research into flexible working patterns in Poland in 2001–3. The results show that flexible working patterns are not widely used (Konecki 2003: 217) and most of the employers studied are sceptical about their future chances of development.

The most popular pattern found by the researchers was outsourcing: signing a civil contract with the business subject (85 per cent of the companies from the research) and mandating contracts and contracts for a specified service or assignment (freelancing and subcontracting) (68.6 per cent). Over half of the organisations used fixed-term contracts (78.4 per cent) and part-time contracts (66.3 per cent). Cases of organisations using other non-typical working patterns were very rare (from 5-odd per cent to 15-odd per cent) (Kryńska 2003: 239–43).

Flexible working patterns are an important challenge in HRM. The research discussed here helps to identify the obstacles in taking advantage of them. These are not legal barriers but the employees' reluctance to work on such a flexible basis. From the employer's perspective the obstacle is the flexible employees' limited loyalty to the company and a lack of supervision of employees and equipment (especially in the case of telework) (Kryńska 2003:243–9). The most significant obstacle – employees' negative attitude to flexible working patterns and their perception of such work as less stable and failing to give a sense of work stability,

319

training or promotion (Kryńska 2003: 248) – cannot be overcome solely at company level. It requires the cooperation of all the actors in the labour market: government, employers, employees. Moreover, two basic conditions need to be met: provision of the same protection for flexible and traditional employment and avoidance of treating flexible employment as a means to reduce costs (Kryńska 2003: 251). HR specialists can influence corporate culture so that it welcomes flexible working patterns and overcomes prejudices towards flexible workers and, instead, enhances their loyalty and identification with the company and its goals.

Heightened interest in the labour market

In spite of the fact that the results of the research show that flexible working patterns are not widely used, observation of the labour market indicates heightened interest in this area. A sharp upturn can be seen in self-employment and a dynamic increase in temporary work. This is evidenced by legislative action – the bill of 9 July 2003 on the employment of temporary workers Dz.U. Nr 166, poz. 1608 (Official Journal of 2003) – and the establishment of the Association of Temporary Work Agencies in 2002. Its members are the companies providing temporary workers. The Association promotes temporary work in business and government circles and aims to adapt Polish legislative and ethical standards to European ones. In 2003, the Association conducted research on a group of 1,550 candidates for jobs among its company members. The results definitely show that most of the candidates who had worked at least once through a temporary work agency evaluated such work in a positive (54.8 per cent) or very positive way (22.4 per cent). The respondents thought that temporary job agencies are useful in Poland (92.8 per cent) and saw a temporary job as a chance to get a permanent one. It is thus possible to say that the stereotypes and prejudices towards temporary work are slowly being overcome.

Moreover, there is an increasing awareness in companies operating in the new economy that global competition, informatisation and increased demand for knowledge require transformations in processes and structures and, as a result, changes in employment. The Polish authors think, for example, that despite little use being made of telework nowadays, this pattern will develop vigorously within a short time-scale (Bednarski/Machol-Zajda 2003).

The area of flexible working patterns is starting to appear with increasing frequency on the agenda of conferences and symposia organised mainly by the Institute of Labour and Social Studies. This is accompanied by huge interest from employers, managers and personnel specialists, which it is hoped can be translated into more widespread acceptance of flexible working patterns in Polish companies.

Knowledge management

In the mid-1990s, the issue of knowledge management was raised. It reached Poland in the late 1990s. The development of knowledge management in Poland is closely related to the role of Wawrzyniak, Kwiatkowski, Strojny and Kukliński, Poland's first knowledge management academics and authors of Polish publications. The Polish authors usually accept that knowledge management is 'the process by which the organisation generates wealth from its intellectual or knowledge-based assets' (Bukowitz/Williams 1999: 2) and point to the main parts of the process: acquiring knowledge from the environment, taking advantage of the knowledge in the company, maintaining and developing knowledge assets, and selling knowledge as new products.

Polish authors emphasise that knowledge is one of an organisation's most important resources. Both management theoreticians and practitioners agree that it is a basic requirement for corporate competitiveness. Knowledge management signifies the necessity to acquire, create, collect, select and transfer knowledge and consequently the ability to use it in practice in order to gain a competitive advantage. Accordingly, knowledge management in the new economy becomes a key competence within the HR realm. The main tasks of HRM in a knowledge-based organisation are thus: recruiting and maintaining necessary knowledge workers, encouraging employees to share their knowledge and increasing the possibilities of employees acquiring and creating knowledge (Table 11.1).

Table 11.1 Main tasks of HRM in the knowledge management process

Knowledge management area	Main HR tasks
1. Knowledge acquisition	Ensuring knowledge assets currently necessary and required for the future
2. Creating and using knowledge resources	Creating the atmosphere to learn and the motivation to get and use knowledge resources
3. Collecting and transferring knowledge	Creating knowledge bases and ensuring access to knowledge resources in the right form, time and context
4. Sharing knowledge	Building pro-effective organisational culture orientated to develop knowledge-sharing attitudes

The consequence of such an approach is that shop-floor workers decrease as a group and are replaced by knowledge workers (Drucker 2002). According to Polish authors, the productivity of knowledge workers becomes a key factor of corporate success (Pocztowski 2003b: 14).

Knowledge management means new organisational challenges, the most important of which are: changing content and conditions of work, heightened significance of organisational learning, changes in the organisational roles of HR subjects, the search for methods of HC measurement (intangible assets) and support for employees seeking to maintain a work–life balance.

What would you like to teach foreign HR managers? What is important for them to know in your opinion?

- start learning the language;
- you can expect to meet young managers and executives with a great deal of responsibility for their age (especially in internationally geared sectors of the Polish economy);
- try to understand the culture and people. Read up on them before you visit the country; and
- we are very open to international know-how but remember the maxim: 'Think globally, act locally.'

PERSPECTIVES IN THE DEVELOPMENT OF HRM

Even though empirical research has been conducted in the last five years, there is still a great need for more studies of the most important HRM trends in Poland. This requires the cooperation of both practitioners and theoreticians as well as significant funding. The research should help prepare specific models and rules for practitioners to use. Managers and personnel specialists would then be able to explain 'how and why specific HR actions lead to specific results' (Ulrich 2001: 254). In that way they would gain support for their everyday activities, scientific justification of their effectiveness and an argument to use in discussions with boards and managers.

There are many reasons for HRM having such a weak position in Poland; one of them is definitely the lack of a coherent HRM theory, another the lack of knowledge and scant use of HRM effectiveness indicators. The issue of measuring HR effectiveness is quite new in Poland, yet managers and personnel specialists are increasingly aware of the opportunities created by these instruments and their value. This is underlined by their participation in conferences on the subject and the wave of publications and discussions at meetings of the Polish Human Resources Management Association. This is a positive signal because building the position of the HR department as a business partner would be impossible without defining a measurement system for the results achieved.

It seems that the chance of improving the quality of HRM in Polish companies lies in cooperation between HRM practitioners and theoreticians. Such a dialogue has been going on for a number of years, resulting, for example, in the 21st Century Personnel Initiative conferences, where practitioners and theoreticians give lectures, conduct workshops and stage discussions together or, in cooperation with many universities, with the representatives of companies. The activities of Leon Koźmiński Academy of Entrepreneurship and Management (WSPIZ) are a good example of this: organisation of meetings between students and top-notch specialists, mandatory internships in companies, consultation with noted practitioners on the content of syllabuses, and participation of practitioners in curriculum councils, e.g. of postgraduate programmes.

What are you and other Polish people extraordinarily proud of with respect to HRM?

- considerable progress and development of HRM: from a purely administrative function before the 1990s to competences and knowledge management with sophisticated methodologies today;
- strong position of HR experts in more and more companies: HR directors play the role of management board members, advisers to executive boards, become partners in business management; and
- remarkable change in the approach to people management and the perception of the human resource as a company's most important asset.

CHALLENGES

The research conducted under the heading 'The experiences of personnel directors – the HR challenge' by the Conference Board and Capgemini Poland in 2004 showed that Polish managers perceived the following to be the most important challenges of the following three years:

- development of HR competences in the managerial team (46 per cent indications);
- development of internal communication (41.9 per cent); and
- implementation of innovative working and reward patterns (31.5 per cent).

Analysis of these results clearly shows a congruence between HR challenges noted by personnel directors and the development of the HR concept in Poland as discussed here. Polish HRM can take advantage of the work of authors studying the development and application of flexible working patterns. In the trends seen developing in strategic HRM and knowledge management, theoreticians stress the significance of a redefinition of the roles of managers and personnel specialists, which as this section shows is also important for practitioners and for creating the right corporate culture. One crucial factor in creating that culture – a key element in promoting the values in the company – is, as the personnel directors state, communication. This is especially important in the face of changes in the strategy and transformation of organisational structures currently ongoing in many companies in the Polish market.

It is thus fair to say that in-depth cooperation between academics and practitioners is beneficial for both sides and constitutes an opportunity for developing the science of HRM in Poland and meeting the current challenges for Polish HRM.

.pl

EAPM AFFILIATE: POLSKIE STOWARZYSZENIE ZARZĄDZANIA KADRAMI

Looking at the HR issues and trends in any of the emerging economies of Central and Eastern Europe, one can see similar patterns to those observed during the recent decades in the West. Virtually no solution that proved effective in the West has not been implemented in Poland since 1989. However, one factor remains undoubtedly different – the rapid pace of change. No economy in Western Europe or North America has undergone such dramatic change as Poland in the last two decades. Moreover, another one is imminent, due to the country's accession to the European Union. The way a state-owned company operated in the 1980s is completely different from the way a company needs to act today. The values, behaviours and traits necessary for success have changed. The 'headline legends' of socialism are today forgotten. Most probably, our accession to the EU will also set new challenges and requirements, although not as profound as those since 1989.

(Herman/Motyl 2003: 2)

TEN YEARS OF PHRMA ACTIVITIES IN POLAND

In recent years, HRM in Poland has also experienced change due to its economic transformation. Polskie Stowarzyszenie Zarzadzania Kadrami (PSZK), the Polish HRM Association (PHRMA), has been participating in these processes for years.

In 2004, PHRMA celebrated its tenth anniversary. In its mission statement, PHRMA says: 'Our mission is to integrate, develop and support human resource management professionals and be a leader for the HR environment in Poland. Our aim is to be seen as an effective and important partner for business in development planning and the realisation of corporate strategies.'

Strategy, goals and members

PHRMA's aims are focused on establishing the experience-sharing platform between HR world representatives in Poland. Particular goals are to:

– represent members' interests and develop their professional skills;
– promote exchange of information, between HR professionals and government representatives, employers' organisations and other institutions;
– influence the legal system in the field of labour law and other legal regulations important for employers;
– exchange professional knowledge between members;
– promote an ethical code of good behaviours and practices in HRM;
– establish and observe high standards of HRM;
– support the international dimension of HRM in Poland;

    – establish vocational qualification standards in the field of HRM; and
    – cooperate actively with the European Association for Personnel Management (EAPM) and other international HRM associations, promote networking, exchange know-how, and participate in projects.

PHRMA has over 1,000 ordinary members (HR professionals: directors, managers, consultants) and over ten supporting members (companies willing to support the Association's aims).

Main activities

Bearing in mind the goals of PHRMA, many activities linked with the mission and strategy of the Association have been undertaken in recent years.

HR events

The Association is a partner for the prestige and important events of HRM in Poland: PHRMA members participate in the jury of professional contests such as the annual competitions for HR Director of the Year, Leader of HRM, training Manager of the year, Global Management and Global Management Challenge – Euromanager.

Seminars, conferences, workshops

Every year PHRMA organises many seminars, conferences and workshops on HRM, including 'HRM Convent' – a cycle of seminars on the most important HRM topics such as: managerial coaching, effective motivation, the European Labour Code, etc., coordinated and organised by PHRMA with the participation of noted experts and professionals. In 2004, PHRMA teamed up with the Management Institute to organise the first international HR congress in Warsaw, which featured over fifty speakers from Poland, Europe and the USA combining a wealth of experience in business, academic inquiry and HRM.

Knowledge transfer

PHRMA also participates actively in knowledge transfer. Members of the Association cooperate with professional magazines in Poland and publish articles to spread best practices and knowledge among HR professionals. Every member of PHRMA receives a newsletter containing the most important information on HR matters, events and contacts. The meetings of the regional units are linked with presentations, panel discussions or debates on the hottest HR subjects.

Research and surveys

Thanks to the initiative and participation of PHRMA, a variety of research projects have been successfully realised: research on company training policies, survey of HR environment needs, analysis of HR salaries and benefits in Poland, research on the recession and on the gains of intellectual capital in Poland,

325

and research on HR competence models in Europe. The results of the surveys are presented and discussed among PHRMA members.

Cooperation with government bodies

PHRMA is also an important partner for government institutions, providing opinions on critical aspects of the law concerning HRM. Consultations on new legal regulations, on changes in current procedures and on the Labour Code have been requested and considered by government bodies in recent years.

HR professional standards

PHRMA is the first professional organisation in Poland to have taken up the discussion of professional standards and permanent education for HR professionals. The project is under consultation and discussion. The first step map of HR competences has been realised.

IT and people management

This exclusive PHRMA project focuses on the promotion and development of reliable and professional IT systems supporting HRM in organisations. The Association makes recommendations for the highest quality IT systems.

Integration of HR professionals

PHRMA activities are based on the integration of the HR environment in Poland. The Association offers various opportunities for members: apart from a host of conferences, seminars and workshops organised for HR professionals, 'HR pub' has been set up to integrate members in a more informal way – with meetings and discussions not only focused on HR topics but also linked with culture, hobbies, members' personal interests, etc. The monthly meetings of the regional branches also provide an opportunity to share knowledge, network and maintain contacts.

Project teams

To satisfy PHRMA members' different preferences and create opportunities to develop different interests and personal qualifications, five project teams are active in integrating modern HRM, and we consider these in the following sections.

Marketing communication team

This team was created to build the image of the Association internally and externally as the platform for cooperation on the development of modern HRM methods. This project group is focused on developing attractive offers for members, creating a positive image for the Association, and maintaining relations with the media.

International projects group

The main activities here are connected with international cooperation with EAPM and participation in the international projects initiated by EAPM, other associations (young talents, research projects) and the team itself (HR European competences model). The group cooperates with other associations through active networking and projects; it is also a discussion forum and platform for international knowledge exchange.

Knowledge transfer and development team

One of the strategic projects of this team is to set up a model for HR professional standards. The goal of the project is to create a system of permanent education for each and every HR professional in Poland. The group is also focusing on creating a programme of postgraduate studies for HR professionals.

Labour code team

The goal of this team is to support PHRMA members in dealing with legal issues, participate in the legislative process in Poland (different regulations regarding the European Labour Code) and help ensure the Labour Code's proper application in Poland. The activities of the group involve organising seminars and conferences on the Labour Code.

Regional exchange of experience team

The goal of this team is to support and integrate PHRMA regional activities in thirteen branches across Poland. The team supports regional enterprises and the integration of HR professionals in the country through conferences, events and meetings with management board members.

CURRENT AND FUTURE CHALLENGES FOR HR PROFESSIONALS

HR management in Poland today requires a complete rethink. Globalisation, technological development and business effectiveness are creating the need for a profound and intensive transformation of contemporary HR functions. Companies that understand and respect the significance of not only financial but also human, intellectual and social assets perform better. Organisations need to foster an open-mind culture: organisational change, new ideas, new people and their knowledge are the way to achieve competitive advantage. The challenge for HR professionals is to support and lead companies in that direction.

Today, HR managers are able to focus on activities facilitating business strategy and other processes which bring added value to company performance. The role of HR as a corporate strategic partner presents new qualification requirements for HR professionals. On the other hand, the process of integration with the EU makes it necessary to invest in knowledge and skills for Polish HR managers. At the same time, the distance between HR managers and operational managers is being reduced, creating additional requirements for HR professionals in terms of business awareness and business skills.

HR as a business partner constantly needs to prove its effectiveness and 'return on investment'.

> The challenges which the knowledge-based economy presents to the HR manager are very ambitious. Permanent education, new systems of employees' motivation, mobility, increase in rapid implementation of business processes (time-to-market) or the knowledge-based economy strategic build programme (Lisbon Strategy) are just some of the challenges that Polish and European managers face.
>
> (Fazlagic 2004)

PHRMA understands what is needed today. To support the HR profession in Poland, the Association undertakes many activities and efforts to offer its members the opportunity to develop their knowledge and professional qualifications.

In order to fulfil this purpose, the professional qualification standards model is required not only for Polish HR managers but also for representatives of the profession in central eastern Europe. PHRMA has initiated such a project for the local professional environment in Poland.

Other strategic PHRMA activities are connected with EU accession. Through coordination, initiation and realisation of projects, PHRMA is seeking to support the government's sector operational programme. That programme is focused on the development of Polish enterprises in terms of HRM (upgrading of professional qualifications, knowledge-based economy) and the association is involved in wide-ranging promotional activities for the project.

In a few words, what would you say is the one fundamental strategic competitive advantage your country offers compared to others?

- Location in Europe: the bridge between western and eastern Europe with a clean environment and tasty foods made only with natural products.
- Size of the country = size of the market.

HR ACADEMIA: THE KNOWLEDGE-BASED ECONOMY

Polish authors emphasise that in the new economy – often equated with the knowledge-based economy – learning in societies, organisations and among employees becomes the main motor of progress and social development. The awareness that lifelong learning is an integral part of professional activity is growing.

💡.pl

In a knowledge-based company lifelong learning becomes a routine element of everyday work, one which needs to be tailor-made and delivered 'just in time'.

In Polish literature, we increasingly find theses that knowledge management requires the redefinition of the role of HR specialists, line and executive managers. Managers are expected to be proactive in learning (mentoring, coaching), to be able to create business awareness and build a corporate culture promoting the sharing of knowledge within an organisation and creating the values important for clients, employees and shareholders. Personnel specialists, aside from their traditional roles as advisers and performers of personnel processes, should act as creators of change and be an inspiration for the acquisition, generation and promotion of knowledge. At headquarter level especially, the HR department should be a business partner on the Board, oriented towards creating and implementing personnel strategy and new personnel policy methods and tools and assessing the value of human capital in the organisation.

Knowledge management became a subject of research in Poland in 2000–1. The most significant findings have been produced by the Warsaw School of Economics team headed by Ploszajski, the Leon Koźmiński Academy of Entrepreneurship and Management (Wyższa Szkola Przedsiębiorczości i Zarządzania, WSPiZ) and its Centre of Management Studies under the supervision of Wawrzyniak and the Department of Entrepreneurship Kwiatkowski.

This research identifies numerous initiatives connected with knowledge management in some of the companies studied. Most of them, however, did not have knowledge management systems. Using the KPMG knowledge management system construction model – knowledge-chaotic, knowledge-aware, knowledge-focused, knowledge-managed, knowledge-centric – the WSPiZ academics estimated that most of the companies studied were in the second phase, where various 'knowledge' initiatives were undertaken. Very few companies were 'identified as being at the beginning of the third phase: constructing and implementing knowledge management procedures and tools' (Dąbrowski/Koladkiewicz 2003: 176).

The research conducted by the Warsaw School of Economics and WSPiZ indicates that there are many factors impeding the sharing of knowledge and the most important of them is employee reluctance. This is a huge challenge for managers and personnel specialists, especially in view of the need to build corporate cultures that will support knowledge management and create and implement adequate systems and tools, e.g. motivational systems.

Knowledge management, for both the economy of the country and for companies, is of major interest to the Polish government, various institutions, scientists and management practitioners. Some universities have compulsory lectures in knowledge management (this subject formed part of the curriculum in WSPiZ in 2003–4) and numerous conferences are organised on the subject. It is hoped that the outcomes of the discussions and meetings will have a positive influence on companies.

After evaluating the condition of HRM in Poland, we conclude that the intense activities of various Polish universities, the wide-ranging activities of PHRMA, the abundance of publications and HR journals (*Personel j Zarządzanie/* 'Personnel and management', *Zarządzanie Zasobami Ludzkimi* 'HRM') and the existence of a large group of well-educated, experienced managers and personnel specialists are not reflected in a strong position for HR in Polish companies.

BEST-PRACTICE CASE: POLSKA WYTWÓRNIA PAPIERÓW WARTOŚCIOWYCH S.A. – ADAPTING JAPANESE PRACTICES TO POLISH NEEDS

GENERAL COMPANY INFORMATION

Polish Security Printing Works (Polska Wytwórnia Papierów Wartościowych S.A. (PWPW S.A.) is a commercial joint-stock company of great importance for the national economy. Its exclusive shareholder is the State Treasury of the Republic of Poland. The company emerged from the privatised state-owned enterprise State Security Printing Works.

The history of PWPW S.A. started on 25 January 1919 when government ministers of the Second Polish Republic headed by Ignacy Jan Paderewski decided: 'An office of the State Graphics Works will be founded with the executive task of producing banknotes and all kind of stamps for payments to be made to the State Treasury in Poland.'

The first general meeting took place on 10 July 1926 at the head office of the National Bank of Poland. From then on, the company was known as the Polish Security Printing Works. At the same time, construction work commenced on the company's premises at 1 Roman Sanguszka Street in Warsaw.

During the following years, PWPW S.A. delivered top-quality products: banknotes, postage stamps, security papers and documents for financial and government institutions as well as for other clients who attached prime importance to quality, security and on-time production. By the 1930s, PWPW S.A. had created a security printing system turning out products of a high technological and artistic standard: securities, postage stamps and banknotes designed by outstanding artists, such as Zofia Stryjeńska, Józef Mehoffer and Marian Polak.

Because of the high standard of production and the strength of the company's brand, even the occupying Germans kept the copyright note of PWPW S.A. products in Polish.

In the 1950s, as the company was developing, it changed its name to the State Security Printing Works and was the only Polish producer of banknotes, the most important security papers and other clasified documents.

In the early years following the country's political transformation (after 1989), PWPW S.A. went through a very difficult time, unable to meet the demands of the new political environment. First, the company lost the contract for the production of new passports (which went to the UK company Thomas de la Rue).

Nowadays, the company can put all of this behind it. Completely revamped, PWPW S.A. is considered one of the most modern companies of its kind. In 1996, the original name of PWPW S.A. was readopted and added to the list of State Treasury companies with a strategic significance. Furthermore, restructuring and technological modernisation of the company was successfully carried out.

By 2000, the company's turnover had trebled and the number of employees increased from 1,250 to around 1,600. Between 1998 and 1999 alone, productivity rose by more than 20 per cent. On 22 December 1999, PWPW S.A. was awarded the Quality System Certificate ISO 9001. On 19 December 2002, it joined the ranks of companies awarded the Quality Management System Certificate attesting to compliance with PN-EN ISO 9001 (2001) and the Environmental Management System Certificate according to PN-EN ISO 14001 (1998). In 2003, PWPW S.A. appeared on the White List of reliable companies. The White List is a prestigious assemblage of companies noted for high ethical standards in business.

As a result of cooperation with Austria Card-Plastikkarten und Ausweissysteme in 1999, two joint-stock companies emerged: Elkart, providing plastic card personalisation services for customers of PKO BP, PKO S.A., Bank Handlowy, Bank Śląski and PWPW-IT Technologies (August 2001); and PWPW-IT Technologies, responsible for electronic use.

Furthermore, the company is currently gearing up for euro banknote production.

What is your advice for a foreign firm entering your country's market? What should managers especially care about and, what is more, be aware of?

- Polish people are not very mobile: it is difficult to persuade someone to uproot and move somewhere else.
- All terms of negotiations are to be confirmed in writing; there are no 'gentlemen's agreements'.
- There is a lot of bureaucracy for those conducting a business.
- We prefer a tough management style and clear rules.
- We love foreigners to speak Polish (at least a few words).
- We have learned a very special kind of creativity from our historical experience; we do not always follow formal rules to achieve goals.
- We love business cards, titles (Mr, director, doctor).
- 'Ladies first'– we respect women, give them flowers, kiss their hands, but not in business situations!

PRODUCTS AND SERVICES

PWPW S.A. is one of the most modern companies of its kind in the world, employing a wide range of printing methods, from offset, cryptographic, intaglio and rotogravure to electronic (digital) technology.

High-tech, its printing house, a graphic ink production unit, a design and analysis studio and a chemical and paper laboratory make PWPW S.A. self-sufficient.

Basic products of PWPW S.A. are:

– Polish banknotes;
– excise tax bands for distilled spirits packaging, tobacco and wine products;
– transport documents used to register vehicles (vehicle certificates and registration certificates);
– licences, permits, extracts and haulage certificates;
– visas and invitations;
– postage treasury stamps; and
– cheques, shares, coupons and foreign banknotes.

Given the rapid development of digital reproduction and printing techniques, the level of security required is constantly rising. PWPW S.A. products are protected by a variety of safeguards which are continuously upgraded. The quality of security is world-class standard. The company provides security on three levels:

1. Paper security – specific chemical paper substitute which allows paper to be unambiguously identified and makes printing and written text impossible to remove. It also includes the use of multicoloured ink, watermarks, chemical securities, guilloche background and security fibres.
2. Print security – gravure, micro-prints, guilloche, recto and verso prints, rosettes, angle effects in rotogravure prints, termochronic and luminescent inks visible in UV light or at a certain temperature.
3. Optical security – the best-quality holograms, coded images, diffractive transparent foils.

PWPW S.A. also provides modern IT security techniques. Users transmitting information often note a need for better protection. Furthermore, customers' expectations in terms of electronic data security are at least as high as for conventional documents. Customers demand confidence, credibility, undeniability and integrity. It often happens that parties involved in electronic transactions do not know one other and, when using electronic documents, cannot be sure that the contracting party is not an impersonator. This is where a third reliable party enters. The Polish Centre for Electronic Certification, 'Sigillum', was founded by PWPW S.A. as just such a reliable party, issuing certificates guaranteeing a link between signature and the right person.

The mission of PWPW S.A. is to 'maintain a position of leadership in the production of good products designed for the security of the state and its citisens'. In line with that mission, the company's management stresses the importance of human capital and proper recruitment processes to ensure competent personnel with a business attitude who make the company's brand on the market a driving force.

The main tasks in terms of HRM are incorporating HRM systems and tools, maintaining HRM cohesion, improving managers' competences at the PWPW S.A. Managers' Academy, permanent development of qualifications through participation in internal and external training, developing a system of pay based on job appraisal and evaluation, and constructive cooperation with professional organisations.

The company prides itself on many prestigious HRM titles and awards: first prize in the Employer/Organiser of Safe Work contest (7 November 2001), distinction in the Training Development category of the 2001 Training Manager contest and twice awarded the Emblem of Human Capital Investor (in 2001 and 2002).

What would you say one ought not to do? What are the 'don'ts' in your country?

- Be careful with humour, especially in a business context.
- We are sensitive about religion and politics; it is better to avoid these topics.

THE '5S' PROGRAMME

Briefly, the '5S' programme is about housekeeping and thrift management. The method is one of the most important elements of good management with regard to activities relating to work improvement, proper quality of products and work safety.

The name '5S' comes from the first letters of the Japanese words for factors creating a productive workplace: *seri* (selection), *seiton* (orderliness), *seiso* (cleanliness), *seicetsu* (neatness) and *shitsuke* (self-discipline). Despite its Japanese origin, the method can also be successfully applied in other cultures. A concept of the programme and methodological study shows that it can be adjusted to the organisation structure.

Selection: getting rid of unnecessary things in the workplace

Clutter and disorder in a factory or office need to be distinguished in terms of what is necessary and what is not. Certainly, this is not an easy process and its difficulty is due to a conviction that items might be useful in the future. Things identified as necessary need to be sorted for use and application. Unnecessary things should be sorted for storage, because it might turn out that parts of them are sellable or reproducible. The last stage is grouping things for convenience. Where this is done, a workplace becomes pleasant and functional. It needs to be remembered, though, that everything in a factory, as well as in an office, needs to be sorted.

Orderliness: collecting things in the right order

Orderliness means defining where and how all objects that are needed in the unit (tools, means of transport, materials, resources, semi-finished articles, etc.) are sorted. Everything should be placed within reach and in a visible and accessible place. Thus an object is reachable, which increases work efficiency. It helps to provide line markings on the floor, like visibly separate roads, for pedestrians or storage areas. Properly ordered objects should be sorted along straight lines – horizontal and vertical.

Cleanliness: cleaning the workplace

Cleanliness aims at removing dust and dirt from all the nooks and crannies in a company to prevent breakdowns and improve work safety. In other words, it involves thorough cleaning, dusting, tidying, renovating, painting and ordering of the workplace and its surroundings. That is not all, however, because a single cleaning operation is not enough to keep a workplace dirt-free. Regularly repeated, these activities enable abnormal signals, such as oil leaks or burnt-out electric installations to be immediately perceived.

Systematisation: maintaining order in the workplace

Although the first three 'Ss' are placed at the beginning of the programme, the next two – systematisation and self-discipline – must be observed at all times to guarantee the success of the method. This next stage describes conditions needed to enable order and tidiness to be permanently maintained. The key lies in creating a method of autocontrol and specifying how to recognise irregularity. At this stage, plans and graphics showing order in the area are created – these are elements of 'visible management'. Maintaining order is not only the task of cleaning staff; it is a result of conscious, long-term attention by all personnel.

Self-discipline: discipline at work

Discipline is widely understood: it means observing company rules, internal regulations and unwritten standards of conduct and keeping job requirements high. At the same time, every disciplined person is an example to others and encourages participation in the '5S' programme. Self-discipline crowns the 5Ss and should exemplify a reflex which guarantees improvement of working conditions and productivity in the company. The idea of the '5S' programme seems to be clear but application of its rules is not easy. The reason for disorder at the workplace is not slovenliness; it is due to storing things which might turn out to be necessary in the future. Keeping order in a place where many things are not needed often seems very difficult, even impossible. Implementing the '5S' programme means putting in place a series of activities driving productivity. The next anticipated stage is creating so-called 'circles of quality' to integrate employees with similar interests who can rationalise everyday work. Applying the '5S' programme brings concrete benefits, such as better customer perception of the company, interpersonal relations, pleasant and safe working conditions.

PUTTING THE '5S' PROGRAMME INTO PRACTICE

Economic transformation in Poland forced the company to compete and function according to the most modern management rules, which depend on immediate and flexible adjustment to the changes that dictate customers' requirements.

Starting from 1947, while restructuring PWPW S.A., the Executive Board sought a way of involving the largest number of employees in the process. The task of preparing staff for the '5S' programme started in 1997 with training programmes organised for all employees with external consultants and specialists. The training ended up with the founding of an initiative group which had visited the other companies (Zelmer in Rzeszów, Daewoo in Warsaw, Polmo in Lomianki) to investigate '5S' programme methods.

Commitments

On 8 May, the Executive Board secured trade union agreement for the realisation of the '5S' programme. All parties accepted all the commitments to apply the '5S' programme in cooperation with employees.

The trade unions committed to having trade union representatives participate in '5S' training. Moreover, candidates should be recruited from the ranks of the trained employees to promote the productivity programme which would be sent for specialised training. The trade union arranged as well that employees who take part in training have to be prepared to sit on department committees on productivity and that campaigns have to be run to make staff aware of the need for a productivity programme at PWPW S.A. and employees have to be informed about the benefits of the programme. Finally, developing rules for quantifying the financial impacts of the '5S' programme and negotiating those rules with the Executive Board was one of the trade unions' commitments.

The Executive Board of PWPW S.A. also entered into commitments: they agreed on financing training facilities and putting the '5S' programme into practice; on ensuring organisational assistance during the application of the productivity programme; on offering jobs to employees who would be dismissed as a result of the programme and assuring them of their financial status attained thus far; on developing – and negotiating with trade unions – rules for quantifying financial impacts; and at least on engaging with trade unions to negotiate a formula for dividing the anticipated financial impacts on the basis of one-third for employees, one-third for covering costs, one-third for the company development fund.

The '5S' programme currently covers twenty-seven units employing over 1,200 people. The '5S' programme was appointed under an agreement between the Executive Board and trade unions. The result of the agreement was training organised for all employees.

Organisation

The leading group is represented by all departments in the company and its tasks are to promote the '5S' programme, cooperate with employees participating in the '5S' programme and participate in working committees appointed to evaluate units which fulfil the tasks submitted to the programme. The programme team comprises employees with long seniority who know most of the employees and have a thorough knowledge of the company. The main tasks of this team are to maintain the '5S' programme, apply it in new departments and develop the programme in PWPW S.A. So-called '5S' leaders act as liaison officers between the programme team and personnel.

Leaders are elected by departmental staff and represent their colleagues in negotiations with supervisors and the programme team. They are also a driving force for developing proposals for the realisation of the '5S' programme.

Leaders and the manager of the '5S' programme form part of the initiative team (a representative of the programme team sometimes also takes part in the meetings). Their task is to define issues to be solved or improved by department staff in their teams. The teams do not operate on a permanent basis – appointments depend on the scale and complexity of the solutions required. The leaders coordinate the work of the teams.

Apart from implementing and maintaining the '5S' programme, the programme team works permanently on extending the method. The '5S' programme was not just an end in itself; it was mainly a means of increasing productivity and a base for all programmes geared to that goal. The aim was to avoid machine failure and manage work safety.

The first stage of incorporating the programme in the company is essential for the leading group since its main activities are to convince everyone that it is worth managing the workshop. The successful incorporation of the '5S' programme relies on 'islands' in the company created by departments which declare their participation in the programme. These islands produce results that should encourage other departments to embrace the method. They set a good example of what might be achieved with goodwill and employee involvement.

Realisation

In order to encourage other departments to adopt '5S' programme rules, the methods are advertised in the company's internal newsletter *PWPW S.A. Life*. Furthermore, the HR department offers support for solving potential personnel problems.

Certainly, incorporating the '5S' programme in not an easy issue and causes many conflicts, triggered by employee resistance to change and fear of new burdens of responsibility, and especially fear of moving to what is essentially a new way of thinking and having to accept new rules of conduct. In order to convince personnel to join the '5S' movement, leaders need to spend a great deal of time and effort convincing people. The role of leaders is to justify the legitimacy of the programme, build groups that cooperate effectively and help to fulfil all tasks. The first small but essential step to be accomplished is to stop people excluded from the programme interfering with others in meeting targets. It often happens that the biggest grumblers become leaders and coordinate the work of the whole team.

Despite the attraction of the programme (especially at the beginning of its operation) it represents a burden with a tendency to disappear. Difficulties in everyone's work often give rise to mounting discouragement and present a serious risk to the programme by threatening to stifle commitment under the volume of day-to-day duties. Keeping the '5S' programme working is thus less important than extending it to other parts of the company. Indeed, one might even venture that it is more difficult. As affirmed above, departments apply the programme in different periods of time and, while changes are being made in the units, it is necessary to stimulate employee commitment.

Basic tools for stimulating employee commitment at PWPW S.A. are as follows: (a) Ranking departments: every month, specially appointed commissions made up of four people evaluate units and departments according to how far the '5S' programme rules have been incorporated at all levels. Results are published in the company newsletter. Once a year, the top-rated department is awarded prizes by the Executive Board; (b) Conclusions drawn from the '5S' programme: the '5S' programme produces a variety of conclusions declared by employees. Everybody has the right to make a proposal on the forthcoming incorporation of the programme and its acceptance. Each time, the Executive Board rewards departments which translate conclusions into action; (c) Educational trips: each year, special educational trips are offered to the employees most involved in the realisation of the programme. They are mostly foreign trips, including study visits to similar companies.

SUMMARY

Technically, productivity is defined as a function of output and sales from an initial volume of inputs over a defined length of time. We are interested, though, in a wider dimension of productivity, one which could even be called a social dimension of productivity, since it describes a state of consciousness based on a willingness to improve the status quo and harnesses new techniques and methods to steadily improve work processes and conditions.

The '5S' programme is not only a programme which improves the work environment and involves employees in the process of change and rationalisation; above all, it is an incredibly effective motivational and visualisation tool for participating employees.

Despite many obstacles during the realisation of the '5S' programme, PWPW S.A. management achieved rational benefits, as listed below:

- unaided and completely professional self-management of employees' past;
- unquestionable increase in employee involvement in fulfilling tasks and stronger identification with the mission of the company;
- increase in self-assessment level due to activities connected with self-improvement;
- increase in employee creativity; and
- safe and pleasant workplace, well-being of employees and outside customers.

The statement that productivity is a permanent development of positive features of every employed person in PWPW S.A. has changed the mentality and perceptions of employees: they currently want and are consciously able to improve the quality of their work and bring more added value to products and services.

Which people play key roles in your country? Which names should one know?

- Pope Jan Pawel II (died in 2005);
- politicians: President Lech Kaczyński, Lech Walesa, 'Solidarity';
- Nobel prize-winners: Maria Sklodowska-Curie, Wislawa Szymborska, Lech Walesa, Czeslaw Milosz;
- economists: Leszek Balcerowicz, Hanna Gronkiewicz-Waltz;
- sports champions: Adam Malysz, Robert Korzeniowski, Otylia Jedrzejczak, Zbigniew Boniek;
- astronomer: Nicholas Copernicus; and
- composer: Frederick Chopin.

References

Bednarski, Marek/Machol-Zajda, Lucyna (2003): Telepraca, in: Elżbieta Kryńska (ed.): Elastyczne formy zatrudnienia i organizacji pracy a popyt na pracę w Polsce, Warsaw.

Borkowska, Stanisława (1998): Główne wyzwania wobec problemów pracy na przełomie wieków, in: Praca i polityka społeczna w perspektywie XXI wieku, Warsaw.

—— (2001): Projektowanie strategii wynagrodzeń w przedsiębiorstwie, in: Antoni Ludwiczyński/Katarzyna Stobińska (eds): Zarządzanie strategiczne kapitałem ludzkim, Warsaw.

Bukowitz, Wendi R./Williams, Ruth L. (1999): The Knowledge Management Fieldbook, London.

Dąbrowski, Jan/Kołodkiewicz, Izabela (2003): Zarządzanie wiedzą w przedsiębiorstwach działających w Polsce – wyniki badań, in: Bogdan Wawrzyniak (ed.): Zarządzanie wiedzą w przedsiębiorstwie, Warsaw.

Drucker, Peter F. (2002): They're not employees, they're people, in: Harvard Business Review, 80(2): 70–7.

Fazlagic, Amir (2004): Poznan School of Economics, presentation during the First International HR Congress in Poland.

Herman, T./Motyl, P. (2003): Critical Success Factors in Managerial Roles in Poland.

Juchnowicz, Marta (2004): Human Capital and Developing Enterpreneurship, Warsaw.

Juchnowicz, Marta/Rostkowski, Tomasz (2003): Zastosowanie macierzy kompetencji w praktyce, in: Dorota Dobija, (ed.): Pomiar i rozwój kapitału ludzkiego przedsiębiorstwa, Warsaw.

Konecki, Krzysztof (2003): Wpływ polityki personalnej na stosowanie elastycznych form zatrudnienia i organizacji pracy, in: Elżbieta Kryńska (ed.): Elastyczne formy zatrudnienia i organizacji pracy a popyt na pracę w Polsce, Warsaw.

Kryńska, Elżbieta (2003): Elastyczność popytu na pracę w Polsce – synteza, diagnozy i wnioski, in: Elżbieta Kryńska (ed.): Elastyczne formy zatrudnienia i organizacji pracy a popyt na pracę w Polsce, Warsaw.

Listwan, Tadeusz (2002): Przedmiot, ewolucja i znaczenie zarządzania kadrami, in: Tadeusz Listwan (ed.): Zarządzanie kadrami, Warsaw.

Ludwiczyński, Antoni (2001): Metody strategicznego zarządzania zasobami ludzkimi, in: Antoni Ludwiczyński/Katarzyna Stobińska (eds): Zarządzanie strategiczne kapitałem ludzkim, Warsaw.

Official Journal of 2003, Act on Hiring Temporary Employees of 9 July (item 1608).

Oleksyn, Tadeusz (1999): Zarządzanie kompetencjami w organizacji, in: Antoni Ludwiczyński (ed.): Szkolenie i rozwój pracowników a sukces firmy, Warsaw.

Pocztowski, Aleksy (2003a): Zarządzanie zasobami ludzkimi, Warsaw.

—— (2003b): Zarządzanie zasobami ludzkimi w nowej gospodarce, in: Zarządzanie Zasobami Ludzkimi, 1.

Pocztowski, Aleksy *et al.* (2001): Praktyka zarządzania zasobami ludzkimi i jej wpływ na rynek pracy, Warsaw.

Rybak, Mirosława (2003): Zarządzanie kapitałem ludzkim a kluczowe kompetencje, in: Mirosława Rybak (ed.): Kapitał ludzki a konkurencyjność przedsiębiorstw, Warsaw.

Ulrich, David O. (2001): Human Resource Champions, Warsaw.

.pl

The authors

Tina Sobocińska (tina.sobocinska@wp.pl), Sanofi Aventis Poland, HR Manager. Former Board member of the PHRMA.

Antoni Ludwiczyński (aludwi@wspiz.edu.pl), Associate Professor at the Leon Koźmiński Academy of Entrepreneurship and Management (LKAEM), Deputy Dean of the Faculty of Management and Administration at the LKAEM. Main areas of research: HRM, organisation management. Main publications: *Strategic Human Capital Management* (2001, chief editor and co-author); *The Best-Practices in Managing People in Small and Medium Sized Enterprises* (2004, chief editor and co-author); *The HRM Architecture in Companies Awarded the Title of the HRM Leader* (2005, chief editor and co-author).

Ryszard Michalczyk (emr.consult@acn.waw.pl), Signal-Iduna Poland (insurance company), HR Director. Former President of the PHRMA.

Renata Trochimiuk (rtroch@wspiz.edu.pl), Ph.D. candidate and teaching assistant since 1999 at the Department of Human Resources Management at the Leon Koźmiński Academy of Entrepreneurship and Management (LKAEM). Main areas of research: human capital management and the competitiveness of small and medium-sized enterprises, knowledge management. Main publications: *Human Resources Management* (2004, with Justyna Sztukowska); *The Role of HR Department in Knowledge Management in Selected Companies* (2005, with Justyna Sztukowska); *HRM Strategies and Methods: ComputerLand S.A.* (2004).

Joanna Górska (j.gorska@pwpw.pl), Polish Security Printing Works, HR Manager (development and social affairs). Member of the PHRMA.

12 HRM in Spain: reinventing the function

Joaquín Casals Jiménez/Monica Lorenzo Vázquez/Montserrat Luque Pinilla/
Tomás Pereda Riaza/Eva Triviño Acuña

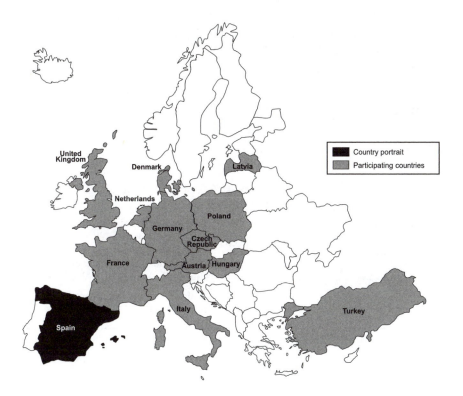

Spain: in a nutshell

In this chapter you will learn:

- that HRM in Spain has changed its role in order to add value to companies by improving its services, strengthening its effectiveness as a business partner and producing quantifiable results;

- that HR academia in Spain can only be understood by looking at its cultural framework; and

- that Banco Sabadell Atlántico accomplished a change project to foster professionals who enhance the company's strategy and defined values.

Capital:	Madrid
Area (sq km):	504,782 (land 499,542; water 5,240)
EU membership:	since 1986
Population:	40,397,842
Languages:	Castilian Spanish (Castellano – official), Catalan, Galician, Basque
Ethnic groups:	Composite of Mediterranean and Nordic types
Gross domestic product:	1.07 trillion USD (2006)
Workforce (in percentages):	21.77 million (2006): agriculture 5.3; manufacturing, mining, and construction 30.1; services 64.6 (2004)
Export commodities:	machinery, motor vehicles, foodstuffs, pharmaceuticals, medicines, other consumer goods

344

BACKGROUND: THE GROWING IMPORTANCE OF PEOPLE

Although the human factor has always been important, it has gained specific weight compared to soil, raw materials, capital, even technology. In this new concept of a global world, human contribution, from top management positions to the lowest job, plays a key role, and is the real protagonist of business projects. The key to managing success lies in the hands of the people who have achieved success by their ideas or performance. HRM can be described as a strategic element of the first order. A company can use the same machinery, the same production systems, the same materials; but the people it employs are not the same, and neither is their contribution. So having a team capable of making a better contribution than the competition makes the difference between success and failure of a company. The problem is that such contributions originate in the employee and are hard to obtain and control. It is thus necessary to create the right environment so that these contributions flow voluntarily.

In Spain, HRM has followed the development of different labour conditions: in the first factories, foremen were the personnel managers but in a totally restrictive sense; they were almost invariably limitative. The creation of personnel departments in the new climate created by stricter labour legislation marked a first step forward, although elements of control and discipline continued to be paramount. The definition and application of motivation, selection and training policies made personnel management more scientific.

In the past few years, HR professionals have been right at the centre of management, becoming a protagonist beyond the traditional scope of their role, clearly linked to the strategic concept of the company. There are four clear stages in the development of the personnel function in Spain (CEDE 2000):

1. Clerk (1950–9)/autarchy: the focus was on bureaucracy, i.e. the day-to-day management of past data, pre-established regulations and instructions. The purpose of the personnel role was exclusively to make workers comply with rules in place.
2. Human relations (1960–76)/development planning: the gearing here was towards technocracy, i.e. an attempt to reach a compromise among contrasting interests through adequate selection and training processes, incentives, correct salary scales and classification according to service. The purpose of the personnel role was to ensure that employees adapted to the technical needs of the organisation.
3. Labour relations (1977–85)/conflicts and agreements: the focus here was social and legal, characterised by the predominance of the collective focus on

the individual. Negotiators and labour lawyers substituted selection personnel and incentive experts. The purpose of the role of personnel was to solve conflicts by negotiating labour conditions.

4. Human resource (1986–present)/merging into the European environment: the orientation here is managerial in character. Efforts are geared to seeking equitable labour relations with the flexibility and integration needed to increase productivity, improve efficiency, create company knowledge and assure total commitment to compliance with the corporate and business objectives within a shifting labour world. The purpose of the personnel function is to integrate the employee into the organisation.

The role of the HR professional or personnel management, as this function has lately been called, is becoming a protagonist in the processes of change, which are becoming a constant feature of present-day economic and business life due to the necessary adaptation to environmental conditions. The HR function is well positioned to become the main facilitator of the competitiveness and added value provided for the organisation by its human capital. Thus the principal task of management is to create a system of human capital to dynamise and maximise such assets.

This challenge is becoming a reality in the Spanish market, where an increasing number of companies are considering action in this field. Nevertheless, because of the apparent intangibility of personnel management systems and the investment effort needed to obtain validated knowledge and experience, as well as the internal effort a company needs to make to change its customary management practices, some organisations take a conservative line when redefining their HR function.

Several studies carried out in Spain (MERCER 2004) reveal that HR leaders are prepared to face the challenge of shaping a new era of excellence in the HR function, establishing increasingly direct links between performance and the profit and loss account, so the HR function is progressing from its present operational role to play the part of a strategic partner in the organisation and bring added value during the transformation process. The transformation process is defined as the refounding or development of the HR function, and includes the following developments:

- establishment of the present model for providing HR services more efficiently in administrative services to employees and executives; and
- development of the person's capacity and measurement of results so as to design and provide human capital systems with a clear impact on business results.

Although the focus is different in each organisation and adapted to local and individual needs, there are common denominators in the different transformation processes (e.g. knowledge and innovation) which are simultaneously regarded as key to the sustainability of competition.

346

The present economic situation has created a need for reorganisation in many companies and the traditional HR department is not considered a strategic partner when managing internal change. Only by changing its role can it add value by improving the services it provides, strengthening its effectiveness as a business partner and producing quantifiable results.

💡.es

What is typical for your country in relation to the country itself (its culture, people, etc.) and its economy?

- sustainable economic growth;
- the transformation from an economy based on the secondary sector to an economy based on the service sector;
- demographic change: declining birth rates, ageing population and growth of immigrant population;
- a high level of unemployment;
- globalisation and displacement of production; and
- diversity.

TRANSFORMATION STATUS OF HR

What are the forces for change? How is the function changing? How will its effectiveness be measured? What stage of the change process have organisations reached? What specific tools are used or are going to be used to assure success?

Studies in Spain show that most organisations are developing or are about to develop HR transformation processes, while a minority say they have no plans for transformation and another minority say they have already completed HR transformation. Among the most frequently cited reasons for developing transformation plans are a desire to change HR into a strategic function and consolidate it as a principal driver for change. Another reason driving HR transformation – a reason advanced by a significant number of companies and organisations – is the wish to line up HR with business targets or respond to business changes within the organisation.

⊞.es

Regarding the yardsticks used to establish the degree of success of the transformation process, the one most frequently used is internal customer satisfaction and, to a lesser degree, direct impact on business results, although a minority of companies are still not sure how this is measured. What all this seems to indicate is that the need to register a positive impact on business performance is acknowledged but the mechanisms needed to measure that impact can still be improved.

CHANGE IN THE HR FUNCTION

Which roles are critical and how much success is the present HR function having? What abilities and qualifications are important for HR personnel and how will such abilities be acquired? What obstacles can prevent the success of these roles and what are the opportunities?

According to Ulrich/Losey/Lake (1998), HR is expected to play four different roles, which are set well apart to promote success through support for business strategy: (a) strategic partner; (b) agent of change; (c) employee champion; and (d) administrative expert.

Data in Spain prompt the following conclusions:

- Mentioned as the most successful roles are those of administrative expert and HR adviser.
- Most HR professionals wish to reduce the time spent working as an administrative expert, because this is the role today that takes up the most time.
- Even where strategic partnership is attained – one of the first objectives of the transformation of the HR function – the vast majority of HR professionals believe they spend little time dedicated to strategic activities and have scant success in these roles.
- The majority of HR directors in Spanish organisations say that they are successful as HR advisers.

Regarding the evaluation of critical abilities and qualifications, studies show that the main strong points of HR personnel in Spain are: expert knowledge in HR issues, interpersonal capacity and teamwork, HR management, HR data filing and company knowledge. However, HR abilities and qualifications are rarely mentioned in relation to success as a strategic partner or agent of change.

.es

Regarding opportunities for improvement and barriers to success, HR leaders identify as the most significant opportunities to improve the role of HR systems: ability of HR personnel, support of top management and technology.

The activities developed by Spanish companies in this sense are investment in developing personnel abilities and development of a staff/personnel strategy within the HR area. Nevertheless, the most urgent matter for HRM is not so much the mechanism for developing qualifications but the task of determining which qualifications need to be developed to achieve success on the HR front by taking on new roles. On the other hand, HR professionals sometimes encounter difficulties in obtaining management support if they try to adopt new roles before showing that they have the capacity to do so. At the same time, it is difficult for HR to adopt new roles without the support of the management. As to barriers that make the transformation process difficult, most professionals mention legal limitations and labour union relations.

STRUCTURE AND TECHNOLOGY

How is the HR function organised and how are the human resources used? What is the contribution expected from technology? What outsourced resources have been organised or planned?

348

Regarding the first question, Spanish HR professionals point to a central administration, HR teams specialised in solving key HR questions, and centralised technical internal consulting abilities as common structural character-istics. Most organisations have HR department representatives in business units, as well as an HR leadership team to develop HR strategy and integrate the work of both specialists and generalists. In most organisations where HR contributes to business strategy and achieves quantifiable results, an HR executive will be involved in the business planning and decision-making process. Studies also show that directors include an HR controller in their HR structure. HR controller implies responsibility for applying business principles and cost management principles to HR operations as well as to HR programmes. Some activities in which the HR controller participates include budget management and staff planning, business decision analysis, supervision of supplier contracts and evaluation of HR practice in the company. To manage efficiently HR expenses, directors need to identify an adequate group of professionals. In studies made, it is evident that the average number of employees for each member of the HR team is 100.

Regarding use of technology and degree of satisfaction, HR professionals and directors evaluate the use of technology as a critical factor for success, and in fact the majority believes that improvements in this area are an opportunity to increase the efficiency of the HR organisation. The great majority of Spanish organisations say they use some form of intranet, and a high percentage also use the internet to provide HR services. Use of more sophisticated technological applications, such as employee self-service, is not as common but is still above the European average, which indicates that there is a great predisposition in Spain to use new technology. Many organisations have invested in sophisticated HR information systems but they have encountered difficulties in achieving the savings promised by such investment. This is due, among other things, to excessive personalisation of applications or to the existence of previous analyses for such investments based on not very practical business suppositions or returns on investment, which include reducing personnel.

Regarding outsourcing, it may be said that although a great number of organi-sations currently outsource some of their functions, such as training, selection or payrolls, there is not a strong tendency in Spain to increase outsourcing. However, some activities may be outsourced in the future, such as relocations and expatriation services, recruiting and selection, and benefits administration.

It is possible that the studies referred to above do not present a full picture of the HR function in Spain because they do not include data from the country's large sector of small and medium-sized companies. But it is a fact, in any case, that the HR or personnel management function is not universal. The processes applied to a company with its own business logic and knowledge, operating in a specific market context, cannot be applied to another with a different logic operating in a different market environment.

.es

Personnel management has to be designed and defined in line with business strategy, clearly crafted for a specific business culture and the circumstances of the labour market at the time.

What are you and other Spanish people extraordinarily proud of with respect to HRM?

The enthusiasm, hard work and passion of professionals for the HR function have won it a strong position on boards of directors. Another very remarkable change is the function's switch from an administrative role (personnel administration, labour relations) to a strategic player with a special focus on organisational change and development.

EAPM AFFILIATE: ASOCIACIÓN ESPAÑOLA DE DIRECCIÓN Y DESARROLLO DE PERSONAS

THE EARLY DAYS (1965–75)

The Asociación Española de Dirección y Desarrollo de Personas (AEDIPE) is the Spanish association for people management and development. Going back to the origins of AEDIPE, we find that its history started in 1965 with a meeting of social secretaries organised by Grupo Acción Social (social action group) in Madrid, from which several work groups on social and labour relations emerged. At the same time, at the Superior School of Business Administration (Escuela Superior de Administración de Empresas (EADA)) in Barcelona, a group was formed out of concern over personnel problems. Later on, these two groups were joined by a third group from Vizcaya, the Asociación Española de Directores y Jefes de Personal (Spanish association of directors and heads of personnel), which helped to make AEDIPE what it is today.

In line with the Spanish system at the time, with its strong element of state control, the principal task of a head of personnel in the 1960s was to develop and apply established regulations within the company. So the function mainly consisted of tasks traditionally described as 'administrative', including wages and salaries, staff selection and disciplinary regulations. In an effort to adapt to economic and social change and in line with the evolution of companies, where personnel management was becoming increasingly important and where the cultural knowledge of incoming professionals was increasing, AEDIPE helped to enhance the knowledge of such professionals and expand their field of action by organising seminars promoting exchange of experiences and knowledge, by producing the first trade publications and publishing what were known at the time as 'personnel notebooks' – the seed that became today's 'leading people' magazine. It also took a clearly international line from the start, which gave it a leading position during the transition years and first-hand knowledge of international experiences at both European and US levels.

In the 1980s, in line with the political changes of the time, the labour situation in Spain underwent a process of profound transformation with regard to the working and labour union environment. Driven by the demands of increased business competition and recent membership in the EEC, greater importance was conceded to the personnel department in companies. Its role expanded, increasing its scope of action in areas such as organisation, performance, qualifications, training, labour relations, salary and wages, and selection. It was also given a specific brief and did not report to any other department in the company. The term 'personnel management' came into being. This is when one of the name changes of the association took place. Adapting to the trends of the time, AEDIPE changed its name to Asociación Española de Dirección de Personal (Spanish association of personnel management).

351

The role of the association developed at two different levels, local/regional and national, through the territorial groups, which, being close to the members, knew the business and social problems of their environment. The association was in charge of organising seminars, exchange meetings (normally practical in character), and, at national level, the annual meetings which became known as *congresos nacionales* (national conventions) from 1972 onwards in Barcelona. These were staged on a rotating basis by the eight different territorial groups that existed in the association at the time, and were soon to become a reference meeting point for experts and professionals in the field, who attended for the purpose of gaining practical knowledge from the experience of their counterparts in other parts of Spain.

The magazine also experienced improvements over time; moving from a work document format it became a quarterly publication, containing research articles, interviews with important persons and practical case studies. This is when the book review section was added, which still exists and helps push forward the traditional frontiers of knowledge. Trade publishing continued to be used as a reference for the association, which published around three or four books a year.

What would you like to teach foreign HR managers? What is important for them to know in your opinion?

- A knowledge of Spanish is a must. Spanish people like to talk, they spend a lot of time in conversation.
- They also spend long hours in the office.
- Lunch is important and you can easily spend two hours having lunch. Dinner tends to be very late and people also leave the office very late (not before 7 p.m.).
- Spanish people do not understand ambiguity; things are white or black.
- Legal aspects are important and complicated.
- Unions have an important social and political role.

GOING INTERNATIONAL (1976–2000)

In 1976, Grupo Eurolatino was created to exchange personnel management knowledge between different cultures. AEDIPE participated actively in Grupo Eurolatino from the outset. Aside from the Spanish association, this is composed of the associations in Italy (Associazione Italiana per la Direzione del Personale (AIDP)), France (Association Nationale des Directeurs et Cadres de la Fonction Personnel (ANDCP)) and Portugal (Associaçào Portuguesa dos Gestores e Técnicos dos Recursos Humanos (APG)). As a consequence of the growing importance of the European Community and the imminent adoption of the 1989 Single European Act, Grupo Eurolatino started to hold bilateral meetings with the UK and with the IPD (Institute for Personnel and Development). The objective: to present a broad view of the developments and trends in the economic, political and social landscape of the two countries, to facilitate an exchange of information and experiences on matters of common interest and to establish links between professionals in both countries.

In the 1990s, new challenges and demands arose for personnel management in Spain: entry into the Single European Market with the consequent mobility of labour, demographic shifts towards an ageing, less active population and greater demands for professional qualifications.

The role of AEDIPE has been to try to present a strategic point of view of the HR manager and to bring professionals into line with the strategic plan of the company, thus making their task more diversified. This led to the establishment of the Foundation for the Development of the Human Resource Function (Fundación para el Desarollo de la Función de Recursos Humanos (FUNDIPE)), an institution focused on the scientific scope of the function and dedicated to empirical studies and research. Since 1989, the European Commission has organised an annual conference for HR directors of major European companies and their business organisations at national or European level. Each conference concentrates on an important subject for businessmen, directors and politicians, and its purpose is to promote good practice.

CHANGES IN HRM (2000 UP UNTIL TODAY)

The role of HRM in the twenty-first century will be to secure the creative and innovative personnel needed to ensure the long-term efficiency of the organisation, to create an HR section which anticipates, organises and looks beyond traditional personnel planning and the outsourcing of activities. How could personnel directors of forty years ago think of this! The profile of an HR director is that of a young professional, in most cases male (although recent years have presented clear evidence of vigorous integration of women in this field) with a university degree and normally a complementary training background.

In AEDIPE, there have also been changes in response to the demands of the new professionals. One of the most important is the association magazine *Dirigir Personas*. Its first issue, in 2003, marked the culmination of a process of change that had commenced several months before. AEDIPE thus took another step towards imbuing the publication with an explicit purpose: to become a key reference in the field of management and development of HR in organisations. The improvements relate to the contents as well as the 'container', and also to the way in which the information is presented. Changes include the name: *Dirigir Personas* ('Managing people'). In the past, the magazine had not had a name of its own; it used the name of the association. The new name seeks to reflect the new trends in the HR function. We are talking about people! It also seeks to sharpen the magazine's profile. A new cover design, changes in the publishing formula, layout of credits and summary. Consideration has also been given to the idea of including at least one article describing a real experience. The idea is to

353

turn the magazine as far as possible into a quality publication: innovative, sleek, attractive as its image, and easy to read – reporting and promoting research on people management and development in organisations.

Another knowledge instrument that the association made available to members – the library – has undergone major change. During the past decade, most of the books published have been translations of foreign authors, normally internationally renowned 'gurus' responsible for most of the known HR theories of recent years – some of them very difficult to apply to Spanish business, which represents 80 per cent of the database of AEDIPE membership. Faced with this situation, AEDIPE considered the possibility of a new editorial project aiming to publish four books a year by Spanish or foreign authors working in companies located in Spain, with eminently practical subjects and with the purpose of driving and encouraging all members to write about their own experiences and thoughts on their profession so as to promote and make known the values contributed by the function and management of the human resource and the creation of our own library.

To acknowledge and stimulate research work in the HR field in Spain, the annual Premio Jóvenes Talentos ('young talent award') has been awarded since 2002 to outstanding young high-flying executives under 35 years of age or at least young professionals with high potential. This initiative is a duplicate of the European 'young talents' project developed by the EAPM in its member countries. The object of the exercise: analysis and comparative study of the HR function at European level. AEDIPE decided to carry out this exercise, limiting subjects to the following areas:

- immigration and demography;
- gender;
- work modes;
- global versus local;
- public versus private; and
- big companies versus small and medium-sized companies.

In 2000, to mark its thirty-fifth anniversary, to stimulate and acknowledge research work in the HR field and promote interest in the association's magazine, AEDIPE got together with HR systems to launch the annual AEDIPE Award for the article on the subject that best meets the criteria of academic excellence, professional interest, clarity, originality and topicality.

New technologies undoubtedly deliver one of the best communication tools the association uses. Its website (www.aedipe.es), in operation since 1997, has also undergone many changes since it started, evolving from a simple information page with data on the institution to a reference portal for HR professionals, offering information about the various facets of the HR function, members, documents, experiences, etc. Aside from that, it has also facilitated the expansion of the association's traditional services, permitting the provision of online services that would otherwise not be possible, for example, an employment bureau and outplacement service. New technologies have also permitted fluid and faster communications, bringing members closer together. In October 2003, to expand the services offered, the association launched the electronic monthly bulletin *Newsletter*, containing general information on HR issues, interviews, surveys, editorials and articles in original versions, as well as information on AEDIPE activities (conventions, awards, agreements). This service to our membership would not have been possible with the traditional costs of a magazine, since it is currently sent out to over 4,300 persons. To facilitate internal communication between members, we publish a regularly updated directory of associations.

For the past few years, we have been working on specialising the services of the association in several areas of this function. This is carried out through work teams, such as the training commission and labour relations commission. This commission focuses on the unequal distribution of positions in Spain, its characteristics and principal obstacles: the problems relating to mediation management in the labour market, the consequences of the lack of adequate qualifications to meet the needs of the labour market, as well as socio-cultural and economic problems. FUNDIPE and AEDIPE, which both support this commission at an international level, promote the purpose and content of the global compact, especially regarding the principles relating to human and labour rights.

Internally, and because of amendments to the Act Regulating Associations in Spain and the consequent adjustments that needed to be made by AEDIPE, a thorough review of the association was carried out in 2004 to check both its legal position and the scope for adapting to new technologies and the requirements of professionals. It changed its name to Asociación Española de Dirección y Desarrollo de Personas, a name that covers not only the management aspects but also the training and development of the function and swaps the anachronistic term 'personnel' – a synonym for 'administrative function' in bygone days – for the term 'people', rather than 'human resources' as they have been called for the past decade. It also underwent an operational transformation, trying to provide more democracy for its internal operations, making more people eligible for membership of the association, which was previously restricted to individuals occupying a management position and thus excluded several groups which are now part of the HR scenario.

 .es

What is your advice for a foreign firm entering your country's market? What should managers especially care about and, what is more, be aware of?

- Spain is a very diverse country. Culture, values and customs differ widely from north to south and east to west. What is more, the high degree of autonomy enjoyed by the country's regions is impacting on legislation.
- Spain is a country with a high level of bureaucracy.
- The labour market is very unstable and the level of unemployment differs widely from one region to another. Spanish people are not very mobile geographically.

HR ACADEMIA: PANORAMA OF SPANISH HRM

CULTURAL FRAMEWORK OF THE HR FUNCTION IN SPANISH COMPANIES

Aware that generalisations ignore very honourable exceptions, HR education in Spain has been partly designed and traditionally influenced by two cultural factors and one event relating to the economic, technological and social environment:

- The European industrial relations model is particularly important because it considers employees as a group (with aims opposed to those of the business-man) arising from trade union models that question the economic and social model, as opposed to the human relations approach predominantly adopted in the USA, which considers the worker as an individual but with aims potentially aligned with those of the business person.
- A certain cultural scepticism regarding what a suitable HR philosophy can contribute to real business as an element of management shared by all the executives in an organisation.
- An orientation of the HR function towards the interior of an organisation as inertia from the times when the outside environment evolved slowly, setting priorities more by being 'guardians of the internal order than agents of change'.

Both initial suppositions have weighed heavily on the expectations placed by Spanish companies on the HR function, placing it in the field of labour relations management and maintenance of instrumental services: selection, compensation, training, etc. This vision of a reduced HRM represents a strategic gap compared to multinational competitors and hinders its process of international expansion.

It will, at some point, be necessary to analyse the reasons for Spanish companies' difficulties in achieving international organic expansion, except by acquiring local companies. With some exceptions, the multinational Spanish managerial fabric is not in balance with its global economic position. Might scepticism regarding HRM be one of the factors making it difficult to go beyond its frontiers?

It is true that thanks to globalisation, HR management in the managerial landscape of Spain is as diverse as the wide variety of national and multinational companies that, with their own philosophies and cultures of management, enrich and stimulate progress in HR thought and practice.

The cultural assumptions of Spanish companies are still too strong to change their perception of people management and incorporate it into their business strategy beyond rhetorical statements such as 'Personnel is our most important asset' – addressed more to the gallery than to a change in its own beliefs.

.es

356

IMPACT ON HR TRAINING: A CRITICAL REVIEW

From these cultural assumptions, it is possible to understand the current situation and the challenge faced by HRM training in Spain.

Logically, a very significant number of traditional HR programmes were inspired on agendas of priorities, activities and matters drawn up by HR professionals. For years, many of the programmes specialising in management or HRM were characterised by an overdose of technical or instrumental matters (labour relations, selection, training, personnel administration, organisational systems, etc.), clearly missing matters at a more strategic level, with the exception of certain HR modules taught in the MBA programmes of prestigious business schools.

If we add to this the special popularity attained by HR training during the last decade in Spain, we find that companies in recent years have added excellent technicians in the management of HR tools, feeding a vicious circle where HR does not quite find its strategic centre of gravity.

This technical approach makes the HR function an unattractive option for MBA students, given its scant leadership, influence and involvement in strategic business management. This feeds the vicious circle even more, because not being an attractive option for top-flight students, HRM remains a second-best option.

THE WORLD CONTINUES CHANGING RAPIDLY

What nobody contests is that the world is still changing very fast, and it seems that talent has a much more relevant role in the process of wealth creation.

It is increasingly necessary to be aware of what goes on outside our companies, because the function develops on the street and not inside the office. Optimisation and efficiency strategies regarding the use of resources are vital for survival; but to be successful, it is necessary to have the qualifications needed to keep us connected with all our interest groups through highly trained and committed professionals. Though it is still necessary to manage a company well, corporate success depends on external relations. This is also true in HR.

These are times for strategists and leaders, who can interpret and turn the expectations of clients, personnel, shareholders, suppliers and the community into valuable offers for all. From the fight for technological connectivity, we have moved on to the challenge of emotional connectivity. The market prefers products and services that generate differentiating experiences, beyond quality and price. To go this extra mile, prepared and committed people are needed; that is to say, people with talent and the ability to connect.

In addition, the environment fortunately – or unfortunately – accelerates change. This is a fact. It is no longer useful to have guardians of the established order; what is needed are agents who firmly stimulate and handle changes. That is to say, people who help individuals in the organisation to develop or change positively at the same pace as the world. That is their *raison d'être*. The risk of becoming obsolete is very high and the cost for the company very dear in terms of survival.

TURNING PERSONNEL MANAGEMENT TRAINING INTO A VIRTUOUS CIRCLE

Specialised training is faced with the great challenge of responding to the expectations temporarily raised by the market: we need to bring in business managers that know how to connect personnel management with their strategy. The age of the administration of men and women has paved the way for that of the management of free individuals committed to a project and intelligent enough to put all their talent at its disposal, a challenge that is as difficult as it is exciting.

Internally and externally geared HR professionals both need qualifications different from those required in the past. They need to be capable of:

- understanding and contributing actively in drawing up and setting up business strategies, dominating financial, commercial and production indicators as well as the key environment factors;
- aligning human resource strategy to the fulfilment of business missions, values and goals;
- directing organisation philosophy and the processes of organisation and change;
- being an expert in human behaviour and organisation, acting as an internal consultant in processes of this nature;
- setting up systems and creating environments generating mutual commitment between the company and the professional, promoting maximum input of such commitment;
- connecting the mutual expectations of the company and its professionals, establishing clear and equitable rules of the game to strengthen involvement and minimise internal uncertainty;
- managing key talent in the organisation effectively, ensuring the necessary qualifications, now and in the future; and
- ensuring the efficiency and effectiveness of instrumental HR processes: labour relations, labour health, compensation and benefits, recruitment and selection, training and development, management of professional careers, etc.

The professional we describe is different from the one the Spanish universities and business schools still produce in their specialised HR programmes today. The principal focus there is on strategy without waiving technology (which may be subcontracted), giving HR professionals greater capacity for authority and influence, clearly raising the level of requirements and preparation. HR also needs to attract the best talent.

It is time for a radical review of the course content of programmes specialising in human relations. The vicious circle needs to be turned into a virtuous circle.

The necessary transformation of the HR function substantially redefines the contents of the specialisation programmes. As a consequence, the programmes should include subjects that qualify future professionals to assume their new roles, and should ensure a profound knowledge of three fundamental subjects:

1. Understanding the business: knowledge at general manager level: management finances and accounting, marketing, commercial management and sales, company strategy, production and logistics, organisation.
2. Understanding the person: human behaviour and organisation: general knowledge and management of change. Philosophy and ethics. Basic knowledge of anthropology, sociology and psychology applied to the company.
3. Understanding the process: policies, systems and HR functional processes: recruitment and selection, training, development, evaluation systems, performance management, compensation and benefits, labour relations, etc.

Aside from this, it is also important to learn the skills that will facilitate effective management: leadership skills, communications, negotiation, effect and influence, project management.

These new training specifications will necessarily require a better profile and a higher level of requirements for those enrolled in the new academic programmes, which will undoubtedly need an initial effort regarding financial investment and structuring of contents, and will sustain an initial decrease in their target public until the market acknowledges the major valuable contribution of these programmes.

Conversely, maintaining the status quo means that no early action is taken to respond to what life demands from the HR function, upholding a dangerous process which diminishes a function that is seriously threatening training activities themselves.

In a few words, what would you say is the one fundamental strategic competitive advantage your country offers compared to others?

- Spain is the natural bridge for the American market, especially the south and the centre of America.
- Spanish is the world's third language.
- Spain receives more than 60 million visitors a year. It is a country with a lot of history and a vast culture.

BEST-PRACTICE CASE: BANCO ATLÁNTICO – THE LEADERSHIP AND PEOPLE MANAGEMENT BANK

LEADERSHIP AND HRM IN A BANKING COMPANY

After a history stretching back 101 years, a company in the banking sector like the one presented in this chapter has a rich cultural background that has characterised and still continues to characterise all its components: the bank employees. Nevertheless, the environment has changed; dizziness and uncertainty mark our era while at the same time providing a background and traditions that until recently set the banking sector apart from all others.

Banco Atlántico employed 3,000 people in twenty different countries and 300 offices in Spain alone when a management change project was introduced in 1999. Because investment in management leadership qualifications was considered the key to achieving the goals change in management, Banco Atlántico implemented a programme called 'Leadership and people management' (*Liderazgo y Dirección de Personas* (LIDD)). After the merger with Banco Sabadell in 2004, LIDD is still valid as one of the key tools for the manager employees of Banco Sabadell Atlántico.

Here, we should like to look at the 2002–3 LIDD programme of Banco Atlántico (Casals Jiménez/Lorenzo Vázquez 2003). Although it is just one part of the ambitious change project launched at the end of 1999 and has to be seen in the context of that background, it provides several successful inputs that are worth noting.

The 2002–3 LIDD programme was involved in a clear effort to train office managers in a bid to promote teamwork and encourage a change project. It was conducted after the launch of a re-engineering process defining strategy, mission, vision and values, and structuring a management system for HR qualifications.

The change project commenced with a re-engineering process, seeking efficiency, quality and image. To this end, the necessary technical and organisational changes were implemented, as well as the tools and processes. Training was also harnessed as a new instrument of people management: the qualification management project.

The management of Banco Atlántico thus defined a business strategy with a triple purpose:

– to direct the organisation towards clear financial objectives;
– to determine the way to achieve such objectives; and
– to improve its operation.

In the strategic approach, two basic principles were always kept in mind: first, 'the involvement of everyone in the project. This is the only way to achieve success.'

For the strategy to be successfully established it is necessary that it be taken up by each and every member of the organisation. To this end, it is necessary to overcome natural resistance to a process of change. The bank developed an internal communications plan that intended to lessen, as far as possible, the thoughts voiced by John P. Kotter (1997): 'The negative aspect of change is inevitable.' In addition, the corporate culture – an organisation's principles, beliefs and values – has a defining impact on business results. This is why we needed to rethink the way we act, decide and feel, which affects daily life and determines whether business targets are met. This is why the values of the bank were defined, so they are coherent with the change project.

What would you say one ought not to do? What are the 'don'ts' in your country?

• Don't underestimate the opinions of the others.
• Don't be distant with the team. In other words, don't be unsociable.

MANAGEMENT THROUGH THE COMPETENCY MODEL

With this vision, the areas of effectiveness determining HRM are:

– HR profitability;
– competitiveness of the organisation;
– organisational efficiency; and
– change of cultural knowledge.

The project for management according to qualifications takes as its starting point the idea that the talent required to achieve the proposed objectives is within the professionals employed by the company. As a result, the project permits us to foster qualities in such professionals that enhance their development, in harmony with the strategy and values defined.

The advantages of working according to qualifications are:

• Valid and objective criteria exist for people management in the organisation.
• Homogeneous criteria can be applied for selection, training, professional development, promotion, performance management and wages and salaries processes. Management according to qualifications contributes to the definition and use of a common language for identifying the actions that are important to different positions and to the organisation. It also permits standardisation of measurement parameters for all processes in which a person's profile needs to be measured.
• Clarity and common expectations act as a 'guide'. It helps if both the boss and collaborators have a clear and shared vision of what is expected of them.

All of these are proven parameters and tools of key importance for people management.

361

Profiles of general qualifications which characterise successful performance in every position have been defined. The company has chosen to tend and work towards excellence, defining not only the general qualifications necessary for standard performance, but also stressing the general qualifications necessary for excellent performance, identified according to the behaviour of those who achieve success in their function. The challenge is great, but the opportunities guarantee greater success.

CORPORATE VALUES

In this context, the management of Banco Atlántico deemed it essential to be explicit about its own corporate values in the change process, as promoting such values would guarantee a clearly defined strategy.

In defining the characteristics and behaviour that need to be strengthened at the bank to achieve business targets, the management considered more than just its own analysis of the situation. It also looked at the fruits of thorough analysis by a representative selection of all the groups in the bank. On this basis, principal goals – the distance between present knowledge and required knowledge that determines which values must be kept and promoted and which ones need to be modified – were assessed.

This analysis concluded with a definition of the eight corporate values of the bank, which were transmitted to the organisation from the top bank management.

THE LEADERSHIP AND PEOPLE MANAGEMENT BANK

Later, the management committee found that the most important value in the short term – the one on which the most effort should be focused as the key to success – was personnel leadership: promoting a management style with participation to achieve highly motivated teams and persons.

This value obviously needs to be promoted in strategic groups within the organisation – those who justify a certain priority because they have a multiplying effect in the organisation and a special importance for the bank's activities: the business unit managers. Leading this change, the management defined the fundamental objectives as:

- activating powerful leadership to contribute added value to the change project of the bank;
- developing the level of general qualifications with a focus on personnel leadership;
- driving values through observable behaviour coherent with the same; and
- providing tools and developing the necessary skills.

In normal HR operations, we have basic tools for day-to-day potential diagnosis: the assessment centre and management development programmes. These are conducted annually for directors and positively rated for attainment of objectives and quantifiable results as well as for their 'prestige', and development and potential as facilities fostering personal ability and management style.

From the diagnosis carried out with these tools, forty-two office managers were elected for the first Superior Management and Leadership Course (LIDD-Bank) at the Bank. The aims of the LIDD-Bank are to develop the level of general qualifications focusing on personal leadership, to promote teamwork and train managers for leadership, supporting the vision and promoting the change project, to increase personal efficiency and productivity for bank profitability and growth for the achievement of business targets, and to provide participants with expertise and skills for optimising the application of the office management model.

INTEGRAL DEVELOPMENT OF PARTICIPANTS

As soon as a group was found to work with, and the targets to be achieved were clearly defined, the great challenge was how to consolidate the purpose and method, especially bearing in mind that while many companies see the need to have leaders in the organisation, many fail in the attempt to produce them, probably because of the leadership training methods they employ.

So the first idea was not to teach what leadership is and how it should be developed but to groom participants for leadership directly. To achieve this, it is essential:

- to strengthen the process of learning – as opposed to the simple learning of content – where knowledge is to be transmitted to others;
- to transfer knowledge and training in theoretical aspects that support the intended framework;
- to have available the experience of others;
- to practise the lessons learned on the job immediately;
- to have an expert for every participant, following his or her steps, helping him or her to correct mistakes immediately; and
- to transfer the lessons to others, persuading and convincing others (including one's own work team) to strengthen learning.

The method that was drawn up and applied has the following benefits:

- It does not show how to improve leadership but develops it. It starts off with sessions where certain knowledge is transmitted, so as to practise immediately that learned on the job. In one year (the estimated length of the programme), it is taught, developed and implemented.
- Several learning channels are combined: meetings, e-learning, personnel coaching. The slogan: we work individually and in groups, and teach collaborators and auxiliaries.
- All the activities carried out in the year apply and develop leadership. Attendees transmit what they learn to their work teams, get daily practice, work in teams with other participants and hold open workshops. In short, they become facilitators/trainers of others in the organisation and thus 'agents of change'. Where knowledge needs to be transmitted to others, the learning process is more efficient than where just content is learned. This implies taking it in, living it and being convinced of it, since later they have to 'sell'

it to others. One of the objectives of the LIDD-Bank is to promote teamwork and train managers for leadership, supporting the vision and promoting the change project.

- It is a 'custom-made' programme. The contents of the programme are essentially geared to the targets to be achieved, the groups to be developed and the methods to be used. The contents are lined up with global business targets. The programme directly affects the participants and the work teams. It also affects a large number of people in the organisation through the workshops.
- Participants complying with the quality requirements of the programme receive a diploma issued by an acknowledged institution: Superior Course in Management and Leadership from CEU San Pablo.
- Every attendee has a personal coach who, as well as conducting regular coaching sessions throughout the programme, acts as a tutor, correcting and providing feedback on the tasks performed.

The effort and dedication of attendees is easy to assess: a great amount of time is required as well as a high degree of involvement. All this is in addition to a normal work schedule. When the programme was presented, prospective participants were informed that an extraordinary amount of effort and dedication would be required, so they should think carefully before signing up for the programme. During the first six months of the project, it became clear that those who decided to participate were putting in a great deal of both.

The programme is designed to last one year, occupying an estimated 300 hours, half of which are flexible as they correspond to individual tasks, meetings with collaborators and coaching sessions. Time which is not flexible is for seminars, workshops and learning groups, which are naturally prearranged and scheduled.

The LIDD-Bank 2002–3 was positively appraised on several counts: (a) the programme aligned with the business strategy; (b) the continued flexibility of the programme was ensured by formulating clear aims which were adaptable in form; (c) the project was tailored to the organisation; (d) the participants acted like 'spilled oil', transmitting what they had learned, becoming involved and involving others; and (e) the programme strengthened the global learning process.

Which people play key roles in your country? Which names should one know?

After the change of government from conservative to socialist, Spain finds itself in a new situation, one which affects international relationships, economics and social life in many ways. Names to note are:

- King Juan Carlos I of Spain;
- bankers Emilio Botín (Banco Santander) and Francisco González (BBVA);
- President of the Spanish government, José Luis Rodríguez Zapatero;
- businessman Amancio Ortega (Inditex); and
- Formula 1 driver Fernando Alonso.

References

Casals Jiménez, Joaquín/Lorenzo Vázquez, Monica (2003): LIDD in the banking sector 2002–2003. Leadership and persons management in a company in the banking sector, in: Capital Humano, 163: 22.
CEDE, La dirección de empresas en el s.XXI (2000): Humanismo y Tecnología, First Congress, Barcelona, 29/30 June.
Kotter, John P. (1997): Leading Change, Madrid, Barcelona, Granada.
MERCER Human Resources Consulting (2004): Utilizando el poder de los Recursos Humanos para crear mayor valor. Estudio sobre la evolución y transformación de la función de los Recursos Humanos en las principales organizaciones españolas, Spain.
Ulrich, David O./Losey, Michael R./Lake, Gerry (1998): El futuro de la Dirección de Recursos Humanos, Barcelona.

.es

The authors

Joaquín Casals Jiménez (fundipe@fundipe.es), Banco Atlántico, Human Resources Managing Director. President of FUNDIPE.

Monica Lorenzo Vázquez (mlorenzo@bancogallego.com), Banco Gallego, Human Resource Development Director. Author of *Coaching. Mitos y realidades*, Madrid, 2004.

Montserrat Luque Pinilla (fundipe@fundipe.es; montseluque@gmail.com), FUNDIPE (Fundación para el Desarrollo de la Función de Recursos Humanos), Technical Secretary.

Tomás Pereda Riaza (tpereda@hertz.com), Associate Professor at various different business schools. Currently Hertz España, S.A, Human Resources Director. Iberdrola, S.A., Human Resources Development Corporate Director. Grupo Leche Pascual, S.A., Human Resources Corporate Vice-President. DuPont Pharma, S.A., Human Resources and Legal Affairs Director. IKEA España, AB (Sucursal en España), Human Resources Country Manager. Laboratorios Serono, S.A., Human Resources Director. Pharmaceuticals holding of the Unión de Explosivos Río Tinto, S.A. (ERT), Legal Adviser and HR Manager Associate. Author of *The individual professional development process by competencies* (*La Gaceta de los Negocios*, 27 September 2004).

Eva Triviño Acuña (eva@aedipe.es), AEDIPE (Asociación Española de Dirección y Desarrollo de Personas), Technical Secretary.

13 HRM in Turkey: the dawn of talent management

Yiğit Duman/Ömer Sadullah/Hande Yaşargil/Lütfi Aygüler

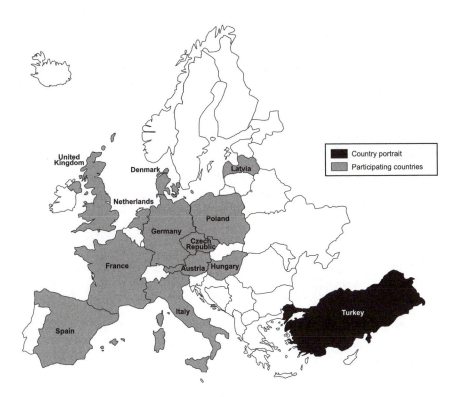

Turkey: in a nutshell

In this chapter you will learn:

- that HRM in Turkey has shifted from personnel management to people management. Accordingly the direction of the HR field is towards the individual and human emphasis of HRM;

- that HR academia in Turkey has undergone a change: HRM is accepted as a strategic partner in organisations. This development is also reflected in business education; and

- that for Balnak people satisfaction is a prerequisite for customer satisfaction. Hence, the transport company makes the highest value-adding investments in HR.

Capital:	Ankara
Area (sq km):	780,580 (land 770,760; water 9,820)
EU membership:	no (Turkey is currently undertaking substantial legal and economic reforms in pursuit of full membership of the EU).
Population:	70,413,958
Languages:	Turkish (official), Kurdish, Dimli (or Zaza), Azeri, Kabardian
Ethnic groups (in percentages):	Turkish *c*. 80, Kurdish *c*. 20 (estimated)
Gross domestic product:	627.2 billion USD (2006)
Workforce (in percentages):	24.8 million (2006): agriculture 35.9; industry 22.8; services 41.2 (2004)
Export commodities:	clothes, foodstuffs, textiles, metal manufactures, transport equipment

BACKGROUND: FROM PERSONNEL MANAGEMENT TO PEOPLE MANAGEMENT

What is your advice for a foreign firm entering your country's market? What should managers especially care about and, what is more, be aware of?

Maintain good public relations. There are some small cultural and social mines scattered around; managers should be aware of them. One bad choice can ruin a product's or service's reputation. People are easily affected by rumours.

From personnel management to people management: since its beginnings the HR profession in Turkey has made rapid progress along a traditional pattern of development. The history of the Turkish Association for Personnel Management and the background of the managers of the HR function show us that pattern clearly. The HR function starts with accounting and administration experts who master the basics of payroll and legal administration. Due to the political dynamics of Turkey, legal experts moved into HR management roles and dealt with labour relations, employee communications and conflicts. Industrial engineers followed the legal experts into the HR field. They worked to improve systems and processes that brought greater profitability and effectiveness. The economic crises of 1994 and 2000 placed employment costs in sharp focus, bringing downsizing initiatives and putting finance managers into the driving seat. As business recovered, companies discovered the impact of organisational behaviour and a new generation of well-equipped psychologists came to the fore in HR.

By the new millennium, everyone had learned that HR is a strategic function rather than a support service. The doors are now open to any manager who has a strategic perspective. Finally and fortunately, HR has a significant role in setting the direction and approach for many Turkish businesses. Today there is a place for both the HR generalist and for specialists who focus in-depth on particular areas of practice.

Overall, the direction of the HR field today is towards the individual and human emphasis implied by the term 'people management'.

 .tr

 .tr

From a broader perspective, predictions for the future should focus on both national and global trends. Turkey has a large and very young population. Driven by the EU inclusion project, many pivotal reforms are being made and new kinds of investment and capitalisation are becoming possible. These local trends will have a positive effect on the business world. Its geographic and political location makes Turkey an attractive corporate headquarters for Middle East and African regions, and even some Eastern Europe operations, but this is not Turkey's only impact on the global economy. One clear trend is that multinational firms are making greater use of Turkish leadership talent. Every year, more Turkish managers are transferred from within the ranks of Turkish subsidiaries to take on executive responsibilities in places like Spain, Canada, South Korea, Indonesia, Latin America, China and the USA (to name but a few recent examples). At the same time, young Turkish traders continue to have an impact on Wall Street and at other equity exchanges around the world, and most of these will eventually bring their expertise and global perspective back home, where it can drive local innovation and growth. As Turkey continues to invest in talent management, its people are well positioned to play a greater role in global business.

Well into the 1980s, a great majority of Turkish organisations and businessmen regarded HRM as a necessary evil. Most people assigned to personnel had no business education at all and some had no BA degree. In fact most organisations preferred retired officers or non-coms for personnel posts because they thought personnel management involved disciplining the employees. More enlightened organisations preferred lawyers. In today's Turkish business environment, the inevitable effects of the firm entrenchment of HRM in higher education can be seen. HRM is regarded as an important function in organisations and, instead of retired officers or lawyers, people with business degrees are being assigned to HR positions – and people in those positions who do not have a business degree are being trained through specialised programmes.

What are you and other Turkish people extraordinarily proud of with respect to HRM?

High ability to adapt to new circumstances both in a social and financial environment is really a matter of pride for the people of this country. It signals a kind of professionalism on the changing management front of modern HRM.

EAPM AFFILIATE: TÜRKIYE PERSONEL YÖNETIMI DERNEGI

GENERAL INFORMATION

The association for personnel management in Turkey (Türkiye Personel Yönetimi Dernegi (PERYÖN)) – the profession's first association – was founded in 1971 by a group of eight volunteers. The founding members shared a belief that the personnel management profession needed to be represented in Turkey. Their aim was to follow the global trends in personnel management and share them with Turkish colleagues, develop the knowledge and coordination between members and increase the importance of the personnel positions in the organisations. The number of individual members in the early 1980s was 312, which jumped to 607 members in the 1990s and then to 1,600 in 2005 – HR professionals, specialists and academic staff.

In 1973, just two years after PERYÖN's foundation, Turkey saw the start-up of its first ever personnel management certificate programme. In 1978, PERYÖN became a member of EAPM (European Association for Personnel Management). During the period from 1991 to 1993, the EAPM president was also the head of the Turkish association. From 1999 to 2001, PERYÖN was represented on the EAPM executive committee. PERYÖN is also a member of WFPMA (World Federation of Personnel Management Associations).

The PERYÖN Quarterly Magazine, published every three months, is distributed to all members and universities in Turkey free of charge. The 11th Annual National Conference staged by PERYÖN on 3–4 October 2003 became a meeting point for some 600 HR professionals. PERYÖN's vision is to become the foremost organisation in the field of personnel management. Keeping in step with social, economical and legal change in both Turkey and the world, PERYÖN is an active and respected non-governmental organisation.

PERYÖN's mission is to serve HR professionals as a guide, to work for the development of personnel management professionals, and to be a powerful reference point in personnel management issues. That mission defines the association's priorities, which are to create active management, to create a wide range of interest and support, to supply the resources required for activities and to continue to serve all social partners effectively. PERYÖN is organised in various work groups: the re-engineering project group, individual and institutional relations, marketing and product management, as well as knowledge management and professional development.

As it is the main idea is to share the knowledge created in PERYÖN across the whole country, PERYÖN has at present five regional offices within Turkey. These branches work separately in their respective regions. To synchronise and maximise the value to members and other partners, PERYÖN organises quarterly meetings with these branch organisations and keeps branch activity plans in synchronisation. The activities of these organisations bring the total number of conferences to four, and the number of training activities to more than twenty. The branches (and years in which they were established) are: Ege (1995), Ankara (1998), Bursa (1998) and Trakya (1998).

In response to financial recommendations and requirements, in 2003 PERYÖN founded its own profit-oriented arm, PERYÖN Ltd. PERYÖN Ltd took charge of all in-house training and congress organisation activities. The main criteria that need to be met by in-house training activity planning are to be innovative and up to date, but not a competitor for any private consulting or training company. The company also secures and handles all advertisements for the PERYÖN magazine and organises HR service provider exhibitions at the annual PERYÖN congresses.

> **In a few words, what would you say is the one fundamental strategic competitive advantage your country offers compared to others?**
>
> Dynamism. Very rapid change is common.

PUBLICATIONS

PERYÖN publishes quarterly, under the slogan 'The Magazine for people pioneering people management', the PERYÖN magazine, with a circulation of 3,000. Besides, PERYÖN has supported many different global and local surveys, including EAPM, SHRM and CIPD surveys and Master's degree research assignments.

The PERYÖN brand and logo were affirmed by the National Patent Institute of Turkey in October 2003. PERYÖN's website, with its novel design, was first broadcast on 20 October 2003. Most PERYÖN members share their professional opinions in a mail group. In addition, a weekly e-newsletter with news and ads is sent out to 960 PERYÖN members.

PERYÖN, as a whole, has accompanied and significantly influenced the development of people management in Turkey. One of the oldest non-governmental organisations in Turkey, it has a good reputation and a well-developed network with both governmental and private organisations. Via its international links, PERYÖN serves members as an institution open to the world.

> **What do you like to teach foreign HR managers? What is important for them to know in your opinion?**
>
> Turkish employees are generally amateur professionals.

HR ACADEMIA: DEVELOPMENT OF HRM EDUCATION

The inclusion of personnel management (PM) as a subject in its own right in higher education can be traced to the founding of the Institute of Business Administration in 1954 with the collaboration of Harvard Business School and the sponsorship of the Ford Foundation. Established within the Faculty of Economics of Istanbul University, the Institute of Business Administration (IBA) is one of the leading institutions of higher education delivering case-oriented business education for graduate students in Europe.

The aim of setting up the IBA was to educate and train managerial candidates to meet the needs of the Turkish business environment. The IBA accepted graduate students with BA degrees in any academic field and, over two semesters (four semesters for night classes), gave them a comprehensive business education emphasising the case method and covering every major field of study. In those early days, personnel management was not included in the curriculum as a distinct subject but functions and issues of PM were included and discussed in human relations and behaviour courses. In addition, legal issues relating to personnel management were covered within the labour law course, again employing the case method. From its establishment in 1954 through to 1968, the IBA was the only institute of higher education providing a formal business administration education that indirectly covered the PM issues and topics in other courses.

FOUNDATION OF THE ISTANBUL UNIVERSITY BUSINESS ADMINISTRATION FACULTY (IUBAF)

In 1968, the Business Administration Faculty of Istanbul University was established from the nucleus of the IBA. This was the first institution of higher education in Turkey to offer a Bachelor's degree in business administration. Another first for the Faculty was the creation of the Chair of Personnel Management as one of several chairs which included finance accounting, marketing and production. From 1968 to 1980, third-year students of the IUBAF were required to choose the discipline in which they wished to graduate. The options were finance, production, accounting, marketing and PM. The courses that had to be taken in the PM discipline at that time were as follows:

- PM;
- wage and salary management;
- job evaluation;
- employer–employee relations;
- social psychology; and
- human relations.

All of these courses were spread over two semesters and four hours a week. Students who chose the PM discipline in their third year had to take these courses alongside the courses that were mandatory for third and fourth years. The discipline system ran for twelve years, being abandoned in 1980.

In 1980, IUBAF adopted a diploma system in which a BA degree in business administration was awarded upon completion of eight semesters of intense business education. Again, from the first year through to the last, all courses took two semesters. Courses relating to HMR began in the first year, skipped the second, then continued through to the last year. These were as follows:

– first year: labour economics and industrial relations;
– third year: personnel management; and
– fourth year: labour law.

Under this system, business students were exposed to the PM discipline in their fresher year through the labour economics and industrial relations course. This course was designed to provide an understanding of the role of human and labour factors in a macroeconomic and organisational context. In the first semester of this two-semester course students learned the concepts of free labour, labour supply and demand, labour mobility, labour markets, wage theories, productivity and unemployment. Industrial relations as a system and concepts such as organised labour and unions, collective bargaining, industrial disputes, resolution methods, strikes and lock-outs were taught in the second semester.

Thus prepared, third-year students took PM for two semesters, in which they learned all the pertinent functions and techniques. The subjects covered in this course were: introduction to PM, history of PM, purpose and functions of PM, organisation of the PM department, job analysis, job design, personnel planning, staffing (recruitment, selection, placement and orientation), performance appraisals, training and development, career planning and development, compensation management, wage and salary systems, job evaluation, health and safety, quality of work life, handling grievances and disciplinary measures.

The legal framework of HRM was covered in the labour law course during the fourth year. This course gave the business students an understanding of the rules and regulations governing HRM practice in the Turkish business environment. Three key acts (the Labour Act, Unions Act, Collective Agreements Strikes and Lock-outs Act) of the Turkish labour law system formed the basis of this course.

This system and curriculum continued at the IUBAF through the 1990s. In 1999, it was changed again. The faculty adapted the semester system and converted the year-long courses into single-semester units. In addition, the number of courses that needed to be taken was reduced to six a year. Elective courses were introduced in the final year. Inevitably, these changes affected the composition of the HR-related courses provided by the chair in HR. In 1998, however, before the changes became effective, the title of the chair and the course was officially changed from personnel management to human resource management. Under the new system, the HR course became a one-semester course taken in the first semester of the third year. The labour economics and industrial relations course was dropped from the first year and again became a one-semester course, as did industrial relations, which moved to the second semester of year three. The labour law course was dropped from the fourth-year curriculum as a mandatory course but was introduced as an elective course on the chair's initiative. In addition, many of the topics that had been covered under the old labour law course were retained in the industrial relations course.

HRM IN GRADUATE STUDIES

In 1978, Master's programmes started at the IUBAF in addition to the existing doctorate studies. These programmes were designed not as typical MBA programmes but rather as M.Sc. programmes. Graduate students with a BA degree in any field were accepted on to these programmes and could choose a discipline in which to specialise. HRM (called personnel management up until 1998) was one of the options. To the authors' knowledge, this was the first time in Europe that HRM was included in a graduate programme as an independent discipline. With the establishment of the Higher Education Board in 1982, the right to open graduate programmes was transferred from the faculties to the newly created Basic Sciences and Social Sciences Institutes at certain universities. In line with this new arrangement, graduate programmes at the IUBAF were turned over to the Istanbul University Social Sciences Institute (IUSSI). However, the actual running of the programmes was left to the faculties. So the IUBAF today is still responsible for the implementation of the graduate programmes and the chair of HRM is still responsible for designing and running the graduate HR programmes. The degrees, however, are awarded by the IUSSI. HRM is also included as a mandatory course in other graduate programmes. The hospital management graduate programme includes HRM among its courses. At the IUBAF alone, over 1,300 theses (M.Sc. and Ph.D.) completed since 1978 have been directly related to HRM.

INSTITUTE OF BUSINESS ADMINISTRATION (IBA)

The IBA, from which the Business Administration Faculty was born, is incorporated into the faculty and today continues to provide general and specific business education on certificate and executive MBA levels. This institute is unique because it is the only institute left to operate after the creation of the Higher Education Board (HEB) in 1982. The IBA offers a variety of programmes which aim to satisfy the needs of the business community. The programmes offered vary from certificate levels to MBA degrees and also from Turkish to English-language programmes. The case method is widely used in every programme. HRM is a mandatory course in almost every programme. Certificate-level programmes are mostly for two semesters and the executive MBA programmes run for four semesters, where HRM is a mandatory course during the second semester.

Students in their third semesters can also elect other courses that relate to HRM such as labour law, performance appraisal, etc. The executive MBA programme does not require a thesis but students are required to complete a graduation project in their fourth semester. The subject of these projects can be in any field and HRM is a popular one. From 1991 to 1995, the IUBAF offered a two-semester certificate-level graduate business programme in Azerbaijan, introducing the concept of HRM to that country for the first time.

In cooperation with the Turkish Personnel Management Association, IBA offers a specialised HR certificate course which mainly targets employees who wish to pursue a career in HRM. It also provides a two-semester tourism and tour operators course for lycée (high-school) graduates, with HRM as one of the mandatory courses.

DEVELOPMENT OF HR EDUCATION AND OTHER INSTITUTIONS

There are over eighty state and private universities in Turkey and every one of them has an economics and administrative sciences faculty with economics and business administration departments. A look at their curriculum reveals HRM as a mandatory course, especially in business administration departments. At major universities, there are also graduate HRM programmes similar to those of the IUBAF. Military academies (army, navy and air force) have included HRM in their curricula both in undergraduate- and graduate-level programmes. The Staff College also includes HRM in its studies.

Most engineering – especially industrial engineering – faculties include HRM in their curricula. Even though HRM is taught in various institutions, it is deeply embedded in business education and faculty members of business schools are invited to conduct HRM courses in non-business schools. Except for the IUBAF, which has an independent HR chair, HRM in other schools is considered as a sub-field of management.

As stated in the opening paragraphs, HRM was not covered as an independent subject in Turkish higher education but was thought to be a subordinate branch of either management or human relations. It is fair to say that business education at Turkish universities is heavily influenced by the US school of thought. This is natural because its roots can be traced to the foundation of the IBA. So the same thinking can also be observed in the development of HRM teaching. With the foundation of the IUBAF, the subject became an independent course, although it went for a very long time (from the mid-1950s to the late 1980s) by the name personnel management. During that period, the staff role of personnel management was mostly underlined.

 .tr

HRM today is accepted as a strategic partner in organisations and this is also reflected in business education.

Professor Selçuk Yalçin, founding member and head of the HR chair of the IUBAF from 1968 until his retirement in 1987, can rightly be described as the pioneer academician in this field. His book *Personel Yönetimi* ('Personnel management') was the first comprehensive textbook of the period and remained so for long time. The first job evaluation projects in public and private sector companies were completed under his leadership. He was the principal figure in the training of today's leading academicians in the field of HRM.

Early research in this field can be defined as descriptive and was concentrated on understanding the functions of personnel management. Today, the scope and variety of research on HRM have increased immensely. One example is the international-level research being carried out by the IUBAF and the Cranfield Network (Cranet-G). The IUBAF and the HRM chair have represented Turkey since 1992 in the Cranet-G, which conducts international strategic HR research.

CONCLUSION

Today, HRM is firmly established as an important field of Turkish business education on both undergraduate and graduate levels at over eighty universities. To these universities the universities of the Northern Cyprus Turkish Republic and a number of universities in Azerbaijan can be added.

What would you say one ought not to do? What are the 'don'ts' in your country?

Do not chat about religion or religious beliefs. Do not criticise people before you develop trust in the relationship.

BEST-PRACTICE CASE: BALNAK NAKLIYAT VE LOJISTIK HIZMETLERI TICARET A.Ş. – LOGISTICS FOR PEOPLE-TO-PEOPLE CONNECTION

INTRODUCTION

The number of companies offering international freight service increased in the mid-1980s when the Turkish economy opened up to world trade. Bal-Nak Uluslararasi Nakliyat ve Ticaret Limited Şirketi was established in 1986 in partnership with the German company Ballauf Spedition by Lütfi Aygüler, who had a keen eye for developing industries and was at the time an executive in a freight company. The company originally employed twelve people and shipped freight by road to and from Germany. The company developed rapidly and in 1994 turned into an organisation offering road, sea and air freight as well as warehousing and storage services. The German shareholders did not wish to invest in Turkey at that time, and sold their shares. With the change in ownership composition, organisational changes also ensued and each department turned into a separate company. In 1995, as the number of group companies increased, Balnak Holding was established to manage and direct the joint organisation of these companies.

The object of the company was originally defined as road transportation, storage and warehouse management but the company is now geared to offering international road, air, sea and rail transport services, warehousing and bonded warehouse services, and logistic services. The current name of the company is Balnak Nakliyat ve Lojistik Hizmetleri Ticaret A.Ş. (Balnak Transportation and Logistics, Inc.; referred to below as Balnak). The company has its headquarters and a warehouse in Istanbul Halkali, branch offices in Izmir and Bursa, a liaison office in Denizli as well as a warehouse and a bonded warehouse in Hadimköy.

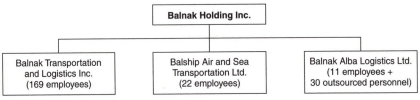

Figure 13.1 The structure of the Balnak Group

Balnak delivers all the operational services of the company and procures support services from the support departments of Balnak Holding. Operating in the international freight and logistics sector, the company does not own any vehicles itself; it offers freight services under its own name and on its own account.

Balnak's customers are resident manufacturing and trading companies in Turkey that export to and import from international markets, as well as representatives in Turkey of international trading companies. Balnak considers the turnover for each customer as an important indicator in customer segmentation. About 50 per cent of Balnak's annual turnover is derived from its 100 largest customers. The quality dimensions of the service received by customers are speed, timely tracking, accessibility, flexibility and use of technology.

People satisfaction is a prerequisite of customer satisfaction. As a service sector company, Balnak also attaches importance to expertise in management, streamlined management levels, wide empowerment, and people awareness of the inextricability of operations (service production) from marketing. This is the only way to create shorter communication channels, achieve close contact with customers and produce 'total solutions to customer needs that are beyond their expectations'.

As of April 2003, the company had 169 employees, 47 per cent of whom are university graduates and 50 per cent speak a foreign language. The company pioneers as a school in its line of business. No distinction is made between blue- and white-collar employees, because all company people are entitled to identical rights. The average age of company employees is 30.8 years.

While many companies fired people in 2001 when the Turkish economy was struck by an economic crisis, Balnak did not lay off a single employee. The company paid salaries and premiums on time, together with the annual rise.

What is typical of your country in relation to the country itself (its culture, people, etc.) and its economy?

Concerning the country, people are typically friendly, generous and warm. Concerning the economy, inflation used to be typical. Nowadays inflation is very low, but people have not yet got used to this new situation.

Q.tr

HR PLANS AND POLICIES

As a company operating in the service sector, Balnak is fully aware that its most important resource are people, and therefore makes the highest value-adding investments in human resources. The CEO and all institutional leaders consider investment in HR and spending time on people every bit as important as external customers. Balnak's management approaches to people are defined in the HRM process, which is a support process (Figure 13.2).

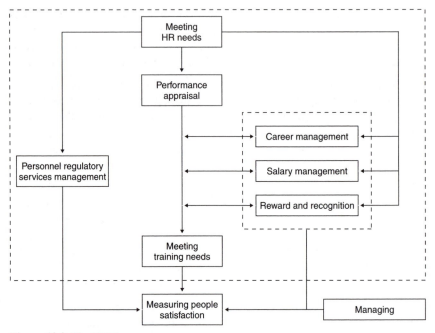

Figure 13.2 The HRM process

RECRUITMENT AND CAREER DEVELOPMENT

The basic principle of the personnel selection and placement system is to employ HR professionals – who are highly qualified, trained and properly competent – at the right time and in the right place. These recruits are capable of adopting and implementing the philosophy, vision, mission and principles of Balnak, and developing themselves, the team and the company. Recruits should be multifaceted, receptive to learning and innovation, and good in human relations – in addition to having the proper skills and competences needed to meet the technical specifications for the job.

An important element of Balnak culture is that an employee should feel esteemed from the first day at work. The following are practised for recruits at all levels:

- The desk, computer, business cards and e-mail address of the recruit are ready on the first day at work.
- A 'welcome letter' is placed on the recruit's desk, as well as a booklet entitled '*Balnakli Olmak*' ('Being a Balnak member').
- A 'welcome letter' containing brief information and a photograph of the recruit is sent by e-mail to all company people on the recruit's first day at work.

- The new Balnak member is personally introduced to the whole management team and employees by the TQHR department.
- A full-day orientation programme is organised by the TQHR department within two months of the new Balnak member's recruitment. All department managers make presentations on processes and operations on orientation day, starting with the CEO's presentation on company culture and objectives.
- All orientation presentations are kept in the intranet as a source of reference for employees.
- On-the-job training is provided according to the department and the type of work. Visits are also made to bonded warehouses, warehouses, customs offices and airport offices.

One of the approaches adopted to ensure that Balnak people are employed in the right job with the expected performance is the career management process.

MEASURING PEOPLE SATISFACTION: PEOPLE SATISFACTION SURVEY

A people satisfaction survey (PSS) is made in April each year to evaluate the management and service quality of the organisation, and to determine the loyalty and satisfaction level of employees. People satisfaction is monitored on a question group basis. Some of the relationships of Balnak PSS questions with the motivation and satisfaction groups of the EFQM Excellence Model are shown in Table 13.1.

Table 13.1 Relation between PSS questions and motivation/satisfaction

Question group	PSS question	M/S
Overall appraisal	I am satisfied with working at Balnak	S
	Company culture is adopted by everyone at Balnak	S
	I am confident that Balnak will adapt to changes and developments in the future	S
	Balnak is a company with total quality and continuing improvement awareness	S
	The company is sufficiently publicised	S
Vision, mission and targets	The company has a vision, which is a clearly defined objective that we wish to reach at the end of a certain period	M
	Our vision and mission have been communicated to us in a way that we can all understand	M
	Information technology support	S
	Social activities	S

M: Motivation; S: Satisfaction

Table 13.2 People satisfaction levels

	1999	*2000*	*2001*	*2002*
Overall appraisal	67.0	80.0	78.0	79.0
Approach to people at Balnak	47.8	60.0	64.0	66.0
Communication and management	58.0	64.8	76.0	77.0
Leadership	57.0	66.0	77.0	74.0
Team spirit	–	–	–	76.0
Vision, mission and targets	–	–	–	85.0
Adequacy and quality of services produced within the company	57.0	67.3	69.0	70.0
Overall satisfaction	58.0	64.0	72.0	74.0

People satisfaction rates (in percentages) on a yearly basis according to Balnak's seven main headings are shown in Table 13.2.

The PPS is conducted to monitor people's perceptions for this purpose, and independent topic-based surveys are carried out as required (Figure 13.3).

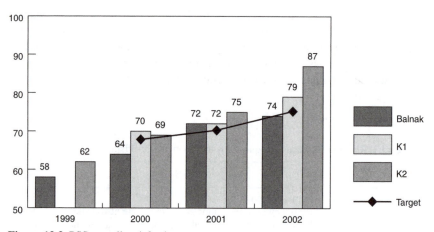

Figure 13.3 PSS overall satisfaction

Survey forms are completed anonymously so that people can fully and objectively express their views. Survey results are analysed on a branch and department basis, and are personally explained in detail to all employees at department meetings by the TQHR manager.

No targets are shown in the chart for the first year because the PSS was only introduced in 1999. The fall in staff turnover from 62.59 per cent in 1998 to 28.57 per cent in 1999 and the new approaches such as social benefits that had been put into practice encouraged the company to target a 15 per cent increase in the satisfaction level in 2000. When personnel regulatory services – a non-value-adding process in the HR system – were outsourced to a specialist firm in 2000, the TQHR manager had more time for people, and new systems such as discussion meetings and performance appraisal were put into practice. The overall satisfaction target for 2001 was therefore set 10 per cent higher than the value realised in the previous year although the target had not been attained in 2000. The overall satisfaction level target for 2002 was set at 75 per cent – which has a symbolic significance – in view of the fact that no Balnak employees had been laid off, salaries had been raised as anticipated and paid on time, and premium payments had been regularly made in 2001 – a year of economic crisis. Comparisons have been made with two companies that won the National Quality Award in the SME category in 2002. These companies are shown above as K1 and K2.

COMPETENCE IDENTIFICATION AND DEVELOPMENT

Seven competency groups have been identified in Balnak for all managers and employees alike. Features of the service sector were taken into consideration in identifying, and in particular defining these competences. As a service sector organisation, Balnak aims to develop employees who are flexible, committed, empathic with customers, regular, sensitive to cost efficiency, effective and efficient on the basis of these competences. Five additional management competences have been described for managers. Competence descriptions are formulated by the TQHR department, and reviewed every six months in performance appraisal discussions by the appraiser and the appraised together.

The annual training plan is prepared by TQHR according to training needs. Annual training plans cover all Balnak people at every level. Necessary arrangements are made in training plans at the strategy meeting each month regarding their adequacy in meeting needs and the new training needs that emerge.

One observer from the TQHR department attends trainings so that hitches in training can be corrected immediately and training effectiveness can be directly studied to identify improvement requirements in future training. Participants complete training appraisal forms after each training to appraise the effectiveness of the training and the trainer. These forms are analysed by the TQHR department and shared with all managers.

Orientation programmes have been systematic in the company since 2001. Participants are asked at the end of the orientation day to express their opinions on an appraisal form so that effectiveness of the orientation day can be reviewed. Trainers revise training notes according to the feedback received. Moreover, employee participation in conferences and fairs is encouraged to help in their development.

INVOLVEMENT AND EMPOWERMENT

Implementations promoting the involvement and empowerment of people are planned according to the principle that 'We manage change and development together'.

In spite of the dynamics of the sector in which Balnak is operating, the company has preferred to make systematic use of employee comments and suggestions through TQM, which it adopted in 1996. The suggestion system (SS) and project groups are the media in which involvement on individual and team levels is ensured. Participation in the SS is taken into consideration during performance appraisal under the 'contribution to the company' heading.

'Problem-solving and initiative-taking skills' is a competence also required for every Balnak member. The motto 'Everyone is a manager in Balnak' encourages people to take the initiative. People involvement is measured in the PSS by the question 'participation of people in decisions at every level', and empowerment by the questions 'proportionally weighted powers and responsibilities in the job description', and 'power to make decisions relating to the job performed'. Competences such as involvement in teamwork, initiative-taking skills, creativity and innovation are used in the performance appraisal system (PAS) to measure involvement and empowerment. The various learning media include self-assessment and visits to companies that practise TQM.

COMMUNICATION

Basic communication in Balnak is defined as speedy and clear communication of feelings, ideas and facts in a way that does not have an adverse effect on cooperation. Communication skills have been adopted as a competency 'required for every Balnak member' and have been defined in detail in view of the above principle.

At Balnak, where efforts to integrate the principle of 'creating a difference through technology' into daily life have become a permanent discipline, the intranet and extensive use of e-mail are among the major communication channels. Head and branch offices and warehouses are interlinked, with access to a joint database based on developments in communication and computer technology (lease line technology). Communication effectiveness is appraised through PSS and self-assessment. Various motivation methods are practised so that the fast-paced and intensive work in Balnak can be fun.

Moreover, the TQHR manager visits national quality award winners to share their good practices with the Board of Directors and institutional leaders at communication and strategy meetings. Leaders of award winners are also invited to Balnak to share their experience. The management works with various consultancy firms in order to transfer the best practices in information systems, law and insurance to Balnak employees.

CARING

Caring for its employees is very important for Balnak. This attitude can be identified in different fields:

- Salaries of employees are determined according to the salary band system and revised twice a year according to inflation and the performance system. Employees also receive performance-based premiums based on the net profit of the company. In addition, each employee leaving Balnak for any reason has a talk with the TQHR manager. Because there is a shortage of trained personnel in the sector, people who have left Balnak may be re-employed – on the assumption that the experience will have taught them the difference between Balnak and competitors' employment practices (care by hiring).

- Participatory management was adopted by Balnak in 1996 to promote and sustain people involvement. The company encourages 'customer satisfaction-focused initiatives' because it is in the service sector and most employees are thus in direct contact with external customers. Dinner or luncheon with institutional leaders after a successful project is also a part of the system (care by recognition).

- Balnak does exemplary work in the field of environmental and social responsibility in line with its social responsibility policy. First-aid, fire and earthquake training is given to all employees in order to develop health and safety awareness. All managers carry on them the addresses and phone numbers of all employees and next of kin so they can be reached in an emergency. Waste-paper and spent battery bins are placed in offices to promote environmental awareness (care by raising awareness).

- As part of the Balnak seniority policy, private health insurance is taken out for each employee who completes one year in the company. All employees are further insured at the time they are hired under a personal accident policy that includes mortality, disability and medical treatment cover. Balnak considers people satisfaction to be a prerequisite for customer satisfaction. The company accordingly provides such facilities as interest-free housing, loans for birth, marriage, cars, mobile phones and computers as well as incentive loans for relocating closer to the company – which would reduce both private and company costs (care through facilities).

- To ensure involvement and deployment in social activities, a committee was set up in 2000. The committee's proposals are taken into consideration in activity planning. Suggested and organised activities are, for example, the New Year's Eve dinner which is attended each year by all employees as well as the Board of Directors and the general manager. All employees are congratulated on their birthday by their respective department/section manager – as well as by the TQHR manager at head office – who personally visits the employee at his/her desk (care in social activities).

To ensure that the department/section managers care for their employees, some of the fields of caring which we have discussed are measured in the PSS. Recognition and care for people is, for example, covered through the question on 'recognition of achievements' and the group of questions on 'adequacy and quality of services produced within the company'.

RESULTS

PSS has been playing an important role since 1999 in identifying areas for improvement so that people satisfaction can be increased. The company monitors various indicators that have an impact on people satisfaction and motivation, in addition to the perception measures shown above. Speed is a major customer expectation in the sector served by Balnak. The company recognises that employee productivity is the cornerstone in providing fast service to customers, and

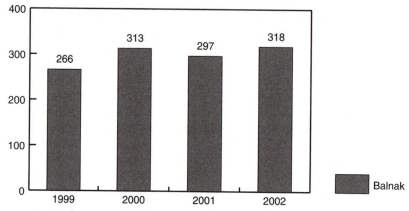

Figure 13.4 Employee productivity

monitors freight per person as a performance indicator. The amount of freight per person realised in the company between 1999 and 2002 is given in Figure 13.4.

The reduced quantity of import freight in 2001 as Turkey's imports fell had a negative impact on employee productivity. Nevertheless, Balnak did not regard the crisis as a chance to lay off people but put up a fight against the effects of the crisis and invested in the post-crisis period by increasing the number of visits and proposals to customers.

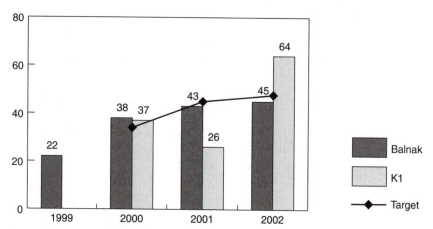

Figure 13.5 Rate of involvement in improvement teams

Balnak improvement teams consist of project groups and committees. Participation is ensured through direct appointment in addition to voluntary participation in improvement teams (Figure 13.5).

The reasons for the positive trend over the years at Balnak – which has adopted the principle of management by project – are the monitoring and coordination of the project management system since 1999, conversion of the system into written form in 2001, promotion and encouragement of participation in projects by the leaders, and the fact that involvement in projects is taken into consideration in the performance appraisal system.

The company places importance on both professional training and individual competences and skills development training, and leaders encourage people to participate in training. Over the years, training hours per person have markedly increased at Balnak as a result (Figure 13.6).

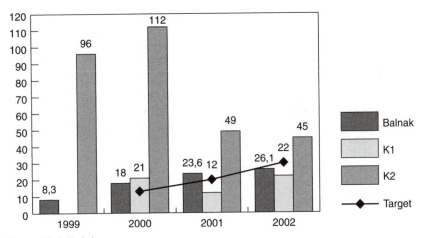

Figure 13.6 Training

Training needs have been more clearly identified since 2000 as a result of the performance appraisal system. The number of training hours can be seen to increase on a year-by-year basis due to the introduction of systematic orientation training in 2001, and training for the software purchased in 2002.

Individuals and teams are rewarded within the framework of the reward and recognition system. At Balnak, this system comprises rewarding members of successful improvement teams with gifts at joint meetings in the presence of all company employees, encouraging individual achievement through material awards, presenting plaques and material rewards for seniority, and other, similar practices.

Balnak believes in the importance of trained manpower, and has adopted a policy of 'staff seniority' since 1999. Operating in a sector with a high staff turnover rate, the company targeted a reduction in this and succeeded in lowering the rate by 74.5 per cent from 1998 to the end of 2002 (Figure 13.7).

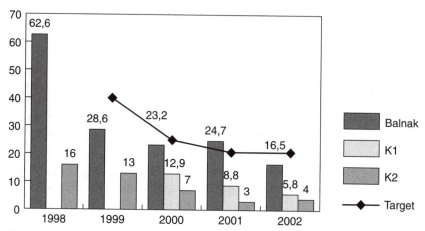

Figure 13.7 Staff turnover rate

Which people play key roles in your country? Which names should one know?

Other than political figures, some top bureaucrats, e.g. Ahmet Erturk, head of TMSF, and media people, e.g. Ertugrul Ozkok, head of Hurriyet, the strongest man in the media, play key roles. And also football commentators . . . .

The authors

Yiğit Oğuz Duman (yigit.duman@kibarholding.com) has his Industrial Engineering degree from the Bosphorus University, and MBA degree from Koç University. He started working at Kibar Holding during his university years, and after several positions and promotions he is the Human Resources Director of this Group. In addition to his professional career, he is the President of the Management Board of PERYÖN (Turkish association for personnel management), the official, leading organisation in Turkey, to develop HR management and increase awereness on the subject.

Dr Ömer Sadullah is an Associate Professor at Istanbul University (www.istanbul.edu.tr), Faculty of Business Administration, Human Resources Department. In his academic career of over thirty years, his main research interests have been in labour law, industrial relations, and organisational behaviour.

Hande Yaşargil (hyasargil@mentor-tr.com) is the founder of Mentor Executive Coaching, Turkey's premier executive coaching and corporate mentoring provider. She originally trained as a psychologist and family therapist, and obtained her BA in Psychology from Istanbul University. She obtained ten years' experience in the human resources profession. She is former Vice-President, Board member and International Manager at PERYÖN.

Lütfi Aygüler, after graduating from the Bosphorus University Industrial Engineering Department, started working in Pada Int. Freight Forwarding. Two years later, in 1986, he started at Balnak Logistics Group. He is still Chairman the Board of Directors of the Balnak Logistics Group (www.balnak.com.tr).

.tr

14 The United Kingdom of Great Britain and Northern Ireland (the UK): between North America and continental Europe

Chris Brewster/Frances Wilson/Nick Holley

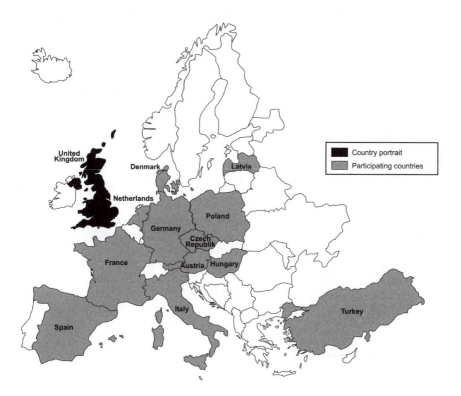

United
Kingdom

Denmark

Latvia

Netherlands

Poland

Germany

Czech
Republik

France

Austria / Hungary

Italy

Turkey

Spain

Country portrait

Participating countries

The UK: in a nutshell

In this chapter you will learn:

– that HRM in the UK is mostly influenced by US HRM practices. Nevertheless, some HRM policies and practices specific to the UK can be identified;

– that HRM academia in the UK is characterised by a debate between two philosophical approaches: one accepting the US approach, and one criticising it; and

– that Vodafone's explosive growth has given HRM some unique challenges: to balance short-term growth with long-term sustainability and to be locally responsive while exploiting its global scale, an effective performance management system has been implemented.

Capital:	London
Area (sq km):	244,820 (land 241,590; water 3,230)
EU membership:	since 1973
Population:	60,609,153
Languages:	English, Welsh (about 26% of the population of Wales), Scottish form of Gaelic (about 60,000 in Scotland)
Ethnic groups (in percentages):	white 92.1 (of which English 83.6, Scottish 8.6, Welsh 4.9, Northern Irish 2.9), black 2, Indian 1.8, Pakistani 1.3, mixed 1.2, other 1.6
Gross domestic product:	1.903 trillion USD (2006)
workforce (in percentages):	31.1 million (2006): agriculture 1.4; industry 18.2; services 80.4 (2006)
Export commodities:	manufactured goods, fuels, chemicals, food, beverages, tobacco

BACKGROUND: THE UK AS A BRIDGE TO THE USA

INTRODUCTION

The United Kingdom of Great Britain and Northern Ireland is a set of small islands off the north-west coast of the European continent: but it retains, as a result of its history, an importance far beyond its size. For the past few years the UK economy has been comparatively successful with low levels of unemployment and steady growth. It is a comparatively open economy, with a strong international bias.

In HRM in particular, partly because of the language, the UK is seen as something of a bridge between the USA – the 'inventor' of the concept of HRM – and the rest of Europe.

For almost a quarter of a century now, practitioners and researchers in the UK have been using the rhetoric of HRM. We have both loved and hated the concept of HRM as it has come to us from the USA. UK conceptions of HRM have been heavily influenced by theory and practice from the USA. This is perhaps not surprising: the USA has been for decades the largest and most powerful economy in the world, the UK shares a language with the USA and the stock exchange has a similarly large impact on the UK economy. The spread of US culture and US business practices has been widely heralded and, in HRM as elsewhere, there are signs of the hegemony of the US model. Prima facie evidence of the power of the US exemplar in HRM may be seen in the spread to the UK of such ideas as downsizing, contingent (flexible) working practices, and employer antagonism to trade unions.

There is an assumption among many observers that the UK is very similar to the USA and that, therefore, the UK is likely to be in the vanguard of HRM practice in Europe. This is an assumption worth exploring.

We need to be careful when discussing HRM in the UK. There is, of course, a diverse range of HRM models and practices in operation – differences between sectors, between organisations within a sector and even differences between the sites of one organisation and, at the most micro level, even between the way that individual managers deal with their subordinates. Discussing HRM in the UK, therefore, involves substantial generalisation.

CURRENT PRACTICES AND TRENDS IN HRM IN THE UK

It is worth noting a few basic and relevant facts about the UK economy before discussing HRM specifically. Patterns of ownership vary between countries. Public ownership, for example, has decreased to some extent in the UK and is now well below the level in some other European countries. However, it is still more widespread in the UK than it is in the USA. The UK is the closest country to the USA in having a 'shareholder economy' under which private enterprise is concerned with maximising short-term profits for investors rather than any broader harmony of interests.

State involvement in HRM is specific to each country. Legislation has been seen as a significant reflector of national values (Hofstede 2001) and it is no surprise therefore to find that the USA, which is characterised by high levels of individualism and comparatively low levels of uncertainty avoidance, has overall comparatively less legislative control over (or interference from, or support for) the employment relationship than is found in Europe. This is a pattern that is widely admired among UK businesses, but in practice the UK is much closer to the European situation than that in the USA. In the UK, recruitment and dismissal, the formalisation of educational certification, and quasi-legal characteristics of the industrial relations framework are all subject to legislation. There are also legislative requirements on pay, on hours of work, on forms of employment contract, rights to trade union representation, requirements to establish and operate consultation or co-determination arrangements – and a plethora of other aspects of HRM. These are all additional to those few areas, such as the legislation on equality or health and safety, which intrude on the employment relationship on both sides of the Atlantic.

In addition to the UK legislature, of course, the European Union, particularly through the Social Charter and its associated Social Action Programme, is having an increasing influence on HRM in the UK. Recent developments include restrictions on the hours that individuals can work and a requirement for larger firms to set up works' councils where employee representatives meet with senior managers on a regular basis to debate a series of subjects laid down in the legislation.

State involvement in HRM in the UK is not restricted to legislation. In broad terms, compared to the USA, the UK state has a higher involvement in underlying social security provision, a more directly interventionist role in the economy, and provides far more personnel and industrial relations services and is a more substantial employer in its own right by virtue of a more extensive government-owned sector. Although, compared to other European countries, the UK may have less state involvement, the country is, in this respect, far more European than Anglo-Saxon.

The position of the trade unions is a third core feature of the UK scene that is different from the USA. As in many other countries, trade union membership in the UK has declined: approximately one-quarter of the members of the UK working population are currently trade union members. More important, perhaps, is trade union recognition: that is, whether the employer deals with a trade union in a collective-bargaining relationship which sets terms and conditions for all or most of the employees (Morley *et al.* 1996). Most large organisations in the UK still work with trade unions on contractual issues.

Closely related to the issue of trade union recognition is the practice of employee involvement. The European Union directive requiring the establishment of employee representation committees in all organisations except the smallest has now been implemented in the UK. As elsewhere in Europe, these tend to supplement rather than supplant the union position (Brewster *et al.* 2006).

Against these background facts, let us examine HRM in the UK.

> **What is your advice for a foreign firm entering your country's market? What should managers especially care about and, what is more, be aware of?**
>
> On a day-to-day level, it is important to understand that the British tend to be closed and non-confrontational compared to some other European countries, with rather formal and direct communications – this is leavened by the use of humour, of which the British are very proud, even though it may appear inappropriate on occasion to visitors. Unlike some other countries, regulations in the UK, while not onerous, are strictly enforced.

The configuration of HRM

It has been suggested that there are major changes going on in HR departments in Britain. HR departments it is argued should be more involved with corporate strategy, focusing more on strategic issues, and with smaller departments working closely, as business partners, with line managers. More and more of the transactional work of the function should be outsourced and/or provided electronically. There is here an issue about the quality of HR professionals: unless the function can attract more of the best people, it will be unable to play the role of strategic partner. In the UK, HR is not seen as a high-status profession. In fact, although some leading UK organisations are taking some very innovative steps in these areas, the reality is that things have not changed much over the past fifteen years. Thus about half of the larger organisations in Britain have their senior HR specialist on their main decision-making board. The rhetoric has outrun the reality (Legge 2005). Despite a lot of discussion by academics, consultants and practitioners about the strategic importance of HRM, that figure has changed very little (Atterbury *et al.* 2004). Rather more have a written HR strategy but these are changing: being simplified and focused on results.

In a similar way, despite much rhetoric about the allocation of HR responsibilities to line managers, the UK remains at the bottom end of this European scale: line managers still tend to rely on their HR departments to handle or help them handle HR issues (Brewster/Larsen 2000). The debate about the growing role of line managers in HRM is widespread in the UK. However, if the notion of line management accepting greater responsibility for HRM is now received wisdom, it is not unproblematic (Brewster/Larsen 2000; Renwick/McNeil 2002). Line managers may not want this responsibility (Gennard/Kelly 1997); they may not have the time to deal with it properly; they may not have the ability to handle HR issues effectively; nor the training for it; they are often ignorant about recent

.uk

developments in thinking about HRM; they may not take a comprehensive organisational or longer term view of the topic; and they are poor at making policy in this area. In the event, much of this work is still left with the HR department.

In addition, as in much of the rest of Europe, the extent of outsourcing of HR activities, while substantial, has not changed much from its traditional levels, the use of e-HRM is still for the future in most organisations and, unsurprisingly, therefore, the size of the HR department in comparison with all the other employees has changed little (Brewster *et al.* 2006).

A few of the HR departments are making substantial changes: getting into substantial outsourcing or developing groundbreaking ideas on e-HRM. Some have service-level agreements with their line managers: their tasks and their standards of delivery are agreed and compared to the costs of providing that service – if the organisation wants them to do more, or wants to reduce the costs of the department, then the other side of the equation must change as well. But these are a minority.

HRM policies and practices

What about the practical policies and practices that UK organisations apply to their management of human resources? Briefly here we review the way that the HRM cycle (from recruiting people to their leaving) works in the UK.

Recruitment and selection

The UK is currently characterised by a tight labour market: unemployment is low and some skills very hard for companies to recruit. There is a shortage of talent and the labour market remains a challenge for recruiters. It is widely felt in the UK that recruitment and selection decisions are the most important of all managerial decisions since they are a prerequisite to the development of an effective workforce, while the costs of poor recruitment and selection can be significant and long-lasting. We consider separately: recruitment, which is concerned with attracting a group of potential candidates to apply for a given vacancy; and selection, the process of choosing the most suitable candidate for employment from the recruitment pool.

The relative merits of an internal and external labour market focus have been seen as somewhat of a 'mixed bag' by UK organisations. An internal labour market emphasis is regarded as cost-effective, both in terms of eliminating the need for external advertising/sourcing and also in terms of reducing the induction or settling-in period, and is considered good HR practice, as a positive motivator for current employees. In addition, it adds credibility to employee development initiatives. On the other hand, it limits: (a) the potential range of candidates; over-reliance on it can (b) lead to a lack of new ideas and perspectives; it has (c) the potential to increase the importance of internal politics; and it can (d) discourage those who are not selected. Reliance on internal labour markets may be most effective in periods of stability, but less so in times of disruptive change when introspection and commitment to an outmoded status quo may be dysfunctional.

The choice between sourcing internal and external candidates is particularly important in regard to management cadres. UK organisations tend to use internal sources for managerial recruitment but, nonetheless, there is a continuing increase in the use of external recruitment for managers, especially for senior managerial positions. One reason for this may be the growing competitive pressures on organisations that may force them to identify and attract 'new blood' from outside the organisation to help meet the competitive challenges facing their organisations (Atterbury *et al.* 2004).

Selection tools available to organisations range from the more traditional methods of interviews, application forms and references, to more sophisticated techniques such as psychometric tests and assessment centres. Storey (1992) suggests that developments in the realm of selection in the UK lend some support to those who propound the HRM thesis, where a key feature has been the increase in selection testing designed explicitly to assess behavioural and attitudinal characteristics.

Application forms, reference checking and interviews continue to be widely used in the UK, despite criticisms of these approaches as methods of selecting between candidates. More sophisticated selection tools, such as psychometric testing and assessment centres, are used by a significant minority (around one-quarter) of larger organisations, but the use of these techniques has traditionally been low in the UK and this has not changed much.

The nature of work

One issue which has attracted increasing attention in Britain is the issue of flexibility in labour patterns. Whether looked at from the point of view of the organisation (as a more cost-effective way of utilising labour) or from the point of view of employees (certain kinds of flexibility have some advantages, for example, working mothers) the subject has become part of the currency of HRM. Flexibility is widespread in Europe to the point where perhaps the term itself may be becoming outmoded as the notion of 'core working time' becomes less common.

The UK has around one-quarter of its workforce in part-time jobs and has seen a steady increase in the percentage of organisations making use of temporary contracts. The proportion of organisations making some use of teleworking has also increased, especially in the public sector, though its use is not widespread. The predictions made in the mid-1990s about the spread of teleworking and the effect it would have on employment and our society have proved to be overly dramatic.

Shift working is a traditional tool for providing a flexible supply of labour, not only in manufacturing and emergency services but also in service sector jobs such as those in call centres. Recent tight labour markets have led to an increase in shift working.

A key issue in relation to working time in the UK concerns hours worked. The figures may not be entirely accurate (employees tend to work much later in the southern European countries than the European Union data records, for example) but in general UK workers tend to work longer hours over a week, to do more overtime, and to work many more hours over a lifetime than most of our European colleagues. This may be related to the poor productivity of much work in the UK and a culture of 'presenteeism', but it is beginning to worry many commentators on HRM.

> **What is typical of your country in relation to the country itself (its culture, people, etc) and its economy?**
>
> The UK is more intuitive and less structured than the rest of Europe. There is a strong belief in the UK that it has less bureaucracy and is more open to entrepreneurs. It is less family oriented and there is a culture of working long hours.

Pay and rewards

National or regional level multi-employer bargaining is now rare in the UK outside the public sector. (Employers' associations in the UK are generally much weaker than elsewhere.) There remain many organisations that still bargain at the national level, especially for manual employees. The predominant level for bargaining, however, is now at the company and individual level, showing the continuing move towards the individualisation of the employment contract.

Share ownership schemes and profit-sharing were relatively widespread in the UK, but have fallen from favour recently, which reflects changes to government rules on tax relief for such schemes.

Other attempts to link rewards to performance have also come under pressure. After achieving a significant increase (though it never reached as many as one-half of even the larger organisations), the use of individual performance-related pay (PRP) has fallen back again. Despite its championing by many consultancies and some academics, some of the problems of PRP have become more apparent and, in particular, its lack of linkage to organisational success has led to its star waning.

On the other hand, the use of individual appraisal – though more perhaps now for general development and performance reasons – has become more widespread.

Training and development

On average, UK organisations spend just over 3 per cent of their labour budget on training, which is just a little above the EU average. HR development practices vary considerably by country in Europe (Tregaskis 1997; Mabey 2004). The UK provision has been much criticised by government and academics, but is probably around the European mode. In terms of training days, managers and professional staff tend to get around five days per year with other staff getting less. The averages are increasing, especially in the public sector.

Communication and consultation with employees

Some of the key questions in HRM are about communication and consultation with the workforce. Employee representation can take individual or collective forms. In the UK, the collective forms include both union-centred and non-union mechanisms. Individually, effective communication, it could be argued, is at the heart of effective HRM. It might, therefore, be expected to be increasingly common everywhere.

The EU's Works Council Directive and the desire of organisations to use as many communications channels as possible has ensured that although there has been a growth in the use of individual channels of communication in the UK, the collective channels are still widely used, among larger employers at least. Direct verbal discussions with employees and direct written mechanisms, made easier by the electronic possibilities, have increased, reflecting the necessity to increase employee commitment in order to achieve organisational success. The use of electronic communication via e-mail and intranets has increased significantly since 1999, particularly in the public sector. This increase, however, runs in parallel with the collective channels, thus supporting the argument that the two are not incompatible.

International HRM

Given the international nature of the UK economy with British people working in many UK multinational corporations (MNCs), in the subsidiaries of foreign MNCs and in organisations with substantial international sourcing or exporting, international HRM is important for the UK. Issues of coordination, shared learning (both top-down and bottom-up) and the dual and conflicting pressures of standardisation and the need to be responsive to local context and culture become critical in this context. In this international environment, a number of new roles of HR departments operating in multinational corporations are emerging based on different HRM internationalisation strategies (Sparrow/Brewster/Harris 2004).

.uk

EAPM AFFILIATE: CHARTERED INSTITUTE FOR PERSONNEL AND DEVELOPMENT (CIPD)

HISTORY OF CIPD

CIPD, today with in excess of 125,000 members, started life ninety-three years ago. It was then the Welfare Workers' Association (WWA), established in 1913, with a membership of just thirty-four. Most of the founding members were women, reflecting their representation in welfare work, concerned with the working condition of female employees in factories.

By the end of the war, there were 600 members of the WWA and at the same time firms were appointing 'labour officers' to assist in the management of recruitment, discipline, dismissal and industrial relations, particularly interpreting the complex legal frameworks. From 1917 to 1924 the association saw splinter groups set up around the country and, concerned at the fragmentation, the WWA adopted a new constitution with a branch structure. The name eventually changed to the Welfare Workers' Institute and in 1920 the first journal, *Welfare Work*, appeared. In the 1920s the numbers in membership went into decline and during this time the 'labour management' movement appeared. Labour managers were responsible for a wide range of employment policies and practices and initially were not keen to join the Institute of Industrial Welfare Workers (IIWW) with its focus on welfare until changes were made in the Institute. Eventually it was renamed the Institute of Labour Management, reflecting its changing focus.

In the USA the term 'personnel management' had been adopted by the 1920s but it was not used in the UK until the 1930s and the new name, the Institute of Personnel Management (IPM), was adopted in 1946, the decision having been deferred when war broke out in 1939. The Second World War provided a stimulus to growth in membership and by 1945 there were almost 3,000 members. In the post-war conditions of full employment, personnel work expanded greatly, particularly in industrial relations and industrial training. Remuneration policy and administration also became part of the personnel remit. In the 1950s IPM made significant developments in the areas of short training courses, publications and membership examinations. The national conference also became more training oriented.

In 1955 IPM moved towards restricting entry into full membership via examination and introduced an education scheme which could be run externally by colleges in preparation for the national exam. From the 1950s the Institute also expanded the books it published on personnel management. The 1960s were characterised by an increasing desire for IPM to be more influential on government employment policy. This was good timing because the traditionally voluntarist role of the state towards these matters was changing. National committees were formed for different areas of personnel management, contributing to the government consultations and the national debate, and they remained in place until 1992.

In the 1970s the debate began about a possible merger between the Institute of Training Officers (later the Institute of Training and Development) and the IPM. The issue remained on the agenda until 1994 when both memberships voted in favour of establishing the Institute of Personnel and Development (IPD). In the year following the establishment of IPD the new Institute had over 75,000 members and it has become the largest body of personnel and development specialists in the world. The next aspiration was chartered status and this was achieved in 2000.

CIPD TODAY

CIPD's aspiration is to lead thinking and practice in the field of people management and development, and this is reflected in all strategies and practices. CIPD aims to be a leading advocate for the profession, demonstrating through research that people management and development play a key role in delivering performance and business success. CIPD's qualifications are designed to equip professionals with the systematically learnable body of knowledge that underpins people management and development in the modern world. Careers in HR are more valued and varied than ever before, and CIPD is committed to providing professionals with the tools to continuously develop their knowledge and skills and to keep up with the changes that surround them.

Research fields and publications

CIPD is a leader of research into people management and development issues. The Institute publishes wide-ranging research reports on the range of HRM and HRD topics. Key areas of research are currently talent management, globalised HR, and human capital. Research is illustrated with practical case studies and research reports are accompanied by practical tools, guides and free summaries and factsheets on the website. CIPD has led research into HRM and HRD, both nationally and internationally, which has provided professionals with leading-edge insights into practice in a range of organisations across many sectors.

Other leading research has been in the field of international HRM, notably the impact of globalisation on the people management function and practices. The research shows how, in companies organised along global lines, HR professionals working internationally create and embed policies and practices to provide global standards and values, while taking into account local needs and diversity. Outlining practice in a range of organisations in different sectors, the research identifies the key mechanisms by which global HRM can deliver organisational capability.

Research is also ongoing into diversity, making sure it is central to an organisation's strategy and business goals. In the area of learning, training and development, the shift is from training to learning and, within that context, looking to see if there is a global learning model. In addition, groundbreaking research into issues such as reward, human capital, employee engagement, talent, technology and managing change is in progress.

CIPD produces a wide range of survey data and other research that is of value to government policy-makers and opinion-formers. CIPD responds to government consultations on proposed legal and regulatory changes and is represented on a number of government committees and task forces.

The CIPD's own magazine, *People Management*, provides members and other subscribers with the latest news and features on the management and development of people in the UK, Ireland and overseas. It also has an associated jobs service. In recent years CIPD's strategic priority has been to establish the CIPD website as a central part of the interface of the organisation with members and the wider community. Online communities enable members to share knowledge, experience and views with each other, and numbers using this facility are increasing each week.

Qualifications and conferences

CIPD offers directly or accredits others to run a wide range of courses, from one-day courses to full postgraduate professional qualifications and certificate programmes. The CIPD's professional standards are the basis for all routes that lead to CIPD professional membership. CIPD's Professional Development Scheme (PDS) forms the basis of CIPD's qualification structure and provides a clear benchmark for employers and professionals. Anyone who has completed the PDS has demonstrated a clear knowledge and understanding of how people management and development contributes to meeting the challenges of modern business management and that they can put that knowledge into practice in the real world. Chartered members have also made a commitment to their own life-long learning, demonstrating to employers that they are constantly up to date with the latest knowledge necessary to fulfil their role.

CIPD is committed to supporting professionals' learning needs, not just through the professional qualifications, but also through informal networks, at professional conferences and other events. CIPD has eight major conferences annually, the biggest being the annual conference in the north of England in October. HRD, which is held in London in April, is the Institute's biggest annual learning and development event, attracting an international audience as well as a domestic one, and CIPD will host the WFPMA World Congress at this event in April 2008.

CIPD's forty-eight branches provide members with local learning and networking opportunities, with some 500 events annually in various locations across the UK and Ireland. Branch chairs are on the CIPD Council, the governing body of the Institute. In addition to branches, CIPD runs specialist interest groups called forums which enable professionals to gain knowledge and exchange experience with other professionals.

As well as researching into international HR and LT&D issues (learning, training and development), CIPD engages in global learning and support networks for the profession. Through affiliation with the European Association for Personnel Management (EAPM), of which CIPD is a founding member, the World Federation of Personnel Management Associations (WFPMA), the European Training and Development Federation (ETDF) and the International Federation of Training and Development Organisations (IFTDO), CIPD works actively to promote the benefits of high standards of people management and development around the world.

What would you like to teach foreign HR managers? What is important for them to know in your opinion?

Most UK HR managers believe that the practical, close-to-the-business, get-on-with-it attitude of the British, rather than reliance on HR theories, would be beneficial in other European countries.

.uk

HR ACADEMIA: THE DEBATES
ABOUT HRM IN THE UK

Two books published in the USA in 1984 (Beer *et al.* 1984; Fombrun/Tichy/ Devanna 1984) heralded a new approach to what had until then been the study of personnel management: 'partly a file clerk's job, partly a housekeeping job, partly a social worker's job and partly fire-fighting to head off union trouble' (Drucker 1989: 269). These texts were the first to conceive of people as 'human resources'. Employees are a resource like any other: they 'are to be obtained cheaply, used sparingly and developed and exploited as fully as possible' (Sparrow/Hiltrop 1994). Attempts have been made to distinguish 'strategic HRM (SHRM)' from HRM generally, but it seems increasingly that definitions of HRM include, intrinsically or explicitly, the notion of a strategic approach to the subject.

Discussing British approaches to this new topic involves substantial generalisation. The many different academics studying the field like to resist being categorised. However, we can say that there are, broadly, two philosophical approaches: one accepting of and trying to replicate the US approach; and one critical of it.

Until recently, many of the academics working in the HRM field had moved across to the topic from industrial relations, as interest in that field began to wane. Some bought wholeheartedly into the notion of HRM as the study of the way that organisations manage their people, having as the objective the need to understand that process better in order to improve the success of organisations. The purpose of the study of HRM and, in particular SHRM (Fombrun/Tichy/Devanna 1984; Ulrich 1987; Wright/Snell 1991; Wright/McMahan 1992), is seen as being about generating understanding in order to improve the way that human resources are managed strategically within organisations, with the ultimate aim of improving organisational performance, as judged by its impact on the organisation's declared corporate strategy (Tichy/Fombrun/Devanna 1982; Huselid 1995), the customer (Ulrich 1989) or shareholders (Huselid 1995; Becker/Gerhart 1996; Becker *et al.* 1997). Further, it is implicit that this objective will apply in all cases.

Others, and a prestigious group of others in British academic circles, worked with a wider and more critical view, seeing HRM as being about the way that people were managed, including a role for regional and national governments, etc., and having as the objective the need to understand the process in order to be able to show that the interests of the employees, or society in general, were not being well served by these organisations (e.g. Guest 1990; Keenoy 1990; Brewster 1999; Legge 2005). Thus, for example, Guest (1990) argued that assumptions of business freedom and autonomy are peculiarly US and are related to the US view of their country as a land of opportunity that rewards success. In HRM, this translates into a view that business owners should be as free as possible to run their businesses the way that they want and that individuals have to take individual responsibility for their situation. This culture of individualism is clearly discernible in the thinking that underpins North American notions of reward systems, with their emphasis on individual performance-based rewards and the US 'hire-and-fire' mentality. In the UK the situation is different, with a widespread feeling that businesses need to be controlled and to treat their employees in a socially responsible way.

Given the differences in what are often assumed to be similar situations, it is worth testing the assumption that HRM in the UK covers the same ground as the concept developed in the USA. In the UK four issues seem to distinguish the way that HRM is conceived and researched by academic commentators:

- the contested nature of the concept (what we are studying);
- the levels at which it can be applied (the range of our studies);
- the focus (what it aims to do); and hence
- the research paradigm.

What are you and our fellow-countrymen extraordinarily proud of with respect to HRM?

The British are proud of being pragmatic, having a stronger affinity with business and practice than with theory. There is a focus on dealing with underperformance. The UK provides opportunities for considerable career flexibility.

THE NATURE OF HRM

HRM is a subject without an agreed definition. The confusion in the appropriate subject matter for HRM has been noted by many UK commentators (e.g. Storey 1992; Legge 2005). Despite the fact that identification of specific activities and policies is central to theoretical approaches to HRM (Weber/Kabst 2004) there is no agreed list of what HRM covers. Some subjects seem to be included in most lists of the topics covered by HRM – resourcing, development, reward – but other topics may or may not be included. Thus, subjects like employee participation, trade union relationships, health and safety, equal opportunities, flexible working, career progression, work design and the countless combinations of HR practices are included in some conceptions of HRM and ignored in others.

US notions of what constitutes 'good' HRM tend to coalesce around the concept of 'high-performance work systems'. These have been characterised by the US Department of Labor (1993) as having certain clear characteristics: careful and extensive systems for recruitment, selection and training; formal systems for sharing information with the individuals who work in the organisation; clear job design; local-level participation procedures; monitoring of attitudes; performance appraisals; properly functioning grievance procedures; and promotion and compensation schemes that provide for the recognition and financial rewarding of high-performing members of the workforce. Alongside similar lists, which all differ to some degree, the Department of Labor list may be taken as an exemplar of the universalist paradigm: most US writers would be broadly in agreement with such a list.

In the UK much of such a list is seen as up for debate. The list is probably commonly accepted among the HRM leaders of most larger international UK firms, but may not be so widely accepted elsewhere. In addition, the terms may have different meanings. For example, 'formal systems for sharing information with individuals' at their workplaces in the US context are significantly different from sharing information at the strategic level with trade union representatives skilled in debating the organisational strategy – a common requirement in at least larger UK firms, where both direct communication to employees and representative communication to trade unions are practised. Clear job design (which can presumably be linked with the performance appraisal and incentive schemes for the individual job holder) can be inimical to the need for flexibility, teamwork and responsiveness to the pace of change seen as important in the debates in the UK.

Common to this debate is the assumption that HRM, and particularly SHRM, is concerned with the aims and actions of management within the organisation. Perhaps in a country like the USA which has as an avowed aim of most politicians the objective of 'freeing business from outside interference', it makes sense to develop a vision of HRM which takes as its scope the policies and practices of management. Researchers in the UK, however, find that the universalist paradigm ironically excludes much of the work of HR specialists and many of the issues that are vital for the organisation – areas such as compliance, equal opportunities, trade union relationships and dealing with government, for example. They are often critical of the universalist model of HRM common in the USA (e.g. Guest 1990; Brewster 1999; Legge 2005).

HRM in the USA typically focuses on the company. For at least the 'critical' school of academics in the UK the nature of HRM is broader, providing better explanations of the potential differences in views about the topic and a better fit with the concerns of the specialists, by including national institutional and cultural issues such as the trade union movement, national legislation and labour markets as not just external influences but as part of the topic.

THE LEVEL OF HRM

A second key question concerns the levels of HRM. As Kochan/Batt/Dyer (1992) and Locke/Piore/Kochan (1995) have pointed out, cross-national comparisons may be made at various levels. We can use the analogy of a telescope (Brewster 1995): with each turn of the screw things that seemed similar are brought into sharper focus so that we can distinguish between, say, the forest and the fields, then with another turn between one tree and another, and then between one leaf and another. Each view is accurate; each blurs some objects and clarifies others; each helps us to see some similarities and some differences.

406

The US tradition works with the organisational or the sub-organisational (e.g. business unit) level of analysis. UK researchers have assumed that HRM can apply at a variety of levels, i.e. that the scope is not restricted to the organisational or sub-organisational level. Thus, there are discussions of the strategic human resource management policies of the EU or of particular governments or sectors. Debates about HRM policies between groups of EU member states are often lively. National governments have HRM policies (for example, reducing unemployment, encouraging flexible working practices) and indeed, some of the strategy literature has located the economic success of organisations, and economies, at the national level (see, for example, Porter 1990). Within a country, specific areas may have HRM policies and practices (raising training standards to attract inward investment, establishing local employment opportunities, etc.). All these levels, which might be seen in much of the universalist tradition as external factors impinging upon HRM, are seen in Europe as within the scope of HRM (Brewster 1995). And at the organisational level, academics in the UK have a long tradition of plant- or site-level, rather than company-level, research – adapted from the industrial relations tradition.

THE FOCUS OF HRM

As indicated, the focus of academic work in HRM in the UK is not always on analysing the management of people as a contributor to finding more cost-effective ways work can be done, in order to ensure that the top management's organisational objectives are met. The UK has a strong tradition of neo-Marxist theorizing (e.g. Friedman 1977; Hyman 1987) that has focused on managerial approaches to controlling potential dissidence. Thus, questions of 'fit' between the organisation's corporate strategy and its HRM are open to challenge at both ends. While not always within the influence of this stream of writing, the willingness to challenge managerial objectives and actions remains relevant. In general terms, UK researchers and writers have been more critical of the concept of HRM than the US experts.

The HRM performance-linked literature is a good example. Most of the critique of that literature from the USA has been concerned with weaknesses in the empirical or statistical data (Huselid/Becker 1996; Rogers/Wright 1998; Gerhart 1999; 2005; Cappelli/Newmark 2001). The critiques of the concept in the UK have tended to be more wide-ranging, examining the assumptions of universalism, of the inevitable 'goodness' of the link and the effects on those other than managers in the system (Guest 1997; Marchington/Grugulis 2000; Guest et al. 2003).

THE RESEARCH PARADIGM

Most researchers in the UK operate within a contextual paradigm. This is not to deny, of course, that there is a substantial minority of academic HRM researchers

407

working from the company perspective. But many work from the contextual paradigm, which is idiographic, searching for an overall understanding of what is contextually unique and why. The researchers are focused on understanding what is different between and within HRM in various contexts and what the antecedents of those differences are. It is the explanations that matter – any link to company performance, for example, is secondary. It is assumed that societies, governments or regions can have HRM policies and practices as well as companies. At the level of the organisation (not firm – public sector and not-for-profit organisations are also included) the organisation's objectives (and therefore its strategy) are not necessarily assumed to be 'good' either for the organisation or for society. There are plenty of examples where this is clearly not the case. Nor, in this paradigm, is there any assumption that the interests of everyone in the organisation will be the same or any expectation that an organisation will have a strategy that people within the organisation will support. Employees and the unions have a different perspective to the management team (Keenoy 1990; Storey 1992; Purcell/Ahlstrand 1994; Turner/Morley 1995). Even within the management team there may be different interests and views (Hyman 1987). These, and their impact on HRM, are issues for empirical study. As a contributor to explanation, this paradigm emphasises external factors such as ownership structures, labour markets, the role of the state and trade union organisation as well as the actions of the management within an organisation.

Methodologically, the research mechanisms used are likely to be inductive. Theory is drawn from an accumulation of data collected or gathered in a less directed (or constrained) manner than would be the case under the universalist paradigm. Research traditions are different: focused less upon testing and prediction and more upon the collection of evidence. There is an assumption that if things are important they should be studied, even if testable prediction is not possible or the resultant data are complex and unclear. The policies and practices of the 'leading-edge' companies (something of a value-laden term in itself) which are the focus of much HRM research and literature in the USA are of less interest to many UK researchers than identifying the way labour markets work and what the more typical organisations are doing. Much more work is, therefore, based on finding out and understanding what is happening: hence there is a stronger tradition of detailed idiographic case studies and, conversely, of large-scale survey work, both of which lend themselves to analyses of the different stakeholders and the environmental complexity of organisations. Similarly, HRM research in the UK is more often focused on the services sector or the public or not-for-profit sectors of employment than is the case for the USA.

We should also note, for completeness, that within the UK there is a diverse range of HRM models and practices in operation – differences between sectors, between organisations within a sector and even differences between the sites of one organisation and, at the most micro level, even between the way individual managers deal with their subordinates.

THE NATIONAL CONTEXT OF HRM

Clearly the practice of HRM cannot be divorced from its institutional context or the way the subject is conceived. The North American model may be a viable possibility for US organisations because of the context within which they operate. Whether it can – or should – be replicated in the UK context is a matter of empirical evidence and opinion.

Different models of HRM have been offered by UK researchers – sometimes working with colleagues from elsewhere (Thurley/Wirdenius 1991; Sparrow/Hiltrop 1994). What they have in common is the need to adopt a multi-level view of the actors in the system and to see business strategy, HR strategy and HR practice located within an environment of national culture, national legislation, state involvement and trade union representation. These factors are seen as part of HRM and not merely as antecedents to it.

More generally, the representative data support theoretical (Smith/Meiskins 1995) and case study evidence (Ferner/Quintanilla/Varul 2001) which indicated the complexity of these issues, the national embeddedness of HRM practices and the dynamic nature of evolving national business systems. Beyond the empirical evidence of difference, compared to the USA, the country of origin of HRM, there are conceptual differences in the way HRM is viewed in the UK. The more critical approach to HRM found in much of the UK literature adds an extra dimension to our knowledge of HRM.

CURRENT ISSUES IN HRM RESEARCH IN THE UK

What are the leading topics for recent HRM research in the UK? The following outlines select just some of the many thousands of projects carried out over the past few years.

The future of work is a subject that began exercising researchers when the UK had extensive unemployment, but has retained its fascination since then. The future of work (or, more strictly speaking, what can be extrapolated from recent trends) has been the focus of extensive research in the UK (www.leeds.ac.uk/esrcfutureofwork).

The HRM–performance link is one that is explored by both the organisational effectiveness and more critical researchers. Purcell and his colleagues (e.g. Kinnie et al. 2005), for example, have explored the links within workplaces. More general analyses have come from Guest (1997), Guest et al. (2003) and Wood (1989). The organisational effectiveness researchers have also spent considerable time, usually, in line with the UK tradition, at workplace level, exploring the notion of a high-performance work system (HPW) (Wood 1999).

Internationalisation or globalisation of HRM is also a significant and developing issue. Britain is one of the most internationally integrated economies. Understanding the effects of this on HRM, therefore, becomes critical.

Hence, there is a significant amount of research being carried out on all aspects of international HRM. There is now a substantial and growing literature in the area (including, for example, CIPD-funded work such as Sparrow/Brewster/ Harris 2004).

There has been a rising tide of interest in the UK in the notion of the psychological contract between employees and their organisations. Employers, consultants and academics are all involved in important projects exploring ways in which engagement and commitment of employees can be achieved through better understanding of the psychological contract.

One of the newer issues in UK HRM is coaching and this is, concomitantly, an area that is receiving increasing attention from researchers. The CIPD is devoting considerable attention and resources to this issue.

As in the USA, and perhaps many other countries, the concept of talent management has been the subject of much practical and academic work. Arguably, in a time of very tight labour markets in the UK, this is absorbing more time from senior HR managers than any other subject.

BEST-PRACTICE CASE: VODAFONE – PERFORMANCE MANAGEMENT IN A TELECOMMUNICATIONS COMPANY

In just twenty years the mobile telecommunications industry has grown into one of the largest and most dynamic sectors in the world. Twenty years ago mobile phones were a status symbol for the few. Today they are a 'must have' of the many. Twenty years ago mobile phones were bulky, barely mobile, expensive and offered little functionality other than voice. Today mobile phones are small, feature-rich and beautifully put together. In an industry that has gone through huge change and massive growth, Vodafone has been at the forefront. It is a young company with a passion for innovation and a can-do attitude that has made it the world's leading telecommunications company.

This history of explosive growth in customer numbers and global reach has given Vodafone some unique HRM challenges. It has meant balancing short-term growth with long-term sustainability and stability. It has meant being locally responsive to its customers and its people while exploiting its global scale and scope. Effective performance management has been at the centre of this challenge, and this case study will highlight these challenges and how Vodafone has overcome them. Please bear in mind that the information was correct at the time of writing in May 2006. Since then there have been a few changes. Nevertheless, the case study shows how the company coped with the main challenges.

> **In a few words, what would you say is the one fundamental strategic competitive advantage your country offers compared to other places?**
>
> A flexible and cosmopolitan workforce.

HISTORY OF VODAFONE

Vodafone was founded in 1982 when Sir Gerald Whent, Chairman of Racal Radio Group, persuaded Racal to bid for the first private sector UK cellular licence. Vodafone was established as a subsidiary of Racal and its new business name was chosen to reflect both the provision of VOice and DAta services over mobile phones. Vodafone launched the first UK analogue network and on 1 January 1985 the first call was made from London to Newbury. Racal-Vodafone Telecommunications plc was floated on the London and New York Stock Exchanges in 1988 and within a year it had 500,000 customers.

Racal and Vodafone demerged in 1991 and in the same year Vodafone made the first international roaming call with Finland and launched the UK's first digital mobile service (GSM). Vodafone also began its global expansion, forming partnerships in South Africa, Germany, Australia, Fiji and Greece. Vodafone grew

411

at an amazing rate from four million customers in 1997 to 100 million by 2003. A lot of this growth came through mergers and acquisitions which established Vodafone as a global player. These included Airtouch in the USA in 1999 and Mannesmann in Germany in 2000. This continued with acquisitions in India, South Africa, Romania, the Czech Republic and Turkey in 2005/6. Vodafone now has equity stakes in mobile networks in twenty-seven countries across five continents, strategic partnerships in another thirty-one countries, over 170 million proportionate customers and 60,000 employees. Based on market capitalisation it is one of the world's largest companies.

HR STRUCTURE

Explosive growth has created a huge challenge in ensuring that the basic HR issues required for the future stability and success of the organisation are dealt with effectively when enthusiastic action-oriented managers and specialists are focused on short-term delivery. HR has also been central to meeting the challenge of balancing Vodafone's global scale and scope with the need to be locally responsive. As a result HR has evolved through several phases over the past twenty years and is structured to reflect the balance between local and global.

HR operates at three levels: global, regional and local. At the global level Group HR sets the Group's people strategy and designs and owns Group HR policies, frameworks and HR IT systems including performance management. Group HR owns talent management and leadership development, for the Board, senior directors and high potentials, and Vodafone's cultural framework. It maintains Vodafone's interfaces with the external world and provides development for the global HR community.

There are two regions within Vodafone reflecting the different business models in emerging growth markets in Africa, Asia and eastern Europe and more mature markets, especially those in western Europe. These regions are span breakers providing two-way visibility and feedback between operating companies (OpCos) and Group, driving change management and integration in each region, capturing and sharing best practice across the OpCos and with Group, and ensuring implementation happens in OpCos in line with global policies and frameworks. They also own talent management and leadership development for directors and high potentials in their relevant OpCos. The OpCos are responsible for operationalising people strategy, policies and frameworks, and providing day-to-day HR support, and talent management for the majority of the people below director level.

This structure works effectively because of the strong relationships between the key players that are fostered through regular meetings and conferences and because of the clear but light-touch governance structure and processes. This ensures that all the players understand where decision-making lies but are also involved in designing and developing global approaches.

HR PRINCIPLES

The organisational design for HR is based on key principles which ensure that HR is playing a strategic role as a true business partner as well as delivering the core HR services such as recruiting, induction, training and development, reward and recognition and of course performance management.

The critical principle is that HR at Vodafone is a customer service organisation. Vodafone's leaders and people are its customers, not HR itself. Many HR functions make the mistake of seeing their own processes as an end in themselves. In Vodafone the priority as a business partner is to influence and achieve the business outcomes set by its customers, the business. This means trying to anticipate and minimise conflicts between different customers, prioritising services, tools and policies that are required to run Vodafone as a truly global business and clearly defining the split of responsibility between Group, regional and OpCo HR. HR activities remain local unless common policies and practices or centralisation of provision provide a demonstrable benefit to customers.

In addition to these principles, if HR is to be close to its customer, it needs to be staffed with people with a mix of backgrounds. At Vodafone this means balancing functional specialists with people, including the new Group HRD (formerly CEO for the Asia-Pacific region), with a strong line background who understand the pressures of the business and the need to provide simple, effective tools to the people managers.

HR PROJECTS

At the start of 2005 this clarity did not exist, and the pace of growth and number of acquisitions had resulted in a proliferation and duplication of HR activities, all well meaning, but in danger of overloading the business and diverting attention from the customer. The new Group HRD established a project prioritisation process, working closely with line customers especially the executive committee (ExCo) that resulted in nearly 250 HR projects being narrowed down to seven.

International mobility

Historically international mobility was managed by Group compensation and benefits and the main focus was on the cost element of a move as opposed to ensuring the right people were sent overseas. As a result there was no integrated link to developing talent and careers. A global business needs effective international mobility processes and policies that encourage its best people to pursue an international career. Over the past eighteen months Vodafone has been at the forefront of creating a new approach to ensure that people on secondment, their families and their host and home countries have a great experience, with the result that Vodafone's best people seek global career opportunities. As a result Vodafone is more choosy about who moves, focusing on those who have been identified as successors for key roles.

413

Internal resourcing

Vodafone seeks to recruit internally for 70 per cent of roles, recognising the importance of cultural fit as well as functional expertise. In the past this was not coordinated. This project has created an internal resourcing forum held monthly where internal recruiters can meet to share vacancies and match them with high-potential internal candidates.

Assessment methodologies for future leaders

As Vodafone continues to grow, and face more demanding markets and customers, so leadership becomes more and more important. This project has established a clear model for what effective leaders in Vodafone need to do and how they should behave. It is not a generic model but has been developed to specifically address the challenges that Vodafone faces and to reflect its internal culture and external brand. In turn this has been used to create an assessment methodology that looks not only at individual style and competence but also at organisational climate and deeper personal values and motives. This methodology is used in all leadership appointments to ensure that all recruits into leadership positions fit Vodafone's style. The same assessment methodology has also been used to provide developmental feedback for all senior leaders that in turn has been used to create and deliver effective individualised leadership development activities.

Functional academies

As the demographic time bomb begins to have an effect and the business continues to grow, Vodafone, like many businesses, faces an increased challenge in finding people with the relevant functional skills in technology and customer-facing areas. This project has created a common framework to help individuals, within a common functional job family, manage their careers and development through a portal that gives them access to common local and global content.

Broad-banding

Since much of Vodafone's growth has been through acquisition the business found itself with numerous grading structures which made it difficult to move people between OpCos. This project established and embedded a common grading structure based on broad bands that enabled common compensation and benefits approaches, and development board and succession planning processes that support international mobility.

Building a high performance culture

Vodafone has a strong customer brand. This stands for three things that its customers should expect when dealing with Vodafone: red which stands for passion, warmth and optimism; rock solid which stands for reliability, quality and integrity; and restless which stands for continuous improvement, best-in-class quality, a willingness to rewrite the rules and a challenger spirit. This project has put in place a culture change programme which engages each OpCo in ensuring that the customer experience provided by every person in Vodafone matches the expectation customers have.

Performance management

The final and key project and the focus for this case study is performance management. This is central to all people processes and was the number one priority. The next few pages outline the rationale behind the decision to create a global process, the need to reflect our global HR approach by balancing the global and the local, the details of the process and, most importantly, how Vodafone has persuaded line managers of the importance of the process and developed their commitment, confidence and competence.

PERFORMANCE MANAGEMENT

Three years ago, as a result of the large number of acquisitions, Vodafone had a plethora of different performance management processes and systems. These ranged from extremely sophisticated IT-enabled processes in some OpCos to the absence of formal performance management in others. Over the past two years Vodafone has piloted and then implemented a single global process and system. This has resulted in 100 per cent completion rates in every OpCo, so that every employee has clear goals, honest, open feedback about their performance, and coaching and developmental support in their roles and for their careers. Surveys show employees have greater clarity about how their roles and day-to-day actions fit with Vodafone's global strategy and local plans, and are receiving more feedback and coaching.

The rationale

A small global team of people, primarily from OpCos, was formed in early 2004 to design and deliver a global process. In researching successful performance management processes around the world from within Vodafone and from external benchmarks the team identified several critical success factors. These were reflected in the key design principles. The most important of these was to recognise that performance management is not an HR process. The driver behind the process was not to create more HR data but to create a high-performing customer-focused organisation. In Vodafone, performance management is therefore a business process facilitated by HR but owned by the line. It is clearly a people process since a high-performing organisation is dependent on motivated people, aligned with group strategy and values, delivering high performance. It also focuses on the majority of motivated people recognising high performance but ensuring that there are also clear consequences for poor performance and behaviour.

Everyone in Vodafone recognised these principles but many asked why Vodafone needed a global process when many OpCos had their own successful local processes and systems. The key was to recognise that performance management is a key element in creating a common approach and feel to Vodafone's management culture, reflecting its values and brand. In addition, in a global business it is an underpinning for matrix working, provides consistent, calibrated ratings as a key input to global talent review boards and gives every employee clarity on what matters to Vodafone.

This provided a rationale at the organisational level; but managers needed to be convinced that they should give time and effort to performance management. For them it helps build a team focused on what they have to do to deliver high performance and is a key to building the capability of their team over time. It supports the development of their skills to manage people effectively and is a tool for feedback and continuous improvement. A global process also gives them access to Vodafone's global talent pool, making it easier to bring in and manage people from other OpCos. In a matrix environment it is also a foundation for remote management. The key for managers was to provide effective, simple, consistent tools to help them manage performance. Once again many HR functions have gone wrong by focusing on their own needs and designing beautiful, elegant processes and systems that do a great job for HR but put an unacceptable burden on busy and stressed line managers. In one example from another organisation the team found a system that required every manager to complete 136 boxes in an online tool for every one of their reports. In this organisation managers used to meet over coffee to share the latest way to short-cut the system. From day one, in the words of Einstein, 'simple enough but no simpler' became critical in designing a successful process.

From the research, individual ownership of performance was clearly important. The manager can provide direction and support but it is the individual who decides how much discretionary effort he/she will put into the job. Having given managers a rationale it was also critical to convince employees of the importance of performance management. For individuals the process provides clarity about and influence over their own goals and contribution to the business. It gives them regular, open feedback on performance with no surprises and ongoing coaching and career development. It provides visibility for their performance and contribution. In a global business it supports international careers and gives every employee a sense of being part of Vodafone. Once again it was also important to give everyone a simple, common process.

The final key stakeholders who needed to be convinced were the HR functions across Vodafone, many of whom already had great processes. One of Vodafone's six strategic goals is to build the 'best global Vodafone team'. Performance management is the key to delivering this and the foundation for people processes in the organisation. It ensures that managers take responsibility for managing their people. It is the foundation of the global employee career proposition and a key support for international mobility. As with the other stakeholders it was also important to meet HR's day-to-day needs so the focus has been on implementation not reinvention, reducing process and system costs. It is also important for all concerned that once the new system was developed changes be kept to a minimum. There is nothing more annoying to line managers than, just when they are used to a new process and system, HR has another brainwave and changes it.

The design principles and great dialogues

As outlined above, in designing the process the real challenge was to produce a high-performing organisation, not a performance management process. This is about mindsets more than processes. The centre of the process is therefore a mandatory performance dialogue between a line manager and his/her people to create this high-performance mindset. The focus throughout is on the dialogue not the process, the form or the system. This dialogue is driven by the individual to relieve managers' workloads and to ensure that individuals are committed to the process and their own performance. This commitment is also dependent on them feeling the process is fair and transparent and delivered in a motivational atmosphere. This means that the skills of managers in holding effective dialogues are critical; which in turn means providing training for all managers and individuals.

A good dialogue is not a quick conversation in the corridor. Managers are expected to set aside a minimum of one hour for the performance dialogue and ensure they are fully prepared. The performance dialogue should be a two-way conversation where the manager not only talks about goals and provides feedback and coaching, but the individual also provides feedback on the manager's performance. Managers should be clear about what is acceptable and what is not and deal with underperformance, supporting underperformers with feedback and coaching. If performance does not improve over time, appropriate action needs to be taken by the manager.

To get the most out of the dialogue, the manager and individual should spend time thinking and preparing for it. Once the dialogue has started, both should endeavour to be attentive, totally focused on the dialogue, spending as much time listening as speaking. They should both be open to feedback. The manager should give specific feedback on behaviour with clear examples as opposed to criticising personality. They should both be open to learning. It is important that both understand what has been learned and how it can be applied in future to improve performance. The dialogue needs to be aligned to Vodafone's values. These are a passion for customers, people, results and the world around us. This should be reflected in the dialogue. It needs to focus not only on performance against business goals, the what, but also on how these goals have been delivered, the how. The dialogue should be encouraging. The focus should be on how to build on the individual's strengths and should be conclusive, leading to concrete outcomes that can be followed through. Above everything, Vodafone wants its managers to hold a deep personal dialogue that focuses as much on the person's dreams, engaging them emotionally, as it focuses on hard measures and key performance indicators (KPIs). It is the magic of a good dialogue which will engage and motivate.

In the rationale we have already outlined some key principles, particularly the focus on the business. This means ensuring that individual goals are aligned to the business and strong links have been made to the high-level strategic and financial planning processes. The calendars of all three processes have been aligned, so once detailed budgets are agreed in February individual goals can be cascaded in March to the top teams in each OpCo and then in April and May to the rest of the organisation.

In addition, the process needs to be flexible, to reflect changing goals during the year. Most organisations, especially ones as dynamic and fast moving as Vodafone, do not stand still for a year for the sake of a system. The process needs to focus on continually improving the organisation, not setting standards in stone. Vodafone's customers are always demanding more, so the performance management process needs to demand more of its people.

> **What would you say one ought not to do? What are the 'don'ts' in your country?**
>
> Writing policies does not create change: that happens through explaining and involving people in why change is necessary and how it will work.

Global versus local

We have already noted the importance in a business like Vodafone of balancing the local and the global. The performance management process has been designed to be globally consistent while reflecting local differences. Some things have been globally mandated. The performance dialogue process itself must be rolled out to all employees at the beginning of the financial year in April and all dialogues have to be completed by 31 May. The core process is mandated globally including the rating scale, definitions, distribution guidelines, guidelines on how ratings are measured, the structure and content of the form and the use of, and the detailed language of, Vodafone's competency framework (known as the performance drivers). Where there are local legal or cultural issues there is flexibility including how goals are cascaded, local exceptions for timings for specific functions to reflect local needs, the use of customer feedback, links to reward and development and the measurement of the process.

The core technology system is mandatory but Vodafone has used a rules-based workflow tool that allows local technology adaptations to reflect different cultural and legal needs. It has also been translated into Albanian, Dutch, German, Greek, Hungarian, Italian, Portuguese and Spanish.

All participants are trained and Group has provided common global materials, but the delivery of the training is localised to fit local culture and language.

Similarly, communications plans and the performance dialogue brand have been set globally but the delivery of communications and stakeholder management is local.

The process

The focus is on the dialogue but there are several elements that sit around it. Prior to the dialogue the individual is expected to prepare a report, referring to his/her role profile to reflect on their core responsibilities, seeking feedback from customers and identifying their development needs and aspirations.

In parallel the manager also prepares a report, reflecting on the individual's performance but also working with peers and line manager to establish goals and calibrated ratings for the team. Goals need to be set to reflect what Vodafone, the relevant business unit and team are trying to achieve so that individuals have a clear sense not only of what they have to do but also why they have to do it and where it fits with the bigger picture. This needs to be done collectively by each business unit management team.

In addition, it is mandatory that a team calibration takes place prior to the performance dialogue. Each manager prepares ratings for his/her team that can be supported with fact-based information and examples including customer feedback where relevant. Calibration looks across the organisation and bands: Group monitors the Vodafone-wide distribution. These team sessions have been very effective in ensuring that managers evaluate their teams properly and become more effective people managers, there is a greater shared knowledge of the people in the group/function, facilitating internal mobility and there is a realistic distribution of performance ratings. It should be stressed that the distribution curve is a guideline and is not intended to force individuals into incorrect ratings.

This distribution has at its centre a 'good' rating which requires that all goals are met or exceeded and the performance drivers are demonstrated consistently and sometimes at a higher level. The distribution curve looks for 85 per cent of people to be rated good or above. This might sound like a tough standard but setting the middle rating as average institutionalises underperformance against goals. Since goals are cascaded out of the detailed budgets, this in turn institutionalises underperformance against plan and Vodafone will disappoint its shareholders. To repeat, the objective of the process is to deliver high performance, so in Vodafone the bar of what is acceptable is set high.

Once these things have been completed, the individual books a dialogue with his/her line boss. This looks initially at the previous year, reviewing his/her performance against last year's goals and agreeing a rating for what needs to be done; reviewing his/her performance against the performance drivers and agreeing a rating for how it should be done; and then agreeing an overall performance rating. In addition, this review looks back at progress against individual development goals, individual aspirations and mobility. After the dialogue (never during) this is entered on a simple one-page online form that goes to the line manager and second line manager for comment and approval. The second part of the meeting is to look at the next year and agree SMART (an acronym of specific, measurable, achievable, relevant, timebound) goals, that are aligned with Vodafone's strategy, and the individual's personal development goals. Once again these are entered on to a very simple form that is then carried over to the next year. Managers are encouraged to spread the dialogue over two meetings to provide enough time to focus on development as well as performance, but it is recognised that this depends on the number of direct reports.

At mid-year there is also a mandatory interim dialogue where progress is monitored, though ratings are not given. It must be stressed that while the dialogue meeting is the centre-piece it is not the end of the process. Performance management is not a meeting – it is a continuous dialogue between the manager and the individual. Managers are encouraged to continue to give feedback throughout the year to ensure that individuals can do whatever is required to improve their performance. It is a nonsense when people have to wait 364 days to give feedback because that is when the next performance management meeting is. Once again it is important to stress that this is not an HR process but the most basic of good management practices.

Performance management is the centre of a holistic approach to HRM. The outputs of the performance dialogues are used to drive reward, though the methodology (base vs. bonus, percentages, etc.) is set locally. The ratings, aspirations and mobility data are fed into the talent review process to establish succession plans and career moves. The development goals are analysed to identify common themes and plan in combination with top-down strategic development needs, organisational development plans and learning interventions.

Engaging line managers

As we have noted, if the dialogue is the core, then it is not the process or system that drives success. Success is dependent on managers' competence (their ability to hold a motivational conversation), their commitment (their willingness to give time and effort to it) and their confidence (their belief that they can deal with difficult situations, especially the consequences of underperformance). This was the biggest challenge, since many line managers had not always seen value in the local performance management processes. In the past many managers had seen it as an HR process that was not relevant for them. Functional managers and specialists in particular did not feel that managing performance was a core part of their job. They did not feel that performance management actually impacted on performance. In many cases, when they looked further up the organisation they saw that their leaders were not carrying out the process. As a result they used the excuse that they were too busy and did not set aside time to sit down with their people. In the original planning stage the team recognised that addressing managers' skills and attitudes was not down to communications alone but required Vodafone to influence them in many different ways, locally and globally, using high-quality branded materials, extensive communications, role-modelling by senior leaders, training, clear measures of success and a simple system.

Communications

A performance dialogue needs more than a form and an e-mail. People need communications that contain key messages that engage them not just intellectually but also emotionally. These need to use multiple-media types since different people respond to different approaches. Starting six months before and throughout the roll-out there was an extensive communications strategy. Every OpCo internal communications team received a communications toolkit on DVD with images, templates, posters, guidelines on look and feel and messaging that could be reused locally. At the centre of these materials is a set of guidelines, short-cut sheets and user guides that are simple and easy to use. These global templates and materials were created to provide a common look and feel, which reinforced the red, rock-solid and restless brand. They save design costs but can be amended locally to fit local cultures and languages. They lean towards pictures, not words, and are in an electronic format that allows redesign and translation.

Globally there were articles in *Vodafone Life!* (the internal newspaper received by every employee) and *Business Life* (the newsletter for all managers used for employee briefings), a *VTV* programme (Vodafone's online global TV channel), *Arun's corner* (the CEO's monthly e-mail to all employees), the intranet and an MMS message sent to employees' mobile phones.

Branding

The dialogue brand is an important part of this communication. Dialogue is not a word in common usage but it works well in different languages, so it could be used to create a specific meaning. The word comes from the Greek *dialogos*: 'dia' meaning 'through' and 'logos' meaning 'the word' – 'through the word'. Dialogue is thus about two people creating greater understanding through sharing information. Most traditional performance discussions are like a game where one party wins and the other loses, while the winning in the dialogue is when two people reach a greater understanding that integrates both participants' views.

Role-modelling

Research shows that effective role-modelling from senior people is one of the most important factors in ensuring that line managers are committed to effective performance management. It was essential that Vodafone's senior leaders bought into and were fully committed to this. The first meeting the team held was with the CEO who, without prompting, talked through not only the importance to the organisation of performance management but also his personal commitment to holding one-to-one meetings with every one of his direct reports. He also ensured

421

that there were clear links between individual performance management and business unit performance management through the PQR (Performance and Quality Reviews) process. Together with his colleagues he created a video where the leadership team spoke about their personal commitments and this was used in all employee training together with local videos from the relevant leadership teams. In each OpCo processes were put in place to ensure that those managers who did not manage performance effectively were helped to ensure that they did so. As Gene Kranz, the mission controller, said in the film *Apollo 13*, Vodafone was clear that 'failure is not an option'!

Champions

Role-modelling came from peers as well as senior leaders. New Zealand had an example of best practice. Local line managers had acted as champions for their 'I Goal' process (the old performance management process in New Zealand) and coached their colleagues in the process and the behaviours. This was very powerful since it encouraged passionate managers, already practising performance management, to mentor/coach their peers, increased credibility and buy-in of performance management as a valuable business tool, offered on-the-spot front-line support on a daily basis, increased the rate of upskilling/uptake of performance management practices and increased the relevance of and application to specific business unit needs. This was adopted globally, though with local flexibility as to whether to apply it. Group provided materials to support it. Where used it was key to building the confidence of all participants in the process.

Measurement

Vodafone needed to show that performance management will make a difference. Vodafone holds a regular global employee opinion survey. Several questions from the global employee survey already measured the impact of the process in terms of people having clear goals linked to Vodafone's strategy, regular feedback, coaching and personal development. These provided a good benchmark and tracker of success. Vodafone developed a simple online survey completed by individuals on their line boss using these questions and a few on the quality of the dialogue (ten in total) which could be used at an organisational level to measure the impact of the process and at an individual level to provide developmental feedback for every manager. This was also used locally to recognise managers who do it well (or not). In addition, Vodafone monitored the percentage of performance dialogues completed and feedback on the tool and the process. Each year a highly interactive and participative (Power Point has been banned!) workshop is held with representatives from every OpCo to reflect on experience, draw key conclusions and plan to do it better the following year. Prior to these workshops every OpCo holds focus groups to ensure that the voice of the customers, leaders, managers and employees is listened to.

HR buy-in

It is essential that the whole HR team bought into the new global approach and become 'ambassadors'. The original core design team went through an exhaustive process of involving the HR community from day one to take their needs into account. In every OpCo the process began with detailed briefings for every HR person to ensure that they fully understood the rationale and bought into the process.

Technology

Technology can drive ease of use and facilitate the tracking of completion rates but it is an enable, not the end goal. Working with the internal IT team Vodafone developed a global technology solution based on a workflow and rules engine that is being used across Vodafone as a process management tool. If the dialogue is the critical success factor, then it was important that the system did not drive the process. It was also critical to keep the system as simple and intuitive as possible.

Line manager skills

As noted earlier, the success of performance management depends on the competence, confidence and commitment of line managers in carrying out an effective performance dialogue. Ultimately the thing that will drive competence is to provide development not just in the process but also in the behaviours. A training group was created with involvement from all OpCos to develop a common approach to these issues and to the training. The outputs from the group dealt with two key issues: why and what the performance management process is (increasing knowledge) and how to carry out the key elements of it and the behaviours to underpin this (developing skills).

The team developed core training materials that used a flexible cascade process. In each OpCo the leadership team was trained in short sessions in small groups using highly interactive materials. Each of the teams then trained their direct reports using the same materials and so on until everyone had been trained. This was very cost-effective since it did not require large numbers of trainers. Using line managers as trainers also gave greater credibility since they were promoting the process at an early stage, while the use of common materials ensured consistent messages. The cascade meant that all target groups were rapidly involved and mobilised to achieve the greatest possible effect. The learning was reinforced since participants, because they are learners and trainers, have to think and reason for themselves rather than being told what to think by a trainer.

Soft-skills training was developed and delivered locally. The global team created an e-room that contained a core 'point of view', which could be used as a framework for delivering skills training, and a resource base of existing best-practice materials from OpCos translated into English which could be modified in local OpCos to suit local needs, cultures and languages. These points of view covered four skill areas: personal and business goal setting, performance monitoring and measurement, continuous feedback, and coaching and development. They also covered key behaviours including how to be attentive, how to give open, two-way, honest feedback, how to bring out the best in others, how to be open to learning and change, how to listen, and how to have mutual respect. This training has not only helped with the success of performance management but has also helped to develop the skills of line managers.

SUMMARY

Vodafone has faced some unique challenges in its short history. It has grown at enormous speed through huge growth in customer numbers and global acquisitions. In HRM terms this has created its own challenge to ensure that Vodafone maintains its customer-focused, can-do, innovative, fresh culture while managing a huge global business. Effective performance management has been at the centre of this drive to ensure that people have clarity about what they have to do and why they have to do it, and are being given feedback and coaching so that they can be more effective in managing their jobs and their careers. The survey shows that the new process has been highly effective in delivering these outcomes. Completion rates have also increased to close to 100 per cent. As an example in the UK, in 2003 roughly one in three people had a dialogue, in 2004 two-thirds and in the past two years this has grown to 99.6 per cent and now 100 per cent.

To finish with an analogy. Walking down a street in medieval Europe, you stop to ask a craftsman what he is doing. He replies, 'I'm carving this stone.' You walk further on and you ask a person dressed in the same way doing the same thing what he is doing. He replies, 'I'm building a cathedral.' The performance dialogue is about inspiring people to be cathedral builders not just stonemasons.

Which people play key roles in your country? Which names should one know?

The City of London, the financiers, plays the key role in business. It is critical for HR people to know who these people are and what their expectations are. (Few HR people in the UK do.)

References

Atterbury, Sarah/Brewster, Chris/Communal, Christine/Cross, Christine/Gunnigle, Patrick/Morley, Michael (2004): The UK and Ireland: traditions and transitions in HRM, in: Chris Brewster/Wolfgang Mayrhofer/Michael Morley (eds): Human Resource Management in Europe: Evidence of Convergence?, London, pp 22–72.

Becker, Brian E./Gerhart, Barry (1996): The impact of human resource practices on organisational performance: progress and prospects, in: Academy of Management Journal, 39: 779–801.

Becker, Brain/Huselid, Mark A./Pickus, Peter S./Spratt, Michael F. (1997): HR as a source of shareholder value: research and recommendations, in: Human Resource Management, 36(1): 39–47.

Beer, Michael/Spector, Bert/Lawrence, Paul R./Quinn-Mills, D./Walton, Richard E. (1984): Managing Human Assets: The Groundbreaking Harvard Business School Program, New York.

Brewster, Chris (1995): Towards a European model of human resource management, in: Journal of International Business Studies, 26(1): 1–21.

—— (1999): Strategic Human Resource Management: The Value of Different Paradigms, in: Management International Review, 39: 45–64.

Brewster, Chris/Larsen, Henrik H. (2000): Responsibility in human resource management: the role of the line, in: Chris Brewster/Henrik H. Larsen (eds): Human Resource Management in Northern Europe, Oxford.

Brewster, Chris/Wood, Geoff/Brookes, Michael/van Ommeren, Jos (2006): What determines the size of the HR function? A cross-national analysis, in: Human Resource Management, 45(1): 3–21.

Cappelli, Peter/Neumark, David (2001): Do 'high-performance' work practices improve establishment level outcomes?, in: Industrial and Labour Relations Review, 54(4): 737–75.

Chartered Institute of Personnel and Development (2006): CIPD Annual Report 2005-2006, Wimbledon.

Drucker, Peter F. (1989): The new realities, in: Government and Politics, in Economics and Business, in Society and World View, New York.

Ferner, Anthony/Quintanilla, Javier/Varul, Matthias Z. (2001): Country of origin effects, host–country effects and the management of HR in multinationals: German companies in Britain and Spain, in: Journal of World Business, 36(2): 107–27.

Fombrun, Charles J./Tichy, Noel M./Devanna, Mary A. (1984): Strategic Human Resource Management, New York.

Friedman, Andrew L. (1977): Industry and Labour, London.

Gennard, John/Kelly, James (1997): The unimportance of labels: the diffusion of the personnel/HRM function, in: Industrial Relations Journal, 28(1): 27–42.

Gerhart, Barry A. (1999): Human resource management and firm performance: measurement issues and their effect on causal and policy inference, in: Patrick M. Wright/Lee Dyer/John W. Boudreau/George Milkovich (eds): Research in Personnel and HRM, Greenwich, Connecticut.

.uk

—— (2005): Human resources and business performance: findings, unanswered questions and an alternative approach, in: Management Revue, 16: 174–85.

Guest, David E. (1990): Human resource management and the American dream, in: Journal of Management Studies, 27(4): 377–97.

—— (1997): Human resource management and performance: a review and a research agenda, in: International Journal of Human Resource Management, 8: 263–76.

Guest, David E./Michie, Jonathan/Conway, Neil/Sheehan-Quinn, Maura (2003): Human resource management and corporate performance in the UK, in: British Journal of Industrial Relations, 41: 291–314.

Hofstede, Geert (2001): Culture's Consequences: Comparing Values, Behaviours, Institutions and Organisations Across Nations, 2nd edn, Thousand Oaks.

Huselid, Mark A. (1995): The impact of human resource management practices on turnover, productivity and corporate financial performance, in: Academy of Management Journal, 38: 635–72.

Huselid, Mark A./Becker, Brian E. (1996): Methodological issues in cross-sectional and panel estimates of the human resource–firm performance link, in: Industrial Relations, 35: 400–22.

Hyman, Richard (1987): Strategy or structure? Capital, labour and control, in: Work, Employment and Society, 1(1): 25–55.

Keenoy, Tom (1990): HRM: a case of the wolf in sheep's clothing, in: Personnel Review, 19(2): 3–9.

Kinnie, Nicholas/Hutchinson, Sue/Purcell, John/Rayton, Bruce/Swart, Juani (2005): Satisfaction with HR practices and commitment to the organisation: why one size does not fit all, in: Human Resource Management Journal, 15(4): 9–29.

Kochan, Thomas A./Batt, Rosemary/Dyer, Lee (1992): International human resource studies: a framework for future research, in: David Lewin/Peter Scherer/Olivia Mitchell (eds): Research Frontiers in Industrial Relations and Human Resources, Madison.

Legge, Karen (2005): Human Resource Management: Thetorics and Realities, Basingstoke.

Locke, Richard M./Piore, Michael J./Kochan, Thomas (1995): Introduction, in: Richard M. Locke/Thomas Kochan/Michael J. Piore (eds): Employment Relations in a Changing World Economy, Cambridge, pp. 359–84.

Mabey, Christopher (2004): Developing managers in Europe: policies, practices and impact, in: Advances in Developing Human Resources, 6(4): 404–27.

Marchington, Mick/Grugulis, Irena (2000): 'Best-practice' human resource management: perfect opportunity or dangerous illusion?, in: International Journal of Human Resource Management, 11(6): 1104–24.

Morley, Michael/Brewster, Chris/Gunnigle, Patrick/Mayrhofer, Wolfgang (1996): Evaluating change in European industrial relations: research evidence on trends at organisational level, in: International Journal of Human Resource Management, 7(3): 640–56.

Porter, Michael E. (1990): The Competitive Advantage of Nations, London.

Purcell, John/Ahlstrand, Bruce (1994): Human Resource Management in the Multi-divisional Company, New York.

Renwick, Douglas/McNeil, Christina M. (2002): Line manager involvement in careers, in: Career Development, 7(7): 407–14.

Rogers, Edward W./Wright, Patrick M. (1998): Measuring organisational performance in strategic human resource management: problems, prospects and performance information markets, in: Human Resource Management Review, 8(3): 311–31.

Smith, Chris/Meiskins, Peter (1995): System, society and dominance effects in cross-national organisational analysis, in: Work, Employment and Society, 4(3): 451–70.

Sparrow, Paul R./Hiltrop, Jean M. (1994): European Human Resource Management in Transition, Hemel Hempstead.

Sparrow, Paul R./Brewster, Chris/Harris, Hilary (2004): Globalising Human Resource Management, London.

Storey, John (1992): Developments in Human Resource Management, Oxford.

Thurley, Keith/Wirdenius, Hans (1991): Will management become 'European'? Strategic choices for organisations, in: European Management Journal, 9(2): 127–34.

Tichy, Noel M./Fombrun, Charles J./Devanna, Mary A. (1982): Strategic human resource management, in: Sloan Management Review, 24: 47–61.

Tregaskis, Olga (1997): The role of national context and HR strategy in shaping training and development practice in French and UK organisations, in: Organisation Studies, 18(5): 839–56.

Turner, Thomas/Morley, Michael (1995): Industrial Relations and the New Order: Case Studies in Conflict & Co-operation, Dublin.

Ulrich, David O. (1987): Organisational capability as a competitive advantage: human resource professionals as strategic partners, in: Human Resource Planning, 10(4): 169–84.

—— (1989): Assessing human resource effectiveness: stakeholder, utility and relationship approaches, in: Human Resource Planning, 12(4): 301–15.

US Department of Labor (1993): High Performance Work Practices and Firm Performance, Washington, D.C.

Weber, Wolfgang/Kabst, Rüdiger (2004): Human resource management: the need for theory and diversity, in: Management Revue, 15: 171–7.

Wood, Stephen (ed.) (1989): The Transformation of Work, London.

—— (1999): Getting the measure of the transformed high-performance organisation, in: British Journal of Industrial Relations, 37(3): 391–417.

Wright, Patrick M./McMahan, Gary C. (1992): Theoretical perspectives for strategic human resources management, in: Journal of Management, 18(2): 295–320.

Wright, Patrick M./Snell, Scott A. (1991): Toward an integrative view of strategic human resource management, in: Human Resource Management Review, 1: 203–25.

.uk

The authors

Chris Brewster (chris.brewster@henleymc.ac.uk), full Chair Professor of International Human Resource Management, Henley Management College, UK. He had substantial experience in trade unions, government, specialist journals, personnel management in construction and air transport, and in consultancy, before becoming an educator and trainer. He has conducted extensive research in the field of international and comparative HRM; written more than a dozen books, including, recently, *Globalizing Human Resource Management*, and over 100 articles. In 2002 he was awarded the Georges Petitpas Memorial Award by the practitioner body, the World Federation of Personnel Management Associations, in recognition of his outstanding contribution to international HRM.

Frances Wilson (f.wilson@cipd.co.uk), Chartered Institute of Personnel and Development, UK, Manager International. She manages major research projects on International HRM and HRD. She leads the International Forum: a network for international people management professionals. Currently she is General Secretary of the European Training and Development Federation (ETDF) as well as representing CIPD at the European Association for Personnel Management (EAPM). Prior to her career at CIPD, Frances had ten years' experience as an HR practitioner in both the public and private sectors.

Nick Holley (nick@nha.uk.com), independent consultant and Visiting Fellow at Henley Management College. He combines an unusual experience as an army officer, a futures and foreign exchange broker and senior HR roles for a number of large global organisations including, most recently, Arthur Andersen and Vodafone, where he was Director of Global People Development.

Index